THE WATERS OF SILOE

9-12-51

Mrs. N. B. Hedges
Paris, Ky   Route 3

THE BARN MONASTERY, GEORGIA

Manning

THE WATERS OF SILOE

THOMAS MERTON

Garden City Books · Garden City, N.Y.

Ex Parte Ordinis

Nihil Obstat: Fr. M. Gabriel O'Connell, O.C.R.
Fr. M. Anthony Chassagne, O.C.R.

Imprimi Potest: Fr. M. Dominique Nogues, O.C.R., Abbot General

Nihil Obstat: John M. A. Fearns, S.T.D., Censor librorum

Imprimatur: ✠ Francis Cardinal Spellman, Archbishop of New York

Garden City Books reprint edition 1951,
by special arrangement with Harcourt, Brace & Company

PRINTED IN THE UNITED STATES
AT THE COUNTRY LIFE PRESS, GARDEN CITY, N.Y.

TO EVELYN WAUGH

THERE IS intoxication in the waters of contemplation, whose mystery fascinated and delighted the first Cistercians and whose image found its way into the names of so many of those valley monasteries that stood in forests, on the banks of clean streams, among rocks alive with springs.

These are the waters which the world does not know, because it prefers the water of bitterness and contradiction. These are the waters of peace, of which Christ said: *"He that shall drink of the water that I shall give him, shall not thirst for ever. But the water that I shall give him shall become in him a fountain of water, springing up into life everlasting."*

These are the Waters of Siloe, that flow in silence.

CONTENTS

The Daily Life of a Cistercian Monk in Our Time

WINTER		SUMMER	
A.M.		A.M.	
2:00	Rise, go to choir, recite Matins and Lauds of Our Lady's Office.	2:00	As in Winter.
2:30	Meditation.	2:30	As in Winter.
3:00	Night Office (Canonical Matins and Lauds).	3:00	As in Winter.
(about) 4:00	Priests say their private Masses, others go to Communion. Then there is time for reading or private prayer.	4:00	As in Winter.
5:30	Prime, followed by Chapter.*	5:30	As in Winter.
6:30 -7:45	Reading, study or private prayer.	6:30	Mixt [breakfast].
7:45	Tierce, High Mass, Sext.	6:45 -9:00	Work. (The students have classes or study.)
9:00 -10:45	Work. (The students have classes or study.)	9:00	Reading or private prayer.
10:45 -11:07	Reading or prayer.	9:30	Tierce, High Mass, Sext.
		11:00	Dinner.
11:07	None [the fifth of the seven canonical hours].	P.M.	
		12:00 -1:00	Meridienne [siesta].
11:30	Dinner.	1:07	None.

WINTER		SUMMER	
P.M.		P.M.	
12:15 -1:30	Reading, private prayer.	1:30 -2:00	Reading, private prayer.
1:30 -3:30	Work.	2:00 -4:30	Work.
3:30 -4:30	Reading or private prayer.	4:30 -5:15	Reading or private prayer.
(about)4:30	Vespers.	5:15	Vespers.
5:15	Meditation.	5:45	Meditation.
5:30	Collation [light refreshment].	6:00	Supper.
5:40 -6:10	Reading, prayer.	6:30 -7:10	Reading, prayer.
6:10	Compline,† *Salve Regina*, examination of conscience.	7:10	Compline, † *Salve Regina*, examination of conscience.
7:00	All go to bed.	8:00	All go to bed.

(The day of a Lay-brother includes more work, less prayer, and not so much fasting.)

* After Chapter in the winter a very light breakfast (*frustulum*) may be taken by those who do not wish to fast until dinner.

† Compline begins with about ten minutes of public reading in the Chapter Room or Cloister.

PROLOGUE

IT IS late at night. Most of the Paris cafés have closed their doors and pulled down their shutters and locked them to the sidewalk. Lights are reflected brightly in the wet, empty pavement. A taxi stops to let off a passenger and moves away again, its red tail-light disappearing around the corner.

The man who has just alighted follows a bellboy through the whirling door into the lobby of one of the big Paris hotels. His suitcase is bright with labels that spell out the names of hotels that existed in the big European cities before World War II. But the man is not a tourist. You can see that he is a businessman, and an important one. This is not the kind of hotel that is patronized by mere *voyageurs de commerce*. He is a Frenchman, and he walks through the lobby like a man who is used to stopping at the best hotels. He pauses for a moment, fumbling for some change, and the bellboy goes ahead of him to the elevator.

The traveler is suddenly aware that someone is looking at him. He turns around. It is a woman, and to his astonishment she is dressed in the habit of a nun.

If he knew anything about the habits worn by the different religious orders, he would recognize the white cloak and brown robe as belonging to the Discalced Carmelites. But what on earth would a man in his position know about Discalced Carmelites? He is far too important and too busy to worry his head about nuns and religious orders—or about churches for that matter, although he occasionally goes to Mass as a matter of form.

The most surprising thing of all is that the nun is smiling, and she is smiling at *him*. She is a young sister, with a bright, intelligent French face, full of the candor of a child, full of good sense: and her smile is a smile of frank, undisguised friendship. The traveler instinctively brings his hand to his hat, then turns away and hastens to the desk, assuring himself that he does not know any nuns. As he is signing the register, he cannot help glancing back over his shoulder. The nun is gone.

Putting down the pen, he asks the clerk, "Who was that nun that just passed by?"

"I beg your pardon, monsieur. What was that you said?"

"That nun—who was she, anyway? The one that just went by and smiled at me."

The clerk arches his eyebrows.

"You are mistaken, monsieur. A nun, in a hotel, at this time of night! Nuns don't go wandering around town, smiling at men!"

"I know they don't. That's why I would like you to explain the fact that one came up and smiled at me just now, here in this lobby."

The clerk shrugs: "Monsieur, you are the only person that has come in or gone out in the last half hour."

Not long after, the traveler who saw that nun in the Paris hotel was no longer an important French industrialist, and he did know something about religious habits. In fact, he was wearing one. It was brown: a brown robe, with a brown scapular over it, and a thick leather belt buckled about the waist. His head was shaved and he had grown a beard. And he wore a grimy apron to protect his robe from axle grease. He was lying on his back underneath a partly disemboweled tractor. There was a wrench in his hand and black smudges all around his eyes where he had been wiping the sweat with the back of his greasy hands. He was a lay brother in the most strictly enclosed, the poorest, the most laborious, and one of the most austere orders in the Church.

He had become a Trappist in a southern French abbey. He

knew no more of hotels or big cities, because he was living now in the monastery that had been built eight hundred years before by Cistercian monks from Burgundy. And he was living pretty much the way they had lived before him, fasting, praying, reading, keeping silence with his tongue in order that the depths of his mind and heart might be free to seek God—the silent, secret, yet obvious presence of God that is known to the contemplative and unknown to anyone else: not so much because it is unintelligible as because its very excess of intelligibility blinds us and makes us incapable of grasping it. Perhaps the fact that he was working on a tractor instead of on an ox-cart might constitute an accidental difference between him and the monks of the twelfth century; but that is a minor point indeed.

The thing that needs to be stressed about this story is that it is true. That lay brother is living today in the abbey of Aiguebelle, and the reason he is there is to be traced ultimately to the fact that one night he walked into a Paris hotel and saw a nun smiling at him, though the clerk told him no nun was there.

A few days later he saw a picture of the very same nun in the house of some friends. They told him that her name was St. Thérèse of the Child Jesus. Of course he had heard of St. Thérèse. Once more he became interested in the religion he had neglected for so many years. And before long his beard had grown and his head was shaved and he was lying underneath a tractor in a brown robe with axle grease all over his face.

Things like that also happen in America. I do not say that men see apparitions and then run off to become Trappists. It is not necessary to have peculiar experiences before you can become a monk. As a general rule you are better off without experiences. However, there are other experiences, more terrible yet easier to explain—the kind produced by war.

There was a young corporal in the United States Marines who found out at very close quarters what happened to the dead bodies of men left unburied at Okinawa. Then he read a newspaper article about Trappist monks who had started a new monastery in Georgia. When he got out of the Marines, he went home to his family in Wisconsin and told them what was on his mind. They were Catholics, but they did not like the idea of his becoming a Trappist. They told him so with emphasis. His uncle offered him a forty-acre farm, ten head of milk cows, and a team if he would give up his foolish notion. The young man said no.

His mother said, "If you go to that place in Georgia, I will never come to see you."

He went out of the house and started for Georgia.

When he arrived, he found that most of the novices in the new frame monastery of pine planks had also left the armed forces to find a peace that could not exist outside a cloister.

He knew that it was the same at the big Trappist monastery in Kentucky, Our Lady of Gethsemani. It was the same at the Trappist monastery in the Blackstone Valley of Rhode Island. It was the same at New Melleray, where the Trappists had settled almost a hundred years ago in the rolling cornfields outside Dubuque, Iowa. Soon there would be two more Trappist monasteries in the United States—one in the Wasatch mountains of Utah and another in the Pecos Valley, at the foot of the Sangre de Cristo mountains, outside Santa Fe, New Mexico.

Life in these monasteries is austere. In fact, when you compare it with the way people live in the world outside, the austerity is fantastic.

Silence. The monks never hold conversations. They use sign language. They talk only to their superiors and to their confessors, which means that they hardly talk at all.

Vigils. They get up in the middle of the night. When they do sleep, they do so not on inner spring mattresses but straw.

Fasting. A shudder goes down the spine of the average American citizen when he learns that the monks never eat fried chicken or apple pie or beefsteak or hot dogs or hamburgers. In fact, they never eat meat, unless they are very ill. Fish is never served in the common refectory, nor eggs, except to the very old or the very young or the sick. They don't even see milk and cheese for weeks at a time during half the year. They subsist on macaroni or sauerkraut or turnips or spinach or some other unappealing item.

There is no point in multiplying the strange facts of Trappist asceticism without qualifying them, otherwise it will be hard for some people to understand the Trappists. The word "Trappist" has become synonymous with "ascetic" and definitely indicates a monk who leads a very hard life. But unless it is explained just why men lead that life and how they came to do it, there is not much point in simply saying that that is what they do.

Penance and asceticism are not ends in themselves. If monks never succeed in being more than pious athletes, they do not fulfill their purpose in the Church. If you want to understand why the monks lead the life they do, you will have to ask, first of all, What is their aim?

One purpose of this book is to answer that question and tell who the Trappists are and where they came from and what they think they are doing. This purpose is the more appropriate in view of one fact which surprises the Trappists almost as much as it surprises everybody else: the amazing growth of the Order in the last twenty years—especially its growth in America.

If ever there was a country where men loved comfort, pleasure and material security, good health and conversation about the weather and the World Series and the Rose Bowl; if ever there was a land where silence made men nervous and prayer drove them crazy and penance scared them to death, it is America. Yet, quite suddenly, Americans—the healthiest, most normal, most energetic, and most optimistic of the younger generation of Americans—have taken it into their heads to run off to Trappist monasteries and get their heads shaved and put on robes and scapulars and work in the fields and pray half the night and sleep on straw and, in a word, become monks.

When you ask them why they have done such things, they may give you a very clear answer or, perhaps, only a rather confused answer; but in either case the answer will amount to this: the Trappists are the most austere order they could find, and Trappist life was that which least resembled the life men lead in the towns and cities of our world. And there is something in their hearts that tells them they cannot be happy in an atmosphere where people are looking for nothing but their own pleasure and advantage and comfort and success.

They have not come to the monastery to escape from the realities of life but to find those realities: they have felt the terrible insufficiency of life in a civilization that is entirely dedicated to the pursuit of shadows.

What is the use of living for things that you cannot hold on to, values that crumble in your hands as soon as you possess them, pleasures that turn sour before you have begun to taste them, and a peace that is constantly turning into war? Men have not become Trappists merely out of a hope for peace in the next world: something has told them, with unshakable conviction, that the next world begins in this world and that heaven can be theirs now, very truly, even though imperfectly, if they give their lives to the one activity which is the beatitude of heaven.

That activity is love: the clean, unselfish love that does not live on what it gets but on what it gives; a love that increases by pouring itself out for others, that grows by self-sacrifice and becomes mighty by throwing itself away.

But there is something very special about the love which is the beatitude of heaven: it makes us resemble God, because God Himself is love. *Deus caritas est.* The more we love Him as He loves us, the more we resemble Him; and the more we resemble Him, the more we come to know Him. And, to complete the circle, the more we know Him, the better we love

Him, and "this is eternal life that they may know Thee, the only true God, and Jesus Christ Whom Thou hast sent." [1]

That is what is called the contemplative life: a life that is devoted before all else to the knowledge and love of God and to the love of other men in Him and for His sake. It is distinguished, therefore, from the active life, which is directly concerned with the physical and spiritual needs of men first of all. The one main concern of the contemplative is God and the love of God.

Members of the active religious orders take care of the sick and directly feed the poor and teach children in schools. The contemplative monk also contributes indirectly to this work, even in a material way, because the surplus of his farm is given to the poor, and the monastery helps to support hospitals and schools when it is able to do so. So, when the monk works in the fields, he knows he is not merely working for himself; he is working to feed others. But no Trappist monastery can accomplish anything much in the material order. Its greatest work is spiritual. In a world in which men have forgotten the value of prayer, it is the monks who pray for the world and for all those in the world who have forgotten how to pray. If there is some small degree of happiness and spiritual joy and faith to temper the despair of our time, it has been obtained by prayer. And if people have been able to discover any ultimate meaning of the chaos of our world, they owe it to the grace of God, which was obtained for them by somebody's prayer.

However, there is much more than that to the contemplative life. The monk does not merely exist from day to day, feeding his interior life on the hope of future felicity or the assurance that someone, somewhere, somehow, is profiting by his sacrifice. The substance of the contemplative life is contemplation itself, the possession of God by knowledge and love. That is why contemplation is the perfection of love, the perfection of

[1] John xvii:3.

Christian charity. And for that same reason, since "charity is the fulness of the law," contemplation is the perfection of Christianity and the highest form of Christian living. And this is most true when contemplation—that is, the wisdom born of charity—becomes so superabundant that it has to pour itself out and communicate to other men what it knows of God and God's love.

But perfect love for God implies perfect sacrifice. God's love is infinitely selfless and disinterested: what can He possibly gain from the love of His creatures? He seeks our love, not in order that we may give Him something, but because He knows that for us the highest happiness consists in loving Him. But in order to love Him perfectly, we have to love Him with something of the disinterestedness with which He loves us: we have to love Him because He is God.

Love is a union of wills. The perfect love of God is a perfect union of wills with God: that means the inability to will anything that God does not will. In the words of the Cistercian mystic, William of St. Thierry: "Man's perfection is to be like God . . . in unity of spirit, whereby man not only becomes one with God in the sense that he wills the same things as God, but in the sense that he is *unable to will what God does not will." Non tantum unitate volendi idem, sed aliud velle non valendi.*[2]

This is not something that is arrived at overnight. Nor can any man arrive at it by the practice of virtues that are accessible to his own powers, even aided by ordinary grace. It is a pure gift of God, and it corresponds to what modern mystical theologians call "transforming union."

But this perfection of love for God is the reason for the existence of Trappist monasteries and of every human soul that comes into the world, because all are created for this union with God and for the tremendous and everlasting joy that it brings with it. Therefore, men who enter Trappist monasteries

[2] William of St. Thierry, *Epistola ad Fratres de Monte Dei*, ii, No. 16.

may seem to be throwing their lives away, and in a sense they are: but only to find them again, immediately and more perfectly. Because this is one sacrifice which terminates in the perfect fulfilment of everything for which we were created.

And this too, says St. Thomas, is the sacrifice that is most pleasing to God: for the closer a man unites himself to God, the more pleasing a sacrifice it is to God. *Quanto autem homo animam suam vel alterius propinquius Deo conjungit, tanto sacrificium est Deo magis acceptum.*[3]

The young army lieutenant who stands uneasily at the gate of Our Lady of Gethsemani and pulls the bell rope and hopes this is the last time he will be standing outside those walls as a stranger, does not clearly know all these things. But the urge in his heart that has brought him to that place to give himself to God by embracing a hard rule that he does not yet understand is destined, by its very nature, to lead to a perfect union of wills with God. That is why God has brought him there. And if he does not arrive at the term of his journey while he is still on earth, he will reach it more quickly and more perfectly after he has passed out of the world and found the God to whom he has sacrificed his life.

Is it any wonder that Trappist monasteries are places full of peace and contentment and joy? These men, who have none of the pleasures of the world, have all the happiness that the world is unable to find. Their silence is more eloquent than all the speeches of politicians and the noise of all the radios in America. Their smiles have more joy in them than has the laughter of thousands. When they raise their eyes to the hills or to the sky, they see a beauty which other people do not know how to find. When they work in the fields and the forests, they seem to be tired and alone, but their hearts are at rest, and they are absorbed in a companionship that is tremendous, because it is three Persons in one infinite Nature, the One Who spoke the universe and draws it all back into

---

[3] St. Thomas Aquinas, *Summa Theologica*, II IIae, q. 182, a. 2, ad 3.

Himself by His love; the One from Whom all things came and to Whom all things return: and in Whom are all the beauty and substance and actuality of everything in the world that is real.

If you ever receive a letter or see a document signed by someone who puts the letters *O.C.R.* or *O.C.S.O.* after his name, you can tell yourself that he is someone who has found out the meaning of life. He is a monk, a Trappist, a contemplative. The initials mean "Order of Cistercians of the Strict Observance" or *Ordo Cisterciensium Reformatorum* ("Order of Reformed Cistercians"). That is the real name of the Order to which these monks belong. The term "Trappist" is only a nickname. And how does it happen that the "Trappist" really ought to be called a *Cistercian?* How is it that, unless a Trappist is a Cistercian, he is not quite what he ought to be?

That is more than a formality and a matter of names. It is a question on which the essence of a religious vocation depends. And that is most important, because the fervor and success of a religious order depends entirely on how close it can manage to keep to the object for which it was founded.

It seems quite probable that the reason why there is such a ferment of new life and spiritual energy in the Trappist monasteries of the world today is that they have become something more than just "Trappist."

The Cistercian Order was founded at the turn of the twelfth century as a reform of Benedictine monasticism. The ideal of the founders was a return to the perfect integral observance of the Rule of St. Benedict: which meant a return to the cenobitic life in all its simplicity. But there was more to the Cistercian reform than that. Under St. Bernard of Clairvaux the Cistercians became the greatest contemplative order of their age: so much so that when Dante sought a guide to the heights of heaven in his *Paradiso*, it was St. Bernard who came to conduct him before the throne of God. The Middle Ages knew of no one better equipped for such a task. Bernard was the contemplative above all others, above St. Bonaventure and St. Francis and Hugh and Richard of St. Victor and the rest.

The Cistercians were the men who lived hidden in the secret of God's face; their speciality was love, and the book of the Bible that treated the mystical union of the soul with God had become theirs by right. *The Canticle of Canticles* was Cistercian territory, as far as Scripture was concerned. St. Thomas of Aquin, when he fell ill at the Cistercian abbey of Fossanova, could think of no more appropriate way of repaying the White Monks for their hospitality than by commenting on the *Canticle of Canticles* for them in their chapter-room.

When the Cistercian Order became too great for its own good, it fell into a decline, and the first thing that went out was the fire of contemplation. In fact, that had been extinct long before the edifice of the Order began to crumble.

In the seventeenth century there was one great reformer among the group who tried to bring the Cistercians back to life. It was Father Jean-Armand de Rancé, the abbot of La Grande Trappe, of whom you will soon hear more in this book. He is famous enough, and if his name means any one thing it means *austerity*. The great Trappist reformer was a severe and ruthless penitent; he was a controversialist; his nature was ardent and active. But the warmth of deep contemplation is wanting in the spirit of La Trappe.

During the eighteenth and nineteenth centuries the Trappists struggled through adventures which the pages of this book will attempt to describe, at least in outline. They were exciting and extremely active lives that these men led. In fact, a kind of active spirit seems to have worked itself right into the Trappist system during those years, until one feels that energetic exertion, labor, bodily penance, and active methods of spirituality seem to have absorbed these monks to the exclusion of everything else.

After the reunion of the scattered Trappist congregations into one Order in 1892, a change began to be noticed. The new Order of Cistercians of the Strict Observance became much more fully conscious of its great heritage. In the half century that has gone by since the reunion, there has been a movement to recapture something of the ardent, contemplative spirit that existed in the monasteries of St. Bernard's day.

At first the development was slow, but since World War I it has been gathering momentum. Its effects are really making themselves felt—at least in the more important centers of Cistercian life, especially in France. However, that life is also pouring itself out obscurely into all the Cistercian houses in the world, and this accounts for the flood of vocations and the growth of new foundations in the United States.

One of the most telling factors in this new growth has been the renewal of intellectual interest in Cistercian history and theology. Father de Rancé, in his ruthless desire to mortify all the natural faculties of his monks, believed that even their brief periods of reading should be a penance. He was suspicious of monks who became too interested in books, and he never permitted them to embark on anything that savored of "investigation" or "research." It is quite true that the Cistercian has no vocation to advanced scholarship or technical theology: but if the Order is to live up to its real vocation, its members must go back to the writings of their fathers and find out what they had to say. There is no hope of a solid contemplative life in a monastic order which does not train its spiritual directors and novice-masters most thoroughly in dogmatic and ascetical and mystical theology, as well as in all the other branches of study necessary for a priest.

Since the reunion of the congregations, the re-formed Cistercian Order has been fully aware of this responsibility and has done its best to discharge it. The names of three great abbots stand out in the first generation since the reunion. Dom Jean Baptiste Chautard is famous for his book *The Soul of the Apostolate*, which is addressed to secular priests and workers in Catholic Action, but which testifies to his own feeling for the need of a deep contemplative life. Like Dom Anselme le

Bail, whom he rather resembles, Dom Chautard infused a new warmth and vitality into the Cistercian spirit by his energetic teaching, which focused the Rule of St. Benedict upon its true object—not so much the love of penance as the love of Christ. And it makes a great difference as to what goes on in your soul, whether you love a Person or an abstraction.

Perhaps the most important effect produced by the three was brought about by the writing of Dom Vital Lehodey. His work on abandonment is the chief modern authority in that field: *Le Saint Abandon*[4] says all that can be said about abandonment without falling into semiquietism. This book has helped to set monks free from their obsession with pious activities, as if these were ends in themselves. It has striven to arouse in them some hunger for a close and personal union with God and has taught men to seek a fresh and vitalizing contact with a real and a living God through His will. Another book, *The Ways of Mental Prayer*,[5] is too little known. It surveys the whole field of active mental prayer and gives a good introduction to infused contemplation—a subject concerning which Trappists of the old school preserved a nervous and unsympathetic silence.

Yet, contemplation in this strict sense is the atmosphere in which the Cistercians of the Middle Ages lived and breathed. It was the source of an amazing fortitude, the fountain of a peaceful and lasting spiritual energy. More than any other monastic body before them, the Cistercians were keenly aware of the joys that Christ had promised to those who drank the living waters of His Spirit. All the strong, pure poetry of Cistercian mysticism, all the strength and clean austerity of Cistercian architecture, all the clear-cut, energetic grace of Cistercian liturgical manuscripts of the twelfth century, bear witness to the intense vitality of the interior life that was lived in the monasteries of the White Monks in those days.

Perhaps the most significant developments in the spirit of the

[4] (Paris, 1919); *Holy Abandonment*, English translation (Dublin, 1934).
[5] *Les Voies de l'Oraison Mentale* (Paris, 1908); English translation (Dublin, 1938).

Order since the reunion can be traced in the changes that were introduced into the semiofficial *Spiritual Directory* of the Order. Again, it was Dom Vital Lehodey who was commissioned by the General Chapter to undertake this work. Since Dom Lehodey was not writing in his own name but as the mouthpiece of the whole Order—and that within twenty years of the reunion, when the ferment was only beginning to be felt—he could not give himself a free hand to reshape the whole book to suit his own farseeing views. On the contrary, he was bound by his position to restrict himself to the most conservative and cautious changes.

He not only preserved the whole structure of the old *Directory*—which was a thoroughly solid piece of ascetical writing—but he even preserved most of the material, rewriting and recasting it in clearer language and purging it of rigidity and harshness. There was no essential change: simply a shift of emphasis. That was all that was needed. Where the old *Directory* stresses externals, the new enters more deeply into the interior spirit of the Rule, without sacrificing anything of the letter. Where the old emphasizes the manner of carrying out various external functions in the monastic life, the new draws attention to the end for which they are to be performed and the spirit of love that should vitalize their performance. Where the old *Directory* places rather a truculent stress on vocal prayers and multiple devotions, the new discreetly strives to simplify the monk's life and reminds him that, since his official day of vocal prayer is quite long, he would do well to refresh his "intervals" with mental prayer and contemplation. Above all, the new *Directory* makes some important and extremely pointed remarks about the essentially supernatural character of the contemplative life, recalling the transcendent part played in it by the Holy Spirit. It is God who sanctifies us, not our prayers and penances by themselves.

Finally, in a chapter devoted to the object of the Cistercian vocation, the new *Directory* revises the notion that the Order is, above all, penitential. In a statement that amounts to an official declaration, we read:

Contemplation is the primary, essential and immediate end to which all our observances are subordinated. . . . A glance at our Rules will show that our life is organized above all for prayer. . . . Everything in our life tends to protect us from the turmoil of the world and of our passions, to guarantee us solitude of the spirit, the heart and the will, in order that our monasteries may be sanctuaries of silence filled with the fragrance of prayer, where nothing is heard but the voice of the soul praising God and of God replying to the soul. . . . However, though contemplation is the chief aim of our Order, we are not obliged to arrive at mystical contemplation, in which the soul, united to God by a simple gaze of love, remains more or less passive under the Divine action and enjoys a repose full of delights. . . . No one can enter into this kind of prayer unless God brings him into it. Since He gives it to whom He wills, He does not demand it of all. The essential thing is to get our vices out by the roots and to climb step by step to the perfection of charity and to strive to be of one will with God; a monk may reach this by the ordinary way, while another may be left far behind in spite of the prayer of quiet and other mystical graces. Nevertheless we must admit that these are a tremendous help to a soul that is humble, detached, and has a good director. We are entitled to ask for such graces if we do so submissively and with a right intention, and we even have the *duty to dispose ourselves to receive them by our detachment and recollection.* There is no better way to these graces than our life of prayer.[6]

Later on, Dom Lehodey quotes, from an anonymous Cistercian writer of St. Bernard's time, a passage that recalls Cassian's first *Conference:*

Above everything else, you should endeavour to keep your soul constantly lifted up in contemplation and your spirit always raised to God and the things of God. Other practises may make more of an outward impression, like vigils, the mortification of the body, fasting, and other such exercises. But you should regard all that,

---

[6] *Le Directoire Spirituel des Cisterciens Reformes* (Bricquebec, 1910), chap. vi, pp. 34-37. Cf. English translation by a Monk of New Melleray (Gethsemani, 1946), p. 34 ff.

necessary as it may be, as a matter of relatively minor importance, and *only valuable in so far as it helps you to purify your heart.*[7] The reason why so few people ever reach true perfection is that they spend their time and their energies on things that have relatively little value, and pay less attention to the things that really matter. So, if you want to reach your goal, enter within yourself and withdraw from everything else, as far as you can. Keep the eye of your heart in tranquil purity by disengaging your thoughts from the forms of inferior beings; set your will entirely free from the cares of the earth and cling to the sovereign Good by fervent love . . . and thus your soul, gathered unto God with all its powers and energies, will come to be one same and single spirit with Him: and this, as we know, is the highest perfection in life.[8]

These quotations are enough to show where the true meaning of the Cistercian vocation is to be looked for. They explain the abounding joy, the beauty, the tranquillity, the peace of the Cistercian life. True, these things demand a great price—nothing less than complete renunciation—not only of the world and its ambitions and its multiple concerns, but also of the monk's own judgment and tastes and his own sweet will. But once the price has been paid, the reward is greater still.

It takes a man above the terrors and sorrows of modern life as well as above its passing satisfactions. It elevates his life to a superhuman level to the peace of the spiritual stratosphere where the storms of human existence become a distant echo and do not disturb the center of the soul—no matter how much they may rage in the senses and feelings.

Fed with the hidden manna of contemplation, the monk finds that the words of Ecclesiasticus are realized in his own soul: "With the bread of life and understanding justice shall

---

[7] Purity of heart, *puritas cordis,* is a technical term in medieval ascetical writing. It harks back to the beatitudes, "Blessed are the clean of heart, for they shall see God" (Matt. v:8). It means detachment not only from all illicit desires but even from licit pleasures and temporal interests and cares. More than that, it signifies the ability to rise above and beyond the images of created things and all dialectical reasoning in order to seize the truth by a pure and direct intuition.

[8] *Op. cit.,* p. 41.

feed him, and give him the water of wholesome wisdom to drink, and justice shall be made strong in him and he shall not be moved." [9]

Those who have tasted joy in the silence of the monastery know what the twelfth-century Cistercians meant when they saw the contemplative life in Isaias's symbol of the *"waters of Siloe that flow in silence."* [10]

[9] Ecclus. xv:3.
[10] Isa. viii:6.

NOTE ON THE FUNCTION OF
A CONTEMPLATIVE ORDER

IF, IN this book, we had attempted a defense of the contemplative life, we would have been expected to explain, above all, how it is that contemplative Orders contribute a very important share to the apostolic life of the Church. However, this has been done often and well, and Catholic doctrine on the subject has been clearly crystallized in Pope Pius XI's *"Umbratilem"* (Apostolic Constitution of July 8, 1924, approving the Statutes of the Carthusians):

From the earliest times [wrote this Pontiff who was famous as the Pope of Catholic *Action*] this (contemplative) mode of life, most perfect and most useful and more fruitful for the whole of Christendom than anyone can conceive, took root in the Church and spread on all sides. . . . Since the whole object of this institution lay in this—that the monks, each in the privacy of his own cell, *unoccupied with any exterior ministry and having nothing to do with it,* should fix their thoughts exclusively on the things of heaven—wonderful was the benefit that accrued from it to Christian society. . . . In the course of time this pre-eminent institution that is called the contemplative life declined somewhat and lost vigor. The reason was that the monks . . . came by degrees to combine active life with their pondering on divine things and their contemplation. . . . It was highly important for the Church that this most holy form of life . . . should be restored to its pristine vigor, so that there should never be lacking men of prayer who, unimpeded by any other care, would be perpetually besieging the Divine Mercy and thus draw down from heaven benefits of every sort upon men, too neglectful of their salvation. . . .

(Contemplatives) give themselves up to a sort of hidden and silent apostolate. . . . We wish that so valuable an institution should spread and increase. For if ever it was needful that there should be anchorites of this sort in the Church of God, it is especially expedient nowadays when we see so many Christians . . . giving rein to their desire for earthly riches and the pleasures of the flesh. . . . But it is easy to understand how those who assiduously fulfill the duty of prayer and penance contribute much more to the increase of the Church and the welfare of mankind than those who labor in tilling the Master's field.

Yet the theme that runs through this history of a contemplative Order is one that will probably shock not only men of the world but many Catholics, and, among them, priests. It is this: the vitality and success of the Trappist monasteries all over the world in our time has been due, among other things, to the fact that the monks have been able to free themselves more and more from apostolic missions, active works of teaching and preaching, which had been forced upon them by circumstances in the past. The Order has recovered its full strength in proportion as it has withdrawn from fields of endeavor into which it never had any business to go. In other words, a contemplative community will prosper to the extent that it is what it is meant to be, and shuts out the world, and withdraws from the commotion and excitement of the active life, and gives itself entirely to penance and prayer.

The pages of this volume will have much to say about this. But before the story begins. it would be well to clarify two important points.

In the first place, it should not be necessary to say that this thesis does not carry with it any criticism of the active life as such. To say that the active life is not the end of a contemplative Order is certainly not to imply that it has no place in the Church. On the contrary, everyone knows that Jesus Christ, sending His Apostles to "preach to all nations" and administer the Sacraments which are the chief instruments of salvation, made the spread of His Kingdom depend on the works of the active apostolate.

But, in the second place, if the contemplative Orders do not engage in teaching and preaching, this certainly does not mean that they have no interest or take no part in the salvation of their fellow-men. On the contrary, the salvation and happiness of men is something they take very much to heart and this is, in fact, one of the ends which their life is directed to obtain, but only as a fruit of contemplation and penance.

The Church stands suppliant before the throne of God, dressed, like the King's daughter in the psalm, "in gilded clothing surrounded with variety." The variety—that is, the designs and ornaments which add beauty to the comely garments of the Church—consists of all the different ways and states of life in which Christians can serve God and give Him glory. Chief among these ways are those which are followed by the different religious Orders and Congregations. The final end proposed to the religious Orders is nothing else but God Himself: which means that their function is to bring their members, in one way or another, to the vision and possession of God, Who is the summit of all reality and the perfection of infinite Truth and the unending fulness of all joy.

The religious state is distinguished from other states of life by the means it uses to obtain this end. Religious consecrate themselves by vow to lives of perfection, and they lead these lives, for better or for worse, in communities.

All religious Orders therefore strive to produce the highest Christian perfection in their members: but they are also dedicated to the spread of the Church. It is a common end of all religious Rules to contribute, in some way, to the salvation of souls.

Contemplation and action necessarily have their part in every religious Rule. The two must always go together, because Christian perfection is nothing else but the perfection of charity, and that means perfect love of God and of men. This is only one love, specifically the same. It cannot be divided into two. But emphasis can nevertheless be placed on one or the other of these two objects. The religious Rules that aim most of all at the love and service of souls are termed active, while those Orders whose members concentrate more exclusively on the contemplation (which implies the love) of God are called contemplative. But the active Orders would soon find that their activity was sterile and useless if it were not nourished by an interior spirit of prayer and contemplation, while the contemplative who tries to shut out the needs and sufferings of humanity and isolate himself in a selfish paradise of interior consolations will soon end up in a desert of sterile illusion.

The fruitfulness of all the religious Orders, and their contribution to the beauty and vitality of the whole Church does not depend on the exterior and material evidence of their energy. The best religious Order is not the one that has the most schools and colleges and orphanages and hospitals: nor is it necessarily the one with the strictest Rule, the most fasting, the severest enclosure, the longest hours of prayer. These are not the standards by which we judge the efficacy of a religious Rule. The best religious Order is the one that has the highest end and the most perfect means for arriving at that end. This, at least, is the abstract standard by which we judge the difference between Orders. But in the concrete, the Order which comes closest to keeping its own Rule perfectly and which, at any given moment, best achieves the end for which it was instituted, will be, in point of fact, the best one in the Church at that moment. And therefore one Order cannot improve itself by suddenly deciding to adopt the institutions and aims of some other Order which has an entirely different purpose in the Church. Instead of becoming better, such an Order would only decline because it would be trying to do a work for which it was never intended.

Now St. Thomas says that the contemplative life is, in itself, the most perfect that can be led by men on earth. (II IIae q. 182 a. 1.) It is, in fact, the life of beatitude, in an inchoate form. When, later on, he adds that the religious Orders dedicated to preaching and teaching are the most perfect, we must remember his explanation that those Orders, although belonging to the active state, perform works which are derived from the fulness of contemplation (*ex plenitudine contemplationis*). (II IIae q. 188 a. 6.)

Dominican theologians, in our own day, assert that even in their life of preaching and teaching, contemplation is not secondary, but is a primary and principal end. It is by no means to be considered as subordinate to preaching. In fact, the value of preaching and teaching will depend on the intensity of contemplation from which it proceeds, and of which it is the overflow. Such is the teaching of Father Garrigou-Lagrange and Father Joret.[1] If contemplation plays a vitally important part in the preaching orders, how much more vital is it to cloistered contemplatives, who cannot offer distracting works as a legitimate excuse for a diminished interior life?

Yet however superior the contemplative life may be in itself, if the Sisters in a hospital suddenly decided to retire for an hour of contemplative prayer just at the time when they were supposed to attend to the welfare of their patients, they might be committing more than an imperfection. In the same way, if some Trappist monks suddenly got the feeling that they could not contain the flood of light which inundated their souls, and hastened to the nearest city to start preaching about it in the streets, they would probably not be adding anything to their increment of merits. So the perfection of each religious Order is defined for it by its own peculiar statutes. In practice, and in the concrete, the most valuable Orders in the Church at any given moment are the ones that are keeping the closest to the letter and the spirit of their own Rules, even though the work they accomplish may attract no outward attention whatever.

As a corollary: it is always a dangerous and insidious temptation for religious to abandon some essential element of their

---

[1] "We must say that *the Apostolic life tends principally to contemplation* which fructifies in the apostolate." (Garrigou-Lagrange, *The Three Ages of the Interior Life*, St. Louis, 1948, Vol. II, p. 492.) "The life of union with God marks the summit of the Dominican life, the apostolate finds its source there." (Joret, *The Dominican Life*, p. 82.)

Rule in favor of something else that seems, from a human point of view, to be much more useful and valuable at the time. The greatest enemy of religious Orders is not the persecutor who closes monasteries and dispels communities and imprisons monks and nuns: it is the noonday demon who persuades them to go in for enterprises that have nothing whatever to do with the ideals of their founders.

Now there is nothing in the Statutes of the Cistercians—that is, the Trappists—to indicate that they ought to preach missions or run parishes or conduct schools. In moments of emergency—for instance, in war-time or in mission countries—they have had to engage in these works for a time: but even then the situation has always been regarded as unhealthy and has too often proved to have been so. An even more obvious danger is the materialism into which monks who are also professionally farmers can sometimes fall when they attach more importance to the business of running their farm than to the contemplative life which is their real end. The necessity to maintain industries in order to support their monasteries has also proved to be a considerable hardship to the Trappists. Teaching school may be a work of the active life, but at least it is a highly spiritual activity compared with the brewing of beer, the manufacture of chocolate, and the large-scale marketing of cheese. It was perhaps excessive materialism which really ruined the Cistercian Order in its golden age. The zeal for manual labor as an adjunct to the contemplative life turned into a zest for land-grabbing and business which utterly ruined the contemplative spirit and introduced avarice, and the confusion of much activity, where there should have been the calm recollection that is born of poverty of spirit.

A Trappist monastery will contribute most effectively to the life and the growth of the Mystical Body of Christ when it forms and prepares all its members for an integral life of silence, prayer, poverty, obedience, manual labor and so on, in order that they may tend to the perfection of contemplation. And the perfection of contemplation means, of course, infused or mystical prayer for those to whom God may deign to grant such a favor.

Now this is precisely the way in which the contemplative Orders perform their apostolic function. Usually people think that the "apostolate" of the monks consists principally in saying many rosaries and offering up many hours of prayer and sweat and hunger for particular intentions recommended to them. All these things count, no doubt. In some lives they play a larger part than in others. But it is not true to say that the apostolic efficacy of a Trappist monastery is measured by the quantity of physical sacrifices or vocal prayer the monks offer up for specific intentions. This conception would be a little crude. It makes one think of the prayer-wheels of the Far East. The monks do pray, and pray with the most ardent charity for the needs of souls in general and in particular—especially of those whom they once knew in the world outside. But the real apostolic "radiation" which goes out from a contemplative monastery springs from the interior purity of the monks' own souls and from the intensity of their contemplative union with the Christ Whose infinite Sacrifice, daily renewed, is the heart of their whole existence. The power of a contemplative monastery is not merely something you assess by counting up the number of Masses said on its altars, but by the perfection with which the community and all its members are *living* the one infinite and perfect Mass.

Anything that interferes with the qualitative intensity and depth of the monk's charity and contemplation of God also cools, by that very fact, the temperature of his apostolic radiation. And therefore when monks engage in works of a more material nature, and lessen their interior union with God, instead of becoming better apostles their apostolate is rendered far less effective.

Now that these things have been said, the reader should be in possession of the underlying truths on which the thesis of this book is based. If the author makes any statements which seem strange or exaggerated, in this respect, let the reader remember that the book was written by one who knows that for his own Order, at any rate, one thing alone is necessary. That one thing—the contemplation of God in silence and detachment from all things—is, for a Cistercian, the supreme apostolate.

PART ONE

I. MONASTICISM; ST. BENE-
DICT; THE CISTERCIANS

A MONK is a man who has given up everything in order
to possess everything. He is one who has abandoned
desire in order to achieve the highest fulfilment of all desire.
He has renounced his liberty in order to become free. He goes
to war because he has found a kind of war that is peace.

Beyond imagination, beyond grandeur, power, wisdom, and
the light of the mind, the monk has found the key to existence
in things without romance and without drama—labor, hunger,
poverty, solitude, the common life. It is the silence of Christ's
Nazareth, in which God is praised without pomp, among the
wood shavings.

The monk's business is to empty himself of all that is selfish
and turbulent and make way for the unapprehended Spirit of
God. That is his ministry and his whole life: to be transformed
into God without half realizing, himself, what is going on.
Everybody who is drawn to visit the monastery and who can
understand what is happening there comes away with the
awareness that Christ is living in those men: "That the world
may know that Thou hast sent me, and hast loved them as
Thou hast also loved me." [1]

It is this thirst for emptiness, for selflessness, that peopled
the deserts of Egypt in the third and fourth centuries. And
the marvelous writing of St. Athanasius and Cassian spread
that fire all over Europe.

When the hermit St. Anthony emerged from the ruined city

[1] "And the glory which Thou hast given me, I have given to them;
that they may be one as we also are one . . . and the world may know
that Thou hast sent me," etc. John xvii:22-23.

in the desert that had echoed for twenty years with the bicker-
ing of the devils against him, his face astonished the men who
had heard of him and had come to be his disciples. They did
not see a dead man or a man twisted by madness and fanaticism
and crude, half-idiot hatreds, but one whose countenance
shone with the simplicity and peace of Eden and the first days
of the unspoiled world. It was a face that would make expressions like "self-possession" and "self-control" look ridiculous,
because here was a man who was possessed, not by himself but
by the very uncreated, infinite peace in Whom all life and all
being lie cradled for eternity. He was more of a person than
they had ever seen, because his personality had vanished within
itself to drink at the very sources of reality and life.

St. Pachomius discovered another kind of solitude. In the
first great monastery of Egyptian cenobites, at Tabenna, the
monk learned how to disappear—not into the desert but into
a community of other monks. It is in some ways a far more
effective way to disappear, and it involves, on the whole, an
asceticism that is peculiarly deep and lasting in its effects.

For centuries the monastic life meant one of two things:
being a hermit or being a cenobite. They were two roads to
the same immediate end—the emptying and purification of
one's heart, setting it free to praise the infinite God for His
sake alone.

No matter what the exaggerations of Tabenna and Nitria
and Scete may have been, the great abbots of Egypt and Syria
laid down the foundations of an asceticism that was full of
wisdom and prudence, good sense and charity. All the sanity
and moderation of St. Thomas Aquinas could find no better
authority on which to rest, no safer model to follow, than the
Conferences and *Institutes* of Cassian.[2]

Nevertheless, if the principles laid down by the masters were
full of truth and strength, the ambition of the disciples ended

[2] Dom Berlière, *L'Ascèse Bénédictine*, p. 4, remarks: "Modern Catholic
asceticism is in direct relation and perfect conformity with that of the
monks of the east." He is referring to the desert fathers.

up in the most fantastic ascetic rivalries—athletic frenzies of fasting and whipping that have given Egyptian monasticism a bad name.

St. Basil, who traveled up the Nile in the middle of the fourth century, was quick to sum up the weakness of the monastic life that he saw. The cenobitic system of Pachomius, he said, was too complex, too noisy, too active. Tabenna was a huge affair—a town, or rather an armed camp, of five thousand ascetics. They were divided up into platoons and regiments, under a hierarchy of military officials dependent upon the abbot, who was the general-in-chief. The vast machine worked efficiently enough, but with a kind of inhuman ponderousness. Labor was so arduous that it resembled modern sweatshop production. So great was the number of monks that all life was depersonalized. There was no intimate contact with superiors. Instead of real spiritual direction, the monks were subjected to a system of formal humiliations and public insults. It was only the extraordinary spiritual vitality of the monks themselves that kept this process from being altogether brutalizing.

It remained for St. Benedict, in the sixth century, to transform monasticism into a life that ordinary men could stand. Instead of letting men harden themselves in confirmed self-worship by striving to become heroes of physical endurance, St. Benedict shifted the whole impact of asceticism to the interior—from the flesh to the will. His monks had plenty to eat and plenty of time to sleep. He reduced the choral offices of the Egyptians by about two thirds and sent the community out to work in the fields for seven or eight hours a day. Extraordinary mortifications were forbidden or discouraged. Virtue consisted in *not* attracting attention rather than in doing things that were conspicuous. The sacrifices that really mattered to him were those that were exacted in secrecy from the deepest veins of selfhood. In such sacrifices, vanity could find no part; they undermined the whole foundation of egoism and self-idolatry. One of St. Benedict's secrets was to purify the hearts of men by acts that were outwardly ordinary, simple, insignificant: the common lot of men, one's daily work, the petty business of getting along peacefully with other people.

At the same time, St. Benedict developed a deep and healthy and Catholic mysticism of grace which is as simple as it is broad and practical. The mortification imposed by obedience, humility, the common life, is not sought for its own sake: it is given us only to open our eyes to the deifying light [3] which God is waiting to pour out upon us, and to make us ready for His action within us, so that in all things the monks may see and praise God. Their every action will be more His work than theirs and will shine with the radiance of His peace. They will taste His presence and thank Him with their praise. *Operantem in se Dominum magnificant.*[4]

St. Benedict's true contribution to European civilization is not that his monks were pioneers and builders and scholars and guardians of the classical tradition. These were only insignificant by-products of the wonderfully simple and Christian communal life that was led in the early Benedictine monasteries. The influence and the example of that life leavened, more than did anything else, the Europe that had been invaded by wave after wave of barbarian tribes. That influence and example kept alive the central warmth of peace and unity among men in a world that seemed to be wrestling with the ice of death.

Monastic perfection was not, of course, uniform and constant. From time to time, reforms were needed. Charlemagne found European monasticism in general decay, and his suggestions of reform were put into effect by a second St. Benedict—of Aniane—after the synod of Aix-la-Chapelle in A.D. 802. This reform put new life into the monasteries of the empire, but it also thrust them into the very center of the social and political arena.

The reform of St. Benedict of Aniane was not able to

[3] *Apertis oculis ad deificum lumen. Rule of St. Benedict,* Prologue.
[4] *Ibid.*

weather the invasions of the ninth century, but in 910 St. Berno and twelve monks founded Cluny in the woods of Burgundy, and the result was the most powerful monastic family that had so far existed in the Church.

Cluny rose up in the thick of the battle over lay investitures. It stood for a certain independence from secular influences, but the independence was to be in the political and ecclesiastical orders rather than in that of the spirit. With Cluny, the monk became, in the fullest sense, a public adorer for the whole of his society and for the entire Church.

There was something very admirable about this wedding of religion and secular life, at least in theory. But in practice the monks no longer led anything like the simple, hidden life of labor and solitude which St. Benedict had prescribed to bring them to the contemplation of God. Though Cluny had many saints in its two thousand abbeys and priories scattered all over Europe, and though it pulled the Church out of the perils of its darkest age, men began, by the end of the eleventh century, to look back with regret to the purity of the old monasticism.

The eleventh century was an age of experiments and trials and new departures in western monasticism. The great founders and reformers manifested their avidity for perfection by wandering from country to country, always in search of a wilder solitude in which to settle down. The journeys of St. Romuald, St. Stephen of Grandmont, St. Bruno, St. Bernard of Tiron, St. Robert of Arbrissel and the rest of them, plotted the map of Europe with crossing and recrossing paths that made of the land a labyrinth. The only one who stayed in one place was St. John of Vallombrosa.

All these men were in frankly open conflict with the conventional monastic and clerical life of their time. St. Bruno and St. John of Vallombrosa endangered their lives by open attacks against simony. It was common for such reformers to be invited to "reform" a monastery, only to be threatened with physical violence when the monks discovered how drastic a

change of life they themselves were expected to contribute
to the process.

St. Romuald wanted men to have the advantages of both the
hermitage and the common life. So he hit upon the expedient
of a combined community of hermits and cenobites. One first
entered the monastery and led the common life. Then, after
a period of trial, the monk could, if he so desired, live in an
enclosed cell in the monastery or go off to a hermitage in the
woods. He remained always subject to the abbot's control and
to obedience. On certain feasts all the hermits came to the
monastery and joined with the others in the choral office.

Two of the other great foundations of the eleventh century
pursued the same kind of purpose: to bring hermits into communities and combine the advantages of solitude and obedience. Grandmont and the Grande Chartreuse sought to give
men that isolation from temporal things that makes a life of
pure contemplation possible and, with the grace of God, even
easy. Grandmont was a much rougher experiment than the
Chartreuse, however, and the order had a stormy history
before it finally ceased to exist at the French Revolution.

The Carthusians founded their order on one of the most
detailed and practical documents in monastic history. After
almost fifty years of experience, the solitaries who had settled
in the lonely Alpine valley of the Grande Chartreuse finally
drew up their *Consuetudines*. These usages were written by
Prior Guigo, but they were probably based on the oral instructions of St. Bruno. Every line of the Carthusian rule [5] con-
vinces the reader that the men who framed it knew precisely
what they were looking for and had a very good notion of
the best means of finding it. They were able to put it all down
in precise terms, even though what they were doing amounted

[5] *Consuetudines*, Migne, *P. L.*, Vol. 153, col. 637 ff. Migne prints
Guigo's text and the extremely interesting commentary by the seventeenth-century general of the Carthusians, Dom Innocent Lemasson.
The two together give a very good idea of the substantial framework
of Carthusian life, its purpose and its ideals.

to a revolution in monastic life. Without any of the complexity of St. Romuald's compromise between the hermitage and the *cenobium*, the Chartreuse was a compact and well-ordered house, a ringed citadel of contemplation. The outworks were occupied by the lay brothers and oblates, and the central keep was a massive block of "cells," or stone cottages, each with its own oratory, workshop, and garden. These, in their turn, clustered around the monastic church.

At the Chartreuse, emphasis was on the monk's private adoration of God in the solitude and silence of his own cell. Here, he not only slept and worked and read and meditated, but also recited all the day hours except Vespers. On feast days, however, the solitaries chanted the whole office in choir, ate together in the refectory, and assembled in chapter. From the very beginning the Carthusians have jealously guarded against too many feasts in order to keep to the purity of the solitary life. They have succeeded better than most orders in keeping to the ideal of their fathers and have been willing to pay the price to do so.

All the other great monastic reforms of the eleventh century explicitly looked back to St. Benedict. Just as certainly as the Camaldolese and the Carthusians wanted to be hermits, St. John Gualbert desired the perfection of cenobitic life. His way was bound to be simpler than theirs: he had only to go back to the letter of St. Benedict's Rule, and there is no denying that this was a matter in which St. Benedict had said the last word.

As far as the good of monasticism as a whole was concerned, St. John Gualbert did precisely what needed to be done. It was all very well for the Camaldolese to experiment in a specialized, restricted vocation: that, too, was something the Church needed. But after all, the life of the solitary, even when it was modified by cenobitic elements, still was a matter of limited appeal. Was there, then, no possibility of monastic life in its purity and simplicity, a life that everyone could live, one that was contemplative, isolated from the world, and

centered entirely upon God, yet not beyond the strength of
ordinary men? That was the question that most needed to be
answered, and the most satisfactory answer was given by
Cîteaux.

The ferment of monastic reform that had brought so many
new communities into existence in the eleventh century cul-
minated, in 1098, with the foundation of a monastery whose
filiations would soon develop into one of the greatest contemplative orders in the Church. Cîteaux is supposed to have
taken its name from the reeds—*cistels*, in Burgundian patois—
which abounded in the marshy woodland where its twenty-
two founders came to settle on Palm Sunday, 1098. The land
was not far from Dijon, and it belonged to the Duke of Burgundy. He made no difficulties about ceding it to the austere
colonists: it was practically useless to anybody in the world
except penitent monks, and he happened to share the general
respect for their abbot, Robert of Molesme.

This Benedictine, who was now close to his nineties, had
acquired an enviable reputation, in the course of his long
career, as an abbot and director of souls. At different times in
his life he had been the center of minor conflicts between
communities of monks that contended with one another for
possession of him as their superior. And these contentions
were not yet at an end. His old abbey, Molesme, would soon
appeal to Rome to recover him from Cîteaux. Perhaps they
hoped that this would finish the new reform at one blow.
Fortunately it did not. For although Robert was ordered to
go back to Molesme, the other pioneers had more than enough
energy and determination to carry on without him. They
began laying down the foundations of what was to prove a
mighty and well-regulated monastic order, and they lost no
time in having it approved by the Holy See.

They knew they would need protection. Cîteaux began its
existence in stormy days. The founders of the new monastery
had walked out of Molesme, publicly lamenting the fact that
they had vowed to keep the Rule of St. Benedict yet found

it impossible to do so in a Benedictine monastery. For some time past they had been complaining of the discrepancies between the Rule, as it was chanted in chapter every morning, and the complex network of monastic usages which had corrupted the primitive simplicity and austerity of that Rule in past centuries. The strong conventional element in the monastery—made up of converted knights and noblemen who were as belligerent as they were shortsighted in spiritual things—had so strongly resented this criticism of the accepted order that they had beaten their prior, Alberic, and thrown him into the monastery jail. This was the man who would take over the direction of the new monastery when St. Robert returned to Molesme. St. Alberic drew up the fundamental *instituta* which were the basis of the Cistercian reform.[6]

In these few points St. Alberic sketched out a program of simplification that seemed wildly revolutionary to the men of his time. His "austerity" raised such an outcry that people paid no attention to the modest claim of the Cistercians that they were attempting nothing new. But the Cistercians were quite right. There was nothing whatever new about Cîteaux. The monks simply wanted to return to the Rule of St. Benedict in all its simplicity. Far from being innovators, they were making it their chief concern to clean house and rid the Order of the many innovations that cramped the monastic life and made contemplation difficult or even impossible.

The first thing that shamed them was the realization that, in the course of centuries, monks had devised specious excuses for softening the Rule and making its burden easier and easier on the flesh. Some of these excuses were legitimate. When the Cluniacs asserted that monks in northern climates ought to be

---

[6] This forms the sixteenth section of the *Exordium Cisterciensis Coenobii*. See Guignard, *Monuments Primitifs de la Règle Cistercienne* (Dijon, 1878), p. 71. This work, called the *Exordium Parvum*, is the official account of the foundation and purpose of Cîteaux, drawn up by St. Stephen Harding when he applied to the Holy See for approval of the basic legislation of the new Order, in the second decade of the twelfth century.

permitted to wear warmer clothing, they had been quite within
their rights. St. Benedict explicitly allowed a certain freedom
in the matter of clothing.[7] However, the Cistercians seem to
have felt that the use of fur coats and fur-lined jackets, not to
mention long, flowing robes and garments that were more or
less ornamental, went beyond the legitimate interpretation of
this rule. For their part, they would allow the monks to increase the *quantity* of their clothing in winter, without any
substantial change in the *quality*. They could wear both their
robes and both their cowls at the same time if they had to—but
no furs! Less legitimate, however, was an interpretation of
the Rule of abstinence from meat. St. Benedict had prohibited
the flesh of four-footed animals.[8] These casuists pointed out
that chickens and ducks and quails and partridges and turkeys
and pheasants had only two feet and therefore were not forbidden. Not everybody made use of this loophole, but the
Cluniacs were notorious for their ingenuity in dressing up fish
and vegetables and serving up spiced and seasoned dishes in
quantities and varieties that made meat unnecessary. One of
the chief concerns of the founders of Cîteaux was to return
to St. Benedict's "two portions" (*duo pulmentaria*), with black
bread and a few extra fruits in season.

Perhaps the Cluniacs had a reasonable excuse for their big
dinners. Their choral offices were four or five times as long
as those prescribed in St. Benedict. To stand in choir, hour
after hour, in a huge, unheated stone basilica, one needed
warm clothes and nourishing food. But the Cistercians were
not interested in that excuse. Their reply was that Cluny had
had no business increasing the length of the office in the first
place. So, Cîteaux took great pains to do what the Carthusians
had done before them. They stripped the office of all the

---

[7] *Vestimenta fratrum secundum locorum qualitatem ubi habitant vel
aerum temperiem dentur: quia in frigidis regionibus amplius indigetur,
in calidis vero minus. Rule,* chap. 53.

[8] *Rule,* chap. 39.

many litanies and processions and "little offices" and additional psalms and ceremonies and returned to the essentials laid down by St. Benedict.

At the same time they swept the sanctuary clean of all useless decorations. St. Bernard of Clairvaux was to launch a devastating attack on the monks who were supposed to be poor but whose churches were covered with gold, whose sanctuaries were illuminated by whole trees of candles, whose walls and pavements and ceilings were covered with paintings and sculptures and mosaics. Pictures and sculpture had their place in the churches and cathedrals open to the faithful at large; but what useful purpose did they serve in the monasteries of contemplatives, who had risen above the life of the senses and whose joy was to find God in pure faith? [9]

Devoured with the same hunger for the authentic, St. Stephen Harding sent two of his monks to Metz on foot to copy out the famous antiphoner that was supposed to contain the genuine notation of the purest Gregorian chant. He sent others to Milan to copy the texts and notation of the Ambrosian hymns from the earliest codices in the city of St. Ambrose himself. He sought to do away with the ornamentation that had crept into the chant in more recent centuries and return to the austere, pure simplicity of the primitive models.

The Cistercians did not always succeed in recapturing the perfection they strove for. The Metz antiphoner, for example, proved to be a disappointment. Nevertheless, St. Stephen Harding showed how serious he was about simplicity by letting the matter rest there. Instead of involving Cîteaux in a series of researches that would have taken the monks into regions of antiquarianism rather than prayer, he was content

[9] *Nos vero qui jam de populo exivimus; qui mundi quaeque pretiosa ac speciosa pro Christo reliquimus; qui omnia pulchre lucentia, canore mulcentia, suave olentia, dulce sapientia, tactu placentia, cuncta denique oblectamenta corporea arbitrati sumus ut stercora, ut Christum lucrificiamus: quorum, quaeso, in his devotionem excitare intendimus? Apologia ad Guillelmum,* chap. xii, No. 38.

to accept the imperfect text as it stood and go no further for the time being.[10]

The result of this liturgical house cleaning was something of a paradox. For, while Cluny had made every effort to encourage all the arts and crafts, and Cîteaux had just as consciously resolved to do without sensible beauty as an aid to devotion, it was the Cistercians who, in the long run, made the more lasting contribution to Christian art.

Cistercian architecture is famous for its energy and simplicity and purity, for its originality and technical brilliance. It was the Cistercians who effected the transition from the massive, ponderous Norman style to the thirteenth-century Gothic, with its genius for poising masses of stone, as it were, in mid-air, and making masonry seem to fly and hover over the low earth with the self-assurance of an angel. Yet, the Cistercians produced a far finer and purer Gothic than the ornate masses of columns and stained glass and flying buttresses that flourished all over western Europe, when the architects of the thirteenth century got drunk on the strong wine of their own virtuosity.

The typical Cistercian church, with its low elevation, its plain, bare walls, lighted by few windows and without stained glass, achieved its effect by the balance of masses and austere, powerful, round or pointed arches and mighty vaulting. These buildings filled anyone who entered them with peace and restfulness and disposed the soul for contemplation in an atmosphere of simplicity and poverty. St. Benedict's doctrine on humility, the basis of his teaching, was written out before them in stone. The monks had not, at first, consciously aimed

[10] The question came up again in the time of St. Bernard. The second generation of Cistercians, who numbered many experts on chant, like William of Rievaulx and Guy of Trois Fontaines, made a burning issue of it. They ended up by introducing a more or less definite reform and codification of norms governing the purity of chant as it was conceived in the monasteries of the White Monks. See *Collectanea Cisterciensium Reformatorum*, April, 1948, and St. Bernard, *De Ratione Cantus*, Tract. xiii.

at any such effect in building their churches. They had arrived
at this result in trying to solve the problem of expense which
the conventional Benedictine church brought up. The static
opulence of Cluny and the Norman builders had expressed itself in huge masses of masonry. These, in turn, cried aloud for
bas-relief and fresco to counteract the tedium of their sheer
weight. One expense led to another, and display demanded
still further display. The union of Cistercian asceticism and
Frankish intelligence, of pure spirituality and scientific brilliance, led to a revolution in architecture when the White
Monks found that, by a judicious concentration of loads and
thrusts and abutments, the bulk of masonry and the conse-
quent expense could be reduced by half.[11]

The churches and cloisters of abbeys like Fontenay, Senanque, Noirlac, Thoronet, and Silvacane, their mellow stones
glowing in a setting of quiet woods, still speak eloquently of
the graceful mysticism of twelfth-century Cîteaux. It was for
the abbot of Fontenay that St. Bernard wrote his tract, *Degrees
of Humility*, with its wonderful twelfth chapter on mystical
prayer. Fontenay itself represents the direct influence of St.
Bernard and is the precise application of his principles on
architecture.[12]

In such settings as these, the purified liturgy of the Cistercians became a thing of tremendous effect. What meanings
men rediscovered in the Mass, now that the essentials of the
Sacrifice stood out in bold relief, liberated from a welter of
confusing decorative details! Simple and eloquent ceremonies,
harmonizing with the style of the sanctuary and dictated
by its very austerity,[13] tied the whole power of the building

---

[11] Cf. Ralph Adams Cram, *The Substance of Gothic*, p. 116. See also
his "Gothic Architecture" in *The Catholic Encyclopaedia*.

[12] "L'influence directe de Saint Bernard et l'application exacte de ses
principes," M. Anselme Dimier, O.C.R., *Revue du Moyen Age Latin*,
Vol. III (1947), No. 3, p. 269.

[13] The different bows prescribed for one ascending from the choir
of the monks up the low steps or "degrees" that divide the "presbytery"
into two sections, the isolation of the altar from the wall, the ceremonies

and the strong chant of the choir to the action that was proceeding at the altar.

Now that the eye was no longer lost in a throng of ministers and a sea of moving vestments, mind and heart could concentrate on the one central thing that really mattered. And the monks in choir contributed their part to the "action" by the vital movement, the systole and diastole of chant, rising and falling with tremendous dignity and austere power to form a background and commentary—a musical meditation on the Mass of the time or the saint of the day.

All contemplative life on earth implies penance as well as prayer, because in contemplation there are always two aspects: the positive one, by which we are united to God in love, and the negative one, by which we are detached and separated from everything that is not God. Without both these elements there is no real contemplation.

The Cistercians did not conceive penance as a system of arbitrary and irritating practices by which the abbot could tease and mortify his monks. The penitential life of the White Monk did not consist in a series of athletic feats of endurance or of systematic flagellations, or even of deliberately-staged public humiliations. The Cistercians were basing their life on the Gospel: and the "austerity" of the life that was led and preached by Jesus Christ is the broad, fundamental, searching austerity of labor and poverty. The penance of the Cistercians is essentially the common penance of the whole human race: to "eat your bread in the sweat of your brow" and to "bear one another's burdens." There would be plenty of cold and hunger and insecurity. Night after night the monk would go to his simple bed of straw, under the stone vaulting of his unheated dormitory, to rest his aching muscles for a few hours.

prescribed for priest, deacon, communicants, etc., going around the altar, etc. (see *Consuetudines*, 53-54), form the elements of a simple, dramatic action that concentrate the attention on the altar itself and on the meaning of the Sacrifice taking place there.

He would rise in the middle of the night and pray and work for a good long time before he got anything to put into his empty stomach. He would know the heat of the sun. His hands would be hard and rough from field work or building or the exercise of a craft.

It must not be imagined that these monks simply indulged in such things out of pious fancy. Underlying the Cistercian insistence on manual labor was a powerful element of what the Communists call "social consciousness." The poverty and labor of the early Cistercians had explicit reference to the social situation in which they lived. Besides being a return to St. Benedict and the Gospel, their way of life was also a protest against the inordinate wealth of so many of the great feudal abbeys.

One of the strongest criticisms leveled by Cîteaux against the Cluniac regime was that it was rooted in social injustice. The Cistercians could not accept the notion of a life of contemplation in which the interior peace and leisure of the contemplative were luxuries purchased by the exploitation of serfs and the taxation of the poor. St. Benedict had prescribed that the monk was to be the poorest of the poor and live by his own labor. Orderic Vital, the twelfth-century Benedictine historian, represents St. Robert chiding the monks of Molesme in chapter for living "on the blood of other men." [14]

If the monk has abandoned the cares and distractions and burdens of life in the world, that does not mean he has renounced the society of other men or the responsibility of providing for himself by the labor of his own hands: far from it. In giving up his possessions, material ambitions, and independence, the monk dedicates his whole life, body and soul, to the service of God in his monastic community. From the moment he makes his vows he gives to God everything that he has and everything that he is or can be. But the gift is not accepted directly by God. God's representative is the abbot of the monastery, *qui Christi agere vices in monasterio credi-*

[14] Orderic Vital, Migne, *P. L.,* Vol. 188, col. 637.

tur.[15] And the monk understands, by the terms in which his vows are made, that his gift of himself to God will consist chiefly in a gift of himself to his abbot and his brothers. He will now live no longer for himself but for the monastic family to which he has been admitted. He will prove his love for God and glorify Him by the simplicity and love with which he obeys his abbot and his brothers, and dedicates his body and soul to the praises of God and to the round of labor and reading and meditation laid down in the Rule. His poverty is so complete that he cannot give or receive or lend or borrow the smallest article, a book or a pen, without permission of his superiors. Indeed, St. Benedict says that the monk no longer has full jurisdiction over the acts of his body and soul. They are no longer his. They belong to God.[16]

But even the monastic family itself was to be poor. The monks owned their own land, and from it they had to earn their living. Their chief source of income was to be their own farm, their flocks, their herds, their vineyards, orchards, and forests, their quarries and fishponds. St. Alberic's *instituta* explicitly forbade the exploitation of tithes or serfs or manorial mills and bakeries; the Cistercians were not to accept the care or revenues of parishes or other benefices. They were to be poor with the poverty of Christ, *pauperes cum paupere Christo.* But this poverty, which amounts to one of the most intimate necessities of the contemplative life, something without which contemplation cannot achieve a vital development, always has its communal aspect for a Cistercian. The White Monk's poverty is not merely a negative self-stripping: it also has a positive function, the support of others in charity.

That was why an anonymous Cistercian writer of the twelfth century could go back to the fourth chapter of the Acts of the Apostles and point to the communism of the early Christians as an exemplification of the Cistercian ideal. "The

---

[15] *Rule,* chap. 2.
[16] . . . *quippe quibus nec corpora sua nec voluntates licet habere in propria potestate. Ibid.,* chap. 32.

multitude of the believers had but one heart and one soul; neither did any one say that aught of the things that he possessed was his own: but all things were common unto them. Neither was there any needy among them. For as many as were owners of lands or houses sold them and brought the price of the things they had sold and laid it down before the feet of the Apostles. And distribution was made to each one according as he had need." [17]

This complete, uncompromising totality of the common life, in which absolute poverty paved the way for a pure union of charity, was considered by the early Cistercians to be the safest and most comprehensive formula for spiritual perfection. The author we are citing, the unknown writer of the *Exordium Magnum*, calls this Christian communism the *formula perfectae poenitentiae*,[18] and the expression is full of meaning. The poverty, obedience, self-renunciation, humility, and fraternal love implied by the common life of the Apostles and monks sum up all that is most efficacious in Christian penance. But more than that, his term *poenitentia* has a positive ring about it, in its context, which makes it mean not mere penance but sacrifice. To give up everything and devote yourself without compromise to the love of Christ in the common life is to glorify God and offer Him the worship that most pleases Him, because it most resembles His own infinite generosity and the gift of Himself to us in the Incarnate Word. It enables us to love one another as He has loved us.

One of the most striking features of this ascetic ideal is that

[17] Acts iv:13. St. Benedict also refers to this passage in *Rule*, chap. 33.
[18] *Exordium Magnum*, Dist. i, cap. 1. The *Exordium Magnum* is a much more lengthy document than St. Stephen's *Exordium Parvum*, to which we have referred, but it has far less authority. It was probably written by several hands, and much of it is legendary. However, it is full of living and accurate details of Cistercian life in the twelfth century. For the authorship of the *Exordium Magnum*, see Vacandard's *Vie de Saint Bernard*, p. xlix. It is considered certain that the latter part of the *Exordium Magnum* was written by the German monk Conrad of Eberbach, but the author of the first sections is an unknown monk, probably of Clairvaux.

it is open to everybody. It is a way of perfection from which no one is excluded. No special vocation, no abnormal spiritual equipment, is required. The purity of the Gospel is open to all Christians, and the Cistercian life is the purity of the Gospel. When the founder of an independent monastic congregation, St. Stephen of Obazine, tried to have his communities affiliated to the Carthusians, whose way of life is more distinctly "special," Guigo, the prior and legislator of the Grande Chartreuse, advised him to take his application to Cîteaux. "The Cistercians," he said, "travel the royal road and their statutes lead to all perfection." [19]

In the course of the twelfth and thirteenth centuries, thousands of ordinary men, together with some of the intellectual and spiritual élite of western Europe—men who might otherwise have been swept away on the strong tides of violence and passion that swelled in the semicivilized world of their time—settled down in Cistercian cloisters to become peaceable and industrious beings—gentle, unselfish, and meditative men whose hard work changed the face of many a wilderness and whose prayers affected the spiritual history of their world in ways that will never be known this side of the tomb.

It would not do to paint too idealistic a picture of the monks in an order as large as that of Cîteaux was soon to become. They did not all turn into great saints. Some of them preserved many of the rough edges they had brought into the cloister from the world. Documents of the time leave us evidence that great sacrifices were demanded to get along with some of the people who were admitted to Cistercian monasteries. But such vocations were not only not excluded, they were taken for granted by the Rule. [20]

[19] See Migne, *P. L.*, Vol. 153, col. 583.

[20] In the prologue, St. Benedict starts out with an explicit declaration that his Rule is addressed to anyone who wants to save his soul: *Ad te meus sermo dirigitur, quisquis abrenuntians propriis voluntatibus, Domino Christo vero regi militaturus, oboedientiae fortissima atque praeclara arma sumis.* In various later chapters we find him making provision for those who argue with the abbot (chap. 3), who not only disobey the

A monastery is not a social club, and it would not be fitting to exclude genuine vocations because of bad manners or imperfections of character, as long as there is the sincere good will that St. Benedict demands.[21] The basic idea in Cistercian asceticism is chanted by the monks at the *mandatum*, when they wash one another's feet every Saturday in the cloister. *Congregavit nos in unum Christi amor*. It is Christ's love that has brought us here together in this house. The sanctity of each one is somehow bound up, in the inscrutable designs of God, with the sanctity of the others. We did not come here for the scenery, the architecture, the fresh air, the music, the country life, or for human friendship. We were brought here to be sanctified by the Holy Ghost—first, no doubt, as individuals but also together as a community. We were brought here that God's love might live in us: that God's grace and the constant daily contact with one another might ground us in a deep, experimental knowledge of what we ourselves are and what all men are, that we might learn patience and unselfish, gentle obedience and be filled with the humility and mutual forbearance without which it is impossible to ascend to the higher reaches of contemplation.

One of the early works of St. Bernard, *Degrees of Humility*,

Rule but make trouble for everybody and are at the same time too stupid to appreciate the force of excommunication (chaps. 23, 28). There is the possibility that honors like the priesthood or the office of prior may turn certain spirits into intriguers and troublemakers (chaps. 60, 63). Divisions may arise in the community from monks taking one another's defense in quarrels (chap. 67), and the saint even foresees the possibility that some of his subjects may lose their tempers and get into a fight (chap. 68). Yet, with all these possibilities in full view and calmly considered, the Rule lays down prescriptions for preventing disorder and for healing any harm that may be done, and urges everyone to practice mutual obedience in an atmosphere of honor and respect that is nothing short of heroic (chaps. 69, 70).

[21] The signs of a vocation, according to St. Benedict, are: a real desire of union with God (*si vere Deum quaerit*), a healthy interest in the liturgical prayers of the monks (*si sollicitus sit ad opus Dei*), willingness to learn obedience and to accept the humiliations and hardships of the common life. *Rule*, chap. 56.

lays down the foundations upon which Cistercian spirituality was to be built up into a powerful but very simple edifice. The abbot of Clairvaux, fond of divisions and degrees, like most of his contemporaries, shows his monks their way to God in "three degrees of truth." Under the guidance of divine grace, in the school of charity, in the silence of the cloister, we are to be gradually initiated into a deep and experimental knowledge of the truth—first, as it is found in ourselves, then as it is found in other men and, finally, as it is in itself.

The beginning of the ascent is self-knowledge. This is more than an academic acquaintance with the names of the things we have done or might be capable of doing. St. Bernard's humility, like that of St. Benedict, is a deep and searching and, on the whole, a very vital and healthy thing, because it enters into the very recesses of the spirit. It is an experimental knowledge, a deep-seated sense not of mere shame, not of mere confusion, but also, curiously enough, of love and peace at the recognition of the human weakness and insufficiency that are in us all. It is not only intellectual, this self-knowledge, it is also affective. It is something accepted by the will. What it means, in practice, is a profound quietude and self-effacement, the disposition of a man who has gone far beyond mere callow disgust with his own failures and has begun at last to pass out of himself and attach no more importance to himself. He has become without value in his own eyes, *ipse sibi vilescit*. And when you recognize that something has no value, you cease to bother about it.

It is in this atmosphere of humility that the way to contemplation begins. It is only through this deep and pacifying sense of his own unimportance that the monk can be set free for the blissfully happy occupation of attending to God, Who alone is all reality and in Whom all values are sublimated, transcending every concept to which the mind has access.

The atmosphere of genuine humility is termed by St. Bernard the *spiritus lenitatis* ("spirit of kindness, gentleness").[22]

[22] *De Gradibus Humilitatis*, No. 14.

Perhaps no one who has not lived in a monastery can quite savor the rich implications in those two words. No one who has not tried to follow St. Bernard and St. Benedict and enter into their peace can quite grasp the spiritual beauty and moral harmony that are contained in that idea. Yet, visitors to Trappist monasteries who have been struck by the sight of some old, hard-handed, white-bearded lay brother absorbed in his job, completely unconscious of himself and radiating the innocence and prayerful gentleness of a good child, because he is obviously in communion with God even while he works, will recognize something of what St. Bernard is talking about. The *spiritus lenitatis* is a tenderness born of the experience of suffering, and it expands and reaches out to embrace all other men, filling our hearts with a delicate and Christian considerateness for their sufferings. When you have a broken leg, you are careful of your movements; if you have any natural sympathy, you will be just as careful of other people when you see them in the same kind of trouble. In the same way, Cistercian humility makes you very circumspect in your actions when you know your will to be weak and wounded and your intellect to be often blinded by selfishness and passion. Once you have experienced the pain of your own infirmity (and to feel the pain is the first step on the way to a cure), you soon learn compassion and a corresponding tenderness toward other people.

Now, in the common life, all the men God has brought to the monastery to be sanctified by His Spirit are thrown together with their various spiritual infirmities, their impatience, their inconsiderateness, their petty vanity, their bad tempers perhaps, and their pride and all the failings of which they are so largely unconscious. St. Bernard sees in all this a tremendous occasion for spiritual growth.

The abbot of Clairvaux seized upon this most characteristic Cistercian doctrine and gave it a crucial position in his mystical theology. The problem of mysticism is to endow the mind and will of man with a supernatural experience of God as

He is in Himself and, ultimately, to transform a human soul into God by a union of love. This is something that no human agency can perform or merit or even conceive by itself. This work can be done only by the direct intervention of God. Nevertheless, we can dispose ourselves for mystical union, with the help of ordinary grace and the practice of the virtues. We have just seen that, for St. Bernard, the two principal steps in this active preparation were humility and charity, or meekness and compassion. They both are "experiences" of the truth: the truth about ourselves and the truth about others. But since contemplation is an "experience" of God by connaturality, by union of love, St. Bernard sees that a connatural appreciation of the sufferings and sentiments of other men is an excellent preparation for the mystical knowledge of God in the obscure "sympathy" of infused love. After all, contemplation is an intimate knowledge of God that flows from a loving union with His will. And God Himself has told us that the ordinary way to that union of wills with Him is union of wills with other men for His sake. "Let us love one another, for charity is of God. And everyone that loveth is born of God, and knoweth God. He that loveth not, knoweth not God, for God is charity. . . . He that loveth not his brother whom he seeth, how can he love God whom he seeth not? . . . If we love one another God abideth in us, and His charity is perfected in us." [23]

St. Bernard gives another reason why this charitable compassion is a perfect preparation for mystical prayer.

It is, he says, because the Holy Ghost takes a more transcendent part in the acts of such a soul and intervenes more directly in the work of preparation. He shows us how, in the vicissitudes and trials of community life, the Spirit of God, the Spirit of Unity, is at work in the souls of the monks, visiting and purifying each will with fire and sweetness, to make it merciful, *dignanter visitans, suaviter purgans, ardenter*

[23] I John iv:7, 8, 20, 12.

efficiens misericordem facit. The final result, in the soul that submits to this action of God, is that the will softens and is made smooth and pliant and tractable, like well-greased leather. It can be "stretched," says the saint, even to the extent of loving its enemies. Then it is ready for the higher experience, the supernatural union in which it will pass out of itself entirely and be absorbed in the pure love of God.[24]

We can see that, for St. Bernard and his contemporaries, the true fulfilment of the Cistercian life was something more than the literal observance of the Rule of St. Benedict, more, even, than the practice of perfect fraternal charity in a common life like that of the first Christians. Both of these were only means to a more perfect end: mystical contemplation and union of the soul with God. This must be well understood by anyone who hopes to grasp the full meaning of the Cistercian vocation, whether in the twelfth century or in the twentieth. The Cistercian Order is essentially contemplative, and it is contemplative in the purest and strictest sense of the word.

St. Bernard saw that, in actual fact, there would always be many in the monastery who would be penitents or active laborers rather than pure contemplatives. They would find their peace in a humbler degree of prayer, but perhaps (as the modern *Spiritual Directory* of the Order tells us)[25] they still might reach a higher degree of perfection than someone who was a mystic. However, if the monastery, like the house where Christ was received in Bethany, was a mixed family of penitents and active laborers and pure contemplatives, it was the contemplatives, sitting like Mary Magdalen at Christ's feet, who were the real glory of that house. *Felix domus et beata semper congregatio est ubi de Maria Martha conqueritur.*[26]

St. Bernard opened his long series of sermons on the *Canticle of Canticles* with a clear statement that the monks of Cîteaux

---

[24] *De Gradibus Humilitatis,* vii, 20.
[25] *Spiritual Directory,* Translation (2nd ed.; Gethsemani, 1946), p. 36.
[26] St. Bernard, *Sermo iii de Assumptione,* No. 2.

were called, at least in a general way, to breathe a higher and more rarefied spiritual atmosphere than Christians in the world outside.[27] The best modern historians agree [28] that the truly characteristic note of the Cistercian vocation is that it understands the Rule of St. Benedict as, above all, a preparation for the mystical life and that it travels toward contemplation by a purely cenobitic way.

It is this that truly explains the strict legislation of the first Cistercians, St. Alberic's *instituta* on fasting and poverty, and the jealous zeal with which the White Monks hid their monasteries in deep woods and mountain valleys to keep away from "the world." It explains the great reluctance of the Cistercians to undertake the direction of nuns and their absolute refusal, for many years, to have anything to do with parishes. Even in the thirteenth century there is repeated legislation in the General Chapter against the tendency of some monasteries to mix in the exterior ministry. And the basic collection of statutes made in 1134 even forbade the monks to hear the confessions of seculars or to give them Communion or burial unless they were actually guests in the monastery or hired hands working with the monks.[29] For the same reason, to preserve their silence and peace, the Cistercians refused to undertake the education of boys, even to prepare them for their own cloisters. When some of the Cistercian saints began to acquire reputations that attracted pilgrims to their tombs, the monks walled up the doors that gave access to their places

---

[27] *Vobis frates alia quam aliis de saeculo, aut certe aliter dicenda sunt* (*In Cant.* i, No. 1). These are the opening words of the first sermon. St. Bernard appeals to the authority of St. Paul who "spoke wisdom among the perfect" (I Cor. ii:6) and tells his monks that he knows them to be well exercised in asceticism and wishes them to proceed with him to more contemplative studies—*Jam acceditur ad hunc sacrum theoricum sermonem* (*Ibid.*, i, No. 3).

[28] Gilson, *Mystical Theology of St. Bernard*, pp. 13-17. Dom David Knowles, *The Monastic Order in England*, p. 218.

[29] Canivez, *Statuta*, 1134, No. 7. See also 1234, No. 1; 1235, No. 2; 1236, No. 3.

of burial and suppressed the accounts of their miracles.[30] The early Cistercians had no desire for publicity and made no attempt to draw attention to the austerity of their lives or to the sanctity of their members.

At the same time, this desire for contemplation as the final consummation of the monastic life was what led the first Cistercians to reestablish the original sane balance of the Benedictine Observance, which is divided into three essential parts: the Divine Office, or liturgical praise of God in choir; manual labor, and *lectio divina*. *Lectio divina* means spiritual, meditative reading, especially of Scripture or the Fathers of the Church. It excludes the intense, analytical application of the scholar and aims less to endow the mind with information than to lead the whole soul to an affective union with God in contemplative prayer. The Cistercians made sure that the two or three hours a day allowed in the Rule for the *lectio divina* were not replaced by public vocal prayers or manual labor, under the guise of giving more glory to God. They frankly admitted that they found the inordinately long offices of the Cluniac monks an insupportable burden.[31]

The Cistercian life, in the Order's Golden Age—which lasted until the middle of the thirteenth century—was a life of marvelous simplicity and joy. Later on in this book we will consider its harmony and balance in greater detail. For the moment it will be enough to remark on the monuments which the Cistercian spirit of the twelfth century has left for us to admire today. We have already spoken of the White Monks' architecture. The same mixture of solidity and luminous order and supernatural joy is found in the magnificent theological prose of St. Bernard's school. True, there were also many poets

[30] M. Seraphin Lenssen, *La Vénération des Saints Cisterciens dans l'Ordre de Cîteaux, Collectanea, O.C.R.*, vi, 1, p. 24.

[31] *Imbecillitatem suam ad tantum pondus sustinendam judicantes . . ."* *Exordium Parvum*, 12, Guignard, p. 68.

in the Order of Cîteaux.[32] But the greatest Cistercian poets
did not write in verse.

There is in the Latin of St. Bernard, Blessed Guerric, or
William of St. Thierry a melody and a freshness that are
incomparable, even in the Middle Ages.[33] But the vitality of
their writing does not lie merely in their poetic prose, enriched
with all the deep music of Scripture. It is not so much the way
they say things, as what they have to say, that wakes up the
mind and heart of anyone capable of appreciating them and
leads him to a rediscovery of the old Cistercians' paradise of
peace. Their prose does not talk, it sings: but it would not have
such an effect if it did not have so much to sing about. Anyone who will go to the effort to master their language will find
in the twelfth-century Cistercian writers the pure joy of souls
in possession of God, souls to whom God has revealed His
secrets in luminous and simple experience. . . .

They play only a few variations on the same fundamental
theme: the love of God, the knowledge of God in contemplation, the life of virtue, humility, and obedience that prepares
the soul for contemplation. Yet, although they are writing,
most of all, of the *experience* of God, these deeply speculative
minds could not pass over their subject without analyzing the
nature of charity itself and the make-up of the soul in which
this experience was received. The Cistercians were the greatest
psychologists of their age. Most of the writers of the
Order have left us tracts *De Anima;* all of them have gone
deeply into the nature of love. Generally, they found themselves inevitably discussing both at the same time, as St. Bernard so frequently does in his sermons on the *Canticle,* or St.
Ailred of Rievaulx in his *Speculum Caritatis.* However, since
it is not enough to have a soul that is capable of love, and love

[32] For instance, Bl. Helinand of Froidmont, Bl. Foulques of Marseille,
Serlo of Wilton.

[33] In many passages of St. Bernard's prose the lines may be broken
down into complex and subtle metrical patterns, and even into standard
verse-forms; cf. M. Anselme Dimier, "Les Amusements Poetiques de
S. Bernard," *Collectanea, O.C.R.* xi, n. 1, Jan. 1949.

which is capable of filling it, there must be a Mediator to bring the supernatural love of God down to man and raise man up to God. The Cistercian writers, therefore, find the exemplar, the efficient and meritorious cause of all contemplation in Christ, the Word Incarnate, Who was, in Gilson's happy phrase, "a concrete ecstasy in Himself." [34]

At the very heart of Cistercian spirituality lies a poignant devotion to the sufferings of Christ and to His death on the Cross. St. Bernard and his disciples entered deeply into the mystery of the Passion—more deeply than any one before their time, except perhaps St. Paul. They saw in the Passion the greatest proof of God's love for men. Constant meditation on Calvary, or rather an uninterrupted contemplative awareness of the love of Christ for men, expressed by His Cross, was one of the characteristics of the interior life of St. Bernard. Compassion for the crucified Savior was as important a means to dispose the soul for mystical prayer as compassion for one's neighbor.[35]

Finally, St. Bernard and his school were the greatest of the medieval panegyrists of the Mother of God. Indeed, it is the Blessed Virgin herself who seems to have been mostly responsible for the magnificent vitality and freshness of the Cistercian spirit. The White Monks were not slow to recognize their indebtedness to her. They were the most explicit in proclaiming Mary as the mediatrix of all graces, through whom came all God's gifts to men.

When the Cistercian Order was at the height of its spiritual vigor and this rich surge of the contemplative spirit was filling the young mystical vine of Cîteaux in all its widespread branches, Eugene III, himself a White Monk, wrote to the General Chapter from Rome, warning them that the life and death of the Order depended on their fidelity to the contemplative ideal.

[34] *Op. cit.*, p. 110.
[35] Cf. *Serm.* 53 *In Cantica.*

Look back, I beg you, to the Fathers who founded our holy
Order and consider how they left the world and contemned all
things, left the dead to bury their dead and fled to solitude; consider how they deputed to others all care to be busy with much
serving of souls, and for their own part sat like Mary at the feet
of Jesus: and thus the further they departed out of Egypt, the
more richly did they receive manna from heaven.[36]

It was more than a hundred years after this letter was written that the Order entered upon a decline visible enough to
be recognized by historians. But if we look for causes of the
decline only in the period after it had already taken place,
we will not stand a very good chance of finding them. That
is why the Black Death and the Hundred Years' War and, last
of all, the *commendam*, were not responsible for the corruption of Cîteaux. The corruption was already secretly at work,
even at the end of the twelfth century, when the Order, outwardly so powerful, still was at a high tide of interior fervor.

Yet, the decline had already begun. Even though there were
many great contemplatives in the Order during the early thirteenth century—and afterward, for that matter—the vast expansion and material power of the Cistercians could not help but
corrupt the simplicity of their original spirit. The General
Chapters put up a magnificent reaction, and the forces of
decay were held in check for many years to come; but they
were definitely working.

It was not the austerity of the monks themselves that began
to weaken. Their fasts, their personal poverty, their manual
labor, continued for two centuries in all the rigor of St.
Alberic's *instituta*. But if the monks themselves did not get
rich, their monasteries did, and one of the first fundamentals
of the Cistercian reform to be disregarded was the prohibition
of parishes and other sources of income, like tithes. Even
before the end of the twelfth century it was not infrequent
for abbeys to accept benefices and sources of revenue for-

[36] Letter to the General Chapter of 1150, prefixed to St. Bernard's
Letter No. 273.

bidden by the founders of the Order. What was worse, the very virtues of the Cistercians tended to contribute something to their decline. The man power of huge abbeys, operating in a far-flung system of granges and distant estates, was immensely productive in its labors, and the Cistercians became one of the most powerful economic forces in the Middle Ages. If the Cluniacs had been implicated in worldliness by their feudal estates, the Cistercians suffered the same disaster in the marketing of great supplies of wheat and wine and oil and wool. The important abbeys had to maintain warehouses and commercial agencies—staffed, of course, by monks and brothers —in the nearby cities. The *cellarium,* or agency, of Clairvaux can still be seen in Dijon today. Monks had to travel to the great international fairs to put their produce on the market, and we read of Cistercians manning riverboats to ship cargoes of wine from the Moselle down the Rhine to Holland. Eventually, the contemplative spirit caved in under the pressure of so many active and material interests, and the Cistercians tended to lose themselves entirely in the active side of their lives. Still faithful to their liturgical obligations and their fasts, they also poured out the surplus of their riches in great abundance on the poor and the sick, on travelers and pilgrims. They continued to do a tremendous amount of good for the society of their times, but the *unum necessarium,* the contemplative spirit, was gone.

And when a contemplative order ceases to produce contemplatives, its usefulness is at an end. It has no further reason for existing.

II. DE RANCÉ
AND LA TRAPPE

BY THE middle of the seventeenth century the huge
Cistercian Order made a curious picture, a kind of
ragged patchwork quilt flung over the chilly bones of monastic
Europe. It was still a powerful order, materially, ecclesiasti-
cally. It was an influence that had to be reckoned with in
politics. But for three hundred years it had been a huge shell,
the sepulcher of the spirituality of St. Bernard. It had its great
doctors in the Sorbonne. It had its colleges in the university
cities of Europe—colleges that had begun to appear when the
mendicant orders inherited the dominance of religious life
from Cîteaux in the 1200's.

Of course, there were plenty of Cistercian bishops and
cardinals. There were Cistercian theologians and historians and
moralists, not the least of whom was John Caramuel, whom
St. Alphonsus called "the prince of laxists." It would be wrong,
probably, to say that there were no Cistercian saints: but there
were very few in the Order who would be considered likely
candidates for canonization.

The huge organism had long been too big for the feeble
life that was guttering out in its heart. It had already begun
to split up into small, isolated congregations in the sixteenth
century. That was the only way it could live. There was nowhere in the Order a vital force capable of reforming the
whole body from within: but there were men who had enough
energy and sanctity to reform single houses, then gather
around them groups of ten or fifteen more houses to form a
congregation.

One by one these new organisms would form, against the

feeble, complaining protests of the parent body—complaints which emanated from Cîteaux and the rare General Chapters: and one by one they would break away. Two of the earliest and strongest of these were the congregations of Castille and the Feuillants.

Martin Vargas formed a solid block of regular and fervent Cistercian houses in Spain, which were able to keep something of the spirit of the Order alive. Jean de la Barrière took charge of the abbey of Feuillants, which he held *in commendam,* and introduced a reform that was extremely austere and had practically nothing to do with St. Benedict or St. Bernard. The monks slept on boards and ate on the floor and went barefoot. What they ate when they were sitting on the floor was mostly black bread, and where they went on their bare feet was on processions all over France. They were scarcely Cistercians, and for once even the General Chapter was glad to have no part of them.

For the rest, there were congregations in Tuscany and Lombardy, in Portugal, Aragon, Poland, and Ireland, in southern Italy and northern Germany.

But the reform that really mattered was the one that had made shy beginnings in the abbeys of Charmoye and Chatillon and was soon taken up at Clairvaux by Denis Largentier. By the year 1618 the "Strict Observance" had spread to eight monasteries, and it went on growing, despite the suspicious attitude of the General Chapter. By the middle of the century some sixty monasteries were making a show of keeping the Rule, although it was far from being strict, in the sense of primitive monasticism.

The fact is, this Strict Observance could not break away from the rest of the Order, and its history in the seventeenth century was nothing but a series of petty and sordid intrigues that proceeded from Cîteaux itself and aimed at the abolition of this timid reform. Matters took a somewhat diverting turn in 1636 when the General Chapter elected Cardinal Richelieu

Abbot General of the Order, in the hope that he would do away with the reform: but Richelieu proceeded to expel the Common Observance from Cîteaux and install the reformers in the very heart of the Order. It was a state of affairs that could not last beyond the death of His Eminence. The Strict Observance once more retired and took the defensive, fighting for the privilege of not eating meat.

When nature supplants the spirit of God in the souls of monks, the history of monastic orders can become distressingly Lilliputian.

Physically, however, there was nothing small about the abbey of Cîteaux. The original church of the founders, the church in which St. Bernard had prayed as a novice without discovering that there were three windows in the apse instead of one—this remained only as a curiosity. It was so tiny that one had great trouble finding it in the labyrinth of cloisters and halls and galleries and new wings. It was, in fact, buried under a mountain of architecture that had accumulated in the course of the centuries. In the midst of all this lived the Abbot General of the Cistercians in a house of his own that had all the character of a château. He was, in fact, a great Lord, and he lived in the style that befitted a nobleman, with servants and equipage in proportion to his rank. The monks, without living in supreme luxury, at least had all the comforts of the upper class, with servants and feather beds in their own private apartments. With all this, one is surprised to read that they still got up at four o'clock in the morning for the "night office" and managed to live without meat on certain other days in the week besides Friday.

There was an atmosphere of comfortable and pious respectability in most of the regular monasteries of the Common Observance, as distinguished from the ones that had fallen *in commendam*. The very existence of the Strict Observance had stimulated a new respect for regularity in the whole Order, and the seventeenth century witnessed a real revival in the Common Observance, as such. The revival took place on many different levels: spiritual, intellectual, material. The monks of the Common Observance took stock of their mitigated rules and tightened up their usages, such as they were, and took steps to live up to their obligations. If they could not muster up any enthusiasm for the austere primitive spirit of Cîteaux, they partly compensated for it by studying the history of the Order, not only with enthusiasm but even with intelligence, and it was at seventeenth-century Cîteaux that the Cistercian saints finally came into their own. Most of them had never had feasts in the liturgy of the Order, and their titles had never been officially recognized by Rome. The General Chapters now saw to it that both oversights were remedied. They did not feel that they could even make a gesture of keeping the primitive *instituta* of St. Alberic, but they found a place for the second abbot of Cîteaux in the Cistercian breviary and got his title to sanctity confirmed by the Holy See.

What was the mental attitude of the average monk of the Common Observance? How did he live? What did he live for?

He entered the monastery, usually, because he wanted to save his soul. He became a "Bernardine," a "monk of Cîteaux" —and *not* a monk of the Strict Observance—because he felt that he needed to save his soul in some way that was not too difficult. He balked at the notion of paying too much for his salvation. The monastery was a quiet and not too unpleasant haven, where he would receive care and shelter and could reasonably expect to keep out of trouble.

We have some letters written by an eighteenth-century novice who prepared for profession in a Cistercian monastery in southern France.[1] He is well fed. He has a room to himself and plenty of firewood to keep it warm. He is the only novice in a "regional novitiate" which is destined to supply sixteen southern French monasteries with trained subjects. He is expected to go to choir with the monks, but the rule about manual labor for novices, revived in the seventeenth century, has

[1] Quoted by Mgr. Auvity, *L'Abbaye de Bonneval* (Rodez, 1947), p. 77 ff.

become a dead letter again in the eighteenth. Most of the day he is free to read or walk around in the garden. However, his letters to his friends are curtailed, and he must take time to meditate on the eternal truths—which he does seriously enough. He realizes that God has brought him to the monastery "to weep for his past failings," and he hopes to survive the terrible "year of trial" by the grace of God. After that, things will not be so bad. He will make profession and go to his chosen monastery of Candeil, near Albi, where the prior is a "good fellow" and comes from his own home town. He will have an allowance of fifty *écus* a year for his wardrobe, and if he wants some more money, he can say Mass and preach a sermon each Sunday in one of the parishes controlled by the abbey. He can have a month-and-a-half or two-month vacation each year at any time he chooses and spend it with his family or friends. For the rest, he can receive visitors at the abbey any time he likes and for as long as they care to stay. . . .

On the whole, since he "likes the country," he looks forward to spending the rest of his life in what he euphemistically calls "solitude." As a matter of fact, his life was not too hampered even by the troubles of a community. There were only five monks at Candeil, and although they "got along well" together, they could easily keep out of one another's way if things went awry.

It is easy to see why noble and bourgeois families chose such monasteries as refuges for their less talented sons—the ones who did not stand much chance of making a way for themselves in the world.

With the commendatory abbeys, it was quite a different story. There, all the rich revenues, far from being enjoyed by the monks, were pocketed by the commendatory abbot. Life was not only not comfortable, it was often squalid.

No doubt there could be found traces of respectability in some of these houses. But there was not even that at La Grande Trappe, an old monastery of the White Monks in Normandy. La Trappe had been *in commendam* for about a hundred years. It had survived the Black Death and the Hundred Years' War and got as far as the sixteenth century without losing the essentials of religious fervor and regularity. But the *commende* had done what war and pestilence had failed to do.

In the thick of a marshy wilderness you came upon a group of half-ruined buildings so dilapidated and filthy that you hesitated to enter the wide-open door into the cloister. Cattle were stabled in the regular places. The bailiff of the commendatory abbot lived in a more or less inhabitable wing of the building with his wife and children. The seven tramps who were "the monks" camped where they could under the leaky roofs. The stairways had all collapsed, and if you wanted to go upstairs, you had to climb up to a first-story window by a ladder. The flagstones of the church pavement had worked loose and strayed from their places. The walls were ready to fall down, cracked from top to bottom, and nobody dared ring the bells that still hung precariously in the tottering belfry.

The best-preserved place in the building was the refectory, which the monks now used as a bowling alley in wet weather.

In the designs of Providence, it was the commendatory abbot of this shambles who was to deliver the Cistercians from the threat of final and irreparable corruption and bring the Order from the edge of the grave back to life and health.

Armand-Jean le Bouthillier de Rancé was the son of the secretary of Marie de Medicis and the godson of Cardinal Richelieu. He was a tonsured cleric at the age of nine, and when he was twelve he became abbot of three abbeys and prior of two priories, as well as canon of Notre Dame at Paris. One of the abbeys was La Grande Trappe. The leaky roofs of the ancient monastery, the tumble-down church, and the seven unkempt creatures playing at bowls in the refectory with their rustic friends were the last things in the world to concern this precocious child.

At the age of ten he had already acquired more than a superficial knowledge of the great Greek and Latin poets, and now he was planning a critical edition of Anacreon, with scholarly footnotes, which was to appear when he was thirteen. This child was also dexterous at fencing, was a good horseman, and possessed all the other skills proper to his rank. By the time he was sixteen, he knew the Fathers of the Church so well that the archbishop gave him permission to preach in any church in the city of Paris. In 1643, being seventeen years old, he was a doctor of philosophy, and in 1647 a bachelor of theology. In the contest for the licentiate he came out first on a list which included Bossuet. Bossuet was second.

In 1651 he was ordained priest. The year following, he was a doctor of the Sorbonne. When he was offered the mitre as Bishop of Léon, he refused it, because the diocese was too unimportant. He wanted to be Archbishop of Tours—and that was already in his family. His uncle had that throne, for the moment.

The character of this brilliant and ambitious nobleman demands to be studied a little, because it will help us to understand the special peculiarities that gave La Trappe a physiognomy entirely its own. For when De Rancé made his vows as a Cistercian of the Strict Observance in 1664, it was with the explicit intention of reviving twelfth-century Cîteaux. He did not realize how different La Trappe would be from the Cîteaux of St. Stephen and the Clairvaux of St. Bernard, in spite of all his own efforts and good intentions. The reason for the difference is to be sought in the life and character of the reformer himself.

At the core of De Rancé's nature was a dramatic and insatiable appetite for the extreme. Once he became attached to an idea, he could not rest until he had pushed it to its logical limits and exhausted all its possibilities. A brilliant mind, he was nevertheless dominated not only by inexorable logic but also by his sense of dramatic fitness, his taste for romantic climaxes. There was in him, underneath the outward polish and classical calm of the *grand siècle*, all the impulsiveness and enthusiasm of a romanticist.

In the world, De Rancé had lived a life similar to that led by some hero in Fielding. After he entered the monastery, he found himself in a new role: that of a father of the desert. Scene and formula had been changed completely, but his life still was a fascinating drama in which it was up to him to carry everything out to the limit. In the world, he had been avid for adventure, achievement, experience; now he was just as avid for the negation of these things. He could not rest until he had tried all the penances and fasts and mortifications and humiliations he had read about in the *Vitae Patrum.*

Nevertheless, De Rancé's retirement to La Trappe was anything but the fruit of a natural impulse. Even when he gave up his adventures and resumed his clerical dress and began to live a more retired life, he had great difficulty in overcoming his repugnance for monks. He despised monks. To him, *les frocards* were, at best, futile and useless little people who frittered away their existence in religious houses, never accomplishing anything that mattered. Their lives seemed dedicated to an evasion. The most serious and pious of them only moved him to disdain. The polite erudition of the Benedictines of Saint Maur was altogether too tame for him. He felt a bitter impatience with the quiet enthusiasm with which they browsed over the books they discovered in their wanderings from library to library. In all the monasteries of France he could not discover a monkish life that seemed to be anything but mildly stupid.

The closest he came to considering a monastic vocation, after his conversion first got under way in 1657, was when he thought of entering the Grande Chartreuse—not as a solitary, but as a permanent boarder in the guest house. The Carthusians were the only order that still kept up any kind of austerity; then, too, the wild scenery of the Chartreuse was something terrific. . . .

It was going to be a real struggle for this man to surrender completely to a vocation in which he would no longer be his own master. He dismissed most of his servants and lived in retirement, for the time being, and assuaged his conscience with acts of largesse: for instance, he undertook to feed five hundred poor people for a whole winter.

He retained control over all his property and was free to follow any adventurous fancy in the realm of piety. He could practice manual labor when he felt like it, just as he had gone hunting before. He could give away money to the poor as freely as he had once spent it on himself. If he wanted to pray, he could pray. He fasted when he felt like fasting. It was all very good in itself, but it could not satisfy De Rancé. It was becoming apparent that much more was expected of him. . . .

It took a long time for him to make up his mind what that might be. For five years he hesitated and asked questions. He consulted many different kinds of people—from D'Andilly, the Jansenist hermit of Port Royal, to Bishop du Plessis-Praslin of St. Bertrand-en-Comminges; from Gaston, Duke of Orléans, to a poor shepherd he encountered in a storm when both took shelter under a tree. He traveled to the Pyrenees to confer with the austere Bishop of Aleth, Monsignor Pavillon, who later fell under condemnation as a Jansenist. From there he journeyed to Pamiers to consult the bishop of that place. One of these persons would tell him one thing, and the next, something else. Least appealing, but seemingly the most worthy of consideration, was the advice given him by Monsignor du Plessis-Praslin, who told him flatly that he ought to be a monk.

Meanwhile, he had visited his various commendatory monasteries. He decided to give the richest of them to the Carthusians. He disposed of the others and found himself left with two: the Grandmontine priory of Boulogne in the forest of Chambord, and the Cistercian abbey of La Trappe.

There he was, face to face with a choice which, although he did not realize it, was to turn out a very significant one in the history of monasticism. Supposing he had joined the Grandmontines and revived *their* ancient disciplines: perhaps they would not have gone out of existence at the Revolution, and we would have had another semi-eremitical order today. The priory of Boulogne sounds as though it must have been rather attractive. It was a small place, lost in the forest. There were few cells, not many monks. It would have been real solitude.

But in the summer of 1662 the Abbé de Rancé left his estate at Veretz forever and headed for Normandy and La Trappe.

He still had no intention of becoming a monk. He meant to clean up the abbey and people it with decent monks from some regular monastery of the Strict Observance, while he settled in the manse of the commendatory abbot to look after both them and himself.

Monks were duly brought in from the Strict Observance abbey of Perseigne, and the commendatory abbot settled in his manse, but not for long. One day, just after he had walked out of one of the rooms, the ceiling came down with a crash. The abbé decided this was a providential sign that God did not want him living in that manse. It was time for him to take the regular habit and join the community as its true superior.

Accompanied by his former valet, who desired to enter the monastery as a lay brother, the Abbé de Rancé turned his steps to Perseigne, where he was welcomed into the novitiate. He proceeded to astonish everybody by reviving many austere practices he had read about in the annals of the Order. He finally approached the day of his vows, in the early summer of 1664, with ruined health but with the dogged determination to revive the ancient Rule. Then, having pronounced his vows, he returned to La Trappe and entered upon his office as abbot.

It was the psychological moment for such a step. The new Abbot General of the Cistercians, Claude Vaussin, was also getting ready to go into action. It was his intention to put the Strict Observance once and for all in its place. These malcontents would have to be brought into line and made to forget their nonsense about abstinence from meat and about all the other fasts and austerities they were so attached to. In other words, Providence had raised up a determined defender for the Strict Observance just when it was most needed.

It was to be a long and wearying conflict. The struggle between the two observances has perhaps been overdramatized by historians in order to cover its essential pettiness with a show of interest. From the Trappist side the abbot of Cîteaux and his party have always looked like smooth and polished villains, while from the camp of the Common Observance the Trappist faction has generally looked like a mob of wild-eyed fanatics. But it is certainly true that the Cistercians of the Common Observance were diplomats. They knew all the ins and outs of the legal formality that must necessarily attend litigation before the various tribunals of the Holy See, and in this they enjoyed the advantage over De Rancé in a war of nerves that only intensified the abbé's ruthlessness and confirmed him beyond recall in his devotion to an absolute extreme.

Just at the moment when he had finally given up everything and resolved to devote his entire life to God in solitude and penance and prayer, earnestly determined to do something about the immense evils he had seen in abbeys ruined by the *commende*, he found that the very order he wanted to save had mobilized against him the whole weight of its power and influence in order to defend the mediocrity which he detested.

When he had to leave his monastery and go to Rome and there spend day after day choking down his indignation and cooling his heels in the antechambers of cardinals who always put him off with some evasion, the convictions in the heart of the reformer became a white-hot fire of zeal for the most muscular form of penance, the most bitter and lashing humiliations, the blackest fasts, the longest vigils, the hardest labor.

And so the stage was set. Everything was now ready for the Trappists to lock their doors upon the world and put on their hair shirts and descend into the depths of that penitential silence that was to impress the world of that time more than the loudest outcry of protest could possibly have done.

Yet, we must not exaggerate. Life at La Trappe was not as frightful as it seemed to the men of that time. There were too many rumors. La Trappe got too much publicity. De Rancé's own rhetoric was too forceful. There was too much talk about skulls and gravedigging and brothers passing one another in the cloister with a whispered *memento mori*. But all things considered, life at La Trappe was in some respects easier than it is in the Trappist monasteries of the twentieth century. True, De Rancé attempted to revive the ancient Benedictine fasts, but he had to give them up and return to a timetable that came close to the present one, as far as meals are concerned. There were then only three hours of manual labor in the day. Now there are four or five. De Rancé allowed recreation, which has long since passed out of existence.

However, if the Rule at La Trappe was not particularly hard, the Abbé de Rancé encouraged his monks to compete with one another in extra penances and fasts and mortifications. One of the religious, who was not strong enough to work in the fields, exercised his ingenuity in manufacturing little penitential instruments of sharp wire, which the more zealous monks were allowed to wear about their person. It was considered a virtue to ruin one's health by excessive private fasting, and the religious who did not protest when the superior offered him medicine and rest and extra nourishment when he fell ill was apt to be tacitly considered a weakling. It is said that De Rancé dismissed a novice because he reached out somewhat gingerly for a clump of stinging nettles that he had been told to pull out by the roots.

Then there was the Abbé de Rancé's view of the monastic vocation. He electrified seventeenth-century France with statements like this: "The cloister is a prison in which everybody is held as guilty [before God] whether he has lost his innocence or not." [2] In the same vein, he said: [3]

Monastic congregations are bodies of men reckoned as criminals, men considered, by reason of their very state, as public penitents

[2] *De la Sainteté et des Devoirs de la Vie Monastique*, p. 315.
[3] *Ibid.*, p. 313.

and *who no longer have any claim on the goodness of God until they have made satisfaction to his justice by chastisements worthy of their sins.*

The monks of La Trappe were encouraged to consider themselves as outcasts, rejected by God and men, and to find solace not in contemplation of God's love or of His mercy but only in the grim business of exercising justice upon their own bodies and souls by every kind of austerity and humiliation.

That was why De Rancé placed such tremendous emphasis on the systematic tongue-lashings which he gave his monks in chapter and for which La Trappe soon became notorious. Monks were supposed to treasure above everything else these opportunities to accept "stinging reproaches, words of fire, public humiliation, and everything that could possibly contribute to their abasement." [4]

The superior who did not satisfy the supposed hunger of his monks for such bitter medicine was held to be guilty before God for gravely neglecting his duty. The monks, on the other hand, soon found out that it was all an elaborate game, and the thing to do was to try and outdo the superior in their own accusations of themselves.

Among the recruits who soon came in swarms to embrace this hard life were many who had had none too savory a reputation in the world. For instance, there was the former Grand Provost of Touraine, who, after a near criminal career in politics, came banging on the gate of La Trappe one wild night in the middle of a storm. He had journeyed thirty-five leagues on foot through wasteland and forest. His soaking garments were reduced to rags. His legs and feet were covered with blood. And the two eyes that burned in his great, haggard face spelled out the names of all the sins he was running away from.

It was just the sort of thing the abbé liked. In after years, this Brother Moses groaned so loudly over his sins that he kept his neighbors in the dormitory awake half the night.

[4] *Ibid.*, p. 265.

And he was one of the champions in the chapter of faults, making public confession of all the terrible things he had once done in the world.

The Trappist reform was a tremendous success. The austerity and fervor of La Trappe were a challenge to all the ancient monastic Orders. De Rancé came out with a book that contained all his notions and ideals, *De la Sainteté et des Devoirs de la Vie Monastique*. The book is beautifully written, and the style, except for a few passages, is not too violent. The tone, in general, is dispassionate, persuasive, and every page burns with the deep and sincere enthusiasm of the one who wrote it. But explicitly or otherwise, it attacked every other monastic order in France.

The result was a series of battles that armed De Rancé against everybody in religion who mattered. He got into trouble with the Jesuits by suggesting that they were too easygoing, and he aroused a mild protest from the Benedictines of Saint Maur by throwing scholarship out of the cloister. His books were burned at La Grande Chartreuse, because Dom Innocent Lemasson found they were upsetting the heads of the solitaries and disturbing them with "wild ideas."

But at the same time, monks from every order began to abandon their relatively easy lives and embrace the penances of La Trappe. Above all, there were the dramatic conversions of noblemen, high-ranking army officers, even princes of the royal blood, who left their palaces for De Rancé's cloister: ingredients in a dish that was peppery enough to be savored for many decades, even in a society of sophisticated and jaded palates.

However, when all this has been said, it must be admitted that La Trappe had less in common with St. Benedict and twelfth-century Cîteaux than the reformer imagined. The circumstances of his own life and conversion and all the agitation surrounding his efforts at reform had led De Rancé, in spite of his sincerity and good will, to modify the spirit of the Cistercian life.

Although his books were thoroughly orthodox and De Rancé's statements are carefully documented with the fruit of the most patient study of the Fathers, yet in practice the reformer's emphasis is usually negative. And that upsets the balance of his spirituality, making it a rather one-sided affair.

Nothing could be more faultless than his description of the monastic state as one designed by God to enable men to serve Him "in spirit and in truth," a state in which "the first and principal obligation of the solitary is to apply himself to God in the repose and silence of his heart to meditate upon His law without ceasing, to maintain himself in a perfect detachment from all that might distract him from God, and raise himself up by ceaseless care and application to that perfection for which God has destined him, by the faithful performance of the commandments and the counsels." [5]

There are plenty of passages in which he talks about the love of God, yet, as one of the leaders of the modern Cistercian revival, Dom Chautard, has remarked, they too often read more like literary exercises than anything else.[6] They show a certain abstract esteem for the ideals that are expressed, but they remain cold and without inspiration.

As a result, the contemplative life, in the strict sense of the word, seems to have remained abortive at La Trappe. Once they overlooked the fact that mortification has an object beyond itself—it is designed to set the soul free from its attachments and dispose it for union with God in contemplation and purity of love—the monks tended to pile penance upon penance in a mathematical accumulation of merits. The one who fasted the most, took the most disciplines, slept the least, was thought to have the most merit. He was the best monk. And the whole atmosphere of a Trappist monastery was one of athletic activity rather than of contemplative detachment and peace.

De Rancé himself, with his nervous, active temperament,

[5] *Op. cit.,* p. 55.
[6] *L'Ame Cistercienne, Les Cisterciens Trappistes* (1931).

could not stand long mental prayer. With his restless mind and insatiable imagination, he was anything but a mystic. He was a penitent, a fighter, an organizer, and a leader. His capacity to take punishment must have been tremendous. His courage was certainly heroic, and the heroism was surely supernatural. He suffered many trials and sicknesses with the uncomplaining fortitude of a saint. And his generosity was infectious. It spread through his own monastery and into many other houses of the Strict Observance and caused men to stand—and even demand—unbelievable things for the sake of their vocation. The whole life of this Trappist monk was a courtship of suffering and death. He went out of his way to look for things that would "annihilate" his natural desires and tastes and feelings; he desired nothing but to embrace all sufferings with a grim and exultant satisfaction that was the token of a supreme disdain for the world, the flesh, and the devil.

The mentality of La Trappe was the mentality of a Lost Battalion, of a "suicide squad" of men who knew they were doomed but were determined to go out of the world in grand style, making death and destruction pay so dearly for their triumph that death had no victory left at all.

If this cult of physical and mental endurance had the effect of sometimes making the Trappist take himself a little too seriously, it nevertheless accomplished one important result. And that was the thing De Rancé had been providentially raised up to do. It brought back one of the essential elements of monastic spirituality. It reintegrated the monastic life by reviving that asceticism without which sanctity and contemplation are impossible. The Trappist emphasis was perhaps a little eccentric and extreme, but the fundamental need for austerity in the religious life was something that had to be satisfied at all costs. The sanctity of the Church demanded it. Without the Trappists, the whole monastic Order and perhaps the Church itself, in France, would have been ill prepared to face the storm that was brewing. And one of the main reasons why the Revolution lay ahead was that the spirit of self-denial and mortification and poverty had been so completely forgotten by monks and ecclesiastics and Christians as a whole.

La Trappe made a tremendous impression on the world of that time. The perfumed noblemen who rode down from Paris in their coaches with their lap-dogs and their servants, enlivening the ride with polite slander and indelicate items of gossip and breaking their journey with long rests and carefully prepared meals, were often completely upset by the cold, silent monastery where these monks came gliding into church like shadows in their gray cowls and knelt down and bowed their shaven skulls in prayer after laboring in the fields. The nobles were escorted through the house by the guestmaster. They saw the bare refectory, with its line of earthenware water jugs and its wooden spoons. They were told how little the monks got to eat: only a few vegetables and some bread and, once in a while, some milk and cheese. They walked out into the farmyard and protected their noses against the various smells with dainty lace handkerchiefs, reflecting that the persons who had to labor in all this manure were not mere rustics by birth, men of a lower and more animal order, but beings who had once moved on the same superior level as themselves, with the same refinements, the same tastes, the same delicate sensibilities.

Most of the Court still affected a shiver at the monstrous things that went on in this abbey, where nobody spoke and nobody raised his eyes, but there were a good number who developed a new and surprising seriousness about life and tended to come out of their aristocratic shells and take account of the world of suffering and need and sin that was around them and was partly their own creation. Many noblemen and even great ladies put themselves under the direction of the abbot of La Trappe, like Mme. de Sablière, who was enabled to forget that she was dying of cancer by visiting the sick and helping the poor—or like the Princess Palatine, whom De Rancé ordered to do manual labor.

So, La Trappe made many saints. It reestablished in a clear light the full claims of penance in Christian spirituality. It gave great glory to God. The penances of the Trappists were astonishing; one cannot help being amazed at the stubborn generosity their sacrifices must have demanded.

With all the influence De Rancé himself exercised in his time, it is interesting to speculate on how much wider and deeper and more beneficent that influence would have been if, like St. Bernard, he had been a contemplative.

However, when he died in 1700, after fourteen years of crucifixion by various sicknesses, one of which seems to have been consumption, De Rancé left a group of well-established and fervent monasteries that were living the Strict Observance to the highest degree and were the edification of Christian Europe.

At the same time he had already foretold the punishment that was being prepared for those who had failed in their social and religious obligations, and he had warned Louis XIV against the revolution that must inevitably come.

It was to be a fierce purgation of society which La Trappe would survive, but not without a wonder!

III THE DISPERSAL; FIRST TRAPPISTS IN AMERICA

IN NOVEMBER, 1789, the apostate Bishop of Autun, Talleyrand, proposed in the National Assembly that the property of the religious orders be confiscated. The proposal was quickly adopted, and early the next year it was followed by a law that refused recognition to religious vows. The new revolutionary government had thrown open the doors of the cloister and "liberated" all the monks.

Those monks who had never lived as monks were thoroughly satisfied with the new arrangement. It delivered them from a lot of foolish and inconvenient formalities that seriously interfered with their pleasure and comfort. As for the Trappists, it seems that they were not inclined to worry too much about the new laws. They accepted them, at first, as a kind of long-delayed act of justice aimed at the monks of other orders who had been neglecting their rules for centuries. They almost took it for granted that they themselves would not be affected by the measures.

When the young novice-master of La Grande Trappe, Father Augustin, begged his superiors to be thinking of a place of refuge beyond the French borders, they told him to be quiet and forget his anxieties. They assured him that the friends of the Order were working for them in Paris and that the new government would soon realize that the Trappists were not like other orders: that they worked hard and kept their Rule and were poor and, in general, loved their life and obligations, for the glory of God. "We will not be disturbed," they said, with an all-too-complacent reliance on the fact that everyone had admired their beautiful farm and all the reclaimed marshlands and the rest of the fruits of a hundred years' hard labor. They acted as if they almost expected the new government to pass a vote of thanks for the admirable labors of the Trappist monks. When government investigators came down to make an inspection of the abbey and to question the monks, the Trappist superiors were confident that their plea for official recognition of their vows and manner of life would soon be heard, especially since their petition had been backed by the local municipal governments and by popular sentiment in the whole district.

The investigators talked to all the monks, ate in the common refectory, visited every corner of the house and farm, and came away with a very definite impression that these men were not maniacs, that they knew what they were doing and had indeed found true happiness in their amazing life.

The language of their report is objective and convincing enough to sound something like an official visitation card given by religious superiors belonging to the Order itself. Having questioned all the fifty-three members of the community, the commission sized them up in these judicious terms:

With the exception of five or six monks who seemed to us to be men of a very limited outlook, the choir religious are generally speaking men of strong and well-formed character which fasting and austerity have not weakened. Religion entirely fills their souls. In a few of them, easy to recognize in the way they express themselves, piety is carried to the highest degree of enthusiasm. Others, the greater number, are penetrated with a piety that is more affecting and more serene. These were the ones who seemed, to us, to love their state of life from the very bottom of their hearts. They have found in it a tranquility, a quietude which must, indeed, have a charm all its own.

Those government officials were not so stupid, after all! They had proved the tree by its fruits—the interior peace of those who were really living in union with God. But they also saw that even the cranks in the community could not, by any stretch of the imagination, be said to be waiting for "liberation from monastic despotism." The Trappists belonged in their monastery.

However, the notes of the commissioners were placed in the hands of a local tribunal, whose judges framed the final official report to be forwarded to Paris. And it was at this intermediary stage that all the high-sounding platitudes about "superstition, claustral despotism and natural liberty, morbid love of isolation, criminal and antisocial solitude" all crept in.

The judges all pounced upon a particular item in the report with the satisfaction of hungry lions on their prey. There was one monk at La Trappe who was a neurasthenic and therefore not exactly happy in the monastery. He it was who became the darling of those judges, their hero, their martyr to Trappist frenzy.

"Ah," they cried, "consider the woeful lot of the unfortunate Bertrand, born with a sensitive heart, made for social living and who, having rashly thrust his neck into the noose of a fatal vow, was unable to stifle the voice of nature: and, in the collision between passion and conscience, has witnessed the shipwreck of his poor mind! When an establishment leads men into such misery as this, have we not ample reason for its suppression?"

The report went to the Assembly, which allowed the monks then living at La Trappe to remain there and die there under simple vows: but no more postulants were to be received. It was a great concession, an unusually merciful compromise —but it was the end of the Trappists in France, just the same.

While all this had been going on, Father Augustin, the novice-master, had been pleading with greater and greater insistence for a foundation outside of France, a house of refuge for La Trappe. Instead of listening to him, his major superiors deposed him from his office and silenced him as completely as they could. Father Augustin had been too eager to indoctrinate his novices and his nineteen penitents with his own ideas. Besides, he had been carrying on a correspondence with friends in the world and even with government officials in Switzerland in order to get things under way and prepare the ground for the new foundation. He wanted to be able to go to his major superiors, with plans completed and all necessary arrangements made, and say: "Here it is: when do we start?"

Most of Father Augustin's letters had been intercepted, but fortunately one of them reached its destination. He received word from the Canton of Fribourg, in Switzerland, that if he came in person to present a petition signed by some of the monks who wanted to accompany him, his request would be considered.

It was at about this time that the decision of the National Assembly, which finally condemned La Trappe to slow extinction, became known. The father Immediate of the monastery, Dom Louis Rocourt of Clairvaux, realized his mistake in listening to the calumniators of the novice-master of La Trappe and gave his permission for the journey.

Within a few weeks everything was settled. On April 26, 1791, eighteen choir religious and eight lay brothers left La Grande Trappe. They put all their belongings in a huge covered wagon, a sort of traveling monastery, and most of them followed on foot or on muleback. They headed for Paris wearing their religious habit, in spite of the danger to their lives. In the capital they had an interview with the police, who characterized their departure as an "insult to France" and wanted to throw them in jail for even attempting such a thing. It was all marvelously logical: they did not want the monks in France, and they did not want them to leave France. In fact, they did not want them to exist at all: that was the final solution. . . .

Fortunately, Dom Augustin and his colonists managed to get away, and in a few days they were across the border and struggling to adapt the Cistercian life to the ruined premises of the old Charterhouse of La Val Sainte, from which the

Carthusians had been expelled some years before by the Senate of Fribourg.[1]

Life at La Val Sainte was not easy. The Cistercians who were to live with Dom Augustin de Lestrange so faithfully for twenty years to come, tasted hardships and privations greater than have ever been known in our Order. The life of the monks of La Val Sainte was going to be inhumanly hard. It is almost unbelievable that they were able to follow the regime they did and still go wandering in monastic caravans from country to country all over Europe, flying before the face of the Revolutionary armies. The Cistercian life of the twelfth century was nothing, compared with the privations and difficulties and hardships that were suffered by Dom Augustin and his men.

As soon as they settled at La Val Sainte they inaugurated a new reform. It was a democratic affair that grew out of general discussions of the whole community assembled in chapter. They took the Rule of St. Benedict and discussed it, point by point, from cover to cover, and when they had finished they found themselves with a Strict Observance that was stricter than the original Cîteaux and made St. Benedict look like doting indulgence.

The most important changes affected the sleep, nourishment, and labor of the monks. They renounced even the straw mattress allowed by St. Benedict and slept on boards. The time of sleep was cut down to five and a half hours on big feasts, six and a half on ordinary days. They returned to the strict Benedictine fast and restricted the extra portions which the Rule allowed when there was especially heavy work. Fish and eggs, even butter, were banished from the refectory, and cheese became a rare luxury. As for manual labor, they were not able to return officially to the hours of St. Benedict, be-

---

[1] The Carthusians returned to La Val Sainte in the nineteenth century, and now it is one of the most flourishing monasteries of that order. Pierre van der Meer de Walcheren's book, *Le Paradis Blanc*, gives a good idea of the place in our day.

cause of the choral offices and conventual Masses which had been added to the obligations of the Cistercian monk: but they arrived at a solution that gave the choir monks slightly more work than the Trappists have in our day: six hours in summer and some four and a half in winter.

In actual fact, however, life at La Val Sainte was so difficult, the ground so poor, and the needs of the monks so great that they were working fourteen hours a day, every day, pausing only to say the office in the woods, barns, or fields.

With all this, they found time to add some vocal prayers and devotions to their regular quota of prayer and to intensify their observance of silence and obedience beyond anything that had ever been practiced in the Order. As for poverty, they did not have to look far to find it: they had nothing, and it is hard to understand how they survived the fierce winters of a Swiss mountain valley, with threadbare cowls and robes, blankets of moss, and a single smoky iron stove.

Nevertheless, their physical lot was far happier than that of those who remained at La Grande Trappe.

A French decree of March 23, 1793, imposed on all priests and religious the obligation of swearing allegiance to the con-stitutional government under pain of deportation. Since the government was frankly atheistic, and since it was constantly threatening to wipe out the last traces of the Catholic religion in France, this oath was one that could not make a very strong appeal to a truly Christian conscience. It meant the final dispersal of the monks of the Strict Observance. The ones who had remained behind at La Trappe scattered and made for the frontiers. Most of them headed for Switzerland, to join Dom Augustin if they could. Some found refuge in the Papal States. A few remained in France, and two of the lay brothers even took up arms with the Vendéens. They were captured and executed. The prior of La Trappe, Father Francis Xavier Brunel, and another priest, Father Anthony Joseph Dujonquoi, were arrested in 1793, before they could reach the Swiss border. Like many other Trappists from different parts of France, they were put into one of the numerous chain gangs converging upon Rochefort, where they were interned in the pontoons. These pontoons were ancient hulks moored in the harbor. There were three of them, the "Bonhomme Richard," "Les Deux Associés," and the "Washington." The two last named were under the command of a pair of bloodthirsty degenerates of the kind that not even the pen of a Victor Hugo could exaggerate. The two priests from La Trappe and a lay brother from Sept-Fons are certainly known to have been interned on "Les Deux Associés." We can judge what the conditions must have been, from the remark of a physician who happened to see the prisoners packed together in the dark and airless hold, so tight they could hardly move and could not even lie at full length on the floor. He said: "If you kenneled four hundred dogs in that place overnight, you would find them, the next morning, either dead or mad."

Dressed in rags, the interned priests and monks were kept from death by starvation only by buckets of slops which were thrown to them to scoop up and devour with their bare hands. Eaten up by vermin and plagued with scurvy, they died by the score. The prior of La Trappe and his companion succumbed on succeeding days in the summer of 1794. They had had ample leisure to reflect on the way the Revolutionary government appreciated Trappist labor and poverty, Trappist simplicity and love of the poor.

Nevertheless, the Trappists who were interned on the pontoons at Rochefort or on the Islands of Ré and Oléron were much better off than those who were deported to French Guiana. The penal colony of Conenama was a burning wasteland in the dry season and a fever-ridden swamp in the time of the rains. All the year 'round, it was infested with poisonous snakes and all kinds of vermin. Even the Indians refused to live in such a place, but the idealistic French Republic decided that it ought to be brought under cultivation by deported priests and monks.

There was a strange, unconscious irony in such a sentence.

This was the only answer an enlightened and progressive government had to give to the religious life, to that "tyranny of monasticism" which had so horrified the freedom-loving Jacobins. These monks had committed the crime of living under vows and according to rules which "crushed human nature" and "warped all the best instincts of man." So now they were sent to die in chain gangs in a South American inferno, under the tender care of an officer who happened to be Danton's nephew.

Fever, plague, dysentery, scurvy, and a score of other torments killed them off like flies. Half the time, the living were too feeble to bury the dead. It did not occur to the soldiers of the Republic to do it for them. They were probably deep in ecstatic meditations on the liberty, equality, and fraternity which they were bringing to the world. But the echoes of the rhetoric of 1789 and 1790, the scandalized outcry of the committee that learned that one of the monks of La Trappe had had a nervous breakdown, had all long since been drowned in two reigns of terror, and no one seemed to recall this peculiar inconsistency. If they did, they were too worn out to appreciate the joke.

However, there is one bright spot in the story. The prison ship on which one of the monks of La Trappe was sailing with a cargo of other condemned men to Guiana was intercepted on the high seas by H.M.S. "Indefatigable," under the command of Sir Edward Pellew. He boarded his prize, and, recognizing the nature of his capture, he said, not without a certain unexpected delicacy: "Fathers, this is the richest booty I have ever taken." He transferred them all to the British man-of-war and landed them at Plymouth, where they found freedom and refuge until the fall of Napoleon.

Meanwhile, Dom Augustin had gone into action with all the energy and resourcefulness for which he was to become famous. La Val Sainte had been approved by the Holy See,[2]

[2] The brief of Pius VI, dated January 27, 1792, was not an official approval of the Val Sainte reform. It was only issued in approbation of

was erected into an abbey, and had started to make foundations all over Europe. The first colony went to Spain, and monasteries were established in Brabant, Piedmont, and England. But when it became clear that the Revolution was going to overflow the borders of France and that La Val Sainte itself would be in danger, Dom Augustin looked further afield. Already, in 1794, he had planned foundations in Hungary and Russia, and in 1798, when La Val Sainte had to be evacuated, he entered on that strange and terrible odyssey in which his monks covered Germany, Austria, Bohemia, and Poland and entered Russia, trying to find a safe and permanent home.

The most obvious idea of all had occurred to Dom Augustin from the very first days at La Val Sainte: the vast acres of unexplored and friendly America were crying out to the Trappists to come and find peace in those forests and prairies. An American foundation was to have followed the one in Spain, but the colony had been intercepted by the charity of the Belgians with too good an offer to be refused, and the monks, who had started for Canada, settled at Westmalle.

The second American-bound colony did not get much further. A rich English Catholic, Mr. Thomas Weld, of Lulworth Castle in Dorset, offered to build them a monastery on his lands and they accepted. Dedicated in 1796, it was the first monastery to be built in England since the Reformation. St. Susan's, Lulworth, did not last many years. Official antagonism was to make it impossible for the monks to survive: but they outlived the French Revolution and the reign of Buonaparte. Finally, they returned to France to reestablish the old Cistercian abbey of Melleray, near Nantes, and it was from Melleray that Gethsemani, in Kentucky, would eventually be founded. So, in a long and roundabout way, Lulworth did end up in America after all.

the foundation and was designed to encourage Dom Augustin and his men to persevere in their heroic work of rescuing the Trappists from the Revolution. The usages of La Val Sainte were not completed until the end of 1794 and were never approved by the Holy See.

Only in 1803, when the Trappists had finished their long flight to Russia and were able to return to La Val Sainte, did a group of monks finally set sail for the United States.

Dom Augustin came in person to Amsterdam to bless the departure of the expedition, which he had placed in the hands of Dom Urban Guillet.[3]

This extraordinary man had been the last novice professed at La Trappe before the French Revolution. He had accompanied his novice-master to La Val Sainte and had followed all the austerities of the reform without a murmur, although they brought him nearly to the grave. He was a living miracle. His abbot chose him as superior of a tentative foundation in Hungary when he was half dead. Without a word he set out on foot across Europe. He took part in the Trappists' Russian campaign, and now he was standing on the deck of a three-master ready to weigh anchor and set sail for America. He was surrounded by a colony of forty men and boys. They were setting out for a new land which none of them had ever seen and where they had few friends and no prospects. Neither did they have any money, to speak of. They did not even have a very clear idea of where they were going, except that they knew they would land at a place called Baltimore. After that, God would have to tell them what to do.

But this was not the sort of thing to trouble Dom Urban Guillet. Whether it was an extraordinary trust in God or just sheer, reckless, natural optimism—probably it was a combination of both—this Trappist had a way of walking headfirst into impossible situations without the faintest chance of extricating himself by natural means. He was continually buying things without money, on the chance that some would turn up before his creditors tried to collect. He was a man of restless and insatiable ideals, living in a near future of dreams that

[3] Father Urban Guillet was born at Nantes, in 1766, of a French father and a Creole mother. The title "Dom" in the Cistercian Order is given only to abbots, titular priors and definitors. "Dom" Urban was never, strictly speaking, a titular superior.

were always just about to be fulfilled. The Trappist odyssey across Europe and the example of his dynamic general—the fast-moving Dom Augustin, who marshaled his troops with the speed and decisiveness of a Napoleon—had had a telling effect upon Urban Guillet. It had set something in motion which only death would stop. It had started him on a long and restless journey which ended abruptly at a small town in northern France, just before he could found the one monastery connected with his name that actually stayed founded and still exists: Our Lady of Bellefontaine. For the rest, the trail of Dom Urban Guillet across Europe and America is lined with ghosts, the shadows of monasteries that might have been if Dom Urban had not moved out before they had a chance to develop.

He was consumed with the flames of his own zeal and energy: but they were the zeal and energy, not of a contemplative, but of a missionary. Dom Urban Guillet was so far from being a pure contemplative that even priests in the active ministry thought he was altogether too carried away by activity. He had an innate ambition to be a teacher, to form and guide the young. And his superiors encouraged him in this ideal. Dom Augustin had conceived the idea of a Trappist "Third Order," made up of secular teachers and of young boys who wore the habit of oblates and received a free education from the Trappists. This education was partly academic and partly a matter of practical manual training. The boys learned Latin and they learned a trade. The idea was that, when they were old enough, some of them might enter the Order. The others, of course, would be free to go out and look for jobs in the world.

Groups of these boys accompanied the exiled Trappists wherever they went, and it was hoped that this would provide some vocations for the indefinite number of new foundations Dom Urban was going to make in America. There were fifteen of them on board the "Sally" with the American pioneers. And the mind of the young superior was already crowded with visions of a wonderful Indian school in the forests of the new world.

This love of education was rooted in Dom Urban's own natural temperament, which was that of a scoutmaster or a schoolteacher. It so colored his conception of the Cistercian vocation that he was able to declare, "I have come to America particularly to engage in the education of youth, Indian as well as white." And when he was applying to Congress for permission to buy four thousand acres of land in Illinois, he gave the senator who presented his petition to Congress the impression that "the one great object of the Trappist Order is the gratuitous instruction and education of children either in literature, agriculture or the mechanical arts." [4]

Now, there is no question that Dom Augustin de Lestrange and Dom Urban Guillet were the most sincere men it would be possible to find. Nor is there any doubt whatever that Dom Augustin saved the Trappists from extinction during the French Revolution. However, their conception of the Cistercian vocation had its peculiarities, and this was one of them. The leaders of the Val Sainte reform were essentially active men rather than true contemplatives, and under the stress of an extraordinary situation they allowed their latent activism to run away with them.

There is no reason to be surprised at this, still less to judge them guilty of any conscious fault. There was an extreme need for schools and teachers, especially in America where refugees from Catholic countries were left without priests and without schools to train their children in religion. Nevertheless, the destiny of a religious order depends on its fidelity to the aims of its founders, and in the designs of Providence the Cistercians were intended from the start to be contemplatives. Many other orders had been started to carry on the work of teaching and preaching the Gospel, and the Trappists

---

[4] Quoted from *The Journal of the Senate and House* by Fr. G. J. Garraghan, S.J., in "The Trappists of Monk's Mound," *Illinois Catholic Hist. Rev.*, Oct., 1925, p. 121.

could not hope to find lasting success or true spiritual prosperity if the Superiors suddenly decided to take over a work which God had appointed to orders far better equipped to carry it out with profit to the whole Church and without danger to the interior lives of their members.

So, perhaps the two statements of Dom Urban that we have quoted reveal the real secret of his failure. In spite of the most phenomenal generosity, the most astonishing sufferings and sacrifices and trials—he went through enough tribulation to canonize a dozen saints—Dom Urban failed in America. His work vanished without a trace, and his memory scarcely survives in his own Order. And even there he is recalled less as a saint than as a kind of a phenomenon.

Heroism, he certainly had—a heroism all the more pathetic in the light of its fruitlessness. He needed all of it, if only to stand up under the blows and reverses that he attracted, as a magnet attracts iron.

The voyage of the "Sally" from Amsterdam to Baltimore was typical. During the hundred-and-twenty-six-day crossing, the overcrowded ship was swept by storms that carried away two of her three masts, while several hundred German, Danish, French, Dutch, Belgian, and Swiss emigrants waited for death below decks. A Dutch vessel, she flew the American flag on account of the international situation. She was under the command of a Yankee skipper—one of those old New England misers whom a foolish tradition has tended to soften and somewhat glorify, as if their inhumanity had something quaint and funny about it. His passengers did not appreciate the humor of the situation when they discovered that the skipper had neglected to stock his vessel with enough provisions.

Someone who witnessed the arrival of the "Sally" in Chesapeake Bay said that the passengers, half mad with hunger, were running about from deck to deck—like birds hopping about their perches in an aviary—saluting the land with half-savage cries. A whole ox was sent on board and torn to pieces by the mob. Tradition allows Trappists to eat meat on shipboard:

and the monks nibbled with dignified restraint at what they could get.

The Sulpician fathers in Baltimore took the Trappists under their protection, and presently a place was found where the monks might settle, at least temporarily. Pigeon Hill, fifty miles from Baltimore and near Hanover, Pennsylvania,[5] was a large farm which a friend of the Sulpicians had placed at their disposal. The Trappists settled in a big, roomy house, which the Sulpicians stocked with provisions, and they found the woods full of berries and chestnuts.

Pennsylvania was the obvious place to settle: but Dom Urban could not be quite at ease there. The Dutch boys of the Third Order, now that they had taken advantage of their free ticket to America, were much more inclined to go and look for jobs and money in Baltimore than to stay on a farm with the monks. Dom Urban thought that to remain near the city would arouse too many temptations. Even the boys who stayed on the farm were more of a nuisance than a help. But in any case, it was the Third Order, above all, that made the Trappists think of leaving Pigeon Hill and Pennsylvania.

When a traveler came in from Kentucky and told Dom Urban what life was like in what was then the "Far West," the flames of missionary zeal burned high in the heart of the Trappist superior.

Taking with him a veteran of La Trappe, Brother Placid, and an interpreter, Dom Urban mounted his horse and started on the western trail to take a look at Kentucky.

---

[5] Pigeon Hill, known locally as Seminary Farm, is about a quarter of a mile from the Lincoln Highway, which runs between York and Gettysburg. On April 4, 1794, an exiled French Friar Preacher purchased the place and set up a school there. He later became a Sulpician. After the departure of the Trappists, the Sulpicians started a school on the property. This institution later moved to Emmitsburg, Maryland, and joined with Mount Saint Mary's College.

IV. FOUNDATIONS IN
KENTUCKY AND ILLINOIS

LOUISVILLE was only a village of log cabins among the frog ponds and willows in 1805. It was not even the most important village in an area where villages were apt to be called cities. Lexington was the center of all the social and intellectual life of Kentucky—which did, indeed, have an intellectual life, even in pioneer days. But Dom Urban came down the Ohio on a flatboat to Louisville and rode inland among the thickets of dogwood and redbud, climbing the rolling plateau where great herds of buffalo still grazed in the sage grass. He was heading for Bardstown and Holy Cross, which were the center of a numerous and relatively compact Catholic colony. Formed in the earliest days of the settlement, this colony was now grouped around one young priest, who had been sent out from Baltimore to take over a parish of indefinite limits, about as large as his native France.

It is to Father Badin more than to anyone that Kentucky owes its fervent and persistent Catholic element. This *émigré*, the first priest ordained in the United States, had already built Holy Cross Church at the foot of Rohan's Knob, within sight of the present abbey of Gethsemani. During the next few years many other churches and schools were to spring up in Nelson and Washington counties. Academies like those of the Sisters of Nazareth and the Sisters of Loretto became fashionable among the families of pioneers who had come to Kentucky fully conscious of being ladies and gentlemen, and had formed a local aristocracy. Since those days the Catholics have never been seriously persecuted in Kentucky.

The atmosphere of Kentucky in 1805 was that of a frontier

country. The little stockaded clusters of cabins that nestled among the creeks and cornfields and wooded "knobs," still bore the marks of savage Indian fighting. It was only ten years since the Treaty of Greenville had put an end to those furious wars. Kentucky was teeming with enthusiastic life. It had already found its feet as a State, and the chief lineaments of the Kentucky character were already clearly formed. Dom Urban Guillet, who was a sociable man, must have fallen in well with his new neighbors the first day he arrived.

Vigorous, pleasure-loving, enthusiastic, friendly, impetuous, the Kentucky pioneer was a wild but amiable creature. Yet, it is hard to make blanket statements about him, because he was full of curious contrasts and contradictions. He was apt to be tough: yet the aristocrats down in the Blue Grass country had gentility and refinement, even though they were still living in log houses. Science and culture were by no means universal, but Lexington was already calling itself the Athens of Kentucky, which shows that some people had heard of Athens, Greece. As early as 1799 a Kentucky doctor was going about, vaccinating his fellow pioneers. This was pretty good going: Jenner had started in London only three years before. On the whole, however, Kentuckians were fonder of bourbon than they were of books and knew more about hunting than about philosophy. Then, as now, they were good talkers and often very witty ones as well. An English traveler at the time claimed that the Kentuckians were "the only Americans who could understand a joke."

Nevertheless, it must be admitted that the rich and vital resources of the Kentucky temperament had more or less gone native on the frontier. A single-minded zest for living had involved Kentucky in a cult of horses, dancing, hunting, and whiskey which almost amounted to an obsession. Yet, even here, one detects a certain pathetic charm. The story is told that, during the earthquake which destroyed Louisville in 1811, the men came running out of the taverns convinced that Judgment Day had come. Yet, far from grieving over their sins, they cried, "What a pity that so beautiful a world should be thus destroyed!"

The movies and popular literature have always presented the American pioneer as at least implicitly God-fearing. But it seems that in Kentucky, at the turn of the nineteenth century, barely one man in twelve claimed any interest in religion. However, a reaction was bound to come. And it came with the impact of an explosion. The year 1800 saw the beginning of that "Great Awakening" which swept most of the frontier States like wildfire, and it is not strange that the first of all camp meetings was held in Kentucky. The emotional and sociable pioneers, who would ride four days on horseback to go to a dance, and who loved nothing better than huge, wild parties, fell for the religious revival in droves. The idea caught on, and all the sects took it up. There followed a series of orgies that attracted and united men of every shade of Protestant belief, destroying all distinction between them in a spiritual intoxication which imparted a somewhat terrifying character to the camp meetings of those years.

The wildest of all these sects was one called the Philistines. Their gatherings quickly developed into tempests of queer "exercises" under the influence of a spirit who was evidently less holy than the cultists believed.

There was, of course, plenty of dancing and shouting and screaming. Convulsions and weird, ecstatic "experiences" were quite common, especially among the women. There was a certain Rev. McNamara who would come crawling through the crowd on his belly, crying, "I am the old serpent who tempted Eve." Groups of ministers were seen playing marbles, as a practical application of the text: "Unless you become as little children you shall not enter the Kingdom of Heaven."

The favorite and most appalling of the "exercises" was barking. Scores of the cultists gathered around a tree and barked like dogs. What were they barking at? They answered that they had "treed the Savior"—or else that they had "treed the devil." It did not seem to make much difference which one they had treed. The barking was what really mattered. When they really warmed up to this devotion, they would seize the trees with both arms and beat their heads against the trunks until blood ran down into their eyes. When the noise was over and they came to themselves and staggered home again with their bandaged heads, the revivalists settled again into their old ruts and their old differences and filled the air with interminable arguments about points of doctrine.

In the middle of all this was one sect—besides Father Badin's Catholics, of course—which had nothing to do with barking and convulsions and refused even to get into an argument about theology. These were the Shakers, who settled in Kentucky in the same year as the first Trappists. The Shakers had been brought to America by a certain Ann Lee, a former Quaker, expelled by the Friends because she had some strange ideas. One of her beliefs was that there had to be masculine and feminine principles in the Deity. Word later got around among the Shakers that "Mother Ann" herself was the feminine principle. In spite of their peculiar theology, the Shakers were much safer people to have for neighbors than the Philistines. They were quiet, sober, hard-working men and women who segregated themselves into communistic villages of their own where they lived in celibacy, practiced their religion, and supported themselves by farming and various crafts. In spite of the note of derision in the nickname they received, the Shakers did not go in for violent ceremonies. They did a little sober dancing and hand clapping—the men and women dancing as they lived, in separate groups. Eventually the Kentucky Shakers, who took celibacy seriously, all died out. The plain, solid brick buildings of their old village now remain as a curiosity for sight-seers.[1]

When Father Theodore Badin looked about him at the religious climate of the State where Providence had led him

[1] Shakertown lies between Lexington and Harrodsburg, in the Kentucky River Valley. It is in the heart of the Blue Grass country, the richest land in the State and one of its most charming regions.

to settle, he had good reason to be anxious about the spiritual welfare of the Catholics under his charge. If he could do something to cultivate their reason, he knew it would prove valuable to them in preserving their faith: so, the one thing he needed most of all was a school. However, the intellect and will of man are supernaturally helpless without grace. If it were possible to have such a thing as a monastery from which the penances and prayers and contemplation of the monks would radiate the clean influence of Divine wisdom and charity, then the Catholics would be truly protected against the diabolical mysticisms of the Philistines and their associates. Thus, when Father Badin heard that the Trappists would come to Kentucky and serve both as contemplatives and as teachers, his cup of joy was full.

In July, 1805, Dom Urban's Trappists were once again on the road with their covered wagon, traveling in the same style that had taken them from one end of Europe to the other a few years before. Now they were crossing Pennsylvania in easy stages, keeping the Val Sainte Rule as they went. They rose in the middle of the night to chant the office, ate at the regular times, worked, prayed, and so on. More often than not they slept under the stars or spread their sleeping bags on the ground under the soughing branches of the Appalachian mountain forests.

It is easy to imagine the thoughts of those silent men in their long days of traveling. It was hard, but their hearts were filled with peace—peace in the assurance that this vast, quiet land not only was made for them but needed them. It was made for contemplatives. It needed their voices, their clean hearts on fire with the secret love of God, to complete its own in-articulate and unconscious praise of the Creator, Whose love was mirrored in the perfection of everything that grew or existed under the wide arch of that blue summer sky. God spoke to them in the rugged ossature of the wooded mountains and in the delicate design and frail structure of the hundred kinds of wildflowers that they had never before seen.

God sang to them in the whistling of brightly colored birds —cardinals, orioles, names they could not know—and in the clear voices of the mountain streams. The cool breath of the woods and the mossy rocks and the pine trees was, as it were, the breath of God, sweet as the unction of the Spirit Who breathed within them, the pledge of their union with the God of heaven.

When they reached the Monongahela River, their journey became more hazardous. Dom Urban bought a couple of flatboats for twelve dollars. Someone remarked that that was about all they were worth.

The waters were low, and the river was so dangerous at that season that Dom Urban could hardly find a pilot who would risk the journey to Pittsburgh. Eight or ten times a day the boats ran aground and everybody had to jump into the water and push them off the sand bars. They covered barely fifteen miles a day.

However, when they reached Pittsburgh in a burst of relieved self-confidence at the thought that the big Ohio River would be simple to navigate, Dom Urban paid off his pilot and bought two bigger flatboats, appointed three lay brothers as navigators, picked up what information he could along the Pittsburgh waterfront, and supplemented it all with the purchase of a popular almanac full of information about natural phenomena.

So, the Trappists pushed off into the powerful and swift-moving waters of the Ohio under circumstances that would have made an experienced riverman quake with fear.

One of the flatboats sprang a leak in midstream, and the monks barely got to shore before it foundered on the sand. The abbey of Bellefontaine still possesses some big folio psalters and antiphonaries that bear the traces of this shipwreck on the Ohio River.

The Trappists had no money, and at Cincinnati they had to sell one of the flatboats in order to buy food. They prepared to continue on their way, perilously crowded, on the other boat:

monks, brothers, oblates, horses, and baggage. As soon as they left the shore it was evident that the boat would sink under them. They put in again at once, and the horses went on by land with two brothers.

But the journey was too much for the animals. Most of them died before they ever got to Louisville. The brothers were lucky to reach there alive themselves. As for those on the boat, they floated downstream under the burning sun, starving on the same rations they had enjoyed on board the "Sally."

When they reached their destination in Kentucky, practically the whole community collapsed from undernourishment and exhaustion. It was a miracle that they got to Louisville at all. Only one day's journey from the town they had nearly capsized in the middle of the river.

Of course, they were surrounded by all the solicitude of warmhearted Kentucky hospitality. The Catholics of the town came to meet them with wagons to carry their baggage and offered them all the foods and provisions they had so long needed: corn, flour, vegetables, melons, potatoes, apples. For a few days they were able to get some of the nourishment that the Rule allowed them in the summer season. But it was already September, and the monastic fasts began. For La Val Sainte that meant that even watermelons were forbidden.

For a month the stricken community languished in a condition that gave the doctors great anxiety. Dom Urban got no sleep for thirty days and was practically unable to keep anything on his stomach. Father Badin took some of the worst cases into his own house. Three of Dom Urban's four priests died. They included the cantor and the second superior. One of them, Father Dominic, was an ex-Carthusian. The bodies of Fathers Dominic, Basil, and Robert still lie in the Holy Cross churchyard at the foot of Rohan's Knob.

However, as autumn progressed, the monks and oblates got back on their feet. A school was opened on Pottinger's Creek, and December, 1805, found Dom Urban, to the consternation of Father Badin, back in Baltimore, where he was trying to raise money to buy a farm. While the brothers were working in the fields and the oblates were in school and the monks were at their various tasks (which included teaching), Dom Urban was almost always on the road.

He finally discovered what seemed to be a good site for a monastery on Casey Creek, some thirty miles south of Holy Cross. He bought eight hundred acres of land from the government and, encouraged by the arrival of reinforcements—Father Joseph Dunand and four Trappists arrived at Pottinger's Creek with a Canadian secular priest as postulant in 1806—set about making a foundation on that property.

It was a wild place. The woods still were full of bears and wolves, and a perhaps exaggerated account says that the monks killed eight hundred rattlesnakes there in two summers. Nevertheless, they went to work as only Trappists can work. Several streams flowed together in fields of rich alluvial soil. Soon the monks had a sawmill going on one of the streams and had built themselves a log-cabin monastery and a small chapel for their Catholic neighbors. Also, of course, there was the inevitable school. Sixty acres of land were cleared and grain and corn were sowed and the fields were soon waving with green banners of maize.

The monks set up a watchmaking shop that was the best in that part of Kentucky, and people came from all the region around Bardstown to buy clocks or have them repaired. This alone was enough to keep the community from starving. Dom Urban, meanwhile, had written to France appealing for books. His brother had combed the second-hand bookstores of Nantes to build up a monastic library for the Kentucky Trappists.

What was more important, novices began to arrive. Soon there were two—one Irish and another American—with the prospect of five more priests who wanted to come down from Canada to join the monks.

The monks nearly made a distinguished conquest in Father Charles Nerinckx, who felt a strong attraction to their austere life of silence and labor and contemplation. But that would have been a hard blow for the new diocese of Bardstown, which was formed in 1808.

This energetic priest frequently stayed with the Trappists when he came to those parts on visits to his missions of St. Mary's and St. Bernard's. He was able to observe their life at very close range, since he and his guide slept in the log cabin which was at the same time dormitory, refectory, scriptorium, chapter room, and church for the pioneer community of Cistercians.

He saw how the monks took their five or six hours' nightly sleep on the bare ground, with sacks of straw for pillows. He woke with them at one o'clock and joined in the chanting of Matins and Lauds, and he saw them go out to work in the woods and fields when the sun was coming up and the grass was still silver with frost or dew, according to the season. He saw how they never broke their fast before noon, even in the summer, when they were reputedly not fasting. And he was able to share with them their rude and simple menu of vegetables and black bread.

And Father Nerinckx came away from that silent and peaceful retreat with his heart full of the happiness that breathed in the very atmosphere of the place. Small wonder that he wanted to join them. In fact, he wrote to Bishop Carroll about it, but could not get permission.

Among his letters we still read his impressions of the new monastery at Casey Creek: "Happy men who can find an attraction in tribulation, joy in suffering, abundance in poverty, in spite of the contempt heaped upon them by a false and delusive world. What modest and holy joy is in their faces! And how their silence speaks to one! . . . *Vere haec est generatio quaerentium Dominum.*" [2]

If the priests in Kentucky were edified at the Trappists, the Catholics in general were in awe at the holiness of the monks and their own good fortune in having them there. What a

[2] "Truly this is the generation of them that seek the Lord," Ps. 23. The letter is quoted in *La Vie du R. P. Dom Urbain Guillet,* p. 211.

contrast it was, when you turned from the "Philistines" barking in the woods to these quiet and peaceful and self-contained and modest men, full of the simplicity and charity of the first Christians. And what a privilege it was to hear the solemn, moving tones of the ancient liturgical chant of the Church rising up in the night to high heaven from these Kentucky woods, where nothing had been heard for centuries but the frogs of Casey Creek and the screech owls and whippoorwills.

Some twenty boys from Catholic families around Kentucky were already at the monks' new school, and now the whole community, including monks, brothers, and oblates, numbered forty-five souls. The boys, of course, were lodged and educated free. They did not provide the monastery with any income, but they joined in to some extent with the farm work and earned at least part of their board.

Dom Urban still had to depend on benefactors to pay off his debt on the property. For that reason he once again took the road to Baltimore, where two rich ladies had promised him two thousand dollars. But when he arrived, he discovered that false news of his death had been spread in the city, and the disconsolate ladies had given their money to somebody else.

In Kentucky the streams that watered the bottoms where the monks had planted their wheat and corn and vegetables overflowed in the late summer and carried everything away, sparing only the monastery itself. Later, the monastery burned down. The monks lost most of their library in the fire but saved their choir books and watchmaking equipment.

That was in December, 1808.

However, in March of that year, in spite of the unpaid debt on the land at Casey Creek, the restless Dom Urban and his prior, Father Joseph Dunand, had already been planning to move West to what was still called Louisiana. Dissatisfied for some reason with Kentucky, they were investigating offers that had been made them in Missouri and Illinois.

When Father Badin asked for an explanation as to why they wanted to leave Kentucky before their monastery had had a chance to get itself established, their answer was that they could not continue to teach school in Kentucky, since they did not know English. Sometimes it is suggested that the fire was the work of an incendiary and that the monks left Kentucky as victims of anti-Catholic persecution. But there are no grounds for the persecution story, and in any case Dom Urban was already planning, several months before the fire, to leave.

And so, to the despair of Father Badin and Father Nerinckx, who were by now thoroughly disconcerted by Dom Urban's restless changes of scene, the Trappists began to build their own flatboats on the banks of the Salt River, so that, when the waters rose in the spring of 1809, they would be able to float down to the Ohio.

There does not seem to be much doubt that Dom Urban was making the biggest of all his mistakes. The Trappists had many friends in Kentucky, and even if they had not already received a fair promise of success at Casey Creek, a Mr. Stoddard at Nolin Creek was willing to give them two thousand acres of land for nothing. They belonged in Kentucky.

It seems that the real answer is to be found in the active and missionary spirit that animated both Dom Urban and his prior, Father Joseph. They wanted to be evangelizing the Indians. The prospect of life on what was then the northwest frontier was much more exciting than were the seven Catholic families who frequented the little mission of St. Bernard's at Casey Creek.

The evil reputation of the settlement called St. Louis reacted on the excitable Father Joseph like the smell of powder on an old war horse. The Jesuit missionaries, who had first brought Christianity to that region, had disappeared when their order was suppressed, and the land was without priests. Life on the frontier was wild and uncouth, and when Father Joseph learned that a man in St. Louis had traded his wife to somebody for a bottle of whiskey, he felt in his bones that this was where God was calling him to preach the Gospel.

Father Joseph Dunand was an impetuous man. The story goes that he had been an officer in the French army of the Revolution and had been ordered to take a captive priest out and shoot him. Instead, he had given the man his liberty and then fled for his own life, ending up as a monk at La Val Sainte.

Now, in St. Louis, he showed the same dramatic generosity. One day he happened to pass the jail. Someone told him that a prisoner was about to be executed. He rushed into the building at once and found seven men gathered together in a cell. Six were Protestant ministers and one was the criminal. Father Joseph immediately singled out the wildest in the group, a man with an unkempt beard and a strange glitter in his eyes, dressed in a tattered coat, and began to harangue him on the necessity of preparing for the next life by Baptism.

The man did not seem to appreciate his sermon, and when Father Joseph asked him if he was a Catholic, he replied that he was an Anabaptist minister. The scene developed into a general free-for-all, four hours of incoherent debate which finally ended in the Baptism of the prisoner as a Catholic and the triumph of the Trappist missionary.

In the meantime, however, he was still supposed to be the prior of a community of contemplative monks. It was he who supervised the river journey of the body of the community to St. Louis, where they disembarked and went to Florissant, Missouri. There, John Mullanphy, Missouri's first millionaire, had offered them two houses and some land rent free for a year. While they were trying to decide whether to acquire this property, as they had a chance to do, they were offered four hundred acres across the river at Cahokia, Illinois. They accepted the offer.

They moved over to their new home, in its rather fantastic setting, and settled in a log cabin. All around them on the plain were a series of low, regular, wooded mounds rising out of the prairie. Even covered as they were with trees, one suspected that these hills were not the work of nature. The fact is, they were a group of great Indian burial mounds. Here, among the bones of forgotten tribes, the Trappists settled down and got ready to build. It was the autumn of 1809.

Unfortunately, before they had a chance to dig themselves a well, the polluted waters of Cahokia Creek infected the whole community with typhoid fever.

When Dom Urban arrived in November with the farm animals and a contingent of young Kentuckians who wanted to remain with the monks as oblates, he found his community in desperate condition.

"The first person I met," he wrote in a letter, "informed me that our Fr. Prior was very sick. Although this was not a pleasant bit of news, I thought I was getting off lightly with only one person sick; but on coming up to the monastery I found quite a different condition of things. I observed a priest with death painted all over his face, carrying with difficulty to some others sicker than himself a little soup which he had made with still greater difficulty. All were dangerously sick, and were lying in a wretched shack, without windows or chimney, and with the wind blowing in on every side." [3]

Dom Urban, with his usual enthusiastic devotion to his men, threw himself wholeheartedly into the service of the sick, with the result that he himself soon went down with the fever too. However, the Trappists rebounded from this, as from all their other trials, with the same extraordinary vitality and elasticity. This time only one of them died.

Soon a clean well was dug, cabins were built, and they were taking the rigors of a midwestern winter in their stride.

Dom Urban and Father Joseph would get on their horses and ride across the ice-covered Mississippi to minister to the faithful in St. Louis, St. Charles, Florissant, or Portage-des-Sioux; as usual, Dom Urban spent most of his days on horseback. He would ride across the prairies with the breviary in his hands, reciting his office. Often he was so busy that he did

[3] From a letter to Bishop Plessis of Quebec, Dec. 14, 1809. Quoted in Garraghan, "The Trappists of Monk's Mound," p. 116.

not break his fast until nine o'clock in the evening, and then he would sometimes have to hurry through the Little Hours, Vespers, and Compline before retiring late to bed. Against the icy winds of the northwest, his Trappist robe offered small protection. He had worn the same one for thirteen years, and wool tends to get rather thin with use. And here in Illinois he was able to compare the cold with what the monks had experienced ten years before in Russia.

In the log-cabin monastery that was called Our Lady of Good Counsel, among the Indian burial mounds, the food froze on the tables in January and February of 1810.

In spite of all these obstacles, the courageous energy of the Trappist monks, fed by a heroic faith, soon had just as flourishing a monastery on Looking Glass Prairie as they had once had in Kentucky. Here, too, their main support was watchmaking. They were able to barter watches and clocks for cattle, leather, tallow, blankets, wheat, corn, and everything else they needed. In a short time they had some eighteen log cabins scattered among the mounds, four or five of which were grouped on one of the mounds themselves, constituting the monastery. The rest were stables and shops and barns. Once again the fields were waving with corn and wheat, and on the terrace of the largest mound they had a vegetable garden. Wheat was growing on the top—the site proposed for the future permanent monastery. If it had ever been built, it would have made a rather impressive sight, visible for several miles across the plain.

The traveler and explorer, Henry Brackenridge, whose curiosity drew him to this strange encampment in 1811, has left us a description of it. It is an accurate and living picture which anyone who has lived in a Trappist monastery would recognize, in its essentials, although it is colored by the peculiar subjective dispositions of the writer.

Brackenridge had walked into the farmyard, where the monks and oblates were busy with their work. Because nobody paid any attention to him, he became depressed and came to the conclusion that the monks were extremely gloomy men.

"On entering the yard," he writes, "I found a number of persons at work, some hauling and storing away the crop of corn, others shaping timber for some intended edifice. A considerable number of these were boys from ten to fourteen years of age. The effect on my mind was inexpressibly strange at seeing them pass and repass in perfect silence. What force must it require to subdue the sportive disposition of boyhood! But nothing is so strong as nature!" continues the uneasy explorer, relieved to find something to bolster up his shaken confidence in the animal inside his own skin. "I admired," he says, "the cheerful drollery of a poor malatto lad with one leg who was attending the horse mill. As the other boys passed by he always managed by some odd gesticulation to attract their attention. He generally succeeded in exacting a smile. It was a faint gleam of sunshine which seemed to say that their happiness was not entirely surrounded by the *lurid gloom* that surrounded them." The italics are Brackenridge's own—the quivering protest of his indignant gregarious humanity, still peeved that no one had come to offer him a cigar and shake him by the hand, slap him on the shoulder and draw up a chair to talk about business.

"Fatigued with this scene," he continues—the monks were doing all the work, and *he* was the one who complained of fatigue!—"which I contemplated apparently unobserved, I ascended the mound which contains their dwellings. This is nearly twenty-five feet in height, the ascent aided by a slanting road. I wandered about here for some time in expectation of being noticed. . . ."

However, we must concede that by this time he had some right to expect a sign of that hospitality which St. Benedict prescribed should be offered to all who came to the monastery, as to Christ Himself. Soon Father Joseph, "a sprightly, intelligent man in the prime of life," put in an appearance and began to show the visitor around. Afterward, he offered him a vegetable dinner. Brackenridge was surprised to find a watchmaker's shop "better furnished than any in St. Louis." In the same building he noticed a library that was "indifferent . . . a few medical works of no great repute and the rest composed of the dreams of the fathers and the miraculous wonders of the world of the saints." [4]

In 1811 the monks still were laboring under tremendous difficulties. The year before, when Dom Urban had been in Washington telling the senators about his prospects for an Indian school and trying to obtain title to four thousand more acres of land at Cahokia, the crops had failed and the entire community was mowed down by another epidemic.

This time five of the community died, and they had to sell two mares and their only anvil, to get funds to build and equip an infirmary.

In 1812 the region was shaken with earthquakes, but none of the monks' cabins was destroyed. In the Illinois territory the Indians still outnumbered the whites three to one, and there were many murders and acts of violence in the neighborhood of the monastery. But the monks themselves were never molested. The Indians displayed a friendly curiosity toward these men, so different from the other violent colonists who had come to settle in the land of their fathers. During the War of 1812 volunteer parties of fighters had to be called to arms to resist sudden attacks of Indians from the northwest, and sometimes Third Order members and oblates from the monastery were summoned to join these bands.

The greatest handicap of the monks was their extreme poverty. But they were used to it by this time. They continued to build up their monastery and their farm. They were, in fact, responsible for some innovations in the region. They were the first to introduce mules to the Illinois territory—not a very extraordinary distinction, no doubt—and the first to mine coal there. They had seen the earth burning at the foot of a tree struck by lightning and, having dug into the ground,

[4] Garraghan, *art. cit.*, 129.

discovered a vein of coal, which provided fuel for the monastery blacksmiths.

Far from being depressed by the *"lurid gloom"* which had left such an impression on the tenderhearted Brackenridge, the oblates and Third Order members showed themselves eager to enter into a fuller participation in the austere life. In the terrible year of 1810 a number of the oblates asked to be admitted as novices, desiring to go on and take vows. But they were under eighteen, and the regulations of La Val Sainte prohibited their admission. A lay teacher of the Third Order, twenty-four years old, also asked to be admitted as a religious. So, even at Cahokia, where they were much worse off than they had been anywhere else in America, the monks still stood a fair chance of succeeding.

But in 1813 orders came from Dom Augustin de Lestrange that the community was to close up the monastery in Cahokia and join him in the East. He had brought a group of monks to the United States by way of Martinique, and now his plan was to reunite all his American colonists into one big group and start a single foundation near New York.

In those days it was, indeed, near New York: a pleasant country site on Manhattan Island, a mile or two from the edge of the city. The monks all traveled, accordingly, to New York, where they took over a school that had been abandoned by the Jesuits. It was on a quiet suburban road among gardens and orchards. The Trappists settled there in 1814, and got under way with their farming, their life of prayer, and their schoolteaching. This time, apparently, they were also going to take over an orphan asylum.

However, news came from France that Napoleon had fallen and was interned at Elba. This put an end to the whole American experiment at one blow. Dom Augustin marshaled his men once more, obtained passage for France on several vessels, and prepared to embark.

It looked like a defeat. Nearly ten years of the most bitter hardships were now to be forgotten and left, as it were, without fruit. There might have been by this time a firmly established monastery of Cistercians, building themselves a permanent church and cloister of stone in the hills of Pennsylvania or Kentucky. But no, they were all leaving America—except, of course, Father Joseph Dunand, who had stayed behind among the Sioux Indians.

But Providence knew what it was about. If the monks had settled in America then, their first thought would certainly have been the building of a school—a college. In fifty years it would have been a university. Imagine the Trappists of Kentucky trying to lead the contemplative life with a university campus at their front door—setting out to work with the full-throated roar of a crammed stadium echoing across their fields, or getting up for the night office while their protégés were rolling home from some triumphal celebration and bellowing, "We are the silent men from Casey Creek. . . ."

God definitely foresaw the danger of a St. Bernard's University, Cahokia, and decided that it would have to die before it was even born.

As for the New York site—that was the worst of all. The fields and orchards, where the monks held a Corpus Christi procession among flowering altars in the sunny countryside of June, 1814, are now occupied by towers of steel and stone. The quiet suburban road became, of course, Fifth Avenue. The house which the monks occupied was eventually replaced by St. Patrick's Cathedral, and the fields where they worked for a while have all vanished under the skyscrapers of Rockefeller Center.

The monks had another scare soon after their landing in France. Napoleon broke out of Elba, and the Trappists all scattered into private homes during the Hundred Days. But after Waterloo the Trappists were once more free in their native land. La Trappe was repurchased, and Dom Urban began negotiations to procure the old Feuillants monastery of Bellefontaine. He spent two years begging in France to raise the price of the property and was on his way to pay it down when the last characteristic mishap crowned his life of reverses and accidents.

He stopped at an inn for food. His horse was tethered outside with all Dom Urban's money in the saddlebags. When the guileless Trappist came out from his meal, he was astonished to find that the money was gone.

V. THE TRAPPISTS IN NOVA SCOTIA; PETIT CLAIRVAUX

WHEN Dom Augustin and his monks sailed from New York in the autumn of 1814, the strange story of the Val Sainte Trappists in North America was not quite ended. In fact, its strangest episode was just about to begin. By a Providential accident, the congregation maintained a more or less theoretical foothold in the New World, and eventually the last survivor of Dom Augustin's expedition was able to make a foundation in Nova Scotia. And this was to be the first Trappist monastery in the New World that was actually a success. True, Petit Clairvaux went out of existence in the 1920's: but the monastery of Our Lady of the Valley, in Rhode Island, is of the same transplanted stock and flourishes mightily today.

Father Vincent de Paul Merle had been left behind in New York with six lay brothers to settle the affairs of the Trappists and arrange for the shipment of their heavy baggage—those ploughs and choir books that had wandered all over the Middle West. He and his companions finally took ship in April, 1815. In May they were at Halifax. There, they were told that their vessel had been ordered to turn into the St. Lawrence and sail up to Quebec, so they had to find accommodations on another ship leaving for France. They did so and went on board. However, the wind was in the wrong quarter, so Father Vincent went ashore to buy some provisions.

While he was in town, the wind changed and the ship cast off. When he got back to the waterfront, she was almost out of sight down the long bay.

Father Vincent had a guinea in his pocket and a breviary

which he had brought with him to say some of the day hours between errands. He was wearing his second-best robe. That was all he had.

Nevertheless, he was not completely shattered by this accident. The truth is, Father Vincent was as zealous a missionary as Father Joseph Dunand: so much so that many people in the Order have accused him of getting stranded in Nova Scotia on purpose. And of all those who were disappointed when the American foundations were given up for good, Father Vincent had been the most grieved.

Yet, he was an exemplary Trappist. As a model son of Dom Augustin, his devotion to the will of God amounted to an obsession. Like his General, he was always talking and writing and thinking about *La sainte volonté de Dieu*.[1] He would certainly never have engineered a deliberate plot to disobey his superiors. But from what we know of his character it is not impossible that some unconscious urge kept him lingering in Halifax longer than was necessary that day when the ship sailed for France.

So, he was able to give a sigh that had, perhaps, much secret satisfaction in it, and to resign himself to the fact that it was *La sainte volonté de Dieu* that had placed him in this land, which was almost destitute of priests; where there were numerous colonies of French Catholics and scores of settlements full of Micmac Indians who had once received the faith from missionaries, but who had now been without priests for fifty years and were going completely to pieces. He met dozens of them hanging around the streets of Halifax, half drunk or half starved, waiting to make a touch and pick up some small coin.

Since there were only two priests in that part of Nova Scotia, of whom one was just about to leave for Ireland and the other was half dead, Father Vincent's suggestion that he might pitch in and help with the parish work in Halifax and

[1] Dom Augustin christened his first convent of Trappistines with this name.

its surroundings was received with the greatest enthusiasm by Bishop Plessis of Quebec. Meanwhile, a letter followed Dom Augustin to Europe and brought back permission to stay in Nova Scotia and try to make a Trappist foundation there.

So, Father Vincent de Paul Merle settled down for the winter.

He was well prepared to face all the difficulties of the active life, this Trappist. Father Vincent had received the most austere training as a secular priest in Revolutionary France. Born in 1768 at Chalamont, near Lyons, he was the son of a doctor who was also a pious Catholic. Before the Revolution broke out he had been educated by the Jesuits in Lyons. When the storm came, Dr. Merle was thrown into prison because of his religion, and his son fled to Switzerland to enter La Val Sainte. However, his health broke down. He received minor orders and the subdiaconate somewhere in Switzerland, re-crossed the border, and went to work as a catechist in the archdiocese of Lyons.

Although the persecution had lost some of its virulence, young Merle was taking his life in his hands when he entered upon this work. But such services as his were desperately needed.

A few years of the Terror had practically de-Christianized the land, as far as organized worship and instruction were concerned. The archbishop was, of course, living in exile. The archdiocese of Lyons was being run by a vicar-general who lived in hiding and controlled a widespread but simple organization of secret missions. The territory had been divided into sections, each of which comprised some thirty or forty communes. In each commune, twenty villages or so were portioned out to a missionary. The priests were accompanied by catechists and "scouts" and bodyguards who prepared the way, kept their eyes open for trouble, and arranged for their escape in case they were denounced.

Father Vincent was ordained priest on Holy Saturday, April 7, 1798. There were six others with him, and the ceremony was performed in the parlor of a private house by the Archbishop of Vienne, who had been traveling through the Alpine districts disguised as a peasant, administering Confirmation and the other Sacraments.

Soon after his ordination Father Vincent was caught and imprisoned at Bourg. There, he was sentenced to deportation, but while he was waiting to begin the terrible journey to Rochefort, his jailer announced that the sentence had been changed and that he was to go to the guillotine the next day.

Father Vincent did not have an opportunity to verify this statement, because a certain Father Perret, the "escape expert" of the archdiocese, showed up that night and helped him to break out of jail.

The young priest fled to the woods, where a secret seminary had been formed on an isolated farm. He taught Latin to boys who gathered there under cover of nightfall and sat around him on piles of hay in a barn. After Napoleon's concordat with the Holy See in 1801 the seminary came out into the open and took over the old archbishop's summer home at Meximieux.

By now things had become so quiet in the secular ministry that they had perhaps ceased to be interesting. Father Vincent once more crossed the border into Switzerland and presented himself at La Val Sainte, where he made his solemn vows on October 13, 1805.

This was just the time when La Val Sainte was enjoying a brief interval of favor with Napoleon. The Emperor conceived the idea of establishing some of Dom Augustin's Trappists in one of the Alpine passes, where they would make themselves useful to him by maintaining a kind of hostel and posthouse on a most important military road into Italy.

Father Vincent de Paul Merle was chosen to preside over the new foundation of St. Catherine's in the pass of Mont Génèvre. He went south in 1806 with half a dozen Trappists and some of the usual students to take up residence in an isolated house on the mountainside. Helped by soldiers, they started at once to build a permanent monastery: but the job was never to be completed, at least by monks. Napoleon's affection for Trappists cooled down. They refused to take an oath supporting him in his conflict with the Holy See. It was time for Father Vincent to start traveling. He joined Dom Augustin at Bordeaux, where the police caught up with him: but only the abbot was wanted at the moment. Father Vincent and a few Trappists got on a boat for America.

That was in 1811. Instead of going west to join Dom Urban, Father Vincent attempted foundations in Pennsylvania and Maryland, with poorer results than Dom Urban was enjoying in Illinois. Finally, he joined the main group in New York.

All this background is necessary for an understanding of Father Vincent. He had spent only three years in a regular Trappist monastery. From then on he was either in pioneer foundations with one or two men or else isolated in parish and mission life. The active ministry was in his blood. And this influenced his whole conception of the Trappist vocation.

Like Dom Urban Guillet, when Father Vincent had to explain himself to government officials, he could say without a blush that one of the *principal functions* of the Order was to teach the ignorant. He did not hesitate to suggest making foundations on the express condition that the monks would devote themselves to the care of Indians or Acadian colonists.

He had, therefore, accepted all Dom Augustin's personal ideas and innovations without surprise and without question. It does not seem to have occurred to him that there might be a fundamental difficulty involved in making a contemplative order do the work of an active order. Listening only to his own ardent love of souls and of the active apostolate, he allowed optimists to persuade him that it would be easy to get a Trappist monastery going in Nova Scotia.

His trust in this project was to weather some very severe storms. Tenacity is a Cistercian trait. Monks do not easily give up their ideals, once they have got a good grip on them, and one of the most tenacious Trappists that ever lived was Father Vincent de Paul Merle.

The summer months gave him time to visit the missions along the coast. When the winter of 1815 set in, Father Vincent, wearing his white Cistercian cowl and accompanied by three mysterious Negroes who had followed the monks from New York, entered the little village of Chezzetcook, where he settled down to two years of parish life.

The Acadian settlement of Chezzetcook, whose colonists were jealous of the traditions they had brought over from Normandy, must have been a pleasant little place. It preserved the atmosphere of a small Norman town, and the people soon developed a great devotion for their new pastor. He presided over all their public religious life and entered their Baptisms and Confirmations and weddings in the parish register, in which he signed his name and added "Priest and Religious of La Trappe." Besides, since he was doing what he could to keep the austerities of his Rule, they came to hold his asceticism in great admiration.

Meanwhile, there was much to keep him busy. Long canoe voyages over treacherous waters, and tramps through the woods with an Indian guide brought him to outlying Micmac villages, where he preached and administered the Sacraments and taught catechism all day. At night he slept on a bed of branches, under a bearskin, while the rain came through the roof or the walls of the hut. It would have taken courage for a strong man to do all this: but Father Vincent's health was not good. To add to the laborious life, he was having trouble learning the Indians' language.

Unfortunately, the promised foundation was slow in materializing. The British government made no show of giving official permission, and Dom Augustin, far from offering any help, did not even answer Father Vincent's letters. Least of all did Dom Augustin do anything about Father Vincent's frantic appeals for a complete breviary. The poor man was leading a life that was in every respect semi-Cistercian, even down to the liturgy. For half the year he could recite the proper offices of each day. For the rest—including Advent and Lent—he had to make use of the Common or else borrow a Roman breviary from a secular priest.

In the winter of 1816-1817, when a letter from Dom Augustin suggested his return to France, Father Vincent asked for more time; but when this was granted, it had to be devoted primarily to the Indians. It was not until the spring of 1818, when he made a two-hundred-mile tour to Cape Breton and Antigonish, that he discovered a piece of property that suited him. It was a wooded valley half a mile from the sea, near a settlement called Big Tracadie. He wrote Dom Augustin a colorful description of it, calling the hills "mountains." In October, when all the leaves had fallen from the trees and the cold winds were blowing down from Labrador with clouds full of snow, the Trappist pioneer bought these three hundred acres and put down on paper his notes on the projected Indian village, complete with school, workshops, farmlands, cooperative store, and so on; the village was to grow up in the shadow of the monastery that already existed in his mind. Not only that, but there would be a convent of Trappistines on the slope of the hill—with another school. All he needed now was some money to pay for the land, some buildings to put on it, and some monks to put into the building. Fortunately, one or two stalwart Irishmen expressed a desire to become monks, and this enabled him to write and tell Dom Augustin that "the foundation has been started" and that "postulants are beginning to come in." He asked for a few monks from France, plans of regular monastery buildings, choir books, and all the rest.

Dom Augustin did not answer the letter. Months passed. When a year had gone by, Father Vincent tried again, with no better success. In 1820 and again in 1821 he returned to the charge. Since his letters are in the archives of La Trappe, Dom Augustin evidently received them. Either he did not know what to do about it, or else the answers went astray; in any case, Father Vincent was, practically speaking, abandoned in Nova Scotia, simply living the life of a missionary and dreaming about a monastery in his spare time.

In 1821, determined not to wait any longer, he actually took the first steps to organize his community of nuns. This consisted in sending three solid, healthy Acadian girls up the river to Montreal to make their noviceship in a convent of teaching sisters. After this they would take vows as "Trappistines." However, he only intended them to keep the rules of Dom Augustin's "Third Order," which explains how he was able to get away with plans so charmingly vague.

In October, 1822, he took up his pen, told Dom Augustin all about what he had done, and intoned the same old refrain: "Please send me some monks from France, breviaries, rosaries, plans for a monastery. . . ." This time he got a reply. Dom Augustin told him it was useless to start a foundation in Nova Scotia. Bishop Flaget of Bardstown was still anxious to have Trappists in Kentucky. In fact, he had offered them four hundred acres somewhere in that State. Therefore, the only thing to do was to sell out, send the "Trappistines" home to their mothers, and go to Kentucky.

La sainte volonté de Dieu!

It was not easy to do all this at once. In fact, going to Kentucky seemed out of the question. Instead, Father Vincent followed the advice of Archbishop Plessis, and in October, 1823, he sailed for France.

Dom Augustin was now nearing the end of his troubled and active career. The last years of his life were to be clouded with conflict and suspicion. The great odyssey had long since been left behind. Dom Augustin de Lestrange was a different man from the savior of the Strict Observance—the brilliant, even handsome, Trappist with a genius for adventure who carted his monks and nuns from one end of Europe to the other and ferried them back and forth across the Atlantic, making them keep the Val Sainte usages on riverboats and clippers, in covered wagons and under the trees of the forest. All this had given great scope for his energy, his imagination, his genius for making and changing plans on the spur of the moment. It had also demanded heroic dependence and the blindest possible obedience from his monks. Indeed, the only reasonable thing left for the Trappists to do, in the series of fantastic emergencies confronting them, had been to leave everything in the hands of the one man who could talk to everybody and find out about everything without breaking any of the Rules.

But now that things had settled down to their normal course, and the monks were back in France and established in regular monasteries, it was vitally necessary to return as far as possible to the peace and silence and tranquillity of the Cistercian life, to the traditional interpretation of St. Benedict's Rule. In many cases Dom Augustin seems not to have understood the need for an adjustment. In his own mind and those of his followers the Val Sainte reform had come to be synonymous with "the Rule" and with "Cîteaux." Everything else, even the obvious sense of St. Benedict and the old usages, was "relaxation."

Great uneasiness arose among the Trappists. The monks began to split up into small, isolated congregations, each group trying to find a workable interpretation of the Rule and each one slightly suspicious of the others. Meanwhile, Dom Augustin had been summoned to Rome to explain many points about his administration.

The year 1823 had even brought misunderstandings between the abbot of La Trappe (to which Dom Augustin had returned when Napoleon went to St. Helena) and the Bishop of Séez. In fact, their relations became so strained that the entire community of La Trappe was now living at Bellefontaine, in another diocese.

It was here that Father Vincent found his major superior.

It was a winter evening. The monks were chanting Vespers in the shadows of a darkened choir. Most of them did not have the faintest idea who the old, gaunt, white-haired, used-up stranger was, when they made room for Father Vincent to take his rank of seniority among the veterans of the American campaign. Only when he was actually among them and standing in his stall, did Father Vincent's neighbors recognize their old companion.

Dom Augustin was overjoyed to see him. It must have cheered him considerably to sit and listen to adventures that reminded him of his own best days. He encouraged Father Vincent to write it all down, and his heart was easily moved to reconsider the Kentucky project. When he heard about the Acadians and the Micmac missions and the "Trappistines," he finally gave in and allowed Father Vincent to return to Nova Scotia and take with him enough monks to start at least the semblance of a monastery. They would be six in all, including Father Vincent himself. And he could not have been given a better subprior. Old Father Francis Xavier was a survivor of the Kentucky expedition. He had, in fact, made his vows in one of the log chapels built by the monks in America. He was a ferociously ardent supporter of the "reform" and had abandoned one of the less austere divisions of the Trappist family to throw in his lot with its strictest unit. Like Father Vincent, he was a man of one idea: and once that one idea had been sanctioned by Dom Augustin de Lestrange, it became the holy will of God and was therefore unchangeable.

The reformer of La Val Sainte sent these six men off to Nova Scotia armed with what is technically known as an "obedience"—a kind of monastic passport which serves as the monk's official identification if he presents himself in some other monastery of the Order. Without it, he may be suspected of being out on French leave. The language of this particular document was typical of its writer. It was one of the last flourishes of the grand Val Sainte manner: "Inasmuch as you are inspired with the desire to bring the knowledge of God to a benighted pagan tribe, and in spite of the danger to your own lives, I order you to proceed on this journey. . . ."

They sailed from Rochefort in a French man-of-war on May 10, 1823, and landed in Nova Scotia some thirty days later. It was a fair journey, but it ended in tragedy. Two of the monks fell into the bay as they tried to get into the rowboat to go ashore, and one of them was drowned. That left Father Vincent with four Trappists. His "Petit" Clairvaux was going to be very little indeed.

They settled in a little wooden building near the site Father Vincent had chosen five years before at Big Tracadie and began their official existence in the usual desperate poverty. They had no money, paying for commodities with potatoes, cabbages, and beef. The monks taught school, and the three sturdy Acadian girls who had gone to the novitiate in Montreal were summoned to Tracadie, dressed in habits, and placed in a little wooden house that had taken nine days to build. Thus, they were once again "Trappistines."

When we read the documents that have survived from those days,[2] it is almost incredible that Petit Clairvaux lasted as long as it did. Only the sincerity and personal heroism of the two men who were the life and soul of the monastery really kept it going. Their story is a strange phenomenon, a curious dead end in monastic history. Petit Clairvaux had to do without the vital support of a vigorous and thriving monastic organism, for the simple reason that it was an offshoot of a tree that was already dead. Father Vincent and Father Francis Xavier were trying to prolong the reform of La Val Sainte when the movement had become exhausted and needed only the death of its initiator before it collapsed and vanished entirely from the scene.

As the last gasp of the Val Sainte reform, however, Petit Clairvaux had something to say, without intending to do so,

[2] I take this opportunity to thank the Rt. Rev. Abbot of Thymadeuc, in Brittany, for sending us the material in his archives. The monks of Thymadeuc used Petit Clairvaux as a refuge during the early part of the present century, and, before leaving, one of their number copied all the important documents in the archdiocesan archives at Quebec. Later, this material was supplemented by letters in the archives of La Grande Trappe and incorporated in a manuscript sketch of Fr. Vincent's life, to which I am greatly indebted. Much of the same material has since been printed by the Augustinian fathers, who are the present occupants of Petit Clairvaux. Rev. Luke Schrepfer, O.S.A., *Pioneer Monks in Nova Scotia* (Tracadie, 1947).

about the whole character of that reform. La Val Sainte had
been an emergency measure. Like all emergency measures, it
had many glaring imperfections: but during the time when
it was needed, the vitality and austerity and sanctity of the
monks compensated for the inherent weaknesses and dispro-
portions of the reform. Now that Dom Augustin's peculiarly
active and energetic ideal had outlived its usefulness, the full
stream of spiritual vitality which Divine Providence will always reserve for the contemplative Order of Cîteaux was once
more flowing in its proper channel. And so, the mistakes of
La Val Sainte lay fully exposed to view in the dry bones of
what was called Petit Clairvaux.

The chief weakness of La Val Sainte was its essentially
active spirit. The contemplative life came to mean little more
than a complex of penitential exercises. If these were fulfilled—
and it took plenty of action to carry them all out—then one
was released from the obligation of cultivating a deep interior
spirit of contemplation and could throw oneself wholeheartedly into teaching, preaching, missionary work, and the rest.
That is why Father Vincent, like Dom Urban Guillet, did not
fear to give everyone the impression that one of the chief
objects of the Order was to educate the young. And that was
why Dom Augustin had been so delighted at the project of
the Indian village under Trappist tutelage.

At the moment, Father Vincent was living not at the monastery but in the presbytery which he had already occupied
for so many years as parish priest of Tracadie. Father Francis
Xavier was left in charge of the community and its school, but
the only thing left of the Cistercian life was a bodily austerity
that went beyond the limits of Cîteaux.

The first consequence of the lack of monastic regularity
and enclosure and silence was that Petit Clairvaux was, for
many years, the graveyard of contemplative vocations. In the
end, no European abbot dared send anybody there. There was
no interior life, and without interior life it is impossible to
support the austerities of the Rule. One of the brothers, Bruno,

grew tired of the monastery and went to live at the presbytery
with Father Vincent. Then he tired of that and moved to a
village school some miles away. Finally, he applied for a dispensation of his vows and got married. Another went back to
Bellefontaine. A third, a doctor, spent most of his time prac-
ticing medicine and ranged so freely about the countryside,
to the utter disregard of his monastic duties, that even Father
Vincent was disconcerted. This doctor went back to France,
but by that time no monastery could hold him, and he died
an apostate. And that disposed of the original colony that had
been sent out to Nova Scotia by Dom Augustin de Lestrange.

When the news of all this became known in the Order,
Petit Clairvaux acquired a very unenviable reputation. After
Dom Augustin's death in 1827 no one wanted to have anything to do with the place, and it remained without an immediate superior or a mother house. Since this practically dissolved
all official connection between Petit Clairvaux and the rest of
the Order, Father Vincent and Father Francis Xavier went
their own way, defending the fasts and austerities of La Val
Sainte long after they had all been suppressed in the Order
itself by the Holy See. An occasional friendly Irishman would
give the life a trial, and this would persuade the two veterans
that they really had a monastery to look after. Nevertheless,
in 1836 Father Vincent went to Europe to beg a few professed
Trappists from some of the best monasteries of the Order.
Carefully avoiding Bellefontaine, where he was no longer *per-
sona grata,* he went to La Grande Trappe, where he was in
neutral territory. When the abbot tried to persuade him to
give up Petit Clairvaux and return to a regular monastery and
keep the Rule, he humbly agreed that this was a good idea; but
later he presented his case to the heads of the Foreign Mission
Seminary in Paris and the *Propaganda*[3] in Rome and once

---

[3] The Congregation of the Propagation of the Faith (*De Propaganda
Fide*) is in charge of all the Catholic foreign missions and supervises
all Church organization in mission territories.

again found himself in a position where it was the manifest will of God that he return to Nova Scotia.

He was back at Petit Clairvaux in 1840 after an absence of four years. This time the growth of the missions relieved him of the charge of parish priest, and he was able to retire to the monastery and live with the tiny community he had founded. Before he died, however, he retired to the convent of his "Trappistines" and settled down to await the call of God, surrounded by the devoted attentions of the sisters.

On January 1, 1853, there was a great stir among the Indians on Cape Breton Island. One of the braves came running into the village to report an ominous piece of news. There was a tree that had been marked by Father Vincent years before and had thus become associated with his person. It was "his tree." On this midwinter day it had suddenly fallen to the ground without any apparent cause, as if it had been struck by lightning. The Indians at once decided that Father Vincent must be dead—and that was, in fact, the day of his death.

He had been venerated as a saint even during his lifetime. Now his cult spread all over Nova Scotia and Cape Breton. All kinds of stories were told about him, some of them plausible enough, others more or less legendary, like the "miracle" in which he stopped a great storm by taking off his shoe and throwing it into the sea. Miraculous cures were claimed by people who had prayed at his tomb, and Bishop Cameron of Arichat testified, thirty years after Father Vincent's death, that a Protestant was still living who claimed to have been saved from death by a prayer to the Nova Scotia Trappist.

Meanwhile, Mother Ann Coté, the superioress of Father Vincent's "Trappistines," declared that he had worked "an infinite number of miracles" and that she was not unwilling to part with relics—a finger of one of Father's gloves, a lock of Father's hair, and a bit of paper on which he had written something. The General Chapter of the Reformed Cistercians, in 1903, even considered the possibility of introducing his cause: but the matter went no further.

Father Francis Xavier assumed charge of the monastery, but it soon became clear that Petit Clairvaux could not survive unless some monks came from Europe. He appealed to the Belgian Trappists, and a colony was sent from St. Sixte, under a Father James, in 1857. They introduced regular observance, and at once the original flow of vitality from Cistercian centers in Europe began to stimulate the little Nova Scotia community. For the first time in its existence it began to prosper in the spiritual and temporal orders at the same time. The only unfortunate element was that the Belgian Trappists followed the usages not of La Val Sainte, or even of twelfth-century Cîteaux, but of De Rancé, and this was far too tame for Father Francis Xavier. He therefore followed the road his predecessor had taken a few years before and retired to the "Trappistines," where he could fast as much as he pleased.

With the arrival of the Belgian Trappists, Petit Clairvaux took on an altogether new aspect. It was once more admitted to the Cistercian Order as a daughter house of Our Lady of Gethsemani, which had been founded in Kentucky in 1848. The monks enlarged their farm, built mills and workshops, and put up one of the largest barns in Nova Scotia, with room for a hundred cattle. The Trappists made butter and cheese that fetched the highest price in the markets of the province. They burned bricks and built themselves a simple, rugged monastery around a cloister garth, according to the Cistercian tradition. In 1866 the community numbered forty-five members, but most of these had come from Belgium. The Nova Scotia Catholics, although they had great admiration for the monks, did not seem to want to join them.

In 1862 Petit Clairvaux made a foundation of its own in the Province of Quebec. This, too, had been one of the dreams of Father Vincent de Paul Merle; but Archbishop Turgeon of Quebec had had to restrain the ambitious pioneer by practically forbidding him to accept land that was offered him at Saint Joachim at a time when he could hardly keep his microscopic community alive at Tracadie. Even in 1862 the foundation of Our Lady of the Holy Ghost was premature. Four monks were sent from Nova Scotia to Longevin Township, in Dorchester County, near the Maine border. They built themselves a temporary monastery—the usual log cabin—in which they suffered incredible hardships when winter came. Nevertheless, the community lasted ten years and even began to show signs of prospering: at one point it had twenty-two members. It is not quite clear why the project was suddenly dropped in 1872.

More peculiar still, this monastery of the Holy Ghost tried to make a foundation of its own in the United States. It was the monastery of the Immaculate Conception, founded at Old Monroe, Missouri, a settlement of German farmers. But not much could be expected of this rather temperamental project, which had sprung into existence from the restless mind of a certain Father Gerard Furstenburg. This monk had made his vows at the French monastery of Mont des Cats but was unable to get along there. He found his way to the Holy Ghost monastery, but he did not settle down any too comfortably there, either. The superior sent him on a begging tour in the States, perhaps more to be rid of him than to raise money. Father Gerard managed to persuade two or three Trappists to live with him in Missouri, and there he started to put up a chapel. Unfortunately, he embroiled himself in more trouble here than he had ever had to face before. The nominal "Catholics" of the district were not all in favor of Trappist monks, and when he preached an inflammatory sermon against their rather wild entertainments, one of their number who happened to be drunk at the time came around after the sermon and threw a hatchet at him. Two members of the Trappist community seized the drunkard and held him down until he was in a better mood. He then went off and filed suit against them for assault and battery. The lawyer whom he retained to prosecute the monks delivered a terrific barrage of invective against the Trappists, referring to them as "the bears of the forest" and declaring that they were all worthy of death. In spite of his eloquence, however, the case was dismissed.

In 1875, three years after the Holy Ghost monastery itself had closed down, this Missouri foundation was abandoned as hopeless. Father Gerard, rather than return to Petit Clairvaux, went to Gethsemani. He stayed for a year or two and then wandered off once more to new horizons. Toward the end of the century he was once again seen in the United States, this time trying to collect money for a Trappist foundation in the East Indies.[4]

The wandering life of this unhappy figure is not something that comes up very frequently in the history of the Trappists—and since the introduction of the new Code of Canon Law the species has died out.

Meanwhile, the thirty-odd years of quiet prosperity that had given Petit Clairvaux the distinction of becoming an abbey[5] suddenly ended with a disaster on the Feast of St. Francis, October 4, 1892. On that day a fire started in one of the old wooden buildings put up by Father Vincent de Paul. It quickly spread to the roof of the main monastery. The roof was so high that no ladder could reach it, and the fire got out of control. In a few hours the monastery was a heap of evil-smelling ruins. The monks spent the next four years in wooden shacks, suffering greatly during the winters. Nevertheless, they set about rebuilding the monastery. Before this work was half finished another fire broke out in 1896, this time destroying the temporary wooden monastery in which they were trying to live, as well as the great barn and other farm buildings.

They were by now almost completely ruined, but the monks moved into the unfinished shell of the brick monastery, where they lived in abject misery. In 1898 the General Chapter transferred them to the jurisdiction of Our Lady of the Lake, whose

[4] At Beagle Bay, New Caledonia.
[5] The first abbot, Dom Dominique Schietecatte, was installed by Dom Benedict Berger of Gethsemani on October 26, 1876. *Pioneer Monks in Nova Scotia*, p. 69 ff.

prior, Father John Mary Murphy, moved the whole community to Rhode Island, as we shall see in a later chapter.

The shell of Petit Clairvaux remained empty for five years and was taken over by the abbey of Thymadeuc in Britanny. It was occupied in 1903 by twelve monks, with instructions to prepare it as a "refuge" in case the Order was expelled from France. Petit Clairvaux remained an annex of Thymadeuc until 1919, when it was closed down. The threat against the orders in France seemed to have passed, and there were no vocations in Nova Scotia.

The building again became empty. In 1937 it was bought by its present occupants, the Augustinian fathers, as a refuge for members of their order expelled from Nazi Germany.

VI. THE FOUNDATION OF
GETHSEMANI ABBEY

AFTER the fall of Napoleon it quickly became evident that the austere and restless history of the Val Sainte congregation would soon be a closed chapter in the annals of the Cistercian Order. By a queer paradox, after 1815 France became one of the safest places in Europe for monks, after having been for ten years the most dangerous. As a result, the scattered and more or less flourishing monasteries that had been founded in Belgium, Germany, Spain, and Italy by Dom Augustin de Lestrange closed their doors under stress of persecution, and the monks withdrew once more to their native country.

Of the congregation which existed during the Revolution and to which the Trappists owe their survival, scarcely a house remains today. The only important one is Westmalle in Belgium. The present Cistercian Order of the Strict Observance goes back to a nucleus of monasteries founded or reopened in France after the fall of Napoleon. The most important was, of course, La Grande Trappe. But there were other ancient Cistercian houses among them, like Aiguebelle, above Avignon, near the Rhône. Port du Salut was founded in 1815, and its monks have since become famous for the cheese that bears the name of the monastery.

But when Dom Augustin died in 1827, the most prosperous and fervent of the Trappist monasteries was Our Lady of Melleray, near Nantes. Melleray reopened its doors as a monastery to receive the monks that had been forced to leave the monastery of Lulworth in England. They brought to France not only the austerity of the contemplative life and the ancient liturgical chant but also some English methods of farming that started what amounted to an agricultural revolution in the Vendée. The peasants of the region were astonished to find that a system of crop rotation would save them the trouble of leaving land fallow for eight or nine years. They soon bought the improved ploughs manufactured by the monks on the English pattern, and the first threshing machine ever seen in that part of France attracted a curious crowd of farmers to the monastery.

The community of one hundred and seventy-five was under the direction of an abbot whose wisdom and experience in temporal and spiritual matters were equaled only by his generosity and spirit of faith. Dom Antoine de Beauregard, a gifted and noble cleric who had fled to England to escape the Revolution, had become a monk at Lulworth. Here he had lived through poverty and hardships not altogether unlike those which his Cistercian brothers had had to suffer in Kentucky and Illinois.

After Dom Augustin's death Dom Antoine of Melleray became the Visitor General of the Congregation, and his wisdom has left its stamp upon the Order even till today. Dom Augustin himself had foreseen that the excessively strict regulations of La Val Sainte would not long survive his death, and practically all his innovations had been under fire for some time.

One of Dom Antoine's first wise moves was to abolish that peculiar invention of Dom Augustin, the Trappist Third Order. In getting rid of these secular teachers, Dom Antoine relieved the Order of a most oppressive and unwieldy burden and delivered the monks from the danger of being saddled everywhere with schools and colleges. It has not generally been recognized that this move did as much to save the Cistercian Order as anything that had been attempted since the French Revolution. If teaching had become inseparable from Trappist monasteries, it would have meant a change in the very essence of the Cistercian vocation.

Then there were the famous austerities of the Val Sainte reform, which outdid St. Benedict and Cîteaux in their rigor. In theory, there was perhaps something admirable about them. Let us grant that Divine Providence demanded this special heroism from a few picked men and women in a time of crisis. There can be no question that the life of the monks who followed Dom Augustin and Dom Urban Guillet was as near as you can get to martyrdom by following a monastic rule, when we consider the fantastic situations in which the monks tried to keep to their exceptionally strict usages. It was a moral and physical immolation. We have had little chance to make more than a passing reference to one or two of its victims. Surely, as far as human beings can conjecture, the monks who died in Kentucky and Illinois died as real saints. Much more evident still is the heroism of the monks of La Cervera in Italy who, in obedience to Dom Augustin, made a public retraction of their ill-considered oath of allegiance to Napoleon, fully conscious of the fate that awaited them for doing so. The story of their deportation and imprisonment on a Mediterranean island need not detain us here. Their fate was something like that suffered by the Trappist prisoners of Rochefort.

The question raised by the life of the Val Sainte monks is not merely whether the men of our time are physically capable of such a life. That is not quite the point. Let us assume that you could fill a few monasteries with men quite capable of sleeping on bare boards for five hours a night, fasting until evening every day in Lent, on top of a long workday, with long choral offices and many supplementary vocal prayers into the bargain. The question is, would this regime be the best means for forming *contemplatives?* The aim of the Cistercian life is something more than mere athletic endurance.

Dom Antoine's answer to the question was very simple and full of supernatural prudence—which is inseparable from charity.

He argued that, since St. Benedict had been praised for

centuries as the wisest monastic legislator the Church had ever
possessed, and since the Cistercians of the twelfth century had
very successfully lived the Rule of St. Benedict to the letter
and lived it as a rule for contemplatives, the wisest thing to do
was to go back to St. Benedict and Cîteaux. In fact, one of
Dom Antoine's most sensible observations echoed one com-
plaint of the first Cistercians against Cluny. The life of the
monks of La Val Sainte was overcrowded with activities and
with vocal prayer and with supplementary devotions, so that
the harmonious balance of the Benedictine life was destroyed
and personal meditation and contemplation and spiritual reading were practically forced out of the picture. Granted that
the Divine Office in choir is the principal work of the monk
and that he is also obliged to live by the labor of his hands;
nevertheless, if he is not left free for some personal communion
with God in silence and solitude and recollection, he will
never become a contemplative.

Dom Antoine thought there could be nothing better for his
monks than to keep the Rule of St. Benedict as it had been
written and as it had been interpreted by St. Alberic and St.
Stephen Harding at Cîteaux. In that way he steered a middle
course between the exaggerations of Dom Augustin and the
somewhat abstract and academic reform of De Rancé, for
whom work had never been a material necessity but only a
penance and a humiliation. In other words, it would seem that
this was a solution that came somewhere near the healthy and
harmonious and well-balanced ideal of the first Cistercians.
For them, the monk was a man who labored because he was
poor and was poor because he loved God, and who lived apart
from the world to praise God and to contemplate Him and
to taste the inexpressible joys of His love in silence and in
peace.

At the same time, this solution, which looked so good in
theory, did not seem to work out altogether in practice. There
were some Trappists who found that even the usages of
Cîteaux were too difficult and imposed too severe a burden.

In 1834 the Trappists were divided into two congregations, one keeping the usages of Cîteaux and the other those of De Rancé. Each had its own vicar general, and both were subject to the Abbot General of the Cistercians of the Common Observance—for the Common Observance still survived as an ill-defined conglomeration of fragments. This was not a satisfactory arrangement, and it is quite likely that this division, this unsettled and equivocal state of the reform, inhibited the spontaneous and healthy regrowth of a spirituality that was truly Cistercian and contemplative, and which the strictness and fervor of the monks themselves might have led us to expect.

Meanwhile, things were by no means settled in France. The 1830 revolution had brought trouble to La Trappe and to Melleray, as well as to other houses of the Order. Melleray, being a large and prosperous house, was singled out for special attention. Six hundred soldiers camped in the monastery, and only the firmness of Dom Antoine in insisting on the rights guaranteed him by the laws of the time saved the monastery from complete suppression. As it was, however, most of the community was turned out of doors.

The result was not altogether an unhappy one. There had been many English and Irish monks in the house, and these were no sooner deported than they settled in Ireland to build Mount Melleray Abbey in county Waterford, a house which has ever since been renowned for its prosperity and vigor.

When the troubles of 1830 had blown over, Melleray was once again crowded with postulants and novices, and the places that had been left vacant by the deportees were rapidly filled. By the year 1847 the house was full to overflowing.

That gave Dom Maxime, who was then abbot, two good reasons for deciding to make a foundation somewhere outside of France. He wanted to make room for postulants, and he foresaw another revolution.

And so it happened that once again the eyes of a Trappist superior were turned to the shores of America. God's Providence definitely designed that a monastery of Cistercian monks was to be built, first of all, in Kentucky. And it was to Kentucky that the prior of Melleray, Father Paulinus, went looking for land on which to build one.

It is not altogether curious that the monks should have looked first of all to Kentucky in their second attempt to settle in the United States. They knew what a hard time Dom Urban's colony had had, and they had heard of the eccentricities of the climate. But probably the sanctity of the first Bishop of Bardstown, who had recently transferred his cathedral to Louisville, was the real explanation why God brought Trappists to that diocese.

Bishop Flaget had come to America in 1792 as a refugee with Father Badin, the first priest to settle permanently in Kentucky. The bishop was a Sulpician, and he probably saw something of Dom Urban and his Trappists, not in Kentucky but at Baltimore, where they were received by the fathers of Monsignor Flaget's community.

In 1808 Bishop Carroll, finding the burden of the entire United States too heavy for his own shoulders, asked Pope Pius VII to give him some more bishops. Accordingly, four new dioceses were erected that year: Boston, New York, Philadelphia—and Bardstown, Kentucky. And so Monsignor Flaget became Bishop of Bardstown and head of a diocese that included Kentucky, Michigan, Indiana, Illinois, Ohio, Missouri, Tennessee, Wisconsin, Iowa, and about half of Arkansas.

It was a task that called for more than human courage and energy.

The new bishop did not arrive in Kentucky until Dom Urban and his Trappists had already moved west to Illinois. They still were in his diocese, no doubt, when Bishop Flaget came down the Ohio River on a flatboat in 1811, accompanied by the priests who were to form the nucleus of his diocesan seminary. But by the time he had had a chance to visit the western reaches of his territory, the bishop found the Trappists had taken flight and were at home in France.

Yet, the memory of the monks and their holiness and their

poverty had not died in Kentucky. There were still a few men who had been to the monks' school, and these were among the most solid and hard-working and intelligent and faithful Christians in the bishop's flock. The echoes of the sweet, solemn cadences of Gregorian chant in the monks' log-cabin chapel, in the woods of Nelson County and Casey Creek, still lived in the memories of Kentucky Catholics.

The arrival of Father Paulinus in Louisville in 1847 was the answer to many prayers.

The eighty-six-year-old bishop, white-haired, leonine, beaming with the simplicity and overflowing benevolence of the saints, received the emissary from the French Trappists with open arms and tears of joy. He sent him at once into the country that had once seen the labors of Dom Urban Guillet's men, and his coadjutor, Monsignor Martin Spalding, became the Trappist's guide and adviser.

It was not long before they found a good-sized farm with some buildings on it and plenty of woodland. It was within sight of Rohan's Knob, in whose shadow the Trappists had first settled thirty-two years before in their temporary home on Pottinger's Creek. Gethsemani, as the farm was called, belonged to some religious of a congregation founded by Father Nerinckx—the Sisters of Loretto. The sisters had opened a small orphan asylum in the middle of a valley in Nelson County. But the enterprise proved inconvenient, and they were looking for a less isolated site.

So, Father Paulinus struck a bargain for the fourteen hundred acres of woodland, with a few cornfields and some log cabins in bad repair, and Gethsemani was sold to the Trappists for five thousand dollars.

It was in October, 1848, that the colony was organized to leave the abbey of Melleray. At its head, Dom Maxime placed Father Eutropius Proust, a thirty-nine-year-old priest from the strongly Catholic Vendée district who had not yet been four years in the monastery. He had made profession in 1846, and the next year he had taken over Father Paulinus's office as prior when the latter went on his expedition to Kentucky. He was a thin, wiry, intense little man, this Father Eutropius. He had a quick intelligence and a vivid, dramatic imagination. He was full of ideals, his heart burned with faith and zeal. And he had more courage than physical strength—a common trait among Trappists. He needed all the faith and ardor and enthusiasm and courage he could muster, to carry out the difficult and complicated mission that was entrusted to him. He was to lead forty-four men—monks, brothers, novices, postulants, and familiars—through a France that was once more simmering to the boiling-point with revolution; he was to put them on a boat and take them to America—fighting his way step by step through a most intricate network of obstacles and reverses.

The number and character of the accidents that beset the monks all through their journey bear sufficient witness to the activity of the enemy of all such enterprises as this. The devil does not like monasteries, especially contemplative ones. He has spent a hundred years trying to interfere with Gethsemani—and in the early days the battle was not altogether to his disadvantage.

However, most of the monks who sailed for the United States under Father Eutropius were perfectly chosen for the foundation. But for one or two exceptions—like Father Paulinus, a Basque, and the Italian Father Benezet—the colonists sent to Gethsemani were Bretons and Vendéens.

That meant, first of all, that they were physically hardy, endowed with plenty of strength and endurance—racial characteristics of these sturdy and intrepid farmers and mariners. Of course, they were not prepared for the Kentucky climate, with its unmitigated summer heat and its sudden temperamental changes of warm and cold in the other seasons of the year. But on the whole they would be well equipped to stand up under the vicissitudes of the new foundation. Father Euthymius, who served many years as subprior, died in 1880 at the age of seventy-two, and Father Emmanuel, the cellarer, lived until 1885 and the age of seventy-four. Some of the lay brothers did even better. Brother Charles Potiron, who reputedly died in an aura of sanctity and mysticism, lived to be seventy-seven, and Brother Theodoret was buried in January, 1893, two months short of his eightieth birthday. Finally, Brother Antonine, who was only eighteen when he sailed from France with the rest of the Trappists as a novice, and who was so tempted against his vocation that he more than once left the monastery and returned to begin over again, outlasted them all and saw the golden jubilee of Gethsemani in 1898. He died in 1902, in his seventy-third year.

On October 26, 1848, the monks of Melleray got up as usual for the night office, at two o'clock in the morning. It was over at about four, and those who had been designated for the American foundation went to the dormitory and changed into secular clothing, afterward putting on their cowls over the unfamiliar garb. Then they descended to the cloister with the two blankets that were their individual baggage and bedding for the long journey.

Dom Maxime addressed them for the last time, in terms of which we may find an echo in the act of foundation of the abbey. "Our dearly beloved brothers," he wrote, "will infallibly succeed if they always keep the spirit of their vocation, which will lead them in particular to the study and practice of the virtues of charity, obedience, poverty, mortification, patience, humility. Let our beloved brothers never forget to apply themselves to prayer . . . let them maintain close union among themselves. . . . Then the world and the devil will be able to do nothing against them, for, let them be fully persuaded of this truth: a house divided against itself will fall into ruins. Let them have a cordial and respectful love for their superior and console him in his cares for them by obedience and fraternal union, and let them never put him into the position where the duty of issuing his commands may become a matter of difficulty and embarrassment for him. Let them, in the consideration of their own frailties, remain humble in spirit and in their hearts. Do this and you shall live, my dearly beloved brothers. Amen! Amen!"

The Trappists listened in silence, with lumps in their throats, then proceeded to the church for the traditional blessing that is chanted over "monks going on a journey."

After that, the whole community, those traveling and those staying in France, issued from the monastery gate in procession, chanting the litany of Loretto. It was a bleak autumn morning and rain was falling steadily. Father Eutropius, armed with a wooden cross that was a copy of the one with which Dom Augustin de Lestrange had once led his band of refugees from La Trappe to La Val Sainte, walked forward full of emotion into a gray, wet world of bare trees and stubble fields and puddles and deep mud. The procession continued its solemn progress, chanting in the rain for about a kilometer. At the edge of a wood they came to a small wayside cross. Here they stopped. The monks who were leaving took off their rain-soaked cowls and handed them to the ones who were staying. They all embraced one another in silence, and the two groups parted, one to return to the abbey and the other—a strange band of workingmen with shaven heads and ill-fitting suits—to begin a long day's tramp to the Loire, where they were to take a riverboat from Ancenis to Tours.

That was how the monastery of Our Lady of Gethsemani came into existence. That morning had seen what was technically the foundation of the new house. The community had been formed and had begun to exist and function as an autonomous unit from the moment of its separation from Melleray. Nevertheless, it still had several thousands of miles to go before it was to find the place of its destiny. For two months the community would be looking for its monastery.

The first day's journey ended dramatically at Ancenis, where the news of the monks' embarkation had attracted a large crowd of curious and devout Vendéens. The Trappists chanted Compline and sang their ancient, heart-rending *Salve Regina* in the parish church, which was crowded to the doors. But when it came time to find their way through the crowds to the boat, they became separated in the darkness, and their superior had a hard time gathering them together again. When they were all finally safe on board, three real misfortunes were discovered. Their baggage had not been put on board at Nantes, as had been planned; their provisions had been mislaid somewhere between Melleray and the boat landing, and finally, a brother who had been sent to Nantes to borrow eight thousand francs had returned empty-handed.

It was a wild journey from Ancenis to Le Havre. They changed from boat to train at Tours, changed trains at Orléans and again in Paris. Each stage of their journey was marked by excitement and confusion. Whenever this weird group of rough-looking men with shaven heads collected around their emaciated leader in station waiting rooms, crowds of curious people flocked from all sides, full of questions and comment. Since they could not get anything out of the monks, who refused to speak to them, the bystanders made their own peculiar surmises. Usually it ended with Father Eutropius making a little speech. "Messieurs," he would say, "do not be alarmed or surprised. These are men dedicated to God, Trappist monks who have renounced everything to live in poverty and labor and silence and prayer. They are going to a distant land to build a monastery. They are going to carry the Name and the worship of God to the forests of North America, among the tigers [1] and panthers and wolves of Kentucky. . . ."

Invariably the gendarmes were on the scene before he had uttered more than four or five sentences. All France was on the alert for riots in 1848. But the Trappists did not get into any trouble.

What was more important, at each new stage of the journey Father Eutropius, with an untiring persistence born of faith married to natural tenacity, pushed and cajoled his way into

---

[1] There were still plenty of wildcats in Kentucky in 1848.

the offices of the highest railway officials he could find, in order to beg huge reductions for the traveling monks. Thanks to his efforts, they went most of the way to Le Havre riding second-class and paying only half the third-class fare.

For many of the monks it was the first time they had ever ridden in a train or had, indeed, even seen one. For most of them it was also their last experience of the ferocious *chemin de fer.*

At Le Havre, three days before the departure of the boat, the brothers who had been told to bring the fifteen thousand pounds of baggage from Nantes to the port of embarkation arrived without any of it. They innocently presented to their superior the "written promise" which a nice gentleman at Tours had given them, stating that they would certainly have their baggage with them at Le Havre that same evening. Father Eutropius threw up his hands in a paroxysm of woe and took the first train back to Paris.

He arrived at the capital at five the next morning—little more than forty-eight hours before their ship was due to weigh anchor. He inquired at three stations without finding a trace of the monks' equipment—which included everything from ploughs and bake ovens to folio graduals and antiphoners and straw mattresses. It was not the kind of consignment that would easily be overlooked.

Finally he found it all safe at the Gare d'Ivry. But his troubles had only begun. He had to move this mountain across Paris to the Gare de Batignolles. This would cost much more than he could afford. Soon Father Eutropius was once again seated in the office of the highest and most influential official he could find.

The Trappist abbot has left us a written account, in English, of all this. He says (with a pardonable disregard for syntax): "On telling him that I was a Trappist he appeared totally surprised, and wished to know the life of a Trappist. I gave him a short résumé of our manner of life. . . . I spoke to him of our spiritual exercises, of our different employments, and the happiness experienced in the quiet of solitude. He listened to me with great attention and when I had finished speaking he cried out: 'Ah, Monsieur! That life is beautiful compared with that of the great part of men in the world where we see only sensuality, pride and self-love. I assure you that if I were not married I would embrace your kind of life and accompany you to America!' " [2]

Father Eutropius Proust was a good talker!

However, this particular official could do nothing to reduce the cost of transporting the monks' baggage across Paris. He sent Father Eutropius off with a letter to another official who gave him just as little satisfaction. By that time it was getting late. In fact, it would soon be too late to move his baggage from the station where it was languishing. He managed to obtain special permission to do so.

Seven o'clock in the evening found Father Eutropius hard at work with three teamsters, loading up wagons at the Gare d'Ivry.

Then there was the problem of the *octroi*, the city customs. If they went through Paris, they would be stopped and all their baggage held up for examination. It was now past nine.

Father Eutropius promised his teamsters a good tip if they would go around the city walls. They agreed.

For a terrible half-hour, however, the Trappist superior was tortured with misgivings about the wisdom of such a course. The teamsters pulled up at the first *bistrot* along their way and stopped in for a couple of drinks to give them strength for their journey.

At ten o'clock he was wringing his hands in the street, standing in the lurid glare that issued from the bar and illuminated the heavy wagons and idle horses.

But in the end everything arrived safely at Batignolles and left on the early train for Le Havre.

At one in the afternoon of November 2, 1848, the forty

[2] *Gethsemani Abbey, a Narrative of the Late Abbot Eutropius, O.C.R.* (1899), p. 34.

Trappists and their books and ploughs and supplies for the long Atlantic crossing were safe on board the "Brunswick," an eight-hundred-ton sailing vessel under the command of Captain Thomas of New Orleans.

The ship was crowded. It was the year of the gold rush, and America was more than ever fabulous in the imagination of immigrants. But on this journey the "Brunswick" was bearing a company unusual even in those years. Besides the Trappists themselves, who barricaded themselves off in the steerage and settled in a provisional shipboard monastery to which nobody else had access without their permission, and besides sixty German immigrants of the ordinary kind, there was a party of eighty men, women, and children destined for one of the strange communist "utopias" that were springing up in such profusion in those years.

1848 was the year when the Oneida community was founded. Seven years before, Brook Farm had entered upon the same path of social experimentation. There were not a few Fourieristic phalanxes in the United States, and it was more than twenty years since the English Socialist, Robert Owen, had inaugurated his community at New Harmony, Indiana—a dream of harmony that had been shipwrecked within two years upon the rocks of the same old discord.

By 1848 there was ample evidence that the only ones among these communist groups that stood a fair chance of survival were those that had some kind of religious basis. The Shakers were still flourishing. The Ephrata community, founded in Pennsylvania by a German Protestant hermit more than a century before, was still thriving and continued to do so for many years to come.

The group that sailed from Le Havre at the end of 1848 with the Trappist founders of Gethsemani was destined to be the longest-lived of the explicitly nonreligious communist "utopias" planted on American soil in those optimistic days.

They were Etienne Cabet's "Icarians." The first thing that Dom Eutropius remarked about them was that they were under the direction of a delegate who took the place of Cabet himself, and "to whom the name of representative was given. He was charged with judging the differences that might arise among them, an office of which there was great need during the voyage." [3] In fact, the Icarians were so divided by quarrels and dissensions arising from petty greeds and jealousies that the monks considered themselves fortunate to be separated, by the improvised enclosure, from all communion with their noise.

One of the many things that distinguished the Trappists from the rest of that ship's strange company was the relative efficiency with which they were prepared to meet the emergencies of the voyage. The other passengers, Icarians included, were fasting on hardtack, while the monks had set up their ovens and were drawing out smoking loaves of fresh bread each morning. Caldrons of soup simmered on the ranges of the monks' kitchen, and under the circumstances the lean Trappist fare began to look like luxury indeed in those days before the phenomenal menus of the modern ocean liner.

In a short time the monks found themselves feeding most of the other passengers—at least, all who were sick or weak or needed some special attention. The chief beneficiaries of this charity were some mothers with infants to nurse and an old immigrant who had been left by his companions to starve when he became too weak to prepare his own meals.

The monks had no trouble with the Icarians, whose only hostile act was a decree of their "assembly" forbidding any of their number to hear Mass in the monks' chapel. The Trappists were glad to do some cooking for them on their range, baking pastry, apples, potatoes, and so on for anyone who brought them to the door of the steerage "monastery."

It would seem that Providence threw these two groups, Trappists and Icarians, together just to invite a comparison between them.

After all, they had not a little in common. The ideal of

[3] *Op. cit.*, p. 41.

Cistercian monasticism is a communal ideal which goes back explicitly to the life of the first Christians, who were of "one heart and one mind" and "had all things in common." [4]

As a social and economic unit, the Trappist community bound for Kentucky was just as truly and strictly "communistic" as were the Icarians, who were heading for Texas. The monks owned all their property in common. They were, in fact, vowed to the most uncompromising poverty, forbidden to possess anything whatever as individuals, not even the most insignificant of consumer's goods. Everything they used or consumed came to them from the abbot or through his permission as representative of the Christ, the Life and unifying Principle of the monastic community. But in the moral order the monks were bound to a far stricter and more radical communism than the Icarians had ever dreamed of. The monk's body and his very soul belong to his community, insofar as it is a part of the living, mystical organism Who is Christ on earth—the Church. The monk cannot claim proprietorship over the smallest internal act of judgment or desire that interferes with the life of the community—which is love, the charity of Christ. He does not even claim for himself such acts as do not interfere with the organic functioning of the group; he prefers to consecrate and dedicate them to Christ living in His brethren, Christ living in the abbot, Christ in the monk's own soul, Christ in the Tabernacle, the visible heart of the monastic community.

The Icarians' brand of communism was nothing but a working compromise between conflicting human appetites. Like all other materialistic communists, Cabet's disciples simply accepted human passions and greeds as a matter of course and attempted to neutralize their evil social effects by rationing out satisfactions to each one on a basis of mathematical equality.

But the common life of a Cistercian monk is based on far

[4] Acts ii:44. Cf. Gilson, *Mystical Theology of St. Bernard*, p. 75.

wiser assumptions, on tenets that reject such absurdities from the very start. There is no such thing as mathematical equality in a Cistercian monastery: each one does not strive to raise himself to the level of everybody else by cutting all the others down to his own level. On the contrary, the monk lives on an ideal of self-sacrifice in which he is the servant of all and gives up everything he has, becoming like Christ, his Master, obedient unto the death of the Cross for the glory of God and for the good of his community. It is, in fact, an ideal of self-immolation which the Dictatorship of the Proletariat, the World Revolution, also demands in practice. But the monk sacrifices himself for eternal values and for a reward which he begins to enjoy in the midst of his very act of sacrifice; his reward consists in the supernatural, divinizing selflessness which liberates him forever from the limitations of a narrow and worldly egoism. The whole end and ideal of communism, which aims at an earthly paradise full of comforts and pleasures and temporal satisfactions, necessarily imprisons a man in the materialism which is the source of all his sorrow and unrest. This consecration to physical satisfactions must, in the end, defeat even the temporary sense of liberation, the passing exaltation, which may come in a time of special stress to one who is willing to sacrifice his whole self to the cause of world revolution. It is an exaltation which is limited to the feelings and imagination and which can never taste anything of the intense inner purity of a charity supernaturalized by Christian detachment.

It was this peace and purity of heart which, above all, marked the essential difference between the monks and the communists who were traveling together to their respective promised lands on board the "Brunswick" in 1848. How was it that the monks lived together in such harmony and happiness and peace, while the Icarians were always at one another's throats? There is no explanation to be found in the natural order. After all, the two groups were made up of the same kind of material. Both monks and Cabetians had been recruited from various levels of society, and in about the same proportions. In both groups there was a small percentage of professional men and a larger group of farmers and artisans. Moreover, most of the Icarians had been brought up in the atmosphere of what was still a more or less Catholic culture. The difference, then, was to be found not on this superficial level but deeper down: the monks had Christ living and working in them by faith, by charity. The monks were united by the Holy Spirit in the peace of God, which tames and dominates and sublimates man's nature and ordains it to the highest possible ends. But the Icarians were united only by the frail bonds of an "armed neutrality" of insatiable animal appetites.

Leaning over the rail of the "Brunswick" as she hove to and took the pilot on board in the vast estuary of the Mississippi, Father Eutropius was astonished by the sight of a strange commotion in the waters—a battle of different kinds of fish. Those that belonged to the sea were fighting with those of the river. It was a presage of the violence that was to come.

On reaching New Orleans, the Icarians received bad news. A Cabetian colony that had preceded them to Texas that year had found that the country was not exactly the paradise flowing with milk and honey that they had been led to imagine. In fact, it was a dry and treeless waste, full of bitter hardship, in which many of their number had succumbed to sickness and thirst and hunger. And now there were not a few of them in New Orleans, begging and in rags. The reaction of the group on board ship was characteristic, but it brought with it tragedies that horrified the monks. There was a special meeting of the "assembly." It was decided that they should divide up whatever money they had left, so as to be ready to face emergencies. This was done, but not before one of their number had made a gallant attempt to get away with the whole sum for himself. Another wrote a letter of delirious invective against Cabet and then blew out his brains. A third fell overboard and nearly drowned. He was rescued in time, however, and Father Eutropius had an interview with him afterward.

The blood nearly froze in the Trappist's veins as the man calmly related how, feeling himself on the point of drowning, he had already unclasped his knife to plunge it into his own heart, when a sailor jumped into the river and saved him.

The monk was left with plenty of food for thought by this insight into the communist mentality.

One brighter touch was added to the dismal picture when one of the Icarians presented himself before Father Eutropius and asked if he could be admitted to the Trappist community. The young superior was not unfriendly to this request. Unfortunately, it turned out that the disillusioned Icarian had a wife.

Cabet eventually reorganized his utopia at Nauvoo, Illinois, on the site vacated by the Mormons, who had left for Utah in 1847.

At New Orleans the Trappists transferred their baggage to a big river steamer, the "Martha Washington," and settled on board for the ten-day journey to Louisville. "Settled," however, is only a euphemism, for this time they had no privacy. As soon as they put their straw mattresses down on the deck to go to sleep, other passengers jumped on them and refused to get off. It was another instance of Trappist austerity being luxury in comparison with early nineteenth-century traveling accommodations.

The arrival of the second Trappist colony in Kentucky was far different from that of the first. Dom Urban Guillet and his handful of men and their bewildered oblates had staggered from their flatboats to fall half dead from exhaustion into the arms of those who had come to meet them. But now there was a community of forty-three strong, healthy men.[5] Father Eutropius left the steamer when it was delayed at the falls of

---

[5] One had been lost on the journey, when the aged Father Benezet died on the high seas. The 70-year-old monk, an Italian from Piedmont, had been a Christian Brother before becoming a Trappist and had traveled back and forth across the sea to Isle Bourbon. He had offered himself for the new foundation and had been accepted, although he was really too old.

the Ohio a few miles outside the city, and went to announce
their arrival to Bishop Flaget. The bishop overflowed with the
rich, abounding joy of an Old Testament patriarch, crying,
"Blessed are you who come to us in the Name of the Lord!"

He offered them shelter in two large halls that were used
as schoolrooms, and here they remained for three days while
their superior was making arrangements for the last stage of
their journey—the fifty miles from the city to Gethsemani.

The journey was to end as it had begun—in a torrent of
rain. The monks, huddled together in three wagons, learned
that Kentucky can be very bleak and mournful and cold in
December. It was the twentieth day of the last month of the
year. They peered through the icy rain at the sycamores and
the ruined cornfields. Hour followed hour. They climbed
hills, and drove through flooded bottom-lands in water up to
their axles. They had long since been soaked to the skin. They
took their dinner of bread and cheese and fruit in their
swamped wagons. That was in the middle of the afternoon.
By then they should have been near Bardstown. But there was
still a long way to go. Darkness fell. Still no sign of a town.

At eight o'clock one of the wagons broke down. The monks
alighted and rearranged themselves. The weakest of their number moved into the two remaining wagons. The rest walked
into Bardstown at eleven o'clock that night, up to their knees
in mud.

They were to spend the night at St. Joseph's College as
guests of the Jesuit fathers. They found the college building
in the Stygian darkness of the rainy night. Taking with him
Brother Hilarion, a Kilkenny Irishman, Father Eutropius made
a tour around the walls of the building trying to find the door.
Having found it, they knocked, but received no answer.

The monks were in no mood to waste time. They gathered
together and took a deep breath, and forty-three powerful
voices roared the one word: "T-r-r-ra-PEEST!"

It seemed as if every window in the building flew open on
the instant. The Jesuits and their students and their neighbors

and probably the whole of Bardstown, besides, were now informed that the silent monks had arrived.

The Jesuits soon built a big fire and prepared a hot meal for the travelers, but they had no beds to offer them. The monks were content to roll their blankets around them and sleep on the floor.

The next day—the winter solstice and the feast of St. Thomas the Apostle—they started out in the not-too-early morning, after Mass and Communion, to cover the few miles that remained.

For most of them it was to be the end of all journeys. Within a year one of them would already be buried at Gethsemani. Most of the others would find their rest there also, one by one, in years to come. They were tired of traveling by now!

But if they knew that their journey was ended, they could see by the poverty of the land around them that their labors were just about to begin. The pale winter sun reached its zenith, and shone feebly on the low, wooded hills dominating the brown fields of the plateau. The sight of a forest cheered them after so much relatively bare landscape. Their satisfaction grew to joy when a Negro who was driving one of the wagons told them that the forest belonged to them. That was Gethsemani, their land, their new home.

They slowly advanced, among cedars and hickory trees, oak and maple and walnut, and an occasional sycamore with mottled branches pale as dead men's bones. And now they were among the hills. As the track they followed reached a summit in the undulating land, they perceived that they were entering into a different kind of landscape. Ahead of them was a broad valley, bounded in the distance by another line of blue, wooded hills. The cold air was sweet with the scent of pines.

A sharp descent brought them down to a creek which splashed over brown shelves of shale in a covert of dark cedars. Then they climbed again and came to open fields. They saw ahead of them, on a bare, even knoll, a group of log cabins standing amid cornfields. In one of the fields, the stalks stood brown and dry, the ears still clinging to them. The wind stirred sadly in the dry stalks and dry shucks. A Kentucky mule came up to the fence and semaphored his surprise at them with big brown ears. It was their home, the orphanage of Our Lady of Gethsemani, standing in what the monks now call St. Joseph's field, facing south and west, dominating the wide, blue valley.

It was a beautiful site, vast and silent and full of peace, and the monks let their eyes rove over the undulating woods and fields toward the distant village of New Hope. The view was almost beautiful enough to make them overlook the dilapidated cabins that they would have to live in. But in any case, their long journey was at an end and they were glad and their tired hearts thanked the Living God, Whose inscrutable will had destined them to this place from all eternity.

MONASTERY AT TAMIÉ, FRANCE

MONASTERY AT AIGUEBELLE, FRANCE

MONASTERY AT SÉNANQUE, FRANCE

Jahan

Sauvageot

12TH CENTURY CLOISTER, FONTENAY, FRANCE

Terrell Dickey

19TH CENTURY BASILICA, GETHSEMANI, KENTUCKY

CHOIR MONKS AT OFFICE, GETHSEMANI

READING AT MEALS: REFECTORY, AIGUEBELLE

CHOPPING WOOD (*above*) – POWER SAW, GEORGIA (*below left*)

Manning

Manning

HAYLOFT CHOIR, GEORGIA (*above right*) – CHOIR MONKS, ORVAL (*below*)

MASS

GOD

FEVER

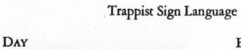

COFFEE

Trappist Sign Language

DAY

EAT

LIBRARY, ORVAL

SCULLERY, AIGUEBELLE

HAYLOFT SCRIPTORIUM, GEORGIA

BULLDOZER, GETHSEMANI

GARDENER, AIGUEBELLE

GOING TO WORK, AIGUEBELLE

MONK'S DINNER, U.S.A.

MONK'S DINNER, FRANCE

Manning

CORNCRIB KITCHEN, GEORGIA

ATHERING GRAPES, AIGUEBELLE

Monks at a Shrine of Our Lady

Manning

ᵒLD WORLD SCRIPTORIUM

NEW WORLD SCRIPTORIUM

Manning

ᵁILDING A TEMPORARY MONASTERY

ACOLYTE SERVING MASS

Low Mass, Gethsemani

Guest House Seen from Entrance to Monastery, Gethsemani

New Monastery: Our Lady of the Holy Trinity, Utah

VII. GETHSEMANI IN THE NINETEENTH CENTURY; OTHER AMERICAN FOUNDATIONS

FATHER EUTROPIUS PROUST and his forty-two Trappists had no sooner reached the primitive farm which they were to take over from the Sisters of Loretto than they had their first taste of Kentucky weather. After the rain that had soaked them the day before, the temperature now took a sudden plunge, and their first evening in the log cabins of Gethsemani left them shivering with the intense cold. In the last few days that remained before Christmas they could do practically nothing but cut firewood in the forest and gather in the corn that still remained to be husked. For the rest, they were content to sit in a cabin and shell corn while one of their number read to them aloud.

The sisters and their orphans stayed to help the Trappists celebrate their first Christmas in America and then moved to a better place, leaving the monks all their farm animals and implements. Unfortunately, the monks' own baggage remained in storage two months in Louisville. Deprived of their big range, with its ovens, they could not bake any bread, and a Frenchman without bread is even more miserable than a Frenchman without red wine. It was not the least of their sacrifices to live for two months on pancakes and hot biscuits.

They tore down the worst of the cabins and used some of the wood to build an addition to the sisters' little chapel, which was far too small to contain the crowds that would come to hear the monks sing High Mass on the big feast days.

They improvised a chapter room and refectory and dormitory, and in the spring of the new year one of the brothers built a bakehouse that was the admiration of Nelson County. The biggest difficulty the monks had to face was clearing their land for cultivation. The existing fields had been newly claimed from the forest, and they had to go over them time after time to root out the briars and blackberries and dogtooth. Buckberries and ironweed sprang up all around them, and in the summer time, if they turned their backs on the corn to look after their potato patch, it seemed that the cornstalks would become a tangle of morning-glories overnight.

Then there was the Kentucky summer! The monks went out to work in woolen robes and scapulars under the furious sun. Their only protection against sunstroke was to pull the black woolen hoods of their scapulars over their heads, and then they nearly smothered in the heat. Meanwhile, their boiling flesh broke out from head to foot in a burning red rash that gnawed at them with an insistence unknown to the hair shirts of the Thebaid.

Life in Kentucky was not altogether easy, they found. Since Gethsemani had been colonized by Melleray, which belonged to the stricter of the two Trappist congregations, the monks were keeping the ancient usages of Cîteaux and thus observing the Rule of St. Benedict in every particular. It was hard, but not altogether impossible: and they could always remind themselves that their predecessors, under Dom Urban Guillet, had had a far harder time of it.

However, all their neighbors and even the bishop himself tried to persuade the monks to take things easier. Almost everyone seemed to think that they would all die if they persisted in trying to live without meat. The monks did not let themselves be worried by such superstitions. But Father Eutropius did think that the foundation could scarcely survive without some small mitigations. The principal one was lighter clothing in summer. The monks were also allowed to go out to work in straw hats, to protect them from the blazing sun. The General Chapter of 1849, convening at La Grande Trappe, heard of the hardships of the Trappist pioneers at Gethsemani and accorded them all the mitigations that had been granted the previous year to the new North African monastery of Staouëli, near Algiers.

In the very first week after their arrival, Father Eutropius was struck down with pneumonia—probably a result of the rainy ride from Louisville to Bardstown and the cold weather that followed—and in a short time he was in real danger of death. Two doctors were called in, and they said that his case was hopeless. They told the prior, Father Paulinus, to give him the Last Sacraments.

As if this were not enough of a blow to the community, three of the weaker members left. One of them was a lay-brother postulant, who was entitled to go whenever he pleased. That was not so bad. But another was a professed choir monk —who apparently received a dispensation from his vows and returned to the world. The third was a professed lay brother. The only notation that follows his name in the very imperfect archives of the abbey is terrible in its brevity: *Mort à Louisville, apostat* ("He died in Louisville, an apostate").

Nevertheless, the majority of the monks were determined to stay in Kentucky and make a success of this foundation, no matter what the cost might be. So great was their resolution to carry out what they were convinced to be God's will for them that Father Paulinus, acting as superior during the sickness of Father Eutropius, made a contract for two thousand bricks to be burned and delivered to Gethsemani in the spring of 1849. The monks were ready to begin their permanent building at once.

Meanwhile, the saintly Bishop Flaget of Louisville, who was himself entering upon what was to be his last sickness, offered the last nine Masses of his life as a novena for the recovery of the Trappist superior. Bishop Flaget was too weak to go to the cathedral, and he said the Masses in his room.

Father Eutropius was lying unconscious in his bed at Gethsemani. The doctor who had come to visit him for what he thought was the last time exclaimed: "It is all over. He has only five minutes to live." He mounted his horse to continue on his rounds and help those who might possibly profit by his services. He had scarcely left the cabin when the patient opened his eyes. Father Eutropius had recovered consciousness, and he felt such a marked improvement that he thanked God for having cured him.

However, it was long before he had any real strength. In fact, his ardent love of the common life led him into imprudences that put off his real recovery for many months. He insisted on going out to work with the monks before he was sufficiently strong to swing an axe or wield a shovel, and soon he was once again in bed. His convalescence lasted until July. In the spring months he could do little else but ride through the woods on horseback, with Father Paulinus to look after him.

On April 8 there came some small consolation for the monks in the log-cabin monastery, when two of those who had crossed the Atlantic from Melleray as novices pronounced the vows that made them permanent members of the community, promising "obedience, conversion of manners and stability [1] in this place which is called Our Lady of Gethsemani, before God and in the presence of His saints whose relics are here present. . . ."

Still, Father Eutropius was by no means convinced that the foundation would last, and one of his first acts on recovering his health was to cancel Father Paulinus's order for two thousand bricks. After all, they had no money with which to pay the Sisters of Loretto for the land, still less to buy bricks.

This fact so preyed on the mind of the young superior that

[1] All monks who make vows according to the Rule of St. Benedict promise "stability." That is to say, they vow to live and die in the monastery of their profession. However, they can be sent by their superiors to start another monastery or to help a struggling foundation elsewhere. In this case, they make a new vow of stability in their new home. The vow is violated by a monk leaving his monastery and going elsewhere of his own accord.

he felt it was absolutely essential for him to return to France to raise money for the monastery. The doctors told him that the journey was out of the question, but he started out, anyway, on the Fourth of July, 1849. He was so weak that it took two brothers to get him into the carriage that was to take him to Bardstown. He had to spend several weeks resting in Louisville, as the guest of Bishop Flaget. From there he went on by easy stages to Cincinnati and New York and finally sailed for Europe.

Although there was no question that the monks needed money, the necessity of such a journey was most unfortunate, since it deprived the community of its superior. It was not the only journey of that kind that Dom Eutropius made when he was abbot of Gethsemani. Later on, when building actually began, other monks of the community, including Father Paulinus, spent months outside the enclosure and traveled many miles trying to raise money to pay for the abbey buildings, whose walls were slowly rising on the knoll above the little creek that ran through the woods of Gethsemani. We find one of the monks as far afield as Montevideo, Uruguay, where he finally became involved in the secular ministry.

These long tours, extending over entire continents, were scarcely in harmony with the Cistercian vocation to silence, stability, and contemplation. There is evidence that the General Chapters viewed them with great disfavor in those days, when begging was still not a violation of the letter of the Rules. (All begging by the monks themselves is forbidden by the present Constitutions of the Order.)

Dom Eutropius, however, had the approval of the Papal Nuncio in the United States.

Even more helpful to the new community than the money collected on these tours were the postulants who presented themselves at the log-cabin monastery. Considering the hardships and poverty of the life, Gethsemani did rather well in attracting vocations in the first year of its existence. During the course of 1849, fourteen men came, at one time or another, to ask the habit of a Trappist novice—nine in the choir and the rest as brothers. Most of them were Irishmen or Germans. There was one Kentuckian, and he turned out to be consumptive and could not stay. Those who applied to become choir novices were mostly priests, and some of them belonged to other religious congregations.

Of the fourteen, four remained to make their vows together on Easter Sunday, April 20, 1851. Meanwhile, a new colony of thirteen priests, monks, novices, and brothers arrived from Melleray. Two of these novices, both priests, also pronounced their vows on that Easter Sunday. They were joined by a novice who had come to Gethsemani with the original pioneers from France, a vigorous and severe middle-aged Breton. He was called Frater Mary Benedict.

Easter Sunday, 1851, must have inspired high hopes at Gethsemani. First, in the chapter room, two lay brothers, Sebastian and Frederick, made their perpetual vows. Then, at the solemn Mass in the monastery chapel no fewer than eight choir monks, three of whom were priests, sang their irrevocable *suscipe*.

They were a curious and interesting group, these men. Most of them were Bretons and had already been formed to the Cistercian life in France. One of them, Frater Theophilus, was a professed monk from the abbey of Aiguebelle, who was only renewing his stability at Gethsemani. Three of them, professed under the names of Fraters Peter, Paul, and Patrick, were all Irish-born and were, so to speak, Gethsemani's own. They had never known any other but the log-cabin monastery. Frater Peter Bannon lived to be seventy-five and died forty-two years later, in 1893, but Frater Patrick Mills survived his profession only two months. As for Frater Paul, whose family name was Murphy, he did not die in the monastery. After his name in the archives there is a laconic note that speaks heaven only knows what volumes of nostalgia. It says, *Parti pour l'Irlande* ("He went back to Ireland").

But Frater Benedict was by far the most important member

of the group who made their vows that Easter Sunday. He had graduated from college with the highest honors and had proceeded to take a seminary course in theology, but had then drawn back from the priesthood, feeling that it was an honor too far above him. The responsibilities brought terror to his austere and rigid soul.

He became a teacher, but life in the world could not give him peace. He turned to the Trappists. At the monastery of Melleray he found what satisfied his soul—a life of rigid, unrelenting penance, of silence, obedience, humiliations. In this powerful and unbending character there was a kind of thirst for humiliations; the ideal of De Rancé was his element. He would have reveled in the chapter of faults in the golden days of La Grande Trappe.

That was what sanctity meant to Father Benedict Berger: the ability to receive outrageous insults, to be cursed, reviled, slapped in the face, spat upon, without twitching an eyebrow. That was the formula for his own sanctification, and that was to be his formula for the sanctification of others when he became abbot of Gethsemani.

But we are getting ahead of our story.

Gethsemani became an abbey [2] very early in her history—long before she was out of her log cabins and into the new brick monastery. Father Eutropius's begging tour of 1849 took him to Rome, where he was received in audience by Pope Pius IX. It was as a result of this visit that Gethsemani was erected in 1851 into an abbey. It was the "proto-abbey" of the New World, an abstract distinction that seems to mean

[2] In the Cistercian Order, an abbey is the highest of three kinds of religious houses. At the present day, permission of the General Chapter and of the Holy See are required before a *foundation* or a *priory* can become an abbey. Permission is granted only to well-established houses where all the elements of a complete monastery are found and where there is a definite chance that the regular contemplative life may be led in all its fulness. When a community is elevated to this dignity, it can elect an abbot, who has certain privileges and responsibilities that give him a high ranking among ecclesiastical superiors in the Church.

more than it actually does. All it really signifies is that the superiors of the monasteries that had been founded in America before Gethsemani, had not thought of going through all the red tape necessary to have their houses raised to this formal position.

In October, 1851, following an election held in May, the first abbot was blessed in old St. Joseph's Cathedral, Bardstown. The first abbot was, of course, Dom Mary Eutropius Proust.

Dom Eutropius had by that time a community of sixty men, and it was high time to begin the permanent monastery. The building was laid out on a scale that surprised those who saw it. Many thought that Dom Eutropius was foolish to build so spacious a church, so large a monastery. The place would be twice as big as he needed. True, postulants were coming; but postulants were also leaving, and novices too, and even some of the professed, some of those who had come from France in the first colony: their health failed, or their hearts, and they got dispensations or managed to be sent home to the mother house. Was it wise to build a place that could house a hundred and fifty men?

But this time Dom Eutropius was really inspired by the Holy Ghost, as we who have come a hundred years later have had ample opportunity to discover. With a community of a hundred and seventy, we have sometimes wondered why Dom Eutropius made the place so small.

However, the pioneer abbot had another inspiration, perhaps not such a good one. Determined to pay off all his debts, he decided to start a school. A school was needed at that time and in that place. Besides, it was a sure way of cementing the good will that bound the monks and their neighbors, both Catholic and Protestant, in all that section of Kentucky.

For a long time this school was more a project than an accomplished fact. Those were the Civil War years. Things were too unsettled for a boys' school in those days, when most young Kentuckians were running off to fight on one side or the other. Besides, the monks were too busy with the vitally important work of building their permanent monastery and making their own living out of the poor land to think of educating the young. As a matter of fact, it was a good thing they did apply themselves so wholeheartedly to what was strictly their own business. Within twenty years of their foundation all the essentials of a complete Cistercian monastery were permanently and solidly built. It was an immense advantage to be able to move into new quarters and keep the Rule in its entirety, from day to day, without any of the weird makeshifts that impose themselves on monks who do not have a real monastery to live in.

Probably this stubborn determination to build a monastery and occupy it as soon as possible finally decided the survival of the Gethsemani community, for, all this time, the fate of the house was hanging in the balance. The father immediate and the General Chapter seem several times to have almost reached the point of calling the whole thing off. But those Breton fathers who had come over to America on the "Brunswick" in 1848 had made up their minds to strike deep roots into the soul of Kentucky, and they were not going to allow themselves to be transplanted any more. The history of Dom Urban Guillet's colony would not be repeated, if they had anything to say in the matter.

The monastery building reflects their state of mind. It is a massive, quadrangular structure without pretension to any special architectural grace. The walls are thick and solid, and it is built around a central cloister garth or *préau*, according to the traditional Cistercian plan. The only attempt at "style" is in the church itself, and there the touch of Gothic Revival is so modest and self-effacing that it is not altogether alien to the Cistercian spirit of simplicity.

The monks of Gethsemani have their poverty to thank for the fact that their monastery has none of the ornate and pretentious ugliness, none of the ponderous vulgarity, that makes most of the architecture of the period so oppressive. True, it would be hard for the buildings to lay claim to any positive beauty, yet this negative freedom from pastiche is a matter for congratulation. To give the place its due, the view of Gethsemani's south front from St. Joseph's Hill is full of real dignity and charm, especially when it is surrounded by the flowers and foliage of summer.

Another thing that clearly reflects the spirit of the founders of Gethsemani was their reaction to Dom Eutropius's resignation. The health of the "proto-abbot" had always been very shaky, and one feels that his confidence in Gethsemani had never been altogether solid. He spent much of his time traveling to raise money, and he could never see the way clear to complete financial security. Finally, he decided that the responsibility was too great for him, and he laid it down to return to Melleray. That was in 1860. Eight years later he was elected abbot of the ancient Cistercian monastery of Tre Fontane, built on the site of St. Paul's martyrdom in the Roman Campagna.

One might have expected the community at Gethsemani to elect Father Paulinus as his successor. After all, Father Paulinus had been prior of the mother house when Dom Eutropius had been no more than a novice, and he had more years of monastic experience behind him than most of the community. But there was one thing against him: he had spent too many months, years even, outside the monastery raising funds.

We can see what was the mentality of the monks of Gethsemani by their actual choice. They did not want a promoter, a businessman, at their head, even though he might also be a good Trappist. They were not concerned about money and financial security before everything else.

Their choice fell upon the austere Breton who had been one of the first to make his vows at the monastery. In electing Dom Benedict Berger, the monks of Gethsemani were fully aware of what kind of abbot they were going to have. They knew what that Napoleonic chin and those steely eyes represented. But they wanted this strict, uncompromising disciplinarian because they knew that he would be a ruthless defender of the rigor of the Rule. Perhaps he would be a hard superior; but one feels that most of the monks were all the happier for it. They were Trappists.

But beyond their concern for the welfare of their own individual souls, they were thinking of the survival of the monastery and of the Cistercian life in Kentucky. For that, it was all important that Gethsemani should have an abbot who would devote his whole life to maintaining the Benedictine regime of prayer, manual labor, and contemplative reading, together with the fasting and poverty and austerity and penance and monastic obedience in all their original purity.

Dom Benedict Berger ruled the monastery for twenty-nine years. And he really ruled it. He stayed with his monks and kept his finger on everything that went on. The new abbot rarely traveled, although we find him attending the two plenary councils of Baltimore besides making several visits to France and Nova Scotia on business for the Order.

During those twenty-nine years Gethsemani became a byword in Kentucky and in the American Catholic Church. It acquired a very definite character and spirit and reputation of its own—not altogether a pleasant one to most minds, it is true. All this was the effect of Dom Benedict and his regime.

The Gethsemani of the nineteenth century came to represent everything that La Trappe had been standing for since De Rancé. It was a place that people at large, even Catholics, were afraid of. Many shivered when they passed it. The monks were not understood. In the first place they were foreigners. Then they led that atrocious life of penance! The belief that most of them were reformed criminals gained authority in most minds from the fact that the guest house of the monastery usually had a quota of fallen priests entrusted to the monks for a period of ecclesiastical penance. The atmosphere of Gethsemani was well calculated to get most of them back into shape to perform their duties conscientiously— it was so forcible a reminder of purgatory!

Finally, the whole community was judged in terms of its

abbot, and Dom Benedict's relations with the outside world—especially with the chancery office in Louisville—were characterized by the same unbending severity, the same dictatorial attitude, that he assumed among his monks.

The exiled French monks were thus all the more isolated, even though their school was now receiving students and making friends who were capable of understanding the monastery and what it really stood for.

Nevertheless, it must have required a very special kind of heroism to live through those twenty-nine years of very hard labor and real poverty, under an abbot whose deliberate policy was to insult and humiliate his monks at every turn. And there were many other discouraging factors in the life. If the monks had had plenty of good books to read, it might have made a big difference, at least to some of them. But they had very little besides conventional books of piety—some of which require almost a special charism unto themselves if they are to be absorbed without twisting the mind into a caricature of sanctity.

The monks had none of the consolation that comes from a novitiate full of good prospects, with postulants coming in every other week. The postulants who came to Gethsemani were few, and the archives show that they practically all left. Dom Benedict took the Rule very seriously in its prescriptions about testing the novices to see if they loved humiliations.

Walled in, then, in this big, isolated fortress of silence, the Breton fathers who had come from Melleray had absolutely nothing to fall back on except a deep interior life. Everything else was literally annihilated. It was God or nothing. And we have reason to believe that for most of them it was God. They had to be saints; otherwise they would have gone crazy.

Of course, the big problem of the house was always its survival. A monastery cannot go on without vocations. And what was most important of all, what would eventually decide Gethsemani's fate, would be its ability to attract and hold *American* vocations. It was not enough that a passing Irishman or Frenchman or German should decide to end his wanderings at Gethsemani; what the monks needed was some evidence that the Cistercian life was capable of capturing the minds and hearts of these adventurous and independent Americans in whose country they had planted their foundation.

In the first days at Gethsemani the excitement caused by the monks' presence in the neighborhood brought them a postulant, a young Kentuckian who wanted to be a lay brother but who had to be sent away because he had consumption. That was in 1849. Not until four more years had passed did another American-born postulant appear. In 1853 a twenty-three-year-old farm boy from New York State applied to the lay brothers' novitiate. Brother John, as he was called, survived the novitiate and made his simple perpetual vows in 1855. This showed that an American could come along at least that far in the Cistercian life. Brother John lasted fourteen years; in 1869 he received a dispensation and returned to the world.

During all these fourteen years there were only two other American-born postulants. One, Brother Lawrence, had been a tax collector, and his stay of one year proved him to be true to the tax collector's professional reputation for hardheartedness. He spent most of his time trying to argue with Dom Eutropius and crowned his monastic career with a twelve-page document full of close-packed invective which the records of the house describe as "diabolical." With this parting shot, he walked out the front gate never to return, and the monks all heaved sighs of relief.

In 1868, exactly twenty years after the foundation, Gethsemani opened her doors to her first American-born postulant for the choir. He was a secular priest, and he made two attempts to become a Trappist at Gethsemani. The first time, he stayed a year and left. He returned in 1881, to spend almost the whole two years' novitiate, but when the time came to take his vows, he fled.

Then Gethsemani acquired another Brother John—from Alabama—in 1876. He made his vows but was afterward dispensed.

He stayed on a short time as a family brother, that is, a kind of farm hand living in the gatehouse and working for bed and board, but he soon left altogether. The same year, another secular priest, this time from Brooklyn, came and gave the life a four-month trial. In 1878 there was another postulant for the lay brotherhood; he left in the same year.

Among the American postulants who thought of becoming Trappists at Gethsemani during Dom Benedict's administration, the most colorful, by far, was a certain Joseph Dutton. Recently converted to the faith, this man had led the kind of life that legend generally tacks on to Trappists. Born of Protestant farmers in Vermont, he had fought in the Union army in the Civil War. He had been unhappily married, then divorced. After that, he had gone through years of misery, drinking and gambling and ruining his life altogether. In the early 1880's he turned up in Memphis, where his reputation earned him, strangely enough, a romantic popularity. With a view to marrying the daughter of a Catholic family in that city, he had begun to take instructions in the faith. Then, soon after his Baptism, he suddenly vanished. Word came back that he had entered Gethsemani.

He remained in the monastery for twenty months. One day, toward the end of his novitiate, he was mowing hay in St. Mary's field, in front of the abbey, when a runaway horse came galloping down the road. The rider, a young girl, fell off as the horse went by. He picked her up and carried her to the monks' school. When he left the monastery a few months later, the rumor went around that he had gone off to marry her.

This story seems to have given the popular Kentucky novelist, James Lane Allen, the theme for his story about Gethsemani. *The White Cowl* has always rather annoyed the monks. There is supposed to be a copy of it around the monastery somewhere, but nobody seems to know where it is, and practically nobody has read it. But the mere thought of the book's theme (which is also that of the Marlene Dietrich movie,

"Garden of Allah") irritates them: so much so that, when we thought of borrowing a copy from the outside, in the hope that it would furnish an amusing page for the present volume, Dom Frederic Dunne, our late abbot, refused permission, saying he "didn't want people to think we had any interest in the thing."

In reality, Dutton left Gethsemani for a very solid reason. The monks, who were accustomed to write remarks in the record of entries and departures, seldom had any admiration for those who left. There is only one exception—Joseph Dutton. He went off to join the heroic Father Damien in his leper colony at Molokai, in the Pacific. It turned out that this was his real vocation. He became the close friend and one of the chief supports of the leper-priest and lived on Molokai for forty-four years—until he was well over eighty. It was a life of much harsher and more terrible penances than anything known at Gethsemani, even under Dom Benedict Berger.

Gethsemani had now been in existence thirty years. It was a fully developed Cistercian community, with a complete monastery and all that was needed to lead the Trappist life in all its details. The pioneer stage had long since been left behind. Those who entered the monastery found all the essentials of the contemplative life that had been led by St. Bernard and the Cistercian mystics of the twelfth century, except for the special spiritual atmosphere and the vital doctrine that pervaded St. Bernard's Clairvaux. Apart from that, they found the same rule, the same kind of life, the same opportunities. But they did not want them. They could not appreciate what they were getting. They could not penetrate beneath the surface of hardships and exterior humiliations to find the inner unction that came with the cross of the ascetic.

In thirty years there had been only eight native Americans at Gethsemani, and they had all run away. Was it true, what they were saying in Europe, that Americans would never make contemplatives? If so, that meant the end of Gethsemani, because the original founders were old men now, and the cemetery behind the apse of the church was beginning to be dotted with gray crosses and green graves bedded in myrtle.

Irish and German and French and French–Canadian novices came from time to time, and enough of them made profession to keep the house going until this, its greatest problem, was finally solved. And some of these had sufficient heroism to make up for what was lacking in those who did not stay.

For instance, there was Father Henry. He is still remembered in Gethsemani and in the neighborhood, for he died in 1919, after many years as confessor to the retreatants in the guest house. Father Henry was a German from Westphalia. He entered Gethsemani as a secular priest. During his novitiate he went blind. This would have been a very good reason for leaving the monastery, but Father Henry did not leave. He made his solemn vows and bound himself to spend the rest of his life in the poverty and obedience and enclosure and silence of a Cistercian—as well as in the perpetual darkness which God had added to his burden for good measure. He knew the psalter by heart, and he not only could say Mass, reciting the Masses of Our Lady and of the Dead by heart, but he even sang the conventual Masses when his turn came as hebdomadary. All he needed was to have someone read the proper of the Mass over to him a few times before he went to the altar. His inability to see anything with the eyes of his body did not impair the inward vision of his soul, but even that was obscured, toward the end of his life, by one of those nameless and dreadful trials with which the Spirit of God visits and purifies the souls of contemplatives. Father Henry accepted that also in the same spirit of peace and resignation with which he took all his other afflictions.

But long before that time, things had changed, and Gethsemani's survival was assured.

Nobody realized it at the time, but the turning-point came in 1885, when a young man who had been born on a farm near Lebanon, in the next county, confronted the ageing Dom Benedict and asked for admission to the lay brothers' novitiate. His name was John Green Hanning, and they put him down as a farmer. That was true; he had just come from his father's tobacco plantation near Owensboro, Kentucky. But when his superiors came to know this bronzed and wiry and laconic man a little better, they found that he had led rather an unsettled, wandering life. He had received the beginnings of an education from the monks themselves at their school on St. Joseph's Hill, but then he had run away from home to become a cowboy in Texas.

It was strange that the first native American to make a complete success of the Trappist life at Gethsemani should be a Texas cowboy. The ten-gallon hat and the lariat and the pair of six-shooters and the high saddle horns of the broncobuster have always symbolized the ultimate in American independence, and this tan and taciturn stranger, who took the name of Brother Joachim when he joined the monks, was no exception to the rule. He was independent and he was wild.

One would think he was absolutely the worst kind of candidate for the formation that Dom Benedict Berger believed in, and the truth is that the abbot's attempts to humiliate this ex-cowboy were met with explosions more proper to the wild west than to De Rancé's La Trappe. In a way, this Brother Joachim was the most unpromising of all the foot-loose wanderers who had stayed a while at Gethsemani to give the life a trial.

Yet, he turned out, after all, to be the very best—so true is it that it is the Holy Ghost Who makes religious vocations and sometimes makes the best of them out of the least likely material.

Brother Joachim had many natural qualities that fitted him to be a Trappist brother. He was strong. He could work. And although for a good part of his life he had not lived as a Catholic, there was a predisposition to solitude, a natural foundation for the contemplative life, something he had acquired in those long, lonely rides on the range. But above all, he was sincere and already had much of the natural humility of men who have been too often beaten down by a dominant passion—of men who know their own weakness.

That, after all, is the most important qualification in a postulant to the Cistercian life: a sense of the *need* of grace, of God's help, of the strict Rule, of solitude and silence and prayer. Without that, no one will really come to the monastery "seeking God," which is the first requirement St. Benedict demands in a novice.

The transformation worked by grace in the soul of this cowboy during his twenty-three years at Gethsemani was so remarkable that it has become the subject of a book that has gone through twelve American editions and is being translated into many other languages.[3] Brother Joachim has become famous with more than the fame of a merely human heroism. Catholics have prayed to God for favors through his intercession and have been answered. One of the first things many visitors to Gethsemani ask to see is his grave.

But long before all this came about, it was already evident that the entrance of John Green Hanning into the lay brothers' novitiate marked the beginning of a new age for Gethsemani. Indeed, his name is the first of a long list of native Americans who entered the monastery and took the Rule and all its hardships and embraced them for the love of God and stayed until the end. He was the first of a new generation that did not completely pass away until 1939, when little Brother Aloysius, the ex-Pennsylvania coal miner who came to Gethsemani two years after Brother Joachim, was laid to rest in the shadow of the monastic church.

The first native American to persevere at Gethsemani as a Cistercian choir monk was a young man of twenty who came to the Trappists from Atlanta, Georgia, in the summer of 1894, received the habit, and settled down quietly to lead the Cistercian life in all its rigor. He went on leading it for well over fifty years; for thirteen of them he was abbot of the

[3] M. Raymond, O.C.S.O., *The Man Who Got Even with God* (Milwaukee, 1941).

monastery, the first American to become a Trappist abbot: Dom M. Frederic Dunne.

While Gethsemani had been working out the all-important problems of survival, two other famous Cistercian monasteries of the Strict Observance had been founded on the North American continent. The first was a cousin of the Kentucky monastery, only a year younger than Melleray's second daughter. Indeed, it was only a few months since the Breton Trappists had moved into the log cabins they had bought from the Sisters of Loretto, when a priest presented himself at their gate and introduced himself as a monk of Mount Melleray in Ireland. Father Bernard McCaffrey was his name, and he had been sent to the United States to find a site for a new foundation. It turned out that Mount Melleray had several of these scouts scattered around in America looking for a building site, and in the summer of 1849 the abbot himself, Dom Bruno Fitzpatrick, disembarked on American soil with the same end in view.

He boldly advanced farther west than any other Trappist, planted a foundation stone on some land that had been offered him by the Bishop of Dubuque and said, "Here is where we will build."

So, in 1849 the Cistercians had a monastery west of the Mississippi. Not that the community was formed, nor that the buildings sprang out of the ground overnight. Our Lady of New Melleray had a slow and painful growth—building on a foundation of poverty and sacrifice.

The first colony of two priests and four brothers needed reinforcements and needed them badly. So, a party of sixteen sailed from Ireland in the fall of 1849. But they had a fateful journey which ended, for six of them, long before they reached the rolling plains of Iowa.

They had set out from New Orleans with four hundred other passengers on a river steamer bound for St. Louis. But when the steamer reached its destination, there were only sixty passengers left. An epidemic of cholera had broken out on

board, and twenty-six had died. The rest had got off the boat
at the earliest possible opportunity. Of the twenty-six victims,
six were Trappists—three buried in Mississippi, one in Tennessee, and two in Missouri. The first to go had been Brother
John Evangelist. Brother Patrick, who had helped bury him,
came back on board and said drily to his superior: "I have
the cholera since morning." With this, he collapsed, and in a
few hours he was dead too. They buried him a little way up
the river, on the following morning.

But in the general panic and despair of the passengers, the
calm and peace of the Trappist monks was so impressive that
by the time they reached their moorings in St. Louis the
silence of the Cistercians was preaching louder than any number of sermons—far louder than the enthusiastic Father Joseph
Dunand had ever done in that same city, nearly half a century before. One of the fruits of this silent sermon was the
conversion of the river steamer's captain, who went off and got
himself baptized.

In a few months this same captain was able to point out
the crosses that marked the graves of the buried Trappists to
another party of monks from Mount Melleray who were on
their way to Iowa.

The monks built themselves a frame church and started a
parish for the local Catholic farmers. As a matter of fact, New
Melleray was destined to play an even more active and important part in the development of Catholicity in the American
Northwest than Gethsemani had ever done in the South. The
Iowa Trappists gave two bishops to the Catholic hierarchy in
the nineteenth century. Father Clement Smyth, the first permanent superior of the new community, was chosen as Coadjutor Bishop of Dubuque in 1856 and later became bishop
of the diocese. Meanwhile, his successor at New Melleray was
also raised to the episcopacy. Father James O'Gorman, who
had led the famous colony through the cholera epidemic, became Bishop of Raphanea and Vicar Apostolic of Nebraska
in 1859.

In 1863 New Melleray became an abbey, and four years later the monks began to build their permanent quarters—two wings of a not unattractive monastery of limestone. They had the good fortune to have a lay brother in the community who had worked under the architect Pugin; thanks to him, the north wing of New Melleray is a tolerably good example of Gothic Revival.

This much of the work was completed in three years, but a series of unfortunate accidents kept the monks from moving in until 1875. By that time New Melleray was going through one of the greatest storms of a stormy history. But for the generous financial assistance of good friends, they might have gone under altogether.

Fortunately for the Order, they survived and went on into the twentieth century under Dom Alberic Dunlea. At his death in 1917 the abbey entered upon another crisis and was only saved from extinction by Dom Bruno Ryan, who summoned the help of volunteers from the Irish monasteries of Mount Melleray and Mount St. Joseph. One of the volunteers, Dom Eugene Martin, a priest from the latter monastery, is today abbot of New Melleray, which is now compelled to expand by the press of vocations and is prospering more than ever before in its long history.

Finally, although it would be beyond the limits of this book to go into a detailed history of the six Cistercian monasteries and convents in Canada, this chapter would not be complete if we said nothing about the well-known abbey of Notre Dame du Lac on the shore of the Lac des Deux Montagnes, close to Montreal.

Like most of the other North American foundations, this new Cistercian monastery was born of French persecution. This time, the mother house was Dom Urban Guillet's Bellefontaine. On the morning of November 6, 1880, citizen Assiot, the prefect of the Department of Maine and Loire, and two other government officials put on their top hats and adjusted their *pince-nez* and started out for the abbey of Bellefontaine at the head of five hundred soldiers and six brigades of gendarmes. They had reason to start out early: it was to be a long, busy morning.

The invaders drew themselves up before the monastery, where the monks, expecting their arrival, had been joined by the Bishop of Angers, who also happened to be a member of the Chamber of Deputies. This complicated matters, no doubt. But citizen Assiot and his gendarmes proceeded to summon the monks, with all the dusty formality of French legal terminology, to vacate the premises peacefully unless they wished to be put out by force. For some reason it took them from six o'clock in the morning until two in the afternoon to say all this, since the bishop and the Trappists had a few things to say in reply. Finally, it became clear that the monks would leave only under duress, so they were escorted out of the monastery one by one, dragged by soldiers and policemen who were at the same time trying to preserve some clumsy appearance of dignity and self-respect.

By five o'clock in the evening the monks were all on the outside and the soldiers were on the inside—and the latter were by far the more embarrassed of the two groups. However, they settled down as best they could in the monastic enclosure, while the Trappists scattered to private homes. This awkward and tedious situation lasted for five weeks. By that time the soldiers were thoroughly disgusted with milking cows and loafing around the cloister, while citizen Assiot had been appropriately humbled by the general amusement of the public at his military "triumph." Finally, the soldiers got themselves together and came forth from the monastic enclosure and marched back to their *caserne* to hide their faces, which by now had assumed several different shades of confusion. The monks were free to return home.

However, this had been enough to convince the father abbot, Dom Jean-Marie Chouteau, that it was high time he investigated certain offers of land for a new foundation in

Canada. In the spring of 1881 he was on the high seas, bound for New France.

By midsummer a small colony of monks and brothers was established in the little four-room farmhouse on a thousand-acre property they had acquired from the Sulpician Fathers by the lake at Oka. The building of a temporary house for the community was begun at once, and thanks to the help of friends among the fervent French–Canadian Catholics and encouragement from the Canadian government, the work moved fast. By the end of the year the half-finished buildings were already blessed, the monastery was canonically erected, and the new superior had already given the white Cistercian habit to his first Canadian novice. Work on the permanent buildings was begun in 1889, and Notre Dame du Lac became an abbey in 1892. In that same year it made definite plans for its own first foundation.

The Province of Quebec was indeed a propitious setting for a Trappist monastery. The new abbey was only ten years old, and already her monks were advancing confidently into the north woods to found Notre Dame de Mistassini at Lac Saint Jean.

But 1892 was a year of jubilation among the Cistercians not alone in Canada but everywhere, for it was in that year that the most significant event in the modern history of the Order took place. It was only then that the Cistercians of the Strict Observance finally became an *Order* in their own right, by the reunion of the three Trappist congregations that had been carrying on in legal subjection to the Abbot General of the Common Observance, each one trying to keep its own interpretation of the Rule.

VIII. REUNION OF THE CISTERCIAN CONGREGATIONS; NEW GROWTH; GETHSEMANI UNDER DOM EDMOND OBRECHT

THE vitality of a religious order comes to it from the Holy Ghost. It is charity—and God Himself is charity—that brings men together and unites them in a common work for the glory of God and for their own peace and for the good of the Church. And the strength and health of an order is proved not by material prosperity, not by numerous foundations and big buildings and many members, but by its internal unity and cohesion and consistency.

When men love one another and live together without fuss, willing to see things in the same light, to sacrifice their own limited views, to share and enjoy the same poverty and the same hardships in eagerness to give up their own interests out of love for one another—then the Spirit of God is working among them.

But there is another spirit, a spirit that does not build up religious orders. On the contrary, it breaks them down. It is a solvent, a principle of disorganization and decay. When it takes hold on a monastery, on an order—on any group, for that matter—the group dissolves into its constituent parts. Communities break up into cliques. Individuals are divided against one another. Each one tries to force his own views on the others. In the end the strongest is the one who succeeds, and all the rest have to submit. But they only swallow their submission in a spirit of hatred and revolt.

This spirit is called the "spirit of the world," but its ultimate expression, its final perfection, is found only in hell. However, even on earth it sometimes achieves all too complete, all too real an embodiment in the political life of men— in the history of Nazi Germany, Fascist Italy, Red Mexico and Russia, for instance, and in the history of the wars of our time.

But if the spirit of the world is always at work, nevertheless the Spirit of God does not leave His children alone and helpless in the darkness of the world. God's love, too, is always working in the Church and in religious orders: and never more powerfully than when all the agencies of destruction seem to be doing their worst.

The nineteenth century had seen the triumph of a dozen different ideologies which denied everything that the Church believes in and stands for. Materialism had reached its self-complacent peak and was ready to send the world skidding down the steep and slippery incline that would bring it to the wars and revolutions of our own day. The Church and the religious orders had been under persecution in Europe for nearly a hundred years.

Yet, the Church and the religious orders were growing stronger and more fruitful all the time. For the truth is that the nineteenth century was the beginning of a great Catholic revival.

The ancient Cistercian Order, which had been reduced to fragments by the weakness of its own members in ages of too great prosperity, was to be brought together and resurrected again, purified and energized in the forge of persecution.

The Reformed Cistercians, that is, the Trappists, rescued by Dom Augustin de Lestrange, had divided into two congregations, not so much because of their own weakness but because the regime of Dom Augustin demanded of men what the Church and the Spirit of God did not want of them. But in these separate congregations the Cistercian life, in its essentials, was led with fervor and charity, and there was a constant desire for reunion.

There were, besides, two smaller groups of monasteries that kept more or less to the Strict Observance. A small congregation had formed around the abbey of Westmalle in Belgium, and two other monasteries clung forlornly to the ancient Cistercian abbey of Casamari in Italy. Of the two big congregations, the larger was at the same time the stricter. That was the group to which Gethsemani, New Melleray, and Our Lady of the Lake belonged. It had twenty houses in all, including one in Syria and one in North Africa, and it was headed by the abbot of La Grande Trappe. The abbey of Sept-Fons presided over the second, smaller congregation, with houses as far afield as China, Palestine, South Africa, and the East Indies. The wide expansion of the two congregations is partly explained by the persecutions of 1880. It was in that year, for example, that Tamié, perched like an eagle's nest in the high Alps of Savoy, had been temporarily closed, like Bellefontaine and, just as promptly as Bellefontaine, had gone out to make a foundation—this time in the arid hills of north China, near Pekin.[1]

In 1878, before this expansion, the vigor of the Cistercian reforms expressed itself in a petition to Rome for reunion. Unfortunately, the petition ran up against a blank wall of stolid inertia. It was said that the move might be prejudicial to the interests of the "whole Cistercian Order"—that is, to the disconnected and nebulous affair that still survived under that title, which had long since lost all meaning. The second half of the excuse was even worse. It stated that the reunion of the strict congregations was an infringement of the rights of the Moderator General. The Moderator General was a Cistercian of the Common Observance who held supreme authority over all the congregations, strict or easy, and whom the Trappists did not even have

---

[1] See below, p. 249 n

a chance to elect. The abbots of the Strict Observance were not even invited to the General Chapters that put this dignitary on his throne. In any case, he did not have much opportunity to interfere in running the reformed congregations, which were governed by their own vicars general.

All this looks complicated on paper. The fact is that it was far more intricate than we have made it seem. And, of course, it all implied wheels within wheels of organizational waste, not to mention the effort that was squandered in speculating on which one of these congregations was the real heir to twelfth-century Cîteaux.

It was characteristic of the genius of a great and saintly pontiff to cut through all such stupid difficulties and to clear the air with a lucid and simple solution. Where the cardinal consultors had failed, Leo XIII himself stepped in of his own accord, without any new petition from the Cistercian abbots, and issued a decree in July, 1892, which summoned all the abbots of the four strict congregations to an extraordinary General Chapter in Rome.

A spirit of exultation and relief spread through all the Trappist monasteries when this news was announced. It was the answer to more than a few prayers. In a new Dutch foundation, Our Lady of Koeningshoeven, a young novice once known in the world as the Baron Van Rykvorsel Van Rysenberg had offered his life in sacrifice for this vitally important reunion, and the offering was accepted.

He died September 20, 1892, when most of the abbots were setting out for Rome.

On October 1, fifty-four superiors of Trappist monasteries, of whom thirty-two were mitered abbots, met in the French Seminary in the Via Santa Chiara, in the Eternal City. Presiding over the meetings of the Chapter was a great Jesuit, Cardinal Mazzella, representing the Cardinal Protector of the Cistercians.

The words with which he opened the first session not only embodied the earnest desires of Leo XIII but echoed the deepest sentiments in the hearts of the earnest and austere men in that room. And when this keynote had been struck, all the discussions proceeded in tune with it; and the music was as the music of the Holy Spirit. The theme was nothing but that which had been first intoned by the founders of the Order, by that religious genius, St. Stephen Harding, and it can be summed up in one word: *unity*. More important than all the minor differences and viewpoints about observance and the accidental details of regularity was this one big essential of Cistercian life: unity in charity, unity in accepting one common interpretation of the Rule of St. Benedict that the average man could follow, so that the weak might not be discouraged and the strong might wish to do more.

In eleven sessions of smooth and peaceful discussion all the petty distinctions and differences of nation, opinion, or temperament which cloaked themselves in different interpretations of the Rule and of the Cistercian usages were sufficiently leveled by the Holy Ghost to permit the final fusion and union so ardently desired by the Trappists and by the Church. Only the three houses that belonged to the little congregation of Casamari refused to take any active part in the discussions and voting; they remained outside the union. For the rest, all the abbots but five voted for the fusion of the three larger congregations.

The news of the successful conclusion of the Chapter filled the Pope's heart with the liveliest satisfaction, and the new Order of Reformed Cistercians of Our Lady of La Trappe formally began its existence amid *Te Deums* and universal joy.

Within six years, thanks to the energy of Dom Jean Baptiste Chautard and the generosity of the Baroness de la Roche Taillée, all that was left standing of the ancient mother abbey of the Order, Cîteaux, was purchased when the French government was just about to take it over, and it once more assumed its rightful place at the head of the new Order.

True, it was a strangely chastened Cîteaux, from the architectural point of view. Gone were the splendid cloisters and the huge abbey church of the days that had been all too sumptuous and great. There remained, in incongruous contrast, a few fragments of the past: a couple of isolated buildings that dated back to the thirteenth century and a big monumental wing put up in the era of lavish spending that had foreshadowed the French Revolution. But the important thing was that at last the Rule was being kept at Cîteaux once again. The Cistercian life was being lived once more inside those walls. Cistercians were working in the level fields that had been cleared and first cultivated centuries before by the saints who had come to that wilderness from the cloister of Molesme for no other purpose than to keep the Rule of St. Benedict to the letter and live isolated from the world in poverty, simplicity, labor, and prayer.

Once again the abbot of Cîteaux was the temporal and spiritual head of a world-wide family of monasteries where the monastic life was lived in its perfection. All the essentials of the Benedictine and Cistercian life were incorporated in the usages of the Cistercians of the Strict Observance, who now dropped the name of La Trappe altogether from their title. The only really striking accidental change was the mitigation of the old Benedictine fast. This had been the greatest sacrifice which the stricter congregation had had to make in order to achieve the reunion. The two groups had made a friendly compromise for the sake of unity, and the hours of meals were now approximately the same as they had been in the arrangements of De Rancé. That meant, in practice, that there would be a strict enough fast to permit the average man of our day to realize that he was fasting; yet, at the same time, it would not be beyond the strength of any mature person in normal health. On the whole, the present timetable is accepted as satisfactory, and the general opinion seems to be that the old fast would be too much for the constitutions of men in our time.

Until the end of his life Leo XIII kept the Cistercians of

the Strict Observance under close and fatherly guidance. He seemed to cherish these poor and austere monks with a special love. He never missed an opportunity to encourage their spiritual growth as well as their temporal expansion.

Whether he intended to do so or not, in actual practice the Holy Father disregarded some of the notions dearest to the heart of the Abbé de Rancé, and Leo XIII can therefore claim much of the credit for the new directions taken by the Cistercians in the twentieth century. It was he, for instance, who insisted that the Cistercians should acquire a sound theological basis for their lives of prayer and contemplation. A house of studies was organized in Rome, and picked men from Cistercian monasteries in every part of the world were to be sent there for training. Whether or not they returned home with doctorates, these men would be fitted to serve their communities as capable superiors, enlightened spiritual directors, or competent canonists. The anti-intellectualism that had been so prominent a factor in Trappist austerity was no longer to dominate the Cistercians. The change made a big difference. Without in any sense pretending to be a nursery of professional theologians or research students, the Order has nevertheless witnessed a spiritual revival that has begun to bear fruit in books on prayer and the interior life as well as in studies of monastic history.

Only a few days after the Cistercian abbots had knelt at the feet of the Pontiff, in the Vatican, to receive his blessing on their newly united Order, another Cistercian monastery was dedicated in the plains of the Canadian West. Near the banks of the Red River, a few miles out of Winnipeg, Bellefontaine's second Canadian foundation had risen among the vast, rolling fields of wheat. It was called Our Lady of the Prairies, and the wide, open vistas of plains and sky that confronted the monks as they went out to work in the early morning of those autumn days symbolized the new horizons that were beckoning to the whole Order of Cîteaux.

As usual, antimonastic persecution soon would powerfully

stimulate the growth of the Order. When French socialism once more moved against the Church in 1903, it would mean four more Cistercian monasteries in North America. And there would be a corresponding growth in every part of the world.

Meanwhile, Leo XIII told the Cistercians that he ardently desired to see them make foundations in missionary territory —Africa, the Far East. He intervened directly to persuade the abbot of Westmalle to accept the invitation of the King of Belgium and make a foundation in the Belgian Congo, near Leopoldville.[2]

The whole Order had already been taking that trend at the time of the reunion. After the foundation in China another monastery of men was begun in Japan, soon followed by a convent of Trappistines. Our Lady of the Lighthouse and Our Lady of the Angels are both near Hakodate. Within the next ten years the Order would spread to South America and would continue to grow in Africa and the Near East. The East Indian foundation had, meanwhile, moved to northern Australia.

The energetic optimism of which these foundations were the expression was not literally produced by the reunion, since it was already in full swing before 1892. But the consolidation of the Order gave it an impetus that reached its peak in the years before World War I. This material expansion was certainly a proof of spiritual vigor; but like all such works, it was not without its dangers. There was always the peril that the intense spiritual energy which the Holy Ghost was accumulating in our Cistercian reservoirs of penance and contemplation would burst the dam and pour out to flood a mission field of our own, instead of providing hidden power for all the other active workers in the Church.

There were two great drawbacks about this growth in mission territory. First, although the houses founded in temperate zones have generally been a success, the Cistercian Rule

[2] This foundation was a failure.

has never been properly lived in the tropics. So many mitigations are required that the life is unrecognizable. The monks of Leopoldville in the Belgian Congo, Beagle Bay in northern Australia, and the monks of Brazil rapidly lost their true Cistercian character. The climate had simply twisted their Rule out of shape. For that matter, it is easy to see how poorly the Rule of St. Benedict is adapted to the Southern Hemisphere, where everything, as they say, is upside down. Since the seasons are reversed, Lent falls in harvest time, and the monks have to fast when they need to eat; then, in compensation, they have plenty to eat when they could easily fast.

The second difficulty of these mission foundations could more easily have been avoided; but it is not altogether possible for Cistercians to refuse to conduct schools and orphanages in lands where helpless children are crying out for care. Not only were these works practically forced upon the monks by colonial governments, which have always appreciated Trappist contributions to agriculture and have frequently asked us to run agricultural colleges, but even Leo XIII himself demanded them in certain cases. It was he, for instance, who wanted the orphanage at El Athroun, in Palestine. He got not only an orphanage but a school and a dispensary as well.

It can be seen, then, that all the good that had been done by reuniting the Cistercian congregations into a new Order, and all the spiritual energy flowing from that union were in serious danger of being poured out in active works which were contrary to the Cistercian spirit and vocation. An orphanage here and there, an occasional chocolate factory or textile mill, and perhaps an agricultural school or a boys' college—these would not seriously harm the Order. But the danger of entering into wholesale missionary activities was serious. And this fact is proved by the story, or rather the phenomenon, of Mariannhill.

Mariannhill was born of a combination of dynamic forces. Trappists from Germany had planted a foundation in Bosnia (Yugoslavia) which had rapidly grown to tremendous proportions. The great new monastery of Mariastern had over two hundred monks and brothers at the turn of the century. It was easily the biggest house the Cistercians had had anywhere since the Golden Age—although its size was no asset. On the contrary, it was too big. Even supposing they all have genuine vocations, a hundred religious are too many for any one superior in the contemplative life. They cannot be guided. The monastery becomes noisy and crowded and full of a bustling life that is hard to keep flowing smoothly in the proper channels. Mariastern, however, was in the hands of an abbot who combined German genius for leadership and German energy with a powerful and deep religious idealism. Dom Franz Pfanner looked like an Old Testament prophet. The eyes that burned in that long, aquiline countenance flamed like the eyes of a visionary, and the sensitive lips that quivered in that prophetic beard were ready to command no one knew what Crusades. In later life Dom Franz completed the picture with long, gray, flowing locks that were combed back from his shining brow to fall in profusion about his shoulders. But by that time his ideals and his energy had led him far away from the Order of Cîteaux.

At Mariastern Dom Franz had been the patriarch of what almost amounted to a small town rather than a mere monastery. The vast population of his community was occupied not in one but in several factories, in addition to working on their vast properties. There were a textile mill, a tannery, a cheese factory, a brewery—and the inevitable orphanage. Yet, all that was nothing to what was to come when Dom Franz found a field where he could really go to work and express his ideals.

One day, before the reunion, he received an invitation to make a foundation in South Africa. He brought the project to the General Chapter of the second largest and second strictest of the existing congregations, that of Sept-Fons, to which he belonged. That was in 1879. He went forth, armed with permissions and blessings, to build in Natal, in the brown hills a few miles inland from Durban. The name Mariannhill manages to do reverence in Dutch to both Our Lady and St. Ann.

Dom Franz and his men, as soon as they had found a suitable site, went to work with all their accustomed energy. The climate was excellent, though subtropical. The rich soil was soon bringing forth an abundance of coffee, sugar cane, pineapples, bananas, and many other fruits and vegetables. A talented lay brother designed a new monastery, and soon not only were a cloister and all the regular places finished and in use, but a multitude of shops had come into existence. Besides the smithy and carpenter shop and the other ordinary "employments" one would expect around a Trappist monastery, there were a printing press and a photographic studio. Furthermore, the brothers were energetically building roads into the interior of the country and casting bridges over the rapid mountain streams.

What was the meaning of all this printing and road building? The answer was to be sought in the jubilant reception that the monks had received from the Kaffirs. Friendliness, sincerity, and joy, as well as intelligence and vigorous artistic talent, combine with all kinds of natural energy and versatility to make these natives ideal subjects for the kind of training that Dom Franz Pfanner could excel in giving them.

Within a few short months Mariannhill had already expanded beyond all Dom Urban Guillet's wildest missionary dreams. The Kaffirs not only accepted the opportunity to send their children to the school that was opened by the monks. They did more than merely consent to come to the parish church that had been opened for them. They literally invaded the property, swarmed down on the monks, and flung themselves into the life of work and prayer with all the zeal and fervor of the monks themselves. Soon the printing press was running off hundreds of Kaffir catechisms, and the roads into the interior were pointing the way for monks to start long missionary trips on horseback inland into the mountains. Chiefs of distant tribes soon were asking Dom Franz to send priests to their villages and start schools and build churches.

The result was one of the most phenomenal chapters in the history of Catholic missions. Mariannhill established mission stations in Natal, Transvaal, Basutoland, Bechuanaland, Cape Colony, and even hundreds of miles up the coast in German East Africa. Recruiting for all these posts was not possible in South Africa itself, of course; Dom Franz had started a seminary at Wurzburg, Bavaria, just to attract and form subjects for his huge South African venture.

Here was the astonishing spectacle of a Trappist mission in which the contemplative monks had achieved, in a few short years, a success more spectacular than many an active Order had dared dream of, and the Cistercians of the Strict Observance woke up to the fact that the reunion of the congregations had brought them an order within an order. There was more energy and more exterior prosperity in the houses that had grown out of this obscure South African foundation than could be found almost anywhere else in the Order.

The most astounding thing about this new mission was that it was operating on purely Benedictine lines. It was an apostolate of prayer and labor, of liturgy and the plough. What was taking place in the outposts established by Dom Franz Pfanner was exactly the same process that had marked the Christianization of Germany and all northern Europe by the Benedictine monks hundreds of years before.

Each mission post was a small monastery with several priests and half a dozen or more brothers. Joined to it was a small community of sisters belonging to a new congregation founded by Dom Franz to teach in the schools he was building. Around each church and school there grew up a whole village of Christian Kaffirs with a guest house for travelers and all kinds of workshops. The monks taught the natives every conceivable craft and instructed them in painting, music, photography, and a dozen other arts. The most promising natives were prepared for the priesthood in a new seminary at Mariannhill. The bulk of the population worked the land on vast cooperative farms. The beauty of the life was not simply in its mate-

rial productiveness but in the fact that all this was centered
on the church and found its fullest culminating expression in
the great liturgical feasts which so delighted the hearts of the
Kaffirs. They filled the churches and sang with their fine
voices and formed huge processions and crowded to the Sacraments with a fervor that took away the breath of the priests
ministering to them. Soon the South African veldt was dotted
with monastic colonies named after all the famous shrines of
Europe: Reichenau, Einsiedeln, Monte Cassino, Lourdes, Czen-
stochau, Clairvaux, Cîteaux . . . and a hundred others.

Clairvaux was a group of kraals gathered around a church
under some eucalyptus and cedar trees in the heart of a rocky
valley. Cîteaux was a small chapel on a bare hillside, facing the
gaunt outline of a distant mountain ridge. Lourdes nestled in
a friendlier landscape of woods and fields, and the two towers
of its church—which had something of the proportions of a
small cathedral—dominated fertile orchards and gardens and a
colony of brick schoolhouses and cottages.

The blessing of God upon this work leaves us no doubt as
to its providential character: but one important and obvious
thing remains to be said. The day the first catechism came off
the brothers' press, and the day the first stone was laid for the
mission church at Reichenau, the monks of Mariannhill had
ceased to be pure contemplatives.

The Rule of St. Benedict, the usages of Cîteaux, were nothing but a dream in that hive of active apostles, who were liable
to be spending days on horseback and nights teaching and
preaching all over South Africa. Silence was forgotten. The
office was never sung except on Sundays. Feasts of two Masses
existed only in theory, and even on ordinary days the monks
were so busy saying Mass for the Kaffirs that a secular priest
was sometimes called in to sing—or rather to say—the conventual Mass for the community. Although the Kaffirs did a
great deal of manual labor under the guidance of the brothers
and sisters, the monks were too busy being missionaries to
have any time for the gardens or the fields. As for fasting—

so far were they from that, that they took two *mixts*, or break-fasts, when the rest of the Order was limited to a tiny *frustu-lum* or nothing at all. The second mixt went by the name of *zwischenbrot*—the snack of bread that came between breakfast and dinner.

The Cistercian Order could not help but be concerned over this state of affairs. Dom Franz had long since decided to retire and was living at a mission station called Emmaus, which was so small that it was practically a hermitage; but it was not until 1904, the year of the death of Dom Sebastian Wyart, the first Abbot General of the new Order, that the Cistercians finally took definite steps to find out what was really going on at Mariannhill and to determine whether they could do any-thing about it.

This brings us at last to the connection between Mariannhill and Gethsemani. It is a long way from Kentucky to Natal: but that great distance was several times bridged by the fourth abbot of the American proto-abbey. He was appointed apos-tolic administrator of Mariannhill by the Holy See, and his real task was to try and see if the missionaries could not be persuaded to retain enough of the contemplative life to be able to call themselves Cistercians. But by that time things had gone too far and the task was hopeless. Mariannhill was lost to the Order and became an independent missionary congregation which, incidentally, has continued to prosper and to carry on its magnificent work in Africa for nearly seventy years.

The man who had the thankless job of trying to work out a compromise between Mariannhill and Cîteaux was to become one of the most important and valuable men to devote their gifts and energy to the service of the reconstituted Cistercian Order in the beginning of the twentieth century. He was Dom Edmond Obrecht. His work in South Africa was only one of a score of similar legations that took him to every corner of the world where a Cistercian monastery existed. Yet, in spite of his crowded activities, it was also due to Dom Edmond that Gethsemani weathered the most serious crisis in its own history and attained the prominence which it occupies in the American Church today.

Dom Edmond Obrecht was a man of big ideas. His mind took in the whole expanse of the world. He was always much more than merely an abbot of a community of monks hidden away in the woods of Kentucky. It was because he had been recognized as a great person that he had been sent to Kentucky in the first place.

However, to understand the situation fully, we must retrace our steps to the years before the reunion. The scene is once more Gethsemani. It is the middle of August, 1890. In the blinding Kentucky heat the monks are moving in a slow file to the cemetery, chanting psalms. In the open bier, the dead Dom Benedict Berger wears a miter. His face is white, with the rigid outlines of something carved out of stone.

At the grave's edge his mitered successor is moving about the bier, gently swinging a censer that curls with the smoke of incense. Prayers are chanted. We consider the face of the new abbot. We see the features of a much milder man, full of gentleness and resignation. The lines in that countenance spell a whole story of suffering. But there is something almost wistful about the expression. It is not a weak face, by any means; but this kind and patient soul seems to be saying: I do not want to be the kind of abbot my predecessor was: in fact, I do not really want to be abbot of this monastery at all. . . .

The third abbot of Gethsemani, the one who intervened between Dom Benedict and Dom Edmond, has lapsed into obscurity, almost forgotten. He was not a powerful personality, and he did not leave much of a mark on Gethsemani. He has vanished like a wisp between the two giants who precede and follow him.

Yet, Dom Edward Chaix-Bourbon was a person of some distinction—not that his name attached him, as some thought, to the royal house of France. He came of well-to-do parents in the Alpine province of Dauphiné. One would have expected him to enter religion at the Grande Chartreuse. But the fact

that he came so far before taking the religious habit is characteristic of him. As a young man, he had tried in vain to
settle down and find himself a place in the world. He wandered from Vienne to Lyons, from there to Paris, then to Le
Havre. A man of his character could not stay long in a seaport
without succumbing to the urge to set sail for distant lands.
Soon he found himself teaching French in New Orleans. When
the Civil War broke out, he left the city and traveled aim-
lessly until, one day, he happened upon the little log-cabin
monastery of Gethsemani. That was in 1860, when the new
buildings were still unoccupied. Edward Chaix-Bourbon was
so impressed by the deep recollection of the Trappist monks
as they filed out to work that he asked to be admitted to the
monastery.

Dom Benedict, who had just assumed power, gave the new
novice the full benefit of his zeal for humiliating others. He
put him through all the tricks, insulted him, mocked him in the
presence of distinguished visitors, and exhausted his ingenuity
in devising penances for Frater Edward to perform in the
refectory. For instance, when the young man confessed a
secret dislike for a certain Brother Lazarus, Dom Benedict
made him go and kiss the brother's feet and then stand in
front of him during the whole time of dinner. No one seems
to have stopped to ask how Brother Lazarus felt about all
this: after all, it was a public penance for a secret fault. But
if this was the same Brother Lazarus who went off to join
the Carthusians over a score of years later, we can sympathize with his desire to take his meals unmolested. Just imagine how it would be if, day after day, as you tried to absorb
your soup and turnips with your wooden spoon, a new and
different religious came and stood before you, hanging his
head in perfect silence and without any evident reason. It
would be enough to give a man a persecution complex, let
alone ruin his digestion.

Frater Edward, on the other hand, seemed to have a wonderful capacity for taking all this without even a shadow of emo-

tion ruffling his meekness and composure. Dom Benedict did not conceal his admiration from anyone except, of course, Frater Edward himself. In fact, when he was in France on a routine visit to the General Chapter, Dom Benedict once spoke to the Cistercian nuns of Notre Dame des Gardes and told them of the wonderful novice he had at Gethsemani. "I can do anything I like with him," he said. "His obedience is perfect; the man is faultless."

One of the good nuns was so moved that she exclaimed, "Oh! Reverend Father! Perhaps one day he will be our chaplain!"

"Not a chance," said Dom Benedict with a dry laugh.

He was already grooming Frater Edward as his successor: but the fact is, Dom Benedict's faultless novice was to die as chaplain of the nuns at Les Gardes, and he was much happier as a chaplain of nuns than as an abbot of monks.

To tell the truth, Dom Edward had qualities that might have made him a very successful abbot if he had been put in charge of some other house at some other time. He was a deeply spiritual person, a saintly man. What Dom Benedict had said about his humility and obedience was quite true. He had astounding patience and good humor, and his friendliness and sympathetic nature, coupled with lively intelligence and a profound understanding of the spiritual life, destined him to be a director of souls.

But he was not equipped to take charge of an abbey like Gethsemani at the very crisis of its history.

Dom Edward Chaix-Bourbon was a sociable man, but his choice of friends was one of the biggest sources of trouble for Gethsemani. Among his friends was a visionary lady from Chicago who was nursing what appeared to be stigmata, in the old farmhouse of Mount Olivet, on the monks' property. Worse still was the man whom Dom Edward had engaged as principal of Gethsemani College. The latter's mismanagement of affairs nearly ruined the college and brought down untold troubles upon the heads of the innocent monks. In the end it became evident to all that Dom Edward had the simplicity of a dove but none of the prudence of the serpent; and Christ had warned His disciples that they must possess both.

Returning from the General Chapter of 1895, Dom Edward found his community in a ferment. The only American choir monk, young Frater Frederic Dunne was immediately put in charge of the college. He managed to restore order, but great harm had been done. Dom Edward finally wrote to Dom Sebastian Wyart, the new General of the Reformed Cistercians, and tendered his resignation as abbot of Gethsemani. It was not a gesture of despair on his own part; rather, the circumstances were such that it was the only thing left to do. But all the same it was with the greatest relief that the simple, peace-loving religious resigned a charge that was odious to him and embarked at once for France.

Soon the ageing abbot was settled in a position that fitted him admirably in every detail. He had a nice quiet room all to himself at the Trappistine convent of Les Gardes. He had plenty of leisure for prayer and contemplation and nothing to do but hear the confessions of the sisters and charm them with his tender, humorous, and fatherly discourses on the ways of prayer and the love of their Divine Bridegroom. There is no doubt that his labors bore rich fruits at Notre Dame des Gardes, where he is still venerated as a most saintly priest. After suffering a long sickness with the most heroic patience, Dom Edward finally died in February, 1901. From every part of the Vendée, crowds came to pay enthusiastic homage to a man whose name was held in benediction among them. He was buried at the convent, and the nuns surrounded his tomb with affectionate veneration.

Three years passed. Gethsemani was under the charge of the prior, a rugged little Frenchman, Father Benedict Dupont. He was passionately devoted to Trappist austerity, a powerful and tireless worker, and a zealous penitent. Under his charge was a confused and somewhat embittered community of sixty-six men, two thirds of whom were lay brothers. Active voice in the administration of the house was more or less limited to the eight priests. Of these, several were toying with the idea of transferring their stability to some house that was in a more settled condition.

It was the gloomiest period of Gethsemani's history, and the gloom was deepened by attacks and calumnies against the monks. One of the liveliest of these was a book called *The Monk of Gethsemane Abbey*, printed in 1893 in Brooklyn by The Reformed Catholic Book and Tract Concern, at the corner of Johnson and Fulton streets. It was by a certain E. H. Walsh, who described himself as an "ex-Trappist" monk. He had, as a matter of fact, been a novice at Gethsemani under Dom Benedict, but there is no record of his having made vows. Consequently he was not, strictly speaking, an "ex-monk."

The book is a voluble piece of invective. "Popery," "The Virgin," and the "juggernaut of priestcraft" all come in for their meed of contumely. During the two years in which he was known as Frater Augustine, Mr. Walsh seems to have made things hum at Gethsemani. Trappist life, under Dom Benedict, was hard enough: but to a man who had delusions of persecution and was convinced that he was being imprisoned in the monastery against his will, it must have been positively hectic. Walsh was under the impression that anyone who entered the novitiate "is obliged to take vows or be imprisoned," and he wrote, "I often sought for a chance to escape, and examined the strongly barred windows in vain for such an opportunity." Perhaps the fourteen years which had elapsed between his eventual "escape" and the writing of his story suggested those bars on the windows, and other details. The poor soul finally died in an asylum for the insane.

Nor were the calumnies against Gethsemani that flowed freely from the pen of the ex-principal of Gethsemani College—as he sat nursing his wounded feelings in the Louisville jail—any more pleasant or profitable for the monks. This was the man who had been put in charge of the monks' school by the guileless Dom Edward. The smooth-spoken stranger, never reticent on the subject of his connection with one of the best families in England, engineered a scandal that almost ruined the monks altogether. When the police took a closer look at his antecedents, they discovered that there was a great deal more to be learned about him from Scotland Yard than from *Burke's Peerage*. Nevertheless, he took advantage of his leisure, while he was behind prison bars, to dash off the first of what he promised would be a series of pamphlets "unmasking" the hypocrisy of the Trappists at Gethsemani. He promised some juicy bits of information, but when his actual statements of fact are sifted out from the abuse and innuendo in which they are embedded, it turns out that the only thing he really had against the monks was that they were keeping their Rule. Naturally the Rule, the silence, penance, and obedience, irritated him and he did his best to prove that anyone who could stand such an existence must be a pharisee.

Gethsemani sometimes received more sympathetic treatment from professional writers. James Lane Allen's *The White Cowl* told everyone who did not already know it that Gethsemani had almost as much of a place in the traditional Kentucky scene as Lincoln's birthplace or Churchill Downs. But the romance of the monk who ran away with the beautiful lady was not precisely what the Trappists considered good publicity for their Rule and their life of penance. The newspapermen of the day, who found the concept of a flight from the world at least intriguing, never seemed to warm up to Gethsemani. They could see that the monks were smiling and seemed to be happy: but what could possibly make them happy, when they were so thin and their house was so cold and they never heard anything about baseball? All this remained a mystery.

Such, then, was the condition of Gethsemani as the fiftieth year of its existence began. Under the circumstances, it was very doubtful whether the abbey would be able to endure for fifty years more. How long would it be before the dwindling community would have to leave the buildings and scatter to other monasteries and turn the place over to the sisters as an orphan asylum?

The reunion of the three congregations into a new Order was ultimately what saved Gethsemani. If the reunion had not taken place, there would hardly have been a chance of Gethsemani's obtaining an abbot like Dom Edmond Obrecht, who was to arrive in Kentucky in 1898 and take charge of the abbey.

He was a perfect man for the job—so perfect, in fact, that only the strong, centralized organization of an Order like that which the Trappists had now become could afford to dispose of him and place him as it did.

Dom Edmond had everything that Gethsemani needed. In his twenty-three years as a Cistercian, he had acquired a wide, practical experience of everything a prelate needed to know. He had begun his religious life at La Grande Trappe, and had, therefore, been formed at the very center of the life of the Order. He had served in administrative posts in two important abbeys, Acey in the Jura region of France, and Tre Fontane outside of Rome. Above all, many years at the Roman headquarters of the Trappists had given him an intimate working knowledge of the way things were done.

Here, then, was a man who knew what the Rule and the spirituality of the Order meant. He understood chant, ceremonies, liturgy, canon law. He was a linguist, a cosmopolitan, a diplomat, a connoisseur of books and manuscripts. He combined dignity with authority and possessed a clear and powerful intelligence. He knew how to make decisions and get them carried out. He was a born abbot, a born leader, a born organizer. He was just the one to put things in order at Gethsemani.

The impact of Dom Edmond's powerful character upon Gethsemani was unimaginable. He burst into the big Kentucky citadel of silence and threw it wide open to the four winds. He flung himself vigorously into the task of cleaning out the mental dust and cobwebs that had been gathering in the community for two generations. He let out all the stuffy atmosphere of Dom Benedict's system of penances and sanctions and let in the fresh air of a more sensible and vital—and more Cistercian—viewpoint. Not that Dom Edmond could not punish faults! His subjects were to find him in many ways as stern as Dom Benedict when occasion demanded. But there was something more human about him. Besides, he was a man whose large views extended far beyond the limits of a spirituality that sought only to crush and restrict human nature, as if there were nothing positive to follow mortification as its true fruit.

The troubled and disunited community was at once fused together into a solid and vital organism under his tutelage as provisional superior. Its first act of gratitude was to elect him abbot unanimously on October 11, 1898.

The monastery entered into a more live contact with the rest of the Church in America. Relations that had become strained under Dom Benedict were more than patched up by Dom Edmond, who knew how to make friends.

The jubilee celebrations, held a year late, in 1899, threw open the monastery to men who had never dreamed of coming there in the old days, and news began to spread that the Trappists were not so bad after all. The monks were really human beings, and the monastery was far better than a penitentiary for censured clerics. Wisely, too, the new abbot had a little book about the monastery printed. And so, Americans at large gradually began to recognize at least the possibility that happiness and a Trappist vocation were not incompatible.

As the years went on, Dom Edmond built up one of the finest monastic libraries in America at his Kentucky monastery. Its nucleus was the bequest of Monsignor Leonard Batz of Milwaukee, from whom the monks acquired some forty thousand volumes. They included Migne's Greek and Latin Fathers, sets of St. Bernard, St. Thomas, Duns Scotus. Dom Edmond acquired many incunabula and even manuscripts of St. Bernard and several ancient Cistercian liturgical manuscripts, most of them antiphoners, the best of which is twelfth-century work. Add to this such great names in monastic history as the Benedictines Dom Martene and Mabillon.

But Dom Edmond did more than this to humanize Gethsemani. During his abbotship the bare, forbidding brick walls of the monastery were coated with a material which was intended to look like stone and did, indeed, mellow the outward appearance of the buildings. On the inside, a new cloister was built, the Church remodeled and redecorated and even embellished with stained-glass windows. Although these are contrary to the Cistercian tradition—in the twelfth century, abbots who put in stained glass did a considerable amount of fasting on bread and water, under penance from the General Chapter —nevertheless Gethsemani really needed something of the kind. Under Dom Benedict the only way for the monks to fight back against the ferocious Kentucky sun was to daub the windows with white paint at the beginning of each new summer season. It was an expedient that bore fruit in a singularly depressing and unsightly shabbiness.

The year 1912 began with one of the most significant events in the history of Gethsemani Abbey. One quiet winter afternoon, just before the monks were due to go out to work, a column of black smoke was seen issuing from the roof of Gethsemani College. The alarm was sounded, and soon monks and students were fighting the fire—but with all too little success. By night, there was nothing left of Gethsemani College but a mountain of angry red embers still crowned with bitter-smelling smoke. When day dawned and showed the monks nothing but four stark fragments of brick wall standing black and grim against the winter sky, nobody mourned. Indeed, the whole thing was accepted in the monastery with grim satisfaction. The monks felt that God had done them a favor. He had purified their monastic life of something that almost amounted to a cancer. The history of the college had been nothing but a long record of troubles and even spiritual perils for the monks. At best, it had never been anything but a white elephant.

The college had been fairly popular among the Catholics of Kentucky, and warmhearted former students at once began raising money to rebuild the old school. However, Dom Edmond wasted no time in returning the contributions as fast as they came in. There was no further need of the school and no possible excuse for the monks to keep on trying to be educators. It had been necessary in the days that followed the Civil War, but this was the twentieth century, and Kentucky was now full of good schools. The Cistercians had their hands full living their rule and following out their own arduous vocation, without shouldering duties of other religious orders.

The last tottering fragments of wall were pushed down, the rubbish was cleared away, and a statue of St. Joseph was planted on a concrete pedestal atop the hill where the college had once stood. It is a stocky, purposeful little statue. St. Joseph seems to have taken his stand there with the Holy Child in his arms, and in his heart the single-minded intention of keeping the school from ever coming back.

After all, St. Joseph is the patron of the interior life.

IX. EIGHT AMERICAN FOUNDATIONS

O N JUNE 17, 1903, Dom Edmond Obrecht was standing on the French Line docks in New York City.
Tugs were easing the liner "La Bretagne" into position for
mooring, and the first hawsers were splashing in the dirty
water of the North River. Among the passengers lined at
the rails was a singular group of men. There were seventeen
of them, with bearded faces and close cropped heads. They
wore secular clothing which fitted them as ill as a disguise.
There was something singular about these travelers.

At least, that is what the newspaper reporters thought. They
surrounded the Trappist abbot and asked him many questions
about the immigrants. Whatever Dom Edmond may have told
them has long since been forgotten, but the story got into the
papers that seventeen Boer generals who had escaped from an
English concentration camp in the Transvaal were being offered a refuge by the monks of Our Lady of Gethsemani. . . .

That was a wild shot. The only thing true about it was
that the bearded men did need a refuge. Far from being Boers,
they were Frenchmen. Not only were they not generals, they
were not even soldiers—except according to the metaphor of
St. Benedict, who described the monk who followed his Rule
as *militans sub regula vel abbate* ("campaigning under a rule
and an abbot").

That brings us to the story of the suppression of the French
abbey of Fontgombault. For that, too, in its own restrained
way, had been a fight.

In 1850 Trappist monks of Bellefontaine took over an
ancient Benedictine monastery that was falling into ruins.

Fontgombault, rich in associations with the past, and especially with the twelfth-century reformer, St. Bernard of Tiron,
stood among the poplar trees on the banks of the river Creuse,
a tributary of the Loire. The ancient buildings, including the
fine old abbey church, were still standing, in spite of the fact
that the neighbors had been quarrying them freely for stone
with which to build their houses and dovecots and barns. It
was a beautiful, peaceful site in the fertile plains of central
France, with no sound to trouble the silence but the rushing
of water over the milldam. Here, a century or so before, the
gentle Benedictine scholar, Dom Edmond Martène, had slipped
on a stone and taken an unexpected bath in the river when he
visited the abbey, collecting material for the monumental
Gallia Christiana.

However, the Trappists could not simply move in and start
chanting the office and working in the fields and meditating
under the repaired arches of the cloister. Things were not that
simple. The curse that has pursued contemplative monasteries
in Europe ever since the French Revolution was on their heels,
too: they had to find some special source of income. There
was nothing they could do but accept the unpleasant choice
that was offered them, so they found themselves in charge of a
small state penitentiary! It reflected the general idea people had
of the Trappists. They shouldered the task bravely, and by a
merciful dispensation of Providence the persecution of 1881
took it away from them again. By that time they were able to
stand on their own feet.

The fact that they escaped expulsion in 1881 did not mean
that they had no enemies. The freemasons and the petty government officials of the department maintained a constant persecution of the Trappists of Fontgombault. But since they
could not do anything important against them, they used all
their power to entangle them in red tape whenever the monks
entered into contact with their little official world.

In 1899 the renovated church of the abbey was due for re-
consecration. The government seized the opportunity to make

a nuisance of itself to the monks and promptly forbade the ceremony. The consecration was begun "privately," and before it was half over it was interrupted by the police. Thus, at the turn of the century the monks were in open hostility with the civil administration.

It was not a comfortable position for them to be in, because certain politicians in the Chamber of Deputies were at that moment cooking up antireligious legislation that was to bear fruit within three years in wholesale expulsions. The laws sponsored by Emile Combes and Waldeck-Rousseau brought armed men to the gates of every Charterhouse in France, from the Grande Chartreuse to Notre Dame des Prés, near Boulogne, on the shores of the Channel, and cleared France of Carthusians.

The Cistercians had every reason to fear that it might be the same with them. In fact, it very probably would have been if one energetic and resourceful abbot of the Order had not thrown himself with unsparing self-sacrifice into the task of defending her monasteries.

A meeting of French Cistercian abbots in Paris, on June 28, 1901, ended with the delegation of Dom Jean Baptiste Chautard to represent the Order in the coming struggle. This rugged Provençal had proved himself an administrator of no mean ability. He had helped no fewer than three important houses of the Order to get on a firm economic basis; now he had succeeded Dom Sebastian Wyart as abbot of Sept-Fons when the first General moved out to occupy the abbacy of Cîteaux, which fell to him as head of the Order.

Dom Chautard was a quick thinker and a tireless man of action. The activities which obedience imposed upon him drew their power from deep founts of spirituality that vivified a soul closely united with God in a life of faith and prayer.

It was this supernatural spirit, even more than his natural personality and impressive character, that finally brought Dom Chautard success in his mission. Georges Clemenceau was by no means a friend of monks, and when, on the eve of the final vote that was to decide the fate of the Cistercians, this abbot was ushered into his presence, the "Tiger" did not spare him. Dom Chautard was greeted with a long tirade which told him, in substance, that the monks were useless and it was high time they were kicked out of the country.

But when it was over, the abbot of Sept-Fons, with no less energy and conviction, told Clemenceau just what the monks were living for. It was a bold and dramatic speech—bold enough to overleap all the accidental excuses with which a less ardent man would have tried to conciliate the politician. Dom Chautard did not waste his breath in arguing that the monks were experts in "scientific agriculture." He simply gave a bald statement of the essence of the monastic ideal which St. Benedict had boiled down to four words: *nihil amori Christi proponere*. Now, Clemenceau was not the kind of man who would be very well prepared to understand what it meant to love Christ beyond everything else, and he probably did not get much light out of what the impassioned Cistercian was saying about his monks' being the "guard of honor of Christ in the Blessed Eucharist." But he did see that Dom Chautard knew what he was talking about and sincerely believed in it and was not afraid to state his position without compromise. In a word, even the man without faith was able to be impressed by the intense faith of this Cistercian monk. The interview ended when the president shook hands with the abbot and declared, "You are my friend."

The entire Cistercian Order could not be saved. One or two of the houses that were most seriously menaced had to be sacrificed. But the fact that the rest remained untouched amounted to a great victory.

Fontgombault, however, was one of the houses that had to go.

Dom Edmond Obrecht had spent more than a year traveling around Europe in search of places of refuge where the expelled monks might go if the whole Order had to leave France. But now that Fontgombault was closed down, he could think of no better site to offer them than an abandoned farmhouse near Gethsemani. Here, the monks could find temporary shelter while they were waiting for a permanent home in the United States. Only about half the community sailed on "La Bretagne." The rest scattered to various houses of the Order in France, while Fontgombault passed once again into secular hands and became a reform school.

On the evening of June 10, 1903, the French Cistercians stepped down from the Louisville train and were greeted by the Gethsemani College band playing the *Marseillaise*. According to a written account that has come to us from the hand of one of them, they "were overcome with emotion." Gethsemani was hung with French and American flags, and the cloister, paved with flowers for the Corpus Christi procession, made allusion to the guests: "Sacred Heart of Jesus," one floral design spelled out, "save France." There was even a big dinner for the travelers in the monastery guest house.

But when the celebration and gaiety of the welcome had died down, the exiles had their hands full trying to establish themselves in a ruined farmhouse in the middle of a Kentucky summer. Mount Olivet—the home of Dom Edward's stigmatic and of a group of nuns before that—was in such bad shape that the roof and walls leaked and cattle wandered into the ground-floor rooms to escape the rain. It took several weeks to make the place habitable. Finally, they were able to settle down and chant the office and work in their garden and make the acquaintance of poison ivy. It was not until the following year, 1904, that a good place was found for a permanent settlement.

The parish of Jordan, in Albany County, Oregon, was in many ways an excellent place for Cistercians to build a monastery. There was plenty of timber—indeed, the pine trees of Oregon grew to a size that astounded these men from France. The orchards on those fertile hillsides yielded abundant crops of huge pears and plums and apples, and the land gave them plenty of grain and forage. It was a mild enough climate, and the only drawback was the heavy annual rainfall: and that did not prevent them from gathering in their crops and making their living.

Unfortunately, the situation into which the monks moved when their first contingent arrived in Oregon on September 24, 1904, was altogether unfavorable from a spiritual point of view.

To begin with, Archbishop Christie of Portland had invited the monks to Jordan with the rather quixotic idea that they would heal a division that had grown up in that parish of German farmers. The parishioners could not agree on the site of their church. Half the farmers, who lived on the plateau, wanted the church up near them. The others, down in the valley, wanted the church in their district. That was where the church had first been built, but it had burned down and had been rebuilt on the plateau.

Now the monks moved into the new church and presbytery. The novelty was expected to make everybody happy, and certainly all these good Catholic farmers were glad to see the monks among them. But as far as permanent peace was concerned, the move was a failure.

Meanwhile, the handful of Cistercian monks and brothers found themselves cooped up in a parish church to which the farmers and their wives and children came to join lustily in the singing of Mass and Vespers. Some of the monks slept in a small barn, others in the sacristy of the little church, and others still in the classroom of the parochial school. The children still were coming to classes, of course. And when the classes were over in the middle of the day, the schoolroom was hastily transformed into a monastery refectory. There was no farm attached to this property, only a field that was intended for a cemetery. In fact, all that the monks had was a parish church and everything that went with it. It was just what a Cistercian monastery ought not to be, and the situation makes one understand fully the strict injunction in the new Constitutions forbidding a new foundation to be made before there are enough buildings and land to keep the Rule and the Cistercian usages.

There was a very good farm near the church, but the owner made them pay his own price for it. The monks took on the burden of this debt and set to work trying to pay it off in yearly installments, at the same time putting up a temporary monastery on their new land. Their generous parishioners helped the monks in every way they could with time and labor and ideas. One neighbor drew up the plans. The monks contributed their own share of the sweat—and the necessary lumber. Work began in the winter of 1905, but until the following Fourth of July some twenty Cistercians remained crowded in the little parish church and school.

Meanwhile, they had put up a large sawmill, which they hoped would support their monastery. Unfortunately, it was badly situated, and the expense of hauling timber to the mill ate up all their profits. Then the mill caught fire and burned to the ground before the monks got around to insuring it.

When Dom Edmond Obrecht came to Jordan in February, 1908, as the regular visitor delegated by the General Chapter, there was only one question in his mind: Would this monastery survive? It did not take him long to find the answer. The ruins of the sawmill, the huge debt, and the almost complete lack of novices and postulants told him all he needed to know of the accidents and errors of the abortive foundation. One year later the unanimous vote of the General Chapter decreed the suppression of Our Lady of Jordan. The pioneers were told either to return to Melleray or join some other Cistercian community of their own choice. That meant the complete extinction of the monastery that had been Fontgombault.

The blow was a hard one for the pioneers. Most of them failed to understand that the command really was a command; it had to be reiterated, in fact it had to be fulminated, with a threat of ecclesiastical censure, before they would consent to give up their labors and leave Oregon. The Abbot General, Dom Augustin Marre, conveyed the command of the

Chapter to the monks in person in November, 1910, and at last they moved out and scattered to the four winds. Some returned to France, some passed over to the Benedictines, who were well established on the Pacific coast; one or two entered the secular priesthood, but most of them went to the monastery of Our Lady of the Lake at Oka.

Three of them, undeterred by the memory of two Kentucky summers at Mount Olivet, asked to be received at Gethsemani. Father Mary died there in 1932, in his seventy-first year. Brother Stephen became Gethsemani's cook. When he could no longer cook he wove baskets until he, too, passed to the reward of good Cistercians in his eightieth year. The third, Father George, sinking his teeth with even greater tenacity into his Cistercian vocation, outlasted them both. He has celebrated a whole procession of jubilees. He still sits in the infirmary mending socks and making disciplines and comes to the conventual Mass in a wheel chair. Early in Lent, 1949, he received extreme unction, not in bed but in the monastery church and at the time of this writing he still says Mass and proves to be in no hurry to go to heaven.

While the first Far West venture of the Cistercians was going to pieces in Oregon, the bitter struggle that Father Vinvent de Paul Merle had started in Nova Scotia was still being carried on in New England. The monks who had been burned out of their home at Petit Clairvaux had retired for a short time to Our Lady of the Lake, in Canada, where they caught their breath and prepared to move on to Rhode Island.

Dom John Mary Murphy, the new superior and former prior at Oka, took ten companions and all the cattle and furniture and books and vestments and pots and pans—in fact, everything that was left of Petit Clairvaux except the shell of the building—and moved to the Blackstone Valley between Providence and Pawtucket. That was in August, 1900. The pleasant fields and woodlands that now surround Our Lady of the Valley were not there to cheer the souls of the pioneers. They found three hundred acres of land that had been stripped of trees and was covered with small growth, brushwood, and tangled briars, with here and there a full-sized oak. What was worse, the land was littered with stones, and one did not have to dig far below the surface of the soil before one hit solid granite. The huge continental ice sheet that once covered New England had scoured this terrain down to its foundations and scattered stones all over the ground—which was euphemistically called "arable." However, in the very heart of their property, by way of contrast, the monks found a quagmire. It was not only unpleasant, but a positive danger. It swallowed up at least three cows before it was finally drained, in recent years, by the labor of the monks. The property was dominated by a lugubrious memorial of Indian days, the "Nine Men's Misery," where the bones of nine men murdered by savages had been found.

The *Annals* of the early years [1] return over and over again to the sad refrain: "This farm, a stony waste, does not pay." If their crops were not ruined by drought, they were washed out by floods. Then, the Trappists were not prepared for cutworms or potato bugs or army worms or corn borers. It was a struggle to save enough of some one vegetable to get through the winter. At times they were reduced to loading their wagons with stones—of which there was always a rich crop—to be sold to the stone crushers for a few cents a load, in order that they might buy some bread.

The orchards were ravaged by insects. Twice the *Annals* lament that "caterpillars stripped our orchards bare." As late as 1915 "the apple crop was a complete failure." Also, the orchards were badly planned. One patch of fruit trees might be half a mile from the other, which meant that spraying was laborious and spasmodic. Picking was complicated by the mixing of trees whose fruit ripened late with trees that gave an early crop.

---

[1] I am greatly indebted to Rev. Father Maurice Molloy, O.C.R., the librarian of Our Lady of the Valley, for making available the fruit of his research into the archives of his monastery.

Of all the hard beginnings in America—and, for that matter, in any other part of the world—Cistercians have seldom had as crude a first home as the sixty-foot shack of planks that was called Our Lady of the Valley in 1900. Through the summer of their first year, however, the founders were busy putting up a two-story wooden house, which gave them satisfactory shelter. After that, they went to work on the first wing of a granite monastery. The three-story building, with verandah and dormer windows and little cupola, and standing back a hundred yards or so from the busy road to Woonsocket and Pawtucket, has become familiar to several generations of New England Catholics. The monastery was, unfortunately, half monastery and half hotel. The visitors' parlor was separated from the monks' chapel by a thin partition. The chanting of psalms was likely to be accompanied by gusts of business conversation, and secular matters would come floating in on the quiet air to complicate the monks' evening meditation. The poverty of the house was so great that the monks were not able to lead a fully contemplative life. They never chanted the full office, seldom sang the conventual Mass: they had to recite the canonical hours in haste in order to get out to work and keep themselves from starving.

It seemed to them that this course was all the more unavoidable because their community was so desperately small. They attracted few postulants and considered themselves fortunate to have a total of twenty-two members in 1910. But while they had had five priests in 1901, there were still only five priests when the founder, Dom John Mary Murphy, died in 1913. Three lay brothers were professed in the first six years, but it was not until 1908 that the first choir novice made his vows. The first priest ordained at Our Lady of the Valley was a certain Father Benedict, a veteran of Fontgombault and Our Lady of Jordan, who was still only a subdeacon when he came to Rhode Island. He was not ordained until 1915.

In the crisis that followed the death of Dom John Mary in 1913, the General Chapter, after considering the proposal to suppress the Rhode Island monastery as a useless venture, turned it over to Dom Edmond Obrecht and Gethsemani. Thus, the Kentucky monastery once more adopted a daughter, as it had adopted Petit Clairvaux half a century before. But it was not this that saved Our Lady of the Valley or made it prosper.

The one solution to all the difficulties of the Valley, the one thing which turned it from a failure into a success, should, after all, have been obvious. Perhaps the founders had not reasoned out their problems with the logic of the first Cistercians. They had thought material success was necessary before they could hope to be true contemplatives. They apparently believed that they would be able to give all the required time to prayer only when they had grown into a big, solid community with many novices. Actually, it was just the other way round. The reason they had no novices was precisely that they were not truly contemplatives. The reason they had such a struggle was that they could not give themselves entirely to the life of prayer that was required of them. . . .

All this was abundantly proved by the work of Dom John O'Connor in the 1920's. In 1924, after rejecting his plan of moving to a richer site, he might well have turned his thoughts to expedients to support the community. He might have built up a big, modern, dairy farm and started producing Port du Salut cheese on a large scale. There were scores of things that Trappists could manufacture—from chocolate to applejack. He might have gone into the production of any one of them with profit, except that Prohibition ruled out applejack for the time being. What he finally did might have seemed like wild luxury to some of his monks: at any rate, he began the construction of a big Gothic church. And that was what saved the monastery.

As soon as the Rhode Island Trappists were liberated from their own guest house; as soon as the Divine Office took the place that belonged to it in their lives, without having to compete with any secondary interest; in a word, as soon as the contemplative element in the Rule received the full attention it deserves in a contemplative monastery—no matter how poor —the community began to get vocations. The mysterious, vital force that attracts men of prayer to a center of the interior life made itself felt. Postulants came in greater and greater numbers to devote their lives to God. During the twenty years that followed the construction of the church, Our Lady of the Valley twice doubled its numbers. Between 1928 and 1938 it grew from thirty-five to seventy-four; during the next ten years it went up to one hundred and forty-two. By that time, the pressure was enough to burst the walls. The monks made a foundation in New Mexico, as we shall see later.

As the community grew, it also put up more and more defenses between itself and the world. It withdrew into its own interior silence and peace. After adding another wing of monastic buildings, the monks put up a new novitiate in 1936. In the same year they set up a gatehouse between themselves and the busy main road. Entrenched in the privacy on which the contemplative life so largely depends, the Cistercians at Our Lady of the Valley have developed a great love for the traditions and austerities of the Order. They have done more than any other house of the Order in the United States to bring their chant and their liturgy up to the required level. They have remodeled and simplified their sanctuary, they have put Cistercian glass in their church windows—not stained, but only tinted, glass, with very elementary geometric designs, in keeping with the customs of the Order. Meanwhile, they still look forward to completing their monastery, which will mean the destruction of the old guest house and one more step toward privacy by the erection of a new one outside the enclosure. Then they will be able to devote the remaining two sides of their cloister to purely monastic uses.

Our Lady of the Valley became a full-fledged abbey in 1945, during the lifetime of Dom John O'Connor. He was, however, a hopeless invalid and had already resigned his office as titular prior into the hands of Dom Edmund Futterer, who was elected and installed as abbot in that same year. Besides his new foundation in New Mexico, Dom Edmund is occupied, at the time of writing, with the building of the first Trappist-ine convent in the United States. The nuns are not in the habit of living in log cabins—although they have had their share of austerity in the past, too—and they will await the completion of regular buildings before they sail from Our Lady of Glencairn, in Ireland, to settle at Wrentham, just across the Massachusetts state line from the Valley.

The foundation of Our Lady of the Valley in 1901 was the beginning of a small procession of foundations in North and South America—a series which made Cistercian history in the New World quite an animated affair for the first few years of the new century. Most of them were the fruit of the anti-religious legislation of Waldeck-Rousseau in France.

In 1901 the French monks of Bonnecombe decided to pre-pare a refuge for themselves in New Brunswick, and so they established an annex in the diocese of Chatham. The monks arrived and settled in the new house, Notre Dame du Calvaire (Our Lady of Calvary), in the fall of 1902.

One sometimes wonders if there is more than a merely poetic appropriateness about the names of Cistercian monas-teries. Are the communities of this Order called to participate intimately in the mysteries in honor of which their respective houses were founded? In the case of Our Lady of Calvary, this would seem to be evident. Even though every Trappist monastery has a great deal of Calvary about it, this little priory, hidden away in the woods of New Brunswick, has had a history of troubles and hardships which have brought its members into close union with Christ on the Cross.

From their first days in a little temporary wooden monas-tery, down to 1948, when their farm buildings burned to the ground, the Acadian Trappists have had a life of exceptional poverty and hard labor. Dom Anthony Piana, the founder of the house, loved Calvary—both the Calvary on which Christ suffered and the community named after it. As he lay dying of an exceedingly painful sickness, he could think of no better prayer to utter than, "Lord, send me more pain!" That was in 1939.

In that year Calvary got a new prior, who came all the way from the famous Dutch abbey of Koeningshoeven at Tilburg, Holland. His name was Dom Cherubin Lennssen, and he left behind him at Tilburg a twin brother who had entered the abbey with him as an oblate at the age of eleven and received the name of Seraphin. Under Dom Cherubin's guidance, the small Acadian community, numbering a bare thirty-five members, has struggled on and strengthened its position to some extent. The French founders have all died, and the majority of the monks are natives of New Brunswick.

Only a few miles from Calvary is another Cistercian house, dedicated to one of the glorious mysteries: Our Lady of the Assumption. It was founded the year after Calvary, 1903. In fact, two new Canadian Cistercian houses were founded in 1903: Our Lady of the Assumption in Acadia and Our Lady of Good Counsel in the Province of Quebec.

Both houses have something very special to recommend them to our interest: they were the first two American convents of Trappistine nuns.

St. Stephen Harding and the early fathers of the Order were at first unwilling to undertake the direction of religious communities of women. That was part of their reaction against the whole scheme of things in contemporary Benedictine monasticism: they wanted to get away from all the cares and responsibilities of the active ministry in order to live for God alone and for His immediate service. However, it was impossible to exclude women altogether from the Cistercian life. Soon a colony of Benedictine nuns from the convent of Jully, near Dijon, founded the convent of Notre Dame de Tart, in the same neighborhood. They were determined to keep the Rule of St. Benedict to the letter, like the monks of nearby Cîteaux, who took them under their protection. From Tart, founded in 1132, arose a magnificent family of convents that was to be one of the glories of medieval Europe. So rapid and widespread was the expansion of the order of Cistercian nuns that in 1228 the General Chapter, meeting at Cîteaux, repented to some extent of having taken on such a responsibility and decreed that no more convents of women would be officially accepted into the Cistercian Order. It is estimated that some nine hundred convents of nuns were under the jurisdiction of the General Chapter, although no one can say for certain how many there were, and this figure is probably too high. But besides them, there were many other houses of nuns who followed the Cistercian usages without the Order's accepting any responsibility for their guidance or direction. Among these houses was the convent of Helfta in Saxony, the cloister where St. Gertrude the Great, St. Mechtilde of Hackeborn, and Mechtilde of Magdeburg all lived in the thirteenth century.

The Cistercian nuns declined with the rest of the Order, and there was no De Rancé to revive them. The first Trappistines owed their existence to Dom Augustin de Lestrange, who founded a convent in Switzerland in 1796 to accommodate refugee nuns from different orders who wanted not only a refuge but a strict Rule. La Sainte Volonté de Dieu (the Holy Will of God) was the name of this motherhouse of all Trappistine convents, and those who dwelt there had seen the Reign of Terror in France. Therefore, they embraced all the austerities of the Val Sainte reform with great good will and found profound consolations in an asceticism as fierce as that of the monks of the Holy Valley, for they desired to offer God some reparation for the crimes that had filled their land with blood.

Of all these daughters of Dom Augustin de Lestrange there was no one who more completely absorbed his spirit of penance than his namesake, Mother Augustin de Chabannes. This nun, professed before the Revolution at the Cistercian monastery of Saint-Antoine des Champs, outside Paris, had been arrested with many of her sisters in religion and imprisoned under the Reign of Terror. Condemned to the guillotine, she was waiting to lay down her life for her faith when the doors of the prison were thrown open. Robespierre had fallen, and she took advantage of the momentary lull in the persecution of Catholics to make for the frontier. She joined Dom Augustin and his Trappistines and crossed the channel to England in 1801. There, accompanied by three other professed nuns and five novices, she founded the first Trappistine community to survive until our own day. Our Lady of the Holy Cross, at Stapehill, Dorset, remains, after nearly one hundred and fifty years, to bear witness to the energetic faith of Madame de Chabannes. Like their neighbors, the Trappist monks of Lulworth, the nuns at Stapehill had to weather many storms in the early nineteenth century. The monks had to flee to France, but the nuns still are there.[2]

One of the foundations of La Val Sainte was La Riedra, and from La Riedra indirectly stemmed a convent in Vaise, a suburb of Lyons, called Our Lady of All Consolation. The date of that foundation was 1816, after the exile of Napoleon.

It was to Vaise that Dom Augustin de Lestrange came one summer day in 1827. The aged abbot, exhausted by years of strenuous labor and penance, had just traveled up the hot Rhône Valley, in spite of a serious accident at the shrine of La Baume, down near the shore of the Mediterranean. But when he got to Lyons he could go no further. Confined to a sickbed in the guest quarters of the Trappistine convent at Vaise, he realized that he had at last reached the end of his labyrinthine journeys. His last official act as Father of the Order was to address the nuns, speaking to them out of a window that overlooked a garden within the enclosure. There was something a little pathetic about the speech, because Dom Augustin himself realized that his reform was not going to last in all the strictness he gave to it. He foretold that they would be deprived of their greatest austerities and would have to go back

---

[2] See *La Trappe in England*, by a religious of Stapehill (London, 1935); reprint, Gethsemani, 1946.

to keeping the Rule as it had been kept by the fathers of Cîteaux (which certainly ought to be enough for anybody!). But he urged them to make up for it by greater obedience and humility. He died the following day, the feast of the founder of the Order, St. Stephen Harding, July 16, 1827.

Vaise was faithful to the injunctions of the fiery abbot and to the traditions of Trappistine austerity and sanctity all through the nineteenth century, especially under the guidance of the saintly Mère Pacifique. Several of the most fervent convents in the Order today can trace their ancestry back to Vaise: among them, Grottaferrata, outside Rome, and Echourgnac in western France. However, when the anti-religious laws of 1903 went into force, Vaise was suppressed. But France's loss was Canada's gain.

The pastor of Rogersville, New Brunswick, whose zeal was mainly responsible for the presence of the Trappists at Notre Dame du Calvaire, found a good farm for the Trappistines in his own parish, and soon the nuns of Vaise were on the high seas, bound for Acadia.

Nineteen of them landed at Quebec and arrived in Acadia in time to celebrate the Feast of the Sacred Heart, 1904, in the little farmhouse that was their temporary home. Monsignor Richard's gallant parishioners went to work to help them build a convent, where the nuns were soon moderately well established.

At Vaise, the sisters had no farm work to do, since they were in a suburb of a big industrial city. They supported themselves by baking Hosts and making liturgical vestments. Although they continued to do this at their new home, the Cistercian nuns of Acadia soon discovered that farming in New Brunswick was a task that demanded no little time and energy. Often the nuns of Our Lady of the Assumption can be seen filing out to work in the fields and woods, the mother abbess at their head, at five o'clock in the morning, to take advantage of the first cool hours of the day. They interrupt their work to recite the office in the fields when the appointed times come around and return to the convent for an interval of reading and private prayer and another office before the noonday meal.

Dairy products, potatoes, and fruits help to support the Trappistine nuns. They also produce Mass wine from dried grapes; but their situation has always been even more precarious than that of the neighboring monks at Our Lady of Calvary. In fact, Dom Augustin Marre, the second Abbot General since the reunion, considered their survival a "daily miracle." Survive they do, however, and their convent is slightly larger than Calvary, with between forty and fifty in the community. This is considered the ideal size for a house of nuns in our Order.

Notre Dame de Bon Conseil (Our Lady of Good Counsel), which came into being in the Province of Quebec in 1903, has had a peaceful and fervent career. In the early days of the house, when there were only ten sisters living in a temporary dwelling, Dom Edmond Obrecht made a regular visitation of the community and came away singing the praises of the Trappistines. They were, indeed, perhaps the most regular house he had found on the entire North American continent, in spite of their poverty and obscurity. So great was Dom Edmond's edification at the nuns of Bon Conseil that he cherished dreams of retiring from office and ending his days as their spiritual director—as his predecessor, Dom Edward Chaix-Bourbon, had done. He must have known it was nothing but a dream. Dom Edmond Obrecht was the last man in the Order who could have been content to hear the confessions of nuns, and there were many years of labor and traveling still before him. He would meet many important personages, make many speeches, and shake many hands—and, incidentally, accomplish a great deal of good for the Cistercian Order—before he was laid away in the shadow of Gethsemani's abbatial church. Dom Edmond had far too much ambition to be a convent chaplain.

Under the protection of their officially appointed cellarer, St. Joseph, the nuns of Bon Conseil have had a quiet and edifying history, filled with the usual labors and hardships. The house is today slightly larger and more prosperous than the Trappistine convent in Acadia, thanks to its situation. One of its sources of income is a chocolate factory.

While we are still in Canada, we cannot ignore the greatest of the Canadian abbeys, whose foundation has already been described in another chapter. Notre Dame du Lac, well-known to French Canadians as La Trappe d'Oka, has developed into one of the most important Cistercian houses in the entire world. There is, perhaps, no other Trappist monastery that exercises such a profound influence in the social life of the nation where it was founded. One reason for this is the famous agricultural school conducted by the monks. It is affiliated to the University of Montreal and has always received the most lively attention and encouragement from the Canadian government. There are few Trappist monasteries in the world that can truthfully boast that they are scientific farmers, but one of the few is certainly La Trappe d'Oka, famous for its prize stock, its apples, and its cheese.

The abbey of Our Lady of the Lake has paid for its greater prosperity by greater trials than any other Cistercian house in Canada. Twice, in 1902 and 1916, the whole monastery has burned to the ground. The second time, the monks were left without a roof over their heads in the rigors of a Canadian winter. More recently, in 1934, a great barn was destroyed by fire; the harvest had just been stored away and a whole year's supplies went up in flames. Providentially, the livestock was saved.

From all these accidents, La Trappe d'Oka has risen up again stronger than she was before. Her abbot, Dom Pacôme Gaboury, is the father of what is perhaps the largest Trappist community in the world. The most recent figures do not allow us to judge clearly whether Notre Dame du Lac is larger than the famous Irish abbey of Mount Melleray. But in any case, it has over a hundred and eighty members, and this is not the fruit of a sudden rush of postulants. It has been a normal condition for many years.

Instead of making foundations, Dom Pacôme has kept his house at this level, only occasionally sending picked men from his community to help the smaller, hard-pressed houses of Canada, such as Our Lady of the Prairies, which is really a filiation of Bellefontaine. In fact, the present abbot of Notre Dame du Lac has most of the houses in Canada under his care in one way or another, since all are deeply indebted to his generosity and solicitude—especially the houses of nuns.

Antireligious legislation in France, besides endowing Canada with three first-class Cistercian communities, was responsible for two new foundations in South America. They were the first ever attempted in that continent, and they did not last. Both owed their origin to Dom Chautard, although one was a convent of Trappistines. The abbot of Sept-Fons had succeeded only partially in his efforts to save the Cistercian monasteries of France. We saw that one or two houses had to be sacrificed. One of them was Fontgombault. Another was Chambarand, in the Alpine department of Isère—of which Dom Chautard himself had been abbot for a while. Dom Chautard had scoured Europe with characteristic energy, looking for a good refuge. He looked for a place in Scotland and he looked for a place in Poland. Then he made his decision: the foundation was to be in Brazil.

On August 19, 1904, a colony of monks from Sept-Fons set sail for South America and settled in the state of São Paolo, Brazil. The monastery was called Maristella (Star of the Sea), and its long, rambling, one-story white buildings straggled among the palms of an upland plantation. The climate was found to be not altogether impossible, at least on high ground, and four years later an entire convent of nuns, Notre Dame du Sacré-Coeur, at Mâcon, was also transferred to Brazil.

Time was allowed for both houses to get a good trial. The years of World War I went by. In all, more than two decades passed before Dom Chautard finally decided that the tropics were not satisfactory for Cistercians. The biggest difficulty was that there were so few suitable vocations. Good recruiting might, perhaps, have compensated for a tiresome climate, but there seemed little point in keeping alive two houses that would never be anything but a drain on the more vigorous communities at home in France. So, in 1927, in spite of the protest of the Brazilian hierarchy, Dom Chautard closed both communities and brought the religious back to France.

Most of the monks went to what was to be one of the most splendid foundations that have been made since the Middle Ages. The generosity of the Belgian Royal House and other wealthy benefactors brought back the Cistercian life to the ruins of a famous old abbey, Our Lady of Orval, in Luxemburg. Nothing that has been built by the Order in our time can even approach the elaborate care lavished upon the plans and construction of the new Orval. The great stone buildings have all the grandeur and simplicity of twelfth-century Cistercian architecture, although they are on a scale that would probably stagger the average Cistercian abbot of our time. Nobody else will be able to afford such buildings, but the taste and dignity of the new abbey as a whole are well worthy of study and imitation.

As for the Trappistines who had been transported from Mâcon to Brazil—when they were shipped back to France, they reoccupied the abbey of Chambarand, which had been vacated at the time of the Brazilian foundation.

It would almost seem that the Brazilian venture brought to an end the great period of Cistercian activity in the tropics— a period which reached its height around the turn of the century. Few attempts, if any, have been made to send Trappists to the equatorial zone since World War I.

Yet, missionaries are still trying to prevail upon Trappists to settle in the jungles, where they themselves are laboring. The latest invitation has come to Our Lady of Koeningshoeven, Tilburg, Holland, begging for a foundation in the Dutch East Indies.

Since some of the monks have begun to study the dialects of those islands, it seems that the offer will be accepted.

X. A CONTEMPLATIVE ORDER
IN TWO WORLD WARS

O N THE Feast of Our Lady's Presentation, in November, 1911, a young Frenchman was walking along a footpath through fields and woods in the rolling open country just across the Belgian border. Through the trees he could see the buildings of the monastery. Just as he was about to emerge from the woods, a bell sounded in the little steeple. It was the noon Angelus. He fell on his knees in the middle of the path.

Michael Carlier was not yet twenty-one, but he had finished his military service, and now he wanted to bury himself in the cloister, to live in silence and prayer, laboring in the fields, fasting, doing penance. Like so many who feel themselves drawn to the Cistercian life, he could not say exactly what it was that brought him there: but it seemed to be the will of God that he should find peace nowhere else but under this roof.

There was little out of the ordinary about this postulant. There have been hundreds like him before and since. But, unlike so many thousands of other members of this silent Order, Michael Carlier—his name in religion was Frater Maxime—has left the world a record of himself.

After he died, his notes and letters were collected and woven together into a book. It is a narrative of deep significance. The story of the vocation and life and sacrifice of Frater Maxime Carlier gives us a better insight than any other document we possess into the real part played by the Cistercians in the wars that have torn apart the world of our time.

Frater Maxime had entered one of the best monasteries in the Order, Notre Dame des Forges, commonly called "Chimay." The master of novices, Father Anselme le Bail, was a man of deep spirituality and learning who had penetrated far into the theology of the Cistercian writers of the twelfth century. Taking them as his commentators on the Rule of St. Benedict, he had evolved a clear and well-ordered spiritual doctrine, by the light of which he was able to give his novices a more thoroughly Cistercian intellectual formation than they could find anywhere in the Order except, perhaps, at Sept-Fons, where Dom Chautard was abbot.

The novitiate at Chimay was filled with a spirit of balance and sanity; a spirit of simplicity, of clarity; it was eminently Benedictine, and one thing dominated all: the love and service of Christ.

No doubt all these things had been present ever since De Rancé's reform, but they were buried, cramped in other elements which might have proved dangerous and had, indeed, had bad effects on temperaments like that of Frater Maxime. There were many like him in France. He was intelligent, generous, yet there was something in his nature that tended to warp the spiritual life out of its true direction—a certain rigorism, a harshness that chilled the heart and bred suspicion of God, instead of love. Perhaps there was some germ of Jansenism there that tended to breed suspicion between his soul and God—but it was only a germ, and in the healthy atmosphere of Chimay the germ did not prosper. Under other circumstances, Frater Maxime might have turned into one of those distressed, nervous monks who say many prayers and do many acts of penance and work hard but never find rest for their souls and never come close to perfection—their lives never seem to acquire any real unity and meaning: there is always something missing. Here, however, in the clean spiritual air and under the strong light that filled the novitiate of Chimay, the soul of this postulant flourished with a rapid and healthy growth. The influence of his father master was supplemented by the reading of St. Gertrude, from whom Frater Maxime learned a doctrine that can be summed up in two words: confidence and love.

No doubt, there were some rough spots at first. The rigidity of Frater Maxime's nature did not become supple and pliant all at once: yet there were surprisingly few exaggerations. True, in times of trial, the young Cistercian could be overcome by an extremely pessimistic view of his own failings, and he was perhaps too quick to proclaim himself the "worst sinner in the world." That is a statement which too many novices try to make, and which few of them succeed in pronouncing with any degree of conviction.

Practices of this kind have a strongly human tone about them, and they lend themselves singularly well to strain and scrupulosity when carried too far. They were in favor at La Trappe in De Rancé's heyday. At Chimay, Frater Maxime quickly outgrew them. Instead of encumbering his spiritual life with imaginative tricks and complexities of method and device, he soon came to that general and peaceful awareness of God which never reached a very precise definition but which grew from day to day and created an aura of peace about him in which he lived and moved and performed all the actions of the monastic day.

It was the normal and logical fruition of the Rule of St. Benedict: a humility that concentrated not on his own self and its miseries but on the greatness and nearness of God, the constant presence of His indispensable grace and the action of His will in all things. Walking the paths of simplicity, humility, obedience, love, Frater Maxime eventually began to live on a completely different level—in a spiritual climate that was altogether new.

One day he realized suddenly that he was a new man. He had learned the real meaning of God's love, and he saw that, until then, he had been crawling along the ground, while now he seemed to fly. Before, he had struggled along by his own efforts, without ever achieving more than a negligible success. Now, the work had been so much lightened that he did not seem to work at all. On the contrary, it seemed that everything was being done for him. All he had to do was abandon himself, give his consent, yield up his confident love, and God in return flooded his soul with grace. *Je sens l'amour qui m'envahit* ("I feel myself invaded by love"), he wrote, "a love that is very tender, very sweet, and carries one away. . . . Somehow, I don't quite know how it was, my soul entered upon a state in which all its desires seemed to be fulfilled. It enjoyed the delight of resting in a feeling of secret happiness. I felt myself to be under the eyes of God, and that they were fixed upon me. I discovered a great facility for loving God in my neighbor and for seeing Him in all things and I no longer did anything except in order to give Him glory. His love became everything to me and I forgot all the rest. . . ."

The context in which these lines were written shows them to be something deeper than the passing sensible consolations of a beginner. The young Cistercian had entered upon the ways of infused prayer; he had been drawn into the close and intimate control of the Holy Spirit and was now in the strict sense a contemplative. His Cistercian vocation had flowered to a rich maturity.

Yet, infused contemplation is only the beginning of a long road. It is not the reward for consummate sanctity: it is a powerful, perhaps even an essential, means to help us attain sanctity.[1]

Having tasted the first clean and intoxicating joys that come with the gift of wisdom, Frater Maxime Carlier entered into the state of passive purification in which the real work of the contemplative life is accomplished. It became impossible for him to pray, yet the need for prayer, for union with God, became a hunger that devoured him to the very roots

---

[1] The question is much discussed by modern theologians, and a good summary of the discussion may be found in the appendix to Dom Vital Lehodey's *Ways of Mental Prayer*. This appendix is found at least in the original French.

of his soul. Unable to understand his impotency, he nevertheless remained at peace, was held in a state of confused, obscure
resignation. Sometimes this mixture of peace and aridity was
deepened and enlightened by a strong sense of the actual
presence of the Blessed Virgin, who played a dominant role
as Frater Maxime's spiritual guide and took charge of his
mystical formation: an office which belongs to her, above
all others, as the Queen of Contemplatives.

On the Feast of the Immaculate Conception, 1913, he made
his simple profession, pronouncing his temporary vows in the
chapter room of Chimay. His dispositions could be summed
up in the two words *ovis occisionis*. He was offering himself
entirely to Christ as a sheep for the slaughter. "I no longer
belong to myself in anything," he wrote. "Total abandonment.
Let me remain in Thy hands, O my God! Do with me whatever Thou wilt!"

And the God of heaven replied to that challenge with a
demand that was terrible.

One day in July, 1914, a messenger came to the silent Cistercian abbey with the news of the declaration of war. Frater
Maxime was one of the first to go. The Church in France and
Germany had not wished to insist on the rights of clerics and
religious to be exempt from military service, because such an
insistence would only mean trouble, suppressions, expulsions.

On August 2, Frater Maxime knelt in the muddy road to
receive the blessing of his abbot while rain poured down on
the drab fields of a Belgium that was already invaded. *Soyez
bon soldat!* ("Be a good soldier!") were the words he carried
with him to the barracks in Lille.

His own answer was: "The Justice of God demands victims.
I am going to be one of them."

But what a sacrifice! It was more than the long, drawn-out
immolation of a bodily life, more than the acceptance of all
the hardships and sufferings and degradation of trench war-
fare that dragged on month after month and year after year.

Within a few days Sergeant Carlier was at the front. But

the Germans had the advantage all along the line in Belgium, and orders were given for a general withdrawal. The French army began an immense retreat. As they retired before the advance of the enemy, the soldier who was also the Cistercian monk, Frater Maxime, soon recognized familiar landmarks. Long before they got there, he knew that his retreating section would pass right through the monastery farm of Chimay!

Soon they were actually in a wood that was sanctified by the memories of silent workdays, and he could still hear the ringing of the axe that had accompanied the deep, peaceful prayers in the soul of the novice he had once been. As they emerged from the wood, his heart knew every step of the way that could have taken him across the fields to the abbey, whose slim white spire rose up over the trees and the cluster of slate roofs. But his orders made it impossible. He could only gaze across the fields which had once grown to be almost part of him, to the place from which he had been so violently uprooted. His brethren were there still, except for fifteen or more who had been called, like himself, to the army. But he could not even stop and say a word to them, exchange an embrace, a sign of affection, a demand for prayers. . . .

He wrote afterward: "For a long, long time, right up to the moment when we went over the rise, I remained with my eyes fixed upon the abbey where I had so hoped to end my days."

One would think it rather unkind of God to drive home His hard demand with such obvious bluntness: but Maxime Carlier was able to understand what it was all about. This was his sacrifice. It was the greatest thing he had to give: the security of his monastery, his very vocation itself and even his hopes of becoming a saint as a contemplative monk. But these are precisely the things that God demands in sacrifice from the ones whom He means to lead to perfection by the contemplative road. They have to be ready to suffer with equanimity the terrifying loss of all that seems to constitute the indispensable means to perfection, and let God alone lead them, in darkness and emptiness, to their end.

Frater Maxime's true vocation was to become a contemplative in the trenches by living his Cistercian life, as best he could, on the battlefield. His sanctity was to consist in suffering the darkness of passive purification amid the chaos and cruelty of organized slaughter, and in passing through all this in the spirit of a monk of St. Benedict. Like all the other Cistercian monks who had had to go to war with him, Frater Maxime Carlier had a very definite mission from God: a mission of sacrifice, first of all, and an apostolate of example.

His sacrifice was one of atonement, and the love with which he accepted the physical and mental sufferings both of a soldier and of a mystic was intended by God as a holocaust of reparation for the sins of all those who had brought this war upon mankind by their greed and their lust. In the furnace of these trials his soul was brought, without his ever knowing it, to a degree of perfect interior purity and selflessness that reacted profoundly on everyone who came in contact with him.

What was true of Maxime Carlier was true, in proportion, of all the other monks of the Cistercian Order in the war, and of all the other religious and all those who shared his faith and his love of God.

For the next three years the young monk passed through most of the hardest fighting in the war. He was twice wounded and was decorated for bravery with the Croix de guerre. This mystic was astonishingly cool under fire, and the whole record of his military life, which has come down to us in considerable detail, is the story of a powerful and well-balanced soul. His long letters describe the fighting with all the vividness and objectivity of the most dispassionate artist. If he had wanted to do so and had lived long enough, Frater Maxime Carlier would have been capable of writing one of the greatest books about that war.

The secret of his courage and unshaken balance and undimmed clarity of mind and firmness of will is to be found not only in his nature but, above all, in his Cistercian spirit. In the soul of Maxime Carlier the war was putting the Rule of St. Benedict to the test. The devil was trying to break a soul that had been formed by that Rule. But the devil suffered defeat.

Frater Maxime's secret was his faith in the presence of God. When seventy-fives were blasting all around him and German machine guns were making the earth jump and dance before his feet, Maxime Carlier was in the presence of God and clinging to God's will by obeying blindly the orders of his military superiors. These two things, obedience and the presence of God, the two foundation stones of Benedictine spirituality, were absolutely all he had left. Everything else had been taken away. He could not pray. Even in quiet sectors or behind the lines or on furlough he was never able to pray in a way that made sense. Yet the immense, insatiable need for prayer kept driving him into the half-ruined churches they came upon in the fighting. There, he would kneel like a blind and dumb creature and turn his paralyzed mind to the Crucifix and remain fifteen minutes, a half hour, an hour, in impotent and anguished silence. Then he was out again on the road or in the trenches.

One Christmas night his men were camping in an unmolested wood, and Frater Maxime seized the opportunity to slip out of the hut. From nine to midnight he thought about the monks who were chanting the vigils of the feast in the monastic choir of his beloved Chimay; he walked up and down, fingering his rosary under the bare branches and the icy stars. Convalescing from his wounds, he had even better opportunities to pray—on the rocks by the sea at Biarritz and even in two Cistercian monasteries where he spent a few weeks: Our Lady of the Desert, near Toulouse, and Our Lady of Sept-Fons. But always the same aridity and helplessness pursued him. It was the dark night of a perfect sacrifice—the dark night of a contemplation too pure for human taste or sight, too pure for emotion, and God was supporting him constantly in the most difficult circumstances by what could only be a moral miracle.

When the work of this purification was done, and when God was content to call the sacrifice complete, it ended in one swift and merciful stroke.

Frater Maxime was ready to go on furlough. He should have left his men hours before, but he remained with them out of charity until the very last minute. Just as he was about to start for the rear sector, a German bombardment opened up, and one of the first shells came screaming down upon the shelter where he was. His practiced ear must have told him, a fraction of a second before the explosion, that this was going to be a direct hit, and his supple, purified will had time for that last act of love, of self-oblation to the will of the ever-present God.

And then the veils of faith were suddenly shattered, and the noise of the world ended forever, as the Cistercian soldier entered into the sounding silence of a contemplation without obscurity and without end.

The story of Frater Maxime Carlier was also the story of all the Cistercian abbeys in the war area. Like the monk who had to be a soldier and who had to struggle to keep hold of the pure essentials of the interior life, many monasteries and convents had to bid farewell to contemplation. All were affected to some extent. Sept-Fons remained well behind the lines. Twenty-one of its monks and lay brothers were under arms by 1915. Dom Chautard, their abbot, with characteristic energy and charity, sought them out even in the front lines, finding his way through all the barriers of military red tape with a Red Cross arm band on his overcoat. He had a hand in starting a special magazine for mobilized priests and contributed regularly to it. Meanwhile, Sept-Fons had opened its doors to refugee Trappists from Belgium, to the orphans from a bombed asylum at Arras, to the inmates of an old men's home, and to the monks of their own daughter house in Palestine, El Athroun, which had been closed by the Turks.

The situation at Sept-Fons was typical. Every monastery

and convent in France had either refugees or wounded soldiers under its roof. Besides that, the monks who were not mobilized left their enclosures to help in parish work, and the rest not only ran their own monastery farms but helped their neighbors as well. In many parts of France the Trappistine nuns helped their peasant neighbors bring in their wheat and wielded pitch-forks with dexterity and energy in the sweet-smelling fields of hay. It was work to which they were accustomed, but it was not quite the usual thing for them to come out and do it in public.

Most of the French monasteries suffered heavily from mobilizations; the most important houses, like La Trappe and Melleray, had approximately one quarter of their personnel under arms. However, they were not all combatants. There were not a few chaplains among them, and more Cistercians served in the medical corps than as combatants. So, Providence saw to it that most of these contemplatives were spared the degradation of shedding human blood and were allowed the privilege of serving Christ in the wounded and the suffering.

The Belgian monasteries were, in a sense, better off. West-malle had only two priests mobilized, and both were chaplains. Chimay was soon isolated in German-occupied territory, and therefore only those who went to the army in the very first days of the war, with Frater Maxime, were actually mobilized. However, in 1916 the Germans took twenty-two members of the community and led them off into Germany for forced labor, so Chimay suffered, too.

Another monastery was in the center of fierce fighting. Mont des Cats, in the Lille sector, was bombarded and gutted by fire.

Saint-Sixte, in the Poperinghe sector in Belgium, was also destroyed but rose from its ruins after 1918. Igny, the monastery where Huysmans used to seek refuge from the noise of Paris, was turned into a hospital for contagious cases and was finally wiped out. When peace returned, it was altogether rebuilt, and a much more complete and regular monastery rose up in the quiet Champagne valley, over the ruins of what had been nothing but a seventeenth-century manor house: but this time it was turned over to Cistercian nuns. Igny is now one of the most fervent Trappistine convents.

Just as Frater Maxime had fought even harder to preserve the spirit of prayer than he had fought to keep the Germans away from Paris, so too the Cistercian Order did everything in its power to maintain the religious spirit of its mobilized monks. And no one devoted himself more effectively to this work than Dom Anselme Le Bail. Frater Maxime's novice master had become abbot of Chimay, but he too had soon been mobilized. He went into the army as a chaplain, and for most of the war he maintained a sort of field headquarters of Cistercian spirituality in Compiègne. He collected a number of books on theology, asceticism, the liturgy, Scripture, and so on and held them in readiness to lend to any Cistercian soldier who wrote in for them. But what was more important, Dom Anselme edited and wrote a small mimeographed magazine called *Le Moine Soldat*. It came out every fortnight and was made up of three sections. The first was a combination of the Cistercian menology and *Ordo*, reminding the soldiers of the progress of the liturgical cycle and of the saints commemorated from day to day. There were also brief sentences on the chapters of the Rule that every Cistercian would normally hear commented on by his abbot in chapter every morning. This was followed by meditations on the liturgy and by a third section which was mainly ascetical and which tackled the immense task of keeping the spirit of Cistercian monasticism alive in the hearts of men who were up to their knees in mud and filth, devoured by vermin, and engaged in the task of hunting one another down like animals.

When the armistice finally came and the cannons were silent and the military chaplain cleared the shelves at Compiègne of their frayed volumes, leaving the town to the great men who signed a certain document in a *wagon-lit* in that very place, the Cistercian Order recovered its balance and its normal existence and went on as if nothing had ever happened to disturb it. There were a few vacant places in monastic choirs when communities once more reassembled; but on the whole, there was no reason for the Trappists to sing a lamentation over their lot. The General Chapter once more began to assemble at Cîteaux, the normal way of the contemplative life was soon resumed, and monasteries that had been obliged to help in the secular ministry during the emergency gradually withdrew their men once again into the cloister. The Order itself began to advance in fervor and prosperity as never before since the reunion of the congregations. Indeed, it seemed that the Cistercians of the Strict Observance, far from being scattered by the storm over Europe, acquired a firmer cohesion and struck their roots deeper than ever into the ground.

The 1920's saw Dom Edmond Obrecht's zenith at Gethsemani. The year 1924 was an unforgettable date in the abbey's history. The Triple Jubilee celebration was Dom Edmond's triumph. One of the jubilees was, of course, the diamond jubilee of the foundation of Gethsemani, which really came at the end of 1923. The celebration was postponed until the following spring and amalgamated with two of Dom Edmond's personal feasts: his fiftieth year as a Cistercian and his twenty-fifth anniversary as abbot of Gethsemani.

In the depths of his expansive heart there was nothing Dom Edmond Obrecht liked better than a big, colorful celebration. In that sense he was definitely a man of his time, and the Triple Jubilee at Gethsemani was, more than anything else, an expression of the fact that the Trappists had caught up with their times and were willing to display some of the booming optimism that flooded the whole of America in the 1920's.

Gethsemani, in 1924, was the ideal size for a Cistercian community. Its eighty-one members were evenly divided between professed monks and lay brothers. There were only a handful of novices, it is true, but the community was just big enough to keep most of the members from being overworked, without being so big that the abbot could not keep his finger on everything that was going on. It was now a thoroughly homogeneous "American" community, although there were still many monks who had come from distant countries to end their days in Kentucky. Above all, it was a regular, industrious, serious community of men who worked willingly for an abbot who made them work hard; they gave themselves wholeheartedly to an obscure and grueling quest for sanctity in the silence and poverty and all the vicissitudes of Trappist life.

Perhaps the outstanding accomplishment of Dom Edmond's regime in the spiritual order was in bringing Gethsemani finally under the unchallenged dominance of St. Thérèse of Lisieux and her "Little Way."

The Little Flower had had her devotees in the house since long before World War I. The undermaster of choir novices, Father Anthony, was a monk from an aristocratic Catholic family in Holland. His father, Senator James de Bruijn, had been made a Papal Chamberlain by Leo XIII, and his sister was a nun in a contemplative order in Italy. It was she who sent the first copy of *The Story of a Soul* ever to enter the citadel of ruthless severity that was *La Trappe de Gethsemani*. From that time on, the spirituality of the little Carmelite saint, who has exercised such a tremendous influence in the Church in our times, impressed itself upon the spiritual élite of the Kentucky abbey, and especially upon its prior. Dom Edmond was interested, but his interest changed to enthusiasm when the newly canonized St. Thérèse cured him of a dangerous illness in 1925.

Dom Edmond had gone, as usual, to the General Chapter but had been struck down by an almost fatal heart attack before the Chapter opened. He barely managed to find his way to his old family home in Alsace, where he was confined to bed for several months, unable even to say Mass.

The illness of one so prominent was a matter of consternation to the whole Order, and a stream of abbots and dignitaries came to visit Dom Edmond in his native village. The Bishop of Strasbourg even made him an honorary canon of his cathedral. The local villagers, in their turn, came to serenade him with a brass band outside his window. But even that did not kill Dom Edmond.

As he lay in bed, too exhausted even to greet his visitors, he placed all his confidence in a relic of the Little Flower—a lock of her hair—which he kept over the head of his bed. When he finally got on his feet again, his first important journey was a pilgrimage to Lisieux.

Then he boarded the liner for America and finally reached Gethsemani. The monks had never expected to see him again alive. In fact, they did not know how fortunate they were: on his recovery Dom Edmond had tried to resign his charge, but his resignation was not accepted by the Abbot General.

The years that followed, 1927 and 1928, were both marked by pilgrimages to Lisieux: and Dom Edmond Obrecht was no ordinary pilgrim! He not only entered the sacred enclosure of Carmel, armed with special permission from Rome, but he conversed with St. Thérèse's three living sisters, cementing with them a warm and lasting friendship. And he not only became their friend; he was officially adopted into the family.

As a result, the Cistercians of Gethsemani and the Carmelites of Lisieux have become brothers and sisters in an especially close sense. The various feasts of each year witness an exchange of greetings and gifts and all the charming courtesies so characteristic of the daughters of St. Theresa. Gethsemani has by no means suffered from this Providential exposure to the warmth and playfulness and finesse of the Carmelites, who so well know how to temper their austerity with good humor.

There can be no doubt that this warmth from across the ocean did something to thaw out the vestiges of chilliness that still lurked in corners of this big, bare Kentucky abbey. More than that, it was after St. Thérèse was appointed *ex officio* novice mistress at Gethsemani that the astonishing flood of vocations began to come in. . . .

Carmel's new saint had not ended her favors for Dom

Edmond when she cured him in France in 1925. Eight years later, after an automobile accident near Gethsemani in which, by rights, everybody should have been killed in the head-on collision, Dom Edmond developed a gangrenous foot. It soon became so serious that the doctor feared he would have to amputate it. But among the abbot's other ailments there was a diabetic condition which made the operation impossible. The community began a novena to the Little Flower, and the father prior slipped a relic of hers into the bandage he put on the abbot's foot.

The next day, he walked in and found the doctor scratching his head and trying to work out some explanation for the fact that the old abbot was out of danger and his foot on the way to being healed. That was in 1933.

Dom Edmond's course was nearly run. Sleepless nights and a body full of pain left the aged Trappist without rest or strength, yet he insisted on going to the General Chapter and making an emergency visit to Our Lady of the Valley, where Dom John was seriously ill. Finally, as 1934 drew on, he had to be altogether confined to his room. His last appearance among his monks was typical. It was November 1, the Feast of All Saints. Dom Edmond came to the morning chapter to address the community, a thing he was seldom able to do in these last days. He made an important change in the officers of the community, and that evening he appeared for the last time in choir. He entered the church in the purple *cappa magna* granted him in 1929 by Pius XI, on the occasion of his golden jubilee as a priest. During the second Vespers of the great feast he sat in the choir of the infirm but stepped into his stall to give the blessing after the *benedicamus Domino*. Then he remained to chant the Vespers of the Dead for the solemn anniversary of All Souls.

Two weeks later he received Extreme Unction, in his room, from the hands of the prior. He managed to live until Christmas and into the new year, but when the monks were entering choir for Prime at five-thirty on the morning of January 4, the prior beckoned them to come quickly to the abbot's room.

The great man died with his monks around him, reciting the prayers for the agonizing.

Many of the Church dignitaries who had applauded Dom Edmond's wit at the Triple Jubilee banquet were once again at Gethsemani on the cold, rainy, January day when his body was lowered into the earth in a nook behind the chapel of Our Lady of Victories, in the apse of the abbey church where he had usually said Mass.

While the eddies of excitement were dying down in the Catholic press of two continents, the monks of Gethsemani prepared for the election of their fifth abbot. Early in February Dom Corentin Guyader, the father immediate, arrived from Melleray, and the vote was taken with all the prescribed formalities. Not much balloting was required to choose as their new superior for life the man who had been Dom Edmond's prior for over thirty years.

Dom Frederic Dunne was the first American to become a Trappist abbot. He was also, incidentally, the first American who came to Gethsemani as a choir monk and actually stayed there until death. In doing so, he buried many others who had entered the novitiate after him. Before his own life ended, full of years and merits, on August 4, 1948, he not only had seen more than half of Gethsemani's hundred years but had played a dominant part in his half of the abbey's history.

Dom Frederic had entered the monastery in 1894, when he was twenty. Physically speaking, he was not a very promising prospect: his build was slight, he was not tall or muscular. Dom Edward, who was then abbot, recognized at once the intelligence and religious fervor of his new postulant, who described himself in the monastery records as a printer and bookbinder. That was the trade his father had exercised, first in Zanesville and Ironton, Ohio, then in Atlanta, Georgia, and Jacksonville, Florida. While Frater Frederic was still a young monk, his father followed him to Gethsemani and spent the

last years of his life in the habit of a lay-brother oblate. Mr.
Dunne brought with him a small hand printing press and some
type and everything needed to bind a book. During the course
of his long and extremely busy monastic career, Father Frederic
found time to bind many of the books in the library.

"Busy" is scarcely the word for his life. Dom Frederic's
labors for the monastery were something monumental. The
natural generosity of his soul and the intense nervous energy
generated in his wiry frame are not sufficient to explain the
persistence and the effectiveness with which he kept Gethsemani going, sometimes single handed, for so many years.

He entered the monastery at a crucial moment. The monks,
ignorant of the English language or of the ways of the world,
or both, and divided among themselves in a community that
was unbalanced and ill at ease, were closer to ruin than they
realized. Dom Edward quickly discerned the blessing that had
come to his monastery in this intelligent and willing worker:
and it did not take him long to make use of him. He put
Frater Frederic to work long before he should have done so.
Even before the poor boy got well into his novitiate, he
was appointed sacristan: and then he was barely professed
when the whole house was turned upside down by the trouble
at Gethsemani College, the public scandal surrounding the
arrest of the principal, Dom Edward's resignation, and the
confusion that followed.

It was young Frater Frederic who was sent up to the school
to take charge of everything, to go over the books, to find
out how much the ex-principal had managed to embezzle, and
afterward to set things right and try to steer the school back
into the proper spiritual and financial channels. It was not a
bad assignment for a boy of twenty-two. But it was one that
had its dangers. After all, the young monk was taken out of
the community before he was fully formed. He had to live
at the college, and he came down to the monastery only at
rare intervals. He was a contemplative only in desire. The fact
that he managed to preserve such an intense and ardent interior

life all that time bears witness to the fervor and power of that desire! For, although he was at the same time one of the youngest and most overworked men in the house, Frater Frederic was also one of the most spiritual.

Underlying a natural courage and tenacity that could be pushed to the limits of heroism by his iron will, Frater Frederic burned with deep and smoldering supernatural fires, and his was the union of grace and temperament that produces Trappist saints. He was a Trappist in all the rigor of his love for the Rule, in all his uncompromising asceticism and love of penance: but he was more than Trappist in his ardent love of Christ, a love that had something of the fire of St. Bernard and St. Gertrude the Great. This love was the supernatural secret of his tireless devotion to Gethsemani and to all who have lived there in the last fifty years or have come within the radius of the Trappists' influence. And beyond that, his love went out to embrace the whole world, for this contemplative, like St. Theresa of Avila, like Thérèse of Lisieux, had the soul of a great apostle.

All his life was centered upon the altar and Christ in the tabernacle. The Blessed Sacrament, the Sacred Heart were his contemplation: if his thoughts turned at every moment from his work to Christ on the Cross, it was only to return again to this unending immolation of work which was to consume his life in sacrifice. Father Frederic loved books and he loved prayer. He had no relish for society and for the business and functions of men. Perhaps few people ever realized how much it cost him to sacrifice so many hours and days in his long life to material things, to contact with the world, to conversations with visitors, and to errands outside the monastery.

Dom Edmond, of course, had found him invaluable. He had him ordained as fast as he decently could and appointed him prior. After that, during Dom Edmond's long absences in Europe, Africa, and Asia, it was Father Frederic who ran things at Gethsemani. Quietly, efficiently, without fuss or noise, submitting everything he could to the judgment of his abbot, Father Frederic found the secret of doing many jobs extremely well—and letting all the credit go to somebody else.

By the time he was elected abbot, he was thoroughly prepared to be not only abbot but everything else: all during his abbotship Dom Frederic carried out most of the functions of cellarer as well. Here again, it was a question of generous sacrifice. He knew how much it cost to go out and do business in the world, and he wanted to spare any one of his monks from such a trial.

The first American-born Cistercian abbot entered upon his new charge in an hour of severe trials; the Providence of God was evidently preparing him and his community for the years of hard work and expansion that were soon to come. On February 7, the day after Dom Frederic Dunne's election, several members of the community who had fallen ill with Spanish influenza had to be isolated. In spite of all the efforts of the local doctor, the contagion spread rapidly through the community. In a few days Father James Fox, the infirmarian, had half the community on his hands in the small monastic infirmary built years before by Dom Edmond. But the monks did not realize the danger of the situation until Father Columban and Brother Placid both died on February 15. While they were being buried on the 16th, Father Anselm died, an eighty-six-year-old Irish monk. More and more of the Trappists fell ill until finally only twenty were left standing to carry on the regular life of the community and look after the others. The infirmary was taking on some of the aspects of a pesthouse, and there seemed to be nothing anyone could do about it. Father Anthony died on the 18th, followed by Brother Michael two days later. By this time the news of the epidemic was all over the countryside, and it was Bishop Floersh in Louisville who finally brought relief to Gethsemani. He appealed to Chicago for help, and two Alexian brothers were sent at once to Kentucky from their Chicago hospital to nurse the sick Trappists. Meanwhile, the monks were moved out of the infirmary into the top floor of the guest house, where the disease was finally checked, with the loss of one more patient, Brother Matthias. Later on, two more died of pneumonia.

The Requiem Masses were sung over the bodies of all these victims by Dom Corentin—a sad task for a father immediate who had come to install a new abbot in his daughter house. For, while all this was going on, the regular visitation was also being held, and confirmation of the election arrived from Cîteaux. Those who were able to get around on February 18 knelt before their new reverend father in the chapter room and renewed their vows, promising him obedience until death.

However, weeks went by, and the monks were able to finish Lent in the usual rigor. May 1 saw the abbatial blessing of the new superior, and that September he attended his first General Chapter. By November the community entered full swing upon the new program of works that had to be under-taken and began excavating a cellar under the monumental, thick-walled east wing of the abbey, built three-quarters of a century before by the pioneers.

Behind the peaceful walls of the Kentucky abbey, no one thought much of the events that were beginning to cause a stir in the newspapers as the year 1936 progressed. Only a rumor reached the Trappists that the February elections in Spain had put in power a regime under which the Church began to feel the pressure of a savage persecution. In the summer it was heard that Spain was on fire with civil war.

Cistercians don't know anything about politics and they did not become much involved in the confusions that clouded the minds of so many others in America. They did not realize that what was taking shape in Spain was really the prelude to a vast international conflict, a new world war on a scale more extensive and more terrible than anything that had ever been known before. They did not hear how the armies and air forces of Italy and Germany on one side and of the Commu-nist International on the other were making this Spanish Civil War a field of maneuvers, a practice campaign before the real thing began. But what they did hear was that thousands of priests and religious were being taken out and killed and that churches and monasteries were being burned.

And so, even though they did not understand politics, these monks grasped one fundamental truth about the Spanish Civil War: that it was essentially religious. The various twentieth-century religions had come to be badly mixed up, but in this conflict—with Fascism and Nazism on one side, and with Communism on the other—it was still essentially a war of modern godlessness against God and against the Catholic Church. That some of the Church's worst enemies happened, for the time being, to be fighting on Franco's side may have obscured the issue but did nothing to change the fact. At the same time the claims of a tolerant "liberalism," which theoretically hoped for religious freedom under the Popular Front, did not alter the facts. Therefore, in practice, the Cistercian monasteries in Nationalist Spain were not molested. The only one that had the misfortune to be stranded in the province of Santander, controlled by the Popular Front, suffered the fate that was to be expected.

Our Lady of Viaceli had been built in 1901 as a house of refuge for the southern French monastery of Our Lady of the Desert, near Toulouse. It was another child of the Waldeck-Rousseau anti-Catholic legislation in France. In the thirty-five years of its existence the community had done quite well for itself and had made a foundation in the province of Soria, Santa Maria de Huerta.

After the February elections of 1936 the monks of Viaceli began to hear of churches being burned in their province, but they were not visited by the F.A.I. until after the July uprising. First of all, they were "investigated." That is to say, groups of Reds walked in and started pushing them around with rifles and revolvers and asking them questions, as if to give a semijudicial character to the plunder of provisions and the stealing of livestock that were to follow.

The next step came on the Feast of St. Bernard, August 20.

That was the last day the monks were allowed the use of their church, which was then padlocked and sealed. They continued to recite the office in their "scriptorium"—a big place like a schoolroom where the monks read and write and study their theology.

Meanwhile, one or two members of the community who were not bound by vows—novices or oblates—returned to their families. The rest stayed. Of those who went home, one was immediately conscripted into the army of the Popular Front, where he was killed, it is thought, by some of his companions in arms. Another died in a forced-labor battalion.

At the monastery there were two or three weeks of relative calm. On September 8, the Feast of the Nativity of Our Lady, the monks were taking the usual siesta which the Rule provides for during the summer months, when there was a disturbance at the gatehouse. Representatives of the F.A.I. had put in an appearance, and this time they had a government order to close down the monastery and arrest the monks. The Trappists were given two hours to get their things together and clear out. The little packages they gathered up were searched. Breviaries, rosaries, and anything else connected with the worship of God—including the spiritual notes and other private papers of the monks—were all destroyed.

The abbot, Dom Emmanuel Fleché, was respected—not so much because of his rank or his age or his health but because the French consul had expressed official interest in his safety. He was sent to the nearby village of Cóbreces. Two priests, secretaries of the monastery, were also held at Cóbreces by the Reds, who felt sure they might be able to extract some useful information from them. But the body of the community—they made two big busloads—went off down the road between the vineyards full of ripe fruit and vanished in the direction of Santander.

The doors swung shut on a deserted monastery, and the dust settled again in the road and everything was very, very silent.

The two secretaries, Father Eugenio and Father Vicente,

seemed to be in the best position of them all. They were not imprisoned, and when they discovered that things were much safer at Bilbao, they began to make arrangements for going there. Before September ended, they had disappeared. But they had not reached Bilbao. Their bodies were found full of bullets on the road between Torrelavega and Santander, at a place called the Cuesta de las Anguilas. The villagers of Rumoroso recognized them as monks of Viaceli and gave them a Christian burial.

Dom Emmanuel Fleché, protected by the fact that he was a foreigner, was taken to a coastal fishing village which had been marked off as an international zone. It was full of refugees, who lived in the barracks of a big summer camp that served in peacetime as a resort for students from Madrid. The place was given a wide berth by the Fascist bombers, and Dom Emmanuel was relatively safe. Someone smuggled Hosts to him from Santander, and he said Mass, using his Cistercian cowl for a vestment and offering the Blood of Christ in a silver-plated cup that had been awarded to some champion football team of the locality. Someone had also brought him a paten that had been picked out of the ruins of a burned church. On December 8, the Feast of the Immaculate Conception, he received notice that he was to sail for France the following day, which he did. He returned to Viaceli when the war was over and finally died there.

As his ship put out to sea, the lonely old abbot of Viaceli may have guessed that these waters had already received into them the bodies of more than ten of his murdered sons.

The two busloads of Trappists who arrived in Santander on September 8 were imprisoned in the college of the Salesian Fathers. After a relatively short time a friend of theirs, not without considerable risk, engineered their release, and they were paroled. They came out into the town, separated into several groups, and lived together wherever they found hospitality in Catholic homes. Many of them escaped to Bilbao.

Father Pio Heredia, the prior, refused his chance to escape

and remained in Santander with the largest group of monks, to do what he could to take care of the dispersed community.

In this sixty-one-year-old Cistercian, who was at once profoundly contemplative and capable of energetic and wise command, the monks found the support and the example of sanctity. Father Pio belonged to that generation of Cistercians whom Divine Providence seems to have brought to the cloisters of the White Monks to carry through the work of transformation and unification that immediately followed the reunion of 1892. He had entered the Order at Val San José in 1890. In his forty-six years of cloistered life, steeped in the atmosphere of Benedictine prayer, humility, constant absorption in the presence of ·God, he had been filled with the spirit and the strength and the peace of the old monastic patriarchs. Although his profound love of the Rule necessarily gave his spirituality the austere and penitential character inseparable from St. Benedict and from Cîteaux, still there was more than mere negation in the soul of Father Pio Heredia. The one element of his spirituality that dominated all the rest and absorbed everything else to itself was love, the love of God: it was a love that transcended all sentiment and emotionality, to attach itself to God's all-wise Providence and His all-loving will. It was a love that pierced the darkness of every tribulation, every contradiction, and recognized the wise action of a God of love behind the superficial evil of secondary causes. It was a love strong enough to win the great grace of martyrdom.

Most of the men who went to their death with him had been formed to the religious life by Father Pio Heredia when he was novice master at Viaceli. The last days they spent with him were the crown and consummation of their monastic lives.

Although Father Pio and his monks were living across the street from the headquarters of the Red secret police, they lived a life that was entirely monastic and contemplative, beginning each morning with Matins and Lauds at five, followed by Mass—which was said at a dining-room table. There was reading, meditation, manual labor. The whole day revolved around Christ in the Blessed Sacrament, just as it had done at Viaceli, except that the Holy Eucharist was hidden in a dining-room cupboard and not in the Tabernacle of a high altar. They even received Mass stipends from the superioress of some Visitandine nuns who had not yet been dispersed.

The two months spent by the Cistercians at 27 Calle del Sol, Santander, were a final retreat, a preparation for the act that was to be the crown of their monastic vocations. Although they had hoped, for a time, that they would be able to return to their monastery—and even, as Dom Emmanuel expressed it in a letter, to "sing Matins there on the Feast of the Immaculate Conception"—they were surely not surprised that Providence, whose mysterious ways Father Pio had taught them all to contemplate and to adore, had arranged otherwise.

On December 1, in the middle of the morning, they were surprised by the sudden visit of a stranger who claimed that he was an electrician and who insisted on being admitted to the apartment, even when he was assured that there was nothing wrong with the lights. They were ready, then, for the worst.

During the day a young monk who was living alone in another part of town, Frater Alvaro, a cleric, came to visit them. That was how he happened to be with them at the time of the arrest. It was late afternoon when the police came to take them to the *comisaría*.

At the headquarters of the anarchist G.P.U. they found that several lay brothers, living in a separate group, had been arrested earlier. Handcuffed, they were sitting in silence, waiting for the "trial."

Commissioner Neila, who was to be their judge, was a bankrupt draper. He had turned Communist and was no exception to the brutality and stupidity of his type: the insignificant functionary who has suddenly acquired the power of life and death over other men. He spent his nights presiding over the baneful tribunal that disposed, according to his fancy, of everyone that came up before him. The only thing he had to worry about was to keep his balance on the Party line and conform to the exact shade of orthodoxy that was dictated for that precise moment.

With monks, of course, there were no complications. Everybody knew that monks were all Fascists and that their monasteries were full of money and machine guns. The main idea was to beat them until they told you where they had hidden their money, and then shoot them.

Like all Spaniards, Neila liked to start his evening's fun quite late. He did not get around to the monks until one o'clock in the morning. The first one to appear was Father Pio, the prior, and the interest of the commissioner of public order was sharpened to the keenest pitch when he found that a letter containing two hundred pesetas, addressed to Father Pio, had been found in the search.

The prior was questioned. That means, he took a beating. He could not talk without giving away the identity of the Visitandine superioress who had been sending Mass stipends. Therefore he said nothing. His face was swollen and full of blood when he came back to the rest of them in their cell.

One by one the monks and brothers were called into the presence of the commissioner. Since they obviously knew nothing about the money, they did not get so much of a beating, and one of them was even released. Apparently they were not quite sure whether or not he was a Trappist, anyway.

This was Frater Marcelino, a twenty-three-year-old novice with a talent for painting and poetry. He had made an earlier entry into the novitiate at Viaceli but had left in 1931, a short time after receiving the habit. Now he had returned, in 1936, just in time for the Red persecution. This time, although he was only a novice and was therefore free to go wherever and whenever he liked, he stayed with the community in prison and in secular life at Santander. Now that he was formally released, he took his departure. But he was not destined to be separated from his brothers for long. He was finally betrayed, recaptured, and shot. And so, he finally made his stability with the monks of Viaceli who were already in heaven before him. . . .

Indeed, when we look at the men who were gathered that night in the Red *comisaría* at Santander, we can find plenty of material for meditation on that Providence of which Father Pio had loved to speak to his novices.

Frater Alvaro, whom we have already mentioned, had been an oblate in the monks' school, closed by the government in 1931. Instead of wandering off into the world and losing touch with Viaceli, he had returned in a year or so to take the novice's habit. Then, after being separated from the rest in Santander, he happened along on the very afternoon of the arrest.

Another prisoner was Frater Antonio. He had been dismissed from a seminary because he did not have enough brains to be a priest. He could not make anything of his books. The Cistercians at Viaceli had not been able to receive him to profession, either. They kept him as an oblate. He could have gone home when the Reds threatened the monastery. He did not. Providence was reserving for him a higher place in heaven than would go to many a brilliant theologian.

Among the lay brothers was Brother Eustaquio. He was forty-five. Years before, when he was very young, he had entered another monastery of the Order, San Isidro, and had even made simple profession there. Before the time came for solemn vows, he had changed his mind and returned to the world. In 1929 he came back to the cloister, this time at Viaceli. He had made his vows. He was an exemplary brother.

Then there was Brother Angel, the oldest, who was sixty-eight. He had lived in the world as a married man. His wife died, and he entered Viaceli in 1931. After his simple profession he was sent to the foundation of Santa Maria de Huerta. Huerta was in Nationalist territory during the war. But just before the trouble started, Brother Angel became ill and was sent back to Viaceli. There, his vows expired. He renewed them. Just before the Reds came, the old brother, knowing what was ahead, made his solemn profession.

If we knew the stories of them all, we would find many strange things to think about. There were two men of superior learning among them: Father Amedeo and Father Juan Bautista. Together they had edited a little Spanish magazine, for monks and friends, about the life and affairs of the Order. It was called *La Voz del Cister*. Others of the group were only boys. Brother Ezequiel was nineteen, Brother Eulogio twenty.

They all appeared before Neila, who cursed them and threatened them and had them pushed around. He could not get anything much out of them. In the end he sent them all back and called in Father Pio Heredia.

"You!" roared Neila when the prior returned. "Either you tell us where you have hidden the money or you can pick your own brand of martyrdom."

Father Pio said: "Do as you please."

So he was again beaten, and the death sentence was passed on the twelve innocent men.

No one knows what happened to their bodies. In two groups —on December 3 and December 4—they were taken out somewhere, shot—no doubt—and thrown into the sea.

Only a young lay-brother oblate was allowed to go free. Thanks to his release, the story of the others was made known to the Cistercians who had escaped to the more Catholic atmosphere of Bilbao, in the Basque country.

When this diabolical little war ceased tearing Spain to pieces, Dom Emmanuel returned. The monks who still survived gathered around him once again, happy to find that there was still something left of their monastery. Empty storerooms and a few desecrated statues in the sanctuary were all that bore witness to the short-lived Red rule of the province.

In the powerful Catholic revival that followed the carnage of the Spanish Civil War, the Cistercian monasteries of the Peninsula have all grown. One of them, San Isidro, made a new foundation in 1942, in the darkest days of the European conflict. It is called Nuestra Señora de los Martires (Our Lady of the Martyrs).

But no sooner was the pressure upon the Church in Spain relieved than it was applied with equal force at another point. The Nazi occupation of Austria led to the suppression of the Trappist monastery of Engelszell on the banks of the Danube. The Gestapo arrived on July 27, 1939, and immediately took the abbot and prior off to prison. The subprior and several monks soon followed, and the monastery was completely suppressed on November 2. The property was confiscated, and several members of the community were condemned to internment at Dachau—a camp whose very name has become synonymous with an earthly hell. Naturally, they did not survive.

It was only in 1946 that a combined death notice for all the deceased of Engelszell finally reached our American monasteries: the interminable list of these innocent men, condemned as enemies of *Reich und Volk*, was read out in our chapter rooms.

They joined their Spanish brethren in the light of glory, victims of the same hatred of God and His Church, although they happened to have been killed by the Nazis instead of by the Reds. It is a strange irony that the Nazis, who had fought the Communists in Spain, were at that moment entering an alliance with Soviet Russia which led to the martyrdom of a whole Catholic nation: as if any further proof were needed as to the futility of political motives, which cannot obscure the real issue in all these chaotic upheavals of our time.

September, 1939, saw the long-dreaded opening of hostilities. The general mobilization in France and Belgium once more drained monasteries and seminaries of men. The archabbey of the Order saw forty religious leave for the front. Bellefontaine lost nineteen out of forty-nine and Sept-Fons sent thirty men to the army. Many monks followed the footsteps of Maxime Carlier and left Chimay for the armed forces: this time there were twenty-five. All down the list of our houses it was the same. Yet, there were surprisingly few casualties. All of Cîteaux's forty came home again. None of the thirty men from Sept-Fons was lost. And Bellefontaine's contingent not only came home intact, but two of them had the Croix de guerre. One of these was the abbot, Dom Gabriel Sortais; he was wounded at Lille, where he went into action with the Twenty-Fifth French Infantry Motorized Division. He was taken prisoner by the Nazis, and starved for a winter in a prison camp in Prussia. In 1941 he returned to his monastery to spend the rest of the war in the quiet routine of Cistercian life.

Ste. Marie du Mont, which had been gutted by a bombardment in the first war, contributed forty men to the various armies. The monastery was again bombarded, and twenty-four of her men went to German prison camps. All eventually returned except one lay brother killed at Hazebrouck. The year 1943 found the monastery repaired and most of the community living a normal life within its walls; and soon postulants began to arrive in considerable numbers, and when the war ended, the house was bigger than it had been in 1939. . . .

When the German armies flooded France in 1940, many Cistercian communities fled before them, and the houses in the south of France began to bulge with refugees. But a relative calm was soon restored, and communities sorted themselves out, ending up more or less in their proper places. Then followed the long, lean, dreary years of the Nazi occupation. Outwardly, everything went on smoothly, but they were years of strain, interrupted by sudden flurries of violence. Few indeed were the monasteries whose peace was not shattered at least once by the incursions of the Gestapo. These guests invariably turned the house upside down looking for concealed weapons and "maquisards," and sometimes they were all too close to finding certain persons they were very interested in apprehending. M. Schumann, who later became French Prime Minister, found refuge at Notre Dame des Neiges, in the mountains of Southern France, where he took the oblate's habit and followed the whole routine of the monastery. If the Gestapo had penetrated the enclosure of the abbey of Belle-fontaine in a certain week of August, 1944, they would have run into a storm of machine-gun bullets, for a detachment of Allied parachutists had landed and were hiding there. As it was, one or two Cistercian monks who had returned from the army had not ceased waging a secret campaign against the Nazis.

Father Guenael, a patriotic Breton, cellarer of the monastery of Thymadeuc, in the Morbihan, was in constant contact with the Free French leaders abroad and offered all the aid he could to Allied agents and parachutists. When compromising papers and a cache of firearms were discovered, Father Guenael was arrested by the Gestapo and disappeared from Brittany for-ever. News finally arrived that he was in the concentration camp of Neuengamme, where he died.

On December 8, 1943, as the pontifical High Mass for the feast of the Immaculate Conception was ending, officers of the Gestapo presented themselves at the abbey of Our Lady of the Dombes, near Lyons, with a demand for their cellarer, Father Bernard. They had to wait for him to unvest, because he had served in the sanctuary as assistant priest during the Mass. Then they led him off immediately to Lyons.

The monk had been denounced because of his contacts with resistance elements, and his captors did not neglect to put him through their most expert treatment in their attempts to get something out of him. Failing in this, they sent him, already half dead, to Compiègne, whence he passed successively to concentration camps at Weimar, Nordhausen, and Belsen-Bergen—where he finally succumbed. Although he died for his country rather than for his faith, nevertheless the courage and supernatural patience and charity with which he suffered all these things made a tremendous impression on his fellow prisoners. When the news of his death was heard, all the vil-lages and small towns in the neighborhood of his monastery held memorial services, which were packed not only with

Catholics but with men of every shade of belief or no belief at all. Meanwhile, the abbey of the Dombes had acquired a very unsavory reputation with the Gestapo, and in 1944 about a hundred Nazi military police and other soldiers broke into the house and put on one of their typical displays of violence. Having first beaten up some of the monks, they lined the entire community up against a wall and kept them there for three hours with their hands up, facing a battery of machine guns. Meanwhile, the abbot was subjected to questioning. He could not understand one tenth of the words that were screamed into his face through a welter of half-French, half-German abuse and profanity. The search of the house having yielded no results, the SS suddenly left, taking with them a few prisoners who eventually came home safely.

Other houses in France, while not subjected to deliberate maltreatment, at least suffered intense inconvenience from the Germans. One day, for instance, the monks of Bricquebec, in Normandy, came out of choir after Prime to discover that their front courtyard was occupied by thirty-nine German army trucks filled with soldiers, who were busy shaving to the tune of radios turned on full blast. They had no intention of bothering the monks: all they wanted was the monastery. The father abbot, in his turn, had stated his position quite definitely: "We won't leave, even if we have to sleep under the apple trees." They did not get that far. The Nazis left them a cellar and their church. To get from the cellar to the church, they had to go around the outside of the buildings and enter their choir through a hole in the wall, as the cloister was occupied by their guests. On rainy days the offices met with considerable competition from the soldiers drilling in the cloister, the roaring of the Nazi sergeants and the crash of rifle butts on the stone floor where monks were accustomed to pace up and down in silent meditation! When the sun came out the visitors disposed themselves comfortably on the roofs of the cloister or in the grass of the cemetery and exposed their pink Nordic nakedness to the warm rays.

But in a few weeks, when the Allied drive began, Bricquebec was turned into a hospital. The refectory became an operating room, where three surgeons were busy day and night. Doubtless it was the red crosses on the roofs that saved the monastery from being wiped out altogether. It lay directly in the path of the advance from Cherbourg and was in the midst of the fighting in Normandy.

Chimay, too, was turned out of doors by the Germans. This time the Luftwaffe wanted the abbey as a base and listening post. Dom Anselme le Bail and his community packed up their belongings and moved in with the Christian Brothers in a nearby town. There they remained for two years, until the American troops arrived and liberated the region. All that time, the Rule was kept faithfully, all the choral offices went on as usual, and the life of a Cistercian monastery was uninterrupted in its essentials. In fact, Dom Anselme was working diligently on the Cistercian writers of the twelfth century to produce a manual of spiritual theology for his young monks. An indult from the Holy See even allowed them to receive novices. They were bothered by the Gestapo, who arrested some of the monks but afterward let them go.

Some of the houses in Belgium and Holland were under more of a strain. The activities of the Gestapo in those parts were under the direction of an apostate priest, a former member of a religious order. With the peculiar psychology such people sometimes have, he concentrated his attention on the religious orders—no doubt to try and satisfy some obscure and torturing sense of inferiority—in other words, to make priests and religious pay for the suffering his own stifled conscience was still causing him. . . .

He saw to it that the Trappists of two monasteries, Echt and Achel, were expelled. The former house, near Limburg, was turned into a school for the Hitler Youth and remained so until 1945, when the Allies arrived. When the monks returned, they found nothing but a gutted building. The Nazis had not even left them a wooden spoon.

Meanwhile, the apostate turned his steps to the big Dutch abbey of Koeningshoeven, at Tilburg. However, he was in a good mood that day and somehow took a fancy to the Cistercians. Finding nothing to object to, he covered his departure with some heavy clowning, saluted the first superior with *"Ave, abbas illustrissime"* and asked the brother at the gate to pray for him, because he was a poor sinner.

Before that, however, Koeningshoeven had had a more bitter taste of Nazi methods. In August, 1942, toward three o'clock in the morning, when the monks were singing the night office, the Gestapo arrived and demanded two fathers and a lay brother who were converted Jews. All three were blood brothers: Fathers Ignatius and Nivard and Brother Linus Loeb. Their two sisters, Mothers Hedwig and Theresa Loeb, were Cistercian nuns in the convent of Berkel. They, too, were arrested, along with another Jewish convert, an extern sister who had been a doctor of medicine in the world. Nothing was heard of them for a long time, until at last word was received, in a roundabout way, that the three Trappists had been shot in Poland on the Feast of Pentecost, 1943. The others vanished without a trace.

It was when the Allies landed on the Continent and began to drive the Nazis back into Germany that the real martyrdom of some of our monasteries began. Perhaps no house in the Order suffered so much as Tegelen, near Venlo, Holland, not far from the Meuse. Half the house was occupied by German soldiers from the first days of the Nazi invasion. There was an airfield nearby, as well as other military objectives. Month after month, year after year, the monks were in constant dread of raids by the R.A.F., and they spent many nights in the crypt of the church, trying to recite Matins while bombs thundered all around them.

In Holy Week, 1943, the monastery caught fire and three wings burned down, together with some of the barns. Nevertheless, the monks stayed on in what remained, along with refugees from Achel and Echt. It was community life with a vengeance! Things got worse with the frequent bombardments of Venlo in 1944. Upward of three hundred civilian refugees found shelter in the monastery. The meager provisions of the monks, shared out among this crowd, were just enough to keep them all alive. In November the Allied forces drew near and then were held in check at the Meuse—just close enough for the monastery to be in the path of a ceaseless artillery fire aimed over their roofs at the Germans behind them. The British gunners unloaded tons of ammunition on the Nazis, sometimes at the rate of sixty thousand shells a day. The monks and refugees, reduced to a state of famine, were living underground. The monastery was struck by shells in several places. One day, just after dinner, a pursuit bomber swooped down and riddled the empty refectory with bullets. The monks were taking what was euphemistically called a "siesta" at that particular moment.

When the Americans finally took Venlo, the monks were so far gone that they could not believe that deliverance had finally arrived. It was a few days before all the guns were silent, and only then did the truth begin to sink in.

Tegelen had had five full years of war. Yet, Our Lady of Refuge, at Zundert, Holland, had five quiet years in which the life of prayer was not interrupted for a minute. One monk was called to the army—an Austrian priest who returned safely to his cloister, "more of a Trappist than ever." For the rest, the only excitement was caused by a bomb falling on one of the barns. The monks scarcely saw a German uniform all that time, and they did not contribute a single member to the forced-labor gangs which were so busily conscripted from Belgium and Holland and France in those days.

The monasteries in Alsace got the war in two doses; it blundered through their territory, then came back again. The nuns of Ubexy had some narrow escapes in the first round and were forced underground when the fighting returned their way in 1944. Many refugees crowded to the convent. There were some bad scares but nobody was hurt.

The big abbey of Oelenberg, which had been destroyed in
World War I and rebuilt afterward, was once again destroyed
at the end of World War II. The French troops had pressed as
far as the neighborhood of the abbey in November, 1944,
when the Nazis established an observation post in the church
tower. For about a month, beginning in December, the French
had to subject the post to artillery fire. The barns and harvest
were destroyed and the church was riddled with shells; all
the farm machinery was destroyed, and the Germans, before
leaving, killed all the livestock and left the monks with a farm
full of mines on which to try and raise themselves something
to eat. . . .

Nevertheless, 1944 was a glad year for the Cistercians of the
Strict Observance in all parts of Europe. They can remember
the happy day when the first American or British divisions
began to move past their fields. Most of the communities in
the actual area of fighting played host to Allied soldiers during
the last stage of the war, with the result that many American
laymen know the Trappist monasteries of Europe better than
do the American Cistercians themselves.

XI. THE RISING TIDE: NEW FOUNDATIONS IN GEORGIA, UTAH, AND NEW MEXICO; THE LAST MASS AT YANG KIA PING

BY THE year 1943 the Trappist protoabbey of the Americas, Our Lady of Gethsemani, was in many ways a different place from the house Dom Edmond Obrecht had left behind him when he went into eternity eight years before. To begin with, it even looked different. True, the monastery itself was still the gray, rugged quadrangle of buildings that brooded among the trees, its silver spire lifting up a huge cross to the Kentucky sky. But it was surrounded by shiny new barns and chicken houses and a hundred-and-sixty-foot water tower. That tower had given the whole place a new character. It did not make the landscape more beautiful. To recapture the European air the old monastery had preserved from the time of its foundation, you had to avoid looking at the water tower. And that was hard to do. But that water tank had had a rejuvenating effect. It made the place look more alert, more American, even though a trifle more grim than before.

When a high concrete retaining wall was put up behind the old monastery and a two-story brick wing added, jutting out pugnaciously on this new parapet, to dominate the night pasture and the mill and the creek, Gethsemani took on all the appearance of an armed camp. And it became very difficult indeed, in these years of war and revolution, to look at the place without realizing, at least vaguely, that Gethsemani too was stripped for action in its own war—the gigantic struggle of spiritual forces which is too superhuman for us to understand but which underlies all human history, and especially the history of our time.

It wås no doubt because Dom Frederic Dunne and his monks were so keenly attuned to the reality of this spiritual struggle that the abbey took on the grim color of their own hard labor —the quick, almost desperate labor of men who are rearing a barricade against a fast-approaching army. A spirit of energy and rugged, austere joy in the teeth of a cosmic tragedy: that was the temper of Dom Frederic Dunne and of Gethsemani in the years when the world of unbelieving materialism began to fall visibly to pieces around them.

Dom Frederic's view of life was at once tragic and optimistic. It was optimistic because the central reality of his life—a reality more real than anything else—was God's infinite love and mercy to men. It was also tragic, because he experienced, with an anguish so acute that it was physical, the terrible truth that most men have rejected that love and have preferred the confusion and misery of their own selfish ends—the fruit of which is suffering, cruelty, hatred, and war. Dom Frederic's view of life could not help being tragic, considering the tragic times in which he lived. But it could not help being optimistic, since he had consecrated his whole existence to a belief whose essential optimism finds the love of God in all things, even the worst, and keeps reminding us that the love of God turns evil into good. *Omnia cooperantur in bonum iis qui diligunt Deum.*[1]

The fruit of this combination of tragedy and optimism was a life of strenuous effort, in which Dom Frederic dedicated himself entirely to the task of opposing evil with good, hatred with love, selfishness with sacrifice, and sin with reparation. His conception of the Cistercian life was dominated by this reparatory character, and the necessity of vicarious

[1] All things work together unto good for them that love God. Rom. viii:28.

penance was to become, at last, almost the sole theme of his spiritual instructions. Although he was essentially a modest and retiring person, hating every form of fuss or excitement, Dom Frederic Dunne would positively blaze with emotion when he talked about the life of the monk *Christo cruci confixus*, nailed to the Cross with Christ—filling up in his own body the things that are lacking to the sufferings of the *Christus totus*.

Although he hated to leave the enclosure of the monastery and never stayed out a moment longer than was absolutely necessary, he had a very clear picture of the needs of the Church in America. In the years of depression and war the correspondence of the abbot of Gethsemani grew to tremendous proportions. Many people—priests and laymen—were writing to the monks to tell them how abjectly miserable life in the world had become and to ask for a share in their penances and prayers. When he had first entered the monastery, fifty years before, Dom Frederic Dunne had found few to sympathize with him in his intense conviction of the important role of contemplative orders in the Church. In fifty years there had been a considerable change, and even men who were not Catholics were beginning to realize that prayer and penance might perhaps be more fundamental and more valuable to the Church and to the whole world than the exterior labors of the apostolate.

In any case, this first American Trappist abbot had shouldered a task of tremendous importance and vast possibilities.

The first thing he had done, on taking over the miter and crozier of his predecessor, was to make sure that all the austerities of the Rule and the Cistercian usages were observed as fully as possible at Gethsemani. The Kentucky abbey had always been one of the most austere in the Order, in any case, and Dom Edmond Obrecht had certainly not allowed any mitigations which he did not feel were amply justified by the difficult climate. Dom Frederic Dunne began to retrench even upon these. Bit by bit and year by year the meals in the refectory dwindled down to their most rudimentary and naked essentials. The two fried eggs that had transformed each monk's Easter Sunday dinner into a banquet of unusual splendor, were relentlessly banished. The somewhat larger portions of corn-meal mush or oatmeal that made the evening collation, in time of fast, somewhat less microscopic, dwindled gradually to a few ounces of applesauce with a chunk of black bread, according to the usages. Even the wine or cider which are universally permitted in the Order disappeared from the table at Gethsemani forever and gave place to a strange concoction made of barley or soybeans, which goes by the name of "coffee."

Far from resenting these changes, most of the monks were eager to see them intensified, and many went to Dom Frederic and pointed out that, in the old Cistercian usages of the twelfth century, there had been no such thing as collation at all: only one meal a day in time of fast, and no extras, not even a bite of dry bread in the twenty-four hours between dinners. To this, Dom Frederic answered that he would be delighted to keep the ancient fasts as soon as they were brought back into effect by the present General Chapter, with the approval of the Holy See. Until then, he would be content to enforce the strict observance of the usages now in force.

One somehow felt that the bare refectory of Gethsemani was Dom Frederic's pride. When he visited other houses and found their meals less austere, he would say softly, "We do not have that at Gethsemani." And European abbots who visited Gethsemani arched their eyebrows at the rusty old tin cans in which the monks received their barley coffee, and they told one another that these rich Americans were certainly making an effort to practice poverty.

Dom Frederic made short work of another peculiar custom that had been tolerated at Gethsemani since the old days: the use of snuff. Smoking had never been countenanced, except that Dom Edmond had felt he could permit himself an occasional cigar on his many journeys. But some of the old monks had supposed they could not get along without a little pinch of snuff once in a while. Dom Frederic gave the community a chance to try. The only trace of the custom that now remains is the existence of the numerous stone jars in which the snuff used to be imported from Holland. These are now distributed around the various altars in the church, and the servers of Mass empty the basins into them at the *lavabo*.

Curiously enough, one of the immediate effects of Dom Frederic's austerity was a considerable increase in vocations. He had not been abbot a year when the great multiplication of novices began. When they were asked why they had come to Gethsemani, most of them replied that they were looking for the hardest kind of monastic life. They wanted to strip themselves of everything, renounce all the pleasures and comforts of the world, in order to make some faint gesture, give some slight token of the fact that they were trying to love God. Many of them did not find the Trappist life austere enough. They had to be held in restraint, taught moderation. Their attention had to be directed to the searching interior asceticism of the will and judgment in perfect obedience, in Benedictine humility, in the acceptance, above all, of the mysterious and crucifying interior trials with which God purifies the souls of those whom He destines for infused contemplation. . . .

But the crowd of young faces, the enthusiasm and joy of so many energetic young monks in the first fervor of the monastic life, gave the abbey of Gethsemani an atmosphere of vitality and happiness which it had not known in all its ninety-five years. Visitors were deeply affected by the current of joy that rioted through the veins of this great community—and by the contrast with the gloom of the world outside. Novices who weakened and forgot, for a moment, the strength of their resolutions and resumed their secular clothes to return to the world, soon regretted their decision, entered other monasteries or seminaries, or ran back, with all possible speed, to Gethsemani.

When he saw all this and recognized that it was not enough merely to enlarge the buildings and make room for crowds of postulants, Dom Frederic Dunne found himself close to the fruition of an ideal that was once thought impossible to realize. The time had at last come for the American Trappists to spread and build monasteries of their own and extend the power of their hidden apostolate all over the plains and mountains and valleys of the New World.

The war in Europe seemed an insuperable obstacle. Before you can make a foundation, you have to go to Rome and to the General Chapter at Cîteaux. Communication with Rome was impossible. There had not been any General Chapters since 1938. What was worse, the Abbot General, Dom Hermann-Joseph Smets, had died in the first days of 1943.

But the situation was desperate. Gethsemani had either to make a foundation or burst. Dom Frederic had never been able to tolerate the thought of refusing admission to a postulant on the grounds that there was not enough room. He would have gone on admitting them until they were sleeping four abreast on the floor of the chapter room and chanting the office in relays.

Meanwhile, many bishops were trying to persuade the Trappists to come to their dioceses. There was plenty of choice. The monks could have picked almost any climate, any environment.

Dom Frederic, who did all the planning and all the deciding, chose the site for the new foundation on principles that were typical of his whole life.

The Bishop of Savannah–Atlanta, Monsignor Gerald P. O'Hara, was urging the monks to come to Georgia. The climate in Georgia is not any too wonderful for people who have to sleep fully clothed in a religious habit and put in a hard day's work in the fields and chant for six hours in choir even in the middle of summer. Then, too, it was questionable whether the population of rigid Protestants, liberally interspersed with members of the Ku Klux Klan and other such societies, would receive a community of Trappists with un-mixed enthusiasm. But Bishop O'Hara was an old friend of Gethsemani, and Dom Frederic had once lived in Atlanta. Besides, he thought of all the strange ideas that the people of Georgia probably had about Catholics and Trappists. . . .

In short, Georgia seemed to him to be the logical place to go. He received the enthusiastic support of his community, who voted for the plan and settled down to see what would happen.

Permission to go ahead was granted by the Apostolic Delegate in Washington.

Dom Frederic made a couple of journeys south and returned to give the monks in chapter an idea of what he had seen. He had been north and south of Atlanta. He had seen a plantation in some hills, which was too big; another one somewhere else that was too small, and another one thirty miles or so from Atlanta which looked all right: it had woods and was watered by a big creek. It was called Honey Creek Plantation. That was the one that was finally bought.

After that, there was not much discussion of the new foundation. Things just quietly developed. Those who happened to be working around the south wing of the abbey noticed that Father James was collecting many boxes and bales, packing them with tools and commodities, and storing them up in the vault where the archives and rare books are kept. Of course, there were one or two experts in the monastery who had decided that they knew who was going to be sent to Georgia, and they communicated the information to one another by sign language, with the help of the abbey laundry list.

However, all surmise was finally set at rest on the feast of St. Joseph, March 19, 1944. The monks assembled in chapter after the matutinal Mass to be addressed by Dom Frederic, who had made one last trip to Georgia. They all knew that he had been giving the new farm a final inspection, and some of them knew that he had taken a New Haven builder, a good friend of the abbey, to Georgia and had left him with instruc·

tions to clear out the hayloft of a big brick barn and try to make it habitable for some twenty Trappist monks and brothers.

And so, that morning, while the pale spring dawn began to light up the frosted windows of the chapter room, the monks listened with amused excitement while their abbot read off a list of twenty names—beginning with a hale old German priest who was just about to celebrate his fortieth anniversary as a Trappist in Gethsemani, and going on down the line to a lay brother who had made his simple profession a month or so before.

It was not until it was all over that the monks realized how fond they had become of one another and of Gethsemani in the years that had passed! The departure was set for two days later, the Feast of St. Benedict—for on that day Cîteaux had been founded nearly eight hundred and fifty years before.

Atlanta woke up to a strange invasion. Twenty men with shaven heads and monastic crowns, in black and white habits, piled out of a railway car, trussed up the skirts of their robes with strings, and were flinging boxes and crates onto the platform and loading them into trucks. They had been up since three that morning, when they rose and recited all their office for the day, and they were too tired and too busy to pay much attention to the crowd or to the flashbulbs of the news cameramen.

By the time the monks had all their baggage loaded and were themselves settled in the cars of priests who had collected from every part of the diocese to help them, it began to rain. And so they started on the last leg of their journey—the thirty miles that remained between the city and their new home, near Conyers, in Rockdale County.

They arrived about one o'clock in the afternoon. They stepped down into the mud of a big barnyard and looked about them at their new home. They were in gray, undulating country, among fields that would be full of cotton when summer came. Over on the crest of a slight rise was the edge of a pine wood. In the other direction, they could see a share cropper's cabin. But right before them was their own home. The big white barn, with a cluster of sheds around it, threatened to compete with the share cropper's cabin, as far as discomfort was concerned.

But there was no room for dismay in their hearts. Most of them felt a thrill of satisfaction and gratitude that they were at last able to live a life that was unequivocally poor and painful, harder and rougher than that of the poorest Negro or the most destitute share cropper in the countryside. It was almost impossible that they should not compare their state with that of the Christ Who was born poor and friendless in a stable and Whose cradle was the feed trough of pack animals and cattle.

With the bulbs of the reporters still flashing around them like an electric storm, they set up their altars in the hayloft and said Mass. After they had all said Mass and received Communion, they broke their fast. It was four o'clock in the afternoon. They were right on time, according to the schedule of St. Benedict for the season of Lent.

The next day the monks were altogether too famous for comfort. Nevertheless, the general impression was that they were welcome. The Atlanta *Constitution* came out with an editorial praising their hard and prayerful life but adding significantly, "They hope to be unmolested."

Rockdale County was taken completely by surprise. There was only one other Catholic family in the vicinity of Conyers, and they happened to be the Trappists' next-door neighbors. The rest of the Protestant citizenry were filled with mixed emotions at the thought of men dressed up in hoods saying Mass in a barn in their very midst. Who knows what else they might be up to out there! Besides, they had bought the plantation from one of the biggest liquor dealers in Atlanta.

So it was not long before a committee came to investigate the monks. It was officially appointed by the county grand jury. It inspected the barn and the hayloft chapel and looked at the wallboard dormitory cells and peered at the bearded

brother shoemaker and the bearded brother cook and asked
Father James, the superior, to explain the rumor that was going around to the effect that some men were being held
prisoner in the hayloft. However, the investigators went away
and reported that there was "nothing out of the ordinary"
going on out at Honey Creek plantation. After that, Conyers
began to get used to the idea of having Trappists so near at
hand.

At first a few cautious visitors came to the barn–monastery.
Occasionally someone stayed for Mass in the hayloft chapel
and listened to the chanting of the monks, punctuated by the
more elemental songs of the mules in the stable below. There
was something very impressive about the way Gregorian chant
and twelfth-century cowls and the Sacrifice that was offered
under the species of bread and wine seemed to fit in with the
poor, crude surroundings: the bare beams, the rough floor full
of cracks, and the smell of hay and animals.

It was here that the Trappists celebrated their first Easter
in Georgia and entered upon a summer that was to provide
them with opportunities for penance they had barely dreamed
of at Gethsemani, although Kentucky summers are by no
means cool.

The last cold weeks of spring in the Conyers barn had
convinced the superior and his colony of men that it would
not be wise to face a winter in a building open to all airs
and without heat. One of the main tasks that summer would
be the building of a temporary monastery. But they also had
to make their living. There were wheat and cotton to be har-
vested, corn to be planted, vegetables to be cultivated, cattle
to be cared for, hay to be mown and put under cover. Twenty
of them could not do it all in the time the Rule allows for
manual labor.

So, the monks spent the summer working by a timetable
that was more like La Val Sainte than Gethsemani or Cîteaux.
Even when the big feasts of the summer came along—feasts of
sermon, on which Cistercians are entitled to a whole day's

rest and reading and private contemplation (and generally get at least half a day of it)—the men in that barn rose at one o'clock and sang the night office, advanced the hour for Prime and the matutinal Mass, hastened through chapter, and started out for a day's work before the sun was hot.

They had bought a sawmill and set it up, and soon it was working overtime. The framework of a quadrangular wooden monastery took shape between a cotton field and a grove of Georgia pine. It is said that trees felled in the morning were going through the mill toward noon and the lumber was nailed in place before nightfall. The whole building would have been finished long before the end of summer if some governmental red tape had not held up work on the chapel. Since the monks were doing all the work themselves and using their own lumber, there was not much trouble about priorities; only the chapel caused a delay. Somehow, there was legislation afoot that believed the chapel might interfere with the war. It was all right for monks to have a monastery: but a *chapel* . . . there, you had to be cautious! However, the barriers fell in the fall, and the monks made a dash for the lumber that was planed and sawed and piled up near at hand. They put their chapel together and had a complete monastery.

The interior was finished in time for them to move in on the Vigil of the Immaculate Conception, December 7, 1944. It was just in time. That morning the water had frozen in the cruets while the priests were saying Mass for the last time in the hayloft.

Meanwhile, the monks had been farming as well as building. In July they had already brought six hundred acres of their farm under cultivation. This included sixty acres of wheat, seventy-five acres of cotton, two hundred and fifty acres of corn, besides their vegetable gardens and the big melon patch, which, although it was right beside the main road, was unmolested the whole summer long.

All this work had not been done without cost. It was not merely a matter of long hours under a blazing sun that seemed

to boil all the life out of them; it was not that the heat left
their skin aflame with a virulent red itch that kept them awake
when they fell at last upon their straw mattresses at night.
Nor was it merely that their muscles ached and their joints
and bones protested after so much toil. More important, there
was also the subtle and costly sacrifice of the hours of prayer
and silence and reading which are so essential to the contemplative life. After all, the real strength of the contemplative
is drawn from the union of his mind and will with God, and
that union is nourished to a great extent by prayer and meditation and reading. When a monk cannot be alone with his
God and rest in His presence, his inner life tends to flag and
wither away. He feels the lack of something essential in his
spiritual diet. However, all these men knew that there is one
thing more fundamental than all the rest: and that is the will
of God. And so they were able to offer even this sacrifice of
the consolation of silent prayer, along with everything else,
and pray to God by their obedience, in the woods and fields
and under the hot sun, instead of before the Tabernacle.

And even then, when they did manage to get a few moments for contemplation, they found that the hayloft chapel
was about the hottest corner of the whole farm. Someone even
suggested that the monastery ought to have been called "Our
Lady of the Frying Pan."

All this while, they had scarcely been conscious of the
effect they were having on all who came in contact with them.
Trappists develop a kind of immunity to the things of the
world which insulates them from the thoughts and moods of
civil society around them. Most of the time, they are supremely unconscious of the fact that other people are interested in them or in what they are doing.

But by the time summer was over, they could not help
becoming aware that they had made many firm friends. The
secret was, of course, the energetic and fervent generosity
with which they had thrown away all care for themselves and
their own comfort, to accomplish the tasks imposed upon them

by necessity. Americans cannot help admiring hard work, especially when it accomplishes a quick, visible result. Here, on the transformed plantation of the Trappists, all these things were very evident. Yet, men felt that these monks were something more than transplanted athletes playing the spiritual equivalent of football in a strange, eleventh-century uniform: from that little pine monastery in Rockdale County there overflowed an intangible but extremely stimulating sense of confidence and happiness and peace. It communicated something of their strength and health and contentment to all those around them who were willing to receive it, and one felt that the monks controlled some secret influence capable of working even on the hearts of those who most opposed them. It was true, of course, they did not win universal sympathy from the whole of the deep South in one summer. The monastery found itself on the mailing lists of several anti-Catholic organizations, and one day, after some visitors had gone through the new chapel, the word "idolatry" was found scrawled in pencil underneath a Crucifix hanging on the wall.

Nevertheless, Our Lady of the Holy Ghost has prospered from the start. Besides reinforcements that were sent from the mother house, it soon began to receive postulants from many parts of the country. Even before the war ended, applications began to come in from men in the army and navy who felt they wanted to become Trappists when the firing ceased.

The temporary monastery was only the first in a long series of building projects. New barns, a laundry, a garage, a water tower, and several other farm buildings went up. Meanwhile, since the community had already outgrown its small dormitory, it overflowed into the first floor of the new garage, which became the lay brothers' sleeping quarters.

When the first postwar General Chapter of the Order convened at Cîteaux in May, 1946, Dom Frederic flew the Atlantic with a paper in his pocket that asked the fathers to make the Georgia monastery an independent abbey. His petition was granted, and Dom James Fox was elected and duly blessed in

October of that year. By that time the community had doubled in size and was still growing. Work on the permanent buildings was already well under way.

The Georgia foundation had hardly ceased to be news in the Order when it was heard that another foundation had been made in Great Britain, in spite of the war that was still going on. This time the founders came from one of the great Irish Cistercian abbeys, Mount Saint Joseph, at Roscrea. Dom Camillus Claffey, newly elected abbot, looked across the Irish Sea to Scotland and determined that Cistercian monks would once again chant the praises of God and till the soil of that land that was once filled with Cistercian abbeys. The site he chose was in the Lowlands and not far from the ruins of Melrose. Nunraw Castle was bought, and in 1945 the first Cistercians to enter Scotland as a community since the Reformation landed at Glasgow and made their way to the quiet valley in Haddingtonshire, which was to be their new home.

The foundation was in many ways a contrast to the one that had been made the year before in Georgia. It was singularly lacking in excitement. Quietly, and without awakening the attention of any news cameras, a small group of men in black suits and Roman collars carried their suitcases into a big, exceedingly solid building, whose thick walls, several centuries old, had been pierced to make windows. They settled themselves in its rooms with no further need to worry about a temporary monastery and started leading the usual life of the Order, thinking, meanwhile, that perhaps, with God's help, they would be able to build themselves a permanent abbey within ten years or so.

Foundations can be made that way in Europe: there are many large estates that have become a burden to their owners, who are looking for schools or hospitals or monasteries to take them over. In fact, the same process had been gone through in Ireland some years before, when Mount Melleray, Gethsemani's elder sister, bought the land on which Mellifont, the first Cistercian abbey in Ireland, had been founded eight hundred years before by men from St. Bernard's Clairvaux under Blessed Christian O'Conarchy. The monks did not move into the ruins of the old abbey, but they did occupy one of those peculiar pieces of late eighteenth-century classicism which are still to be found in so many corners of the British Isles: heavy, boxlike affairs, pseudo temples, whose porticoes rise amid the sleepy elms and pastures of counties where the chief occupation is fox hunting.

Mount Melleray is one abbey that has had even more trouble than Gethsemani in housing all the postulants that have come there. Many of its monks have been shunted off to New Mellifont, making that young community one of the large ones in the Order, with sixty monks or so. It is already nearly as big as Gethsemani was, fifteen years ago.

After celebrating its centenary in 1932, Mount Melleray started to build a new abbatial church. Today, the wide valley where the abbey stands is dominated by the square stone tower of a building whose proportions recall the great days of Fountains and Rievaulx in England. The church is worthy of the abbey itself, which is one of the only Cistercian monasteries in the modern world that plays the same kind of role, in the nation where it stands, as did the abbeys of the twelfth century in England and France and Italy and Germany and Belgium and Spain. Mount Melleray can say without exaggeration that it is the Clairvaux of twentieth-century Eire.

In democratic America, abbots prudently refrain from translating the "Dom" in front of their name to its English equivalent of "Lord." In England and Ireland the abbots are *Lord* abbots (*Dom'ni abbates*). In England it is a title. In Ireland it is something more of a fact. The abbots of Mount Melleray and Mount Saint Joseph count for something in the life of their state. And when one of them learned that his distant daughter house in Iowa had lost its abbot, a world war and an ocean full of U-boats over which all normal communication had been interrupted did not make him hang his hands in despair. He crossed to America on a troopship to preside at the election of a successor.

Meanwhile, at Gethsemani, the date August 14, 1945, found a community that still enjoyed most of the elbowroom that was left by the Georgia pioneers. A few postulants had come, no doubt: priests and men who were not eligible for the army. But also, from time to time, the father abbot had taken someone or other away with him on his overnight trips to Our Lady of the Holy Ghost to swell the ranks of the founders there.

When the monks came in from the cornfields of the Kentucky abbey on that August day, the Vigil of the Assumption, they did not find it hard to guess why the distillery whistle a mile or so down the road was blowing with such insistent continuity. Their abbot had told them in chapter some days before that strange things had happened in Japan which made an armistice almost certain. Now they surmised that it had come. And when the distillery whistle went on blowing and blowing—for one hour and then two and then three—and finally went off into a staccato and hiccuplike series of toots at nightfall, they became morally certain that the fighting had stopped.

But perhaps they did not realize just what that would mean for them.

It took a month or two for the invasion of Gethsemani to begin. But during the late fall of 1945 and the winter of 1946 soldiers were arriving. Men who had fought in the campaigns of North Africa and Italy, men who had seen service in the Pacific or who had crossed the Channel and pressed into Normandy and on toward Paris and then to the Rhine, now came tugging on the bell rope of this silent, lonely Kentucky monastery. Most of them were still in uniform. Soon the choir stalls that had been left vacant by the Georgia foundation were all filled, and more besides. The shortage of huge folio antiphoners and psalters had long ago become acute: now it was overwhelming. For a time they had tried to keep up with the new arrivals by setting someone hastily to copy the antiphons and responsories into manuscript tomes. But that was not enough. In the end some of the novices had to do without books altogether and try to follow the office in breviaries.

By the end of 1946 the community was bigger than it had ever been before; it was rapidly approaching one hundred and seventy. A new foundation was inevitable. But Dom Frederic had seen it coming and was already preparing the way.

There were several offers from bishops in different parts of the country, but the one that most appealed to the abbot of Gethsemani came from Salt Lake City: a huge diocese in area, with a few scattered parishes and missions and a handful of religious communities. It sounded like a spiritual desert. When he traveled west and saw those high, arid mountains and scanned the bare walls of the valleys, Dom Frederic almost changed his mind. Monks have to live off the land, and they usually need timber and green pastures. Compared with Georgia and Kentucky, this forbidding landscape seemed almost impossible. But then his guides told him how extraordinarily rich was the soil of those valleys and what crops grew from the fields when they were irrigated: and finally he came upon a ranch which seemed to have been created for contemplative monks.

Eighteen miles east of Ogden, after a long climb through Ogden Canyon, the valley opened out into a mile-wide bowl between mountains. The clean air of high altitudes breathed silently over those fields. Not a house was in sight. The snowy ridge of Mount Ogden stood up stark against the sky, as if it were the sentinel of this wilderness. Eastward was a no man's land of snow and sagebrush, and there were deer tracks in the snow. There were sixteen hundred acres of land with good springs. More water was available from the Ogden River nearby. A handful of water-right shares came with the land. There were some cattle on it, and the next year would yield some fair-sized crops of wheat and alfalfa. Transforming this desolate, houseless ranch into a Cistercian monastery and farm would be an immense amount of work: but the very silence of the place cried out for Trappists.

The deeds for the purchase of the ranch had been entered in the records of Weber County, Utah, March 4, 1947. The monks expected, at first, to start west at the end of April, on the feast of St. Robert of Molesme. Next, they hoped to be there by Trinity Sunday, at the beginning of June: a most appropriate time, since the new house was to be called Our Lady of the Most Holy Trinity. But Trinity Sunday came and went and the alfalfa was growing higher in the Ogden Valley and the wheat was shooting forth green ears. However, there was no danger of losing the crop, because a neighbor had agreed to harvest it for them in exchange for a share in the returns.

Housing was the biggest problem. Contracts had been made for a complete monastery of metal Quonset huts, but the job was too complicated to be finished overnight. By June everybody realized that, if they waited for the huts to go up, they might not get to Utah before the fall.

So, Gethsemani's father abbot decided to buy some army barracks from an abandoned camp near Ogden. They could be transported cheaply and without trouble, and the monks could move in at once.

The second colony set out from Gethsemani at nightfall, as the first group had done. It was a larger colony, thirty-four in all. Also, they were younger. Eleven were novices, most of them fresh from the army. Twelve of the professed monks and brothers had been in the Order less than six years. However, this group had formed around a solid nucleus of veteran monks and lay brothers, and those who were left behind in the mother abbey felt that they had lost the pick of Gethsemani's men.

That magnificent mountain valley deserved the best Cistercians that America could give. It was a comfort to think of this body of select men, vigorous, happy, already steeped in the Cistercian contemplative spirit, austere without being narrow, silent without being morose, prayerful and full of joy, journeying toward the providential work that God had destined for them from all eternity.

It was a happy foundation from the very start. The colony left Gethsemani on the evening of July 7 and arrived in Ogden Valley in the early afternoon of the 10th. It was just about two weeks before the hundredth anniversary of Brigham Young's arrival in Utah with the first Mormons.

The monks had come up through the Ogden Canyon in a chartered bus. A couple of miles beyond the town of Huntsville they found themselves at the head of the valley, on the land that was to be their home. All around them in the wide fields were bales of alfalfa, waiting to be carted off by buyers. The snow on the summit of Mount Ogden reminded them that they had come a long way from Kentucky. They could see where the foundations of the "Quonset" monastery had been dug, but there was still no sign of a building. What was worse, they had been told at the station in Ogden that only part of their barracks had arrived.

It took about a month for the colony to get settled—a month of confusion and hardship. The day after they arrived they had been up and about their business for several hours, when they saw the rest of their barracks come lumbering up the dusty road on trailers. They set to work at once, preparing the way for a reunion of the dismembered huts, which turned out to have served as prisons in a cantonment of German and Italian war prisoners. There were still various crude works of art on the walls of the barracks—pictures of mountain scenery, German proverbs, and even one inelegant painting of a stein of beer and a set of dice, which contributed absolutely nothing to the perfection of Trappist recollection.

About noon somebody looked up and discerned another solitary traveler coming slowly up their road. He was pedaling a bicycle. And he was certainly heading for the monastery, because there was nowhere else to go on those broad, treeless acres.

It was their first postulant. He had come from New York, but not on a bicycle: he had bought that in Ogden, because it was the surest way of covering the last, transportationless eighteen miles up the canyon to where the monks were. He certified his determination to stay there by selling the bicycle to one of the Mormon carpenters who were helping the monks to get under cover. The proceeds from the sale went into the practically empty treasury of the new foundation. The carpenter took the bicycle home and gave it to his son.

For the first three or four weeks the hours of work were long and the hours of prayer were mixed up and the hours of reading were more or less abstract and the hours for sitting around and taking things easy were nonexistent. (But then, idle hours never exist in a Trappist monastery, anyway.) Above all, the monks were short of food. There was plenty of alfalfa on the property but not much else, and monks have not yet learned to eat alfalfa. It was due only to the generosity of their friends—especially the Benedictine nuns at the hospital in Ogden—that they got anything to eat at all. And it took a long time to assemble the barracks in a way that was completely satisfying. As a climax to everything, the secular carpenters and electricians who were helping them went off to celebrate the centenary of Brigham Young's arrival. But at last the monks were settled in their home and were able to keep the usages as they were written—all the canonical hours and meals and intervals at their proper time of day and no more work than was prescribed by the *Constitutions.*

By that time, those who had made themselves sick by working too hard in the hot sun and at that unfamiliar altitude had got used to their surroundings: and a dealer from Ogden bought the alfalfa for a good sum of money and took it away.

Now at last they slipped back into the old, harmonious, wise round of the monastic day with its beautiful balance of prayer and study and meditation and manual labor: and now they felt themselves beginning to grow into the soil of this valley—

which they were even now flooding with water to get another crop of hay. They watched the clouds gather around the crest of Mount Ogden. They saw the storms travel down over the mountains. They listened to the deep, intense silence of their valley, a mile above sea level and a thousand feet above Ogden. Hardly a sound was to be heard except the momentary song of a meadow lark as it perched for a few moments on a fence post. Toward evening they would hear the coyotes on the mountainside serenading the solemn rising of the moon. The only thing that reminded them at all of the world beyond their valley was the drone of the mailplanes that went over at regular intervals during the day. It turned out that a radio-beam sending station had been built on a corner of the monks' ground.

But most of the time the silence was so complete that if you stood still you could almost feel it seeping into your blood and bones. As the sun went down, canonizing the stark mountain with a great blaze of blood, filling the utterly clean sky with streamers of delicate fire and saffron interwoven with aquamarine, it was easy to settle into the deep recollection of the contemplative, and let yourself be flooded, from within the secret depths of your own being, with the powerful sweetness of the presence of God. . . .

The very landscape was Cistercian, stripped of nonessentials, rugged and austere and simple, with no irrelevant details to arrest the eye. In the middle of it all, the workmen were now putting up the steel framework for the curious quartet of metal igloos that would be their home for perhaps twenty years to come. There was nothing in the Quonsets to remind anyone of the harmonious and simple Cistercian churches of the twelfth century: but here, too, were buildings completely functional and without frills.

Barns and a hay shed and a garage and various shops sprang up and formed a straggling village around the barracks. By fall, when the snow line crept down the hills and closed in on them from day to day, the valley had changed its character altogether.

By that time some more postulants had come, and the over-crowding which they had left Gethsemani to avoid was once again upon them with a vengeance. They overflowed from their barrack–dormitory and found sleeping quarters where they could: some in the guest department, others in the various shops. One young monk, a lover of sleep and warmth, established himself in the hut which had been allotted to the little chicks and was kept at a constant temperature of eighty degrees. . . .

They would not be in the Quonsets that winter. When the snows came, the metal walls and roofing were not yet finished, and it would not be possible to pour any more cement for the floors, now that the freeze had come. But the barracks were well warmed.

The silent little monastery entered snugly upon a new year, 1948, with forty-one members inside its walls, all thinking of the things that remained to be done: of the gardens and orchards that were to come, of the cattle and the sheep that would graze on that mountainside. And then one day there would be a Cistercian monastery of stone, an abbey church worthy of their liturgy.

These first few months had proved one thing: Our Lady of the Most Holy Trinity was turning out to be one of the most successful foundations the Order had made in modern times, materially and spiritually.

But these are things that have to be paid for.

The price of the Utah foundation was something more than a drain on the finances of the mother house.

A religious order is a body, or rather a unified organism, belonging to the Mystical Body of the one Christ. It is a church in miniature. Its life reproduces the life of the whole Mystical Body. It functions according to the same laws.

As with a plant full of vital sap and fruitfulness, when one branch is cut back another one springs forth. And Providence had destined this vigorous, budding new shoot in the arid Wasatch range to replace another branch that had been brutally slashed from the tree in another part of the world.

It seems strange that the monks should have left Gethsemani and traveled to Utah on the precise days when they did. We have already remarked that they should have started much earlier in the spring.

A few months later, news from China made the ways of Providence come clear.

On the morning of July 8, 1947, while the Utah-bound Cistercian colonists were waiting for a connection in the St. Louis station, their car was shunted onto a siding where, by virtue of an indult from the Apostolic Delegate, they offered Mass on a portable altar and all received Communion. It was the first conventual Mass of Our Lady of the Most Holy Trinity.

That same day saw the last Masses offered in the monastery of Our Lady of Consolation at Yang Kia Ping, in the mountains of North China.

This famous monastery—the first one of the Order in China and the largest in the Far East—had been made known to the whole Catholic world when Pope Pius XI singled it out for mention in his encyclical *Rerum Ecclesiae*. Speaking of the need for contemplative monks to support the active clergy in mission countries by their prayers and example, the Pope commented:

In this connection we have in mind the great monastery founded by the Reformed Cistercians of La Trappe in the Vicariate Apostolic of Peking, in which nearly a hundred monks, most of whom are Chinese, devote themselves to the practice of the most perfect virtues, to constant prayer, and by their austere life and hard labor gain the favor of God for themselves and for those who have not the faith, while at the same time their example draws these latter to Christ.[2]

The idea of a contemplative monastery in China went back to the middle of the nineteenth century. For years Monsignor

[2] *Rerum Ecclesiae*, February 28, 1926.

Delaplace, the Vicar Apostolic of Peking, had been trying to find some enclosed order to make a foundation in his territory. Three Carmelite nuns from Bayonne, in southern France, had started on the journey but turned back at Marseilles. Finally, in 1883, the offer was accepted by the lonely little Cistercian abbey of Tamié, lost in the high Alps of Savoie. One lone monk, Dom Ephrem, set out to prepare the way for a colony. The land that had been offered them, he found wilder than the Alps he had left behind. In the lofty mountains of North China, the site of the monastery was a deep, stony valley surrounded by barren peaks. Only in a Chinese painting would he have expected to see such fantastic contours. Loud with waterfalls, the abrupt, jagged hills were wounded by ravines. Dom Ephrem and his Trappists were supposed to grub a living out of them, somehow. After they cleared the rocky soil of its dwarf oak trees, small pines, and wild rhododendrons, they would be able to grow a little millet and some oats. There would be no clover, no rice, no wheat, and very little corn. However, the valley did have one virtue: it was full of apricot trees. In the springtime, when they came out in bloom, they transformed the ravines into Edens of soft color. They grew all by themselves, needed little care, and gave plenty of fruit. But what was most valuable was not the apricots themselves so much as the kernel of their stones, which yielded an oil of a certain market value.

The beginnings of Our Lady of Consolation were every bit as difficult as La Val Sainte or St. Bernard's Clairvaux, but as the years went on, the community prospered. By the time Pope Pius XI wrote *Rerum Ecclesiae*, Consolation was one of the great monasteries of the Order, in point of numbers and fame. Inside the wide enclosure were gardens and orchards surrounding a monastery and hostelry and the usual barns. In the center of it all was a large abbatial church, whose interior had the simplicity and dignity of a true Cistercian house of prayer. It was a large community, consisting of about a hundred, mostly Chinese, with a few volunteers from European monasteries. Here, the Cistercian life was taken in all seriousness, although a few mitigations had to be allowed in favor of the native monks: they are not robust enough to take the full burden of the Rule, even though they are inured to poverty and hardship.

When World War II became general—it had already been going on for several years in China—the superiors in the West began to wonder if the Chinese monasteries were now strong enough to stand by themselves without help from Europe. It was evident that they might soon have to do so. Consolation had sent a colony to a central Chinese province, and that monastery was now under the supervision of a Chinese titular prior, Dom Paulinus Li. The trial seemed to be a success, and the monks of Notre Dame de Liesse (Our Lady of Joy), as it was called, were turning over in their minds plans of expansion into Mongolia, when the Red armies swept down on both our houses and cut short all surmises about their immediate future.

It was after World War II ended that trouble really began for the Church in China. Our Lady of Consolation had not been much molested by the Japanese. A party of troops had spent one night in the monastery, but they left the next day without making any trouble. But when the American army withdrew from China and the Reds began to push back the Nationalist troops, things began to look dark for Our Lady of Consolation and her daughter house.

The only surprise was that the storm waited so long before it broke.

In 1946 the Communists had come and arrested the French abbot of Consolation, Dom Alexis Baillon, and one of his Chinese monks, holding them in jail for several weeks. Everyone expected the Reds to descend upon the monastery and finish their work then and there. But for some unknown reason they did not.

The blow fell in the summer of 1947.

Theoretically, the Communists allow freedom of conscience,.

and the attack on the monastery was not explicitly antireligious. The Reds were interested, most of all, in gaining the hearts of the peasantry by throwing them this most tempting prize. Of course, people believed that the monks were hoarding great wealth in their cloister. The "cruel exploitation" of the peasants by the "capitalist pro-Japanese imperialist Christian monks" was proclaimed with such insistence in so many meetings that people were able to forget, at least in part, the great services the monks had done them for sixty years past. Had not Our Lady of Consolation fed them in years of famine —including the time when the "scorched earth" tactics of the Red army had left them without a harvest or anything else to live on?

Two Chinese priests, Father Seraphin and the cellarer, Father Chrysostom, both of them prominent officers and well known because of their contact with the lay people who had business dealings with the monastery, were summoned to a village Communist court to answer the charges against the monks. That was only the prelude.

The trial, of course, was a joke. It lasted six days, and the monks were not allowed to defend themselves against a battery of fantastic charges covering the whole history of the monastery. It was said, for example, that Our Lady of Consolation had been founded by Europeans in order to help put down the Boxer Rebellion in 1900. (The rebellion had broken out seventeen years after the foundation of the monastery.) For having allegedly given "information to the Japanese," for having "oppressed the poor," "kept firearms," and "sided with the nationalists," the monks were ordered to pay damages to the people of the region.

As the two Chinese Trappists walked the stony road back to Yang Kia Ping, the word was already running like wildfire through the hills, "The monastery is finished!"

That night the Communists gathered for the kill, assembling peasants from miles around to share in the spoils. It was to be a fine party for them while it lasted. It would be their first real

National Travel Club

50, West 57th St., New York 19, N. Y.

1283-2-25-60 MAX-YR
DAPHNE HEDGES
BOX 21
NO MIDDLETOWN KY

is a member in good standing of the National Travel
Club and is entitled to all privileges pertaining thereto.

Valid Until Date
Shown Above

Sheldon Shrave

Secretary

Signature of Authorized Bearer

TO ANY HOSPITAL

A Group Certificate has been issued to the person named on the reverse side. Benefits are payable to the insured but may be assigned upon request. The Company assumes no liability unless benefits payable are verified by

THE NATIONAL TRAVEL CLUB INC.
50 West 57th Street
New York 19, N. Y.

or by the Home Office of the American Casualty Company at Reading, Pennsylvania.

taste of the Red variant of the Roman Emperors' "bread and circuses" technique. They would do well to make the best of it, because there were not many such opportunities in these mountains.

At midnight the gatekeeper of the monastery woke up at the sound of many feet and many voices. There was a loud outcry as men battered on the monastery gate. The brother went out to speak with them and was seized, beaten, and thrown into a corner, while the mob of men and women rushed into the enclosure.

That was the way July 8, 1947, began at Yang Kia Ping. The dark cloister rang with cries and the sound of smashing wood. Glass tinkled on the stones. Feet hit the stairways with a sound of thunder.

The monks sat up in their dormitory cells. Sleep ebbed from their eyes, and their minds filled quickly with the realization of what was coming. There was nothing for them to do but commend themselves to God.

The first attack was not so bad. The crowd threw the monks out of their dormitory cells and ripped up their straw mattresses in order to take the strong serge cloth covering. They seized everything they could lay hands on and ran out with armfuls of bedding, not forgetting to take whatever spare clothes hung in the cells.

By two o'clock the monastery was quiet again. The crowd had gone. Perhaps they were satisfied. When day dawned, the monks would take stock of the damage and try to do something about it. Meanwhile, it was time for the night office, so they assembled in choir.

After four o'clock, as the last Masses were being said, it was noticed that the Reds were filtering back into the cloister, prowling around and helping themselves to what they had not been able to carry away before. The monks consumed the sacred Hosts and left the Tabernacle empty and settled down to wait for the worst.

When the sun had risen, the crowd gathered again. Daylight showed that they had not obtained much by their efforts in the dark, and this time they settled down to do a thorough and businesslike job of cleaning out the abbey storerooms. All the millet and apricots and the rest of the foodstuffs were carted off to feed the Red soldiers, and the farm tools were distributed to the peasants. In the library they ripped the covers off the books to get leather and cloth. The light wind coming through the broken windows blew torn pages about the floor: pages from the Greek and Latin Fathers, pages of Scholastic philosophy, pages from modern books on scientific farming. The only possible usefulness all this could have to the Communists would be to help start the fire that would burn down the monastery which they hated with such peculiar intensity. But before this could happen, the monks would have to play their part in a long burlesque of legal procedure which the comrades had thought up to impress the peasantry.

The community was placed under arrest and imprisoned in its own chapter room for three days, awaiting the first public trial as a group. It was an elaborately planned affair held outside the monastery in the presence of over a thousand villagers marshaled by Red leaders with appropriate banners. The largest banner bore the words, "The trial of Yang Kia Ping by all the villages."

The same charges were repeated, and individual monks were called out to answer questions. Father Seraphin was marked out for particularly cruel treatment because of his authority as one of the official representatives of the Trappists in their dealings with the outside. He would probably have been the first Chinese abbot of Consolation if things had been allowed to take their normal, peaceful course. But on this particular day, July 10, 1947, he was beaten across the back with clubs for two hours in the presence of "all the villages," while the Red leaders shouted out charge after charge, and the cry of "guilty!" came back by acclamation from the crowds, primed by Communists scattered among them.

Then the monks were taken home and locked up once again in their monastery.

The fact that the first trial, in spite of all the noise and out-cry, had proved altogether inconclusive was shown by the events that followed. After two weeks, another trial had to be instituted, this time in the monastery church.

There must have been the most poignant tension in the hearts of those Chinese and European Cistercians as they filed out of the chapter room, along the cloister, and into the choir, as they had so often done before: and the gripping earnestness of their situation must have seized them with great force as they lined up in the middle of the choir, before the stripped high altar and its empty Tabernacle, while the Red soldiers who were to be their judges sat in the choir stalls on either side of them. Here, in this church, where so many of them had given themselves to God by solemn vows, the full, in-escapable meaning of their Cistercian vocation was brought home to them more graphically than they had ever imagined possible. That they should be victims with Christ for the world; that they should fill up, in their bodies, what was want-ing in the sufferings of Christ, for His Church; that they should dedicate their lives to God in a total, uncompromising aban-donment of their whole being into His hands, to do with as He pleased; to lay down their lives as holocausts of adoration to the infinite God as a testimony, as a witness to His great glory . . . they were actually living that out now, in all truth. They were being perfect Cistercians in the fullest sense of the word. They were fulfilling to the letter the Benedictine ideal: to "prefer absolutely nothing to the love of Christ" and to live as men "whose bodies and whose very wills are no longer in their own power." [3]

Once again the charges against the monks were roared out, and the answering roar of the "people" echoed from the bare walls of the choir with singular ferocity. It was a terrible con-

[3] *Rule*, ch. 72, ch. 33.

trast to the peaceful measures of the psalmody that had hallowed this place for sixty years. Again Father Seraphin took the worst of the beatings. When he cried out, "Have a little mercy!" he was answered, with a yell, "The time for mercy is past: this is the hour of revenge!" One of the brothers, whose name was Roch, was clubbed by three or four guards during his long examination. The monks who tried to protect their brethren by throwing their own bodies in the way of the clubs were pushed aside.

Only one person dared to stand up for the monks. A Chinese widow, a Christian catechist, insisted on telling the truth and defending a monk who had had charge of a mission in the hills during the war years. When she flatly denied that he had acted as a spy for the Japanese, she was beaten into unconsciousness and fell to the floor. They threw a banner over her and left her for dead.

The trial ended with the death sentence being passed upon the Trappist monks and brothers. Their wrists bound with wire standing at the presbytery step before the sanctuary lamp, they heard the sentence on the very spot where most of them had chanted their promise of "stability, obedience, and conversion of manners before God and His saints" when they made their solemn vows.

Even the passing of a death sentence was not enough for the Reds. They and the peasants seemed keenly aware of failure. Perhaps they had sincerely believed that the monks were capitalists and imperialists, hoarders of money and firearms, and agents for the Japanese. But by now it was clear that there was not a shred of evidence for any charge except the obvious one of siding with the Nationalists. After all, there was no other quarter from which the Trappists might expect any help!

This great monastery, which the Reds had imagined so wealthy, had yielded surprisingly little plunder. The monks, seen at close range, proved to be simple men who clung tenaciously to their incomprehensible religious ideal. No doubt

their stubbornness was very annoying, but it hardly constituted a formal crime.

So, the passion of Yang Kia Ping entered into a new phase.
The Reds not only did not proceed to an immediate execution,
they changed their tactics. They launched a psychological
attack and followed it up with some crude efforts at "indoc-
trination." Evidently they hoped that, once the monks' eyes
were opened to the brave new world that was peopled with
such creatures as the Communists, they might be converted
to the Red cause, admit the error of their ways, get themselves
wives, and settle down under the Dictatorship of the Proletariat. Fifty secular prisoners were moved into the monastery
with the monks for psychological effect, as the first step in
a possible process of secularization. Then, toward the middle
of August, the community was taken on a long and painful
jaunt through the hills to view a village where the Reds had
taken over the property of a rich landowner.

The Trappists were not impressed. One, the eighty-two-
year-old Chinese Brother Bruno was so unimpressed that he lay
down and died there. It was the Feast of the Assumption, the
golden jubilee of his solemn vows. . . .

On August 29, the Trappists left Yang Kia Ping on a terrible journey whose stages were to be marked by the graves
of more than one. It was the old monks and brothers that died
first, from exposure and starvation and fatigue. Laden with
chains or handcuffed with wire that cut their wrists to the
bone, they tramped into the bleak hills. The young monks
carried the old and weak in litters. It was cold, and an icy rain
fell hour after hour, day after day. They had practically no
food, no shelter. When they were allowed to stop, they fell
down and slept among the stones. Occasionally they would
stop over at a village, and the monks were put on show in
another "trial." No doubt the Reds were trying to save face
by making a political circus out of their band of prisoners.

Their treatment became more brutal from day to day. Many
monks, their hands permanently bound behind their backs,

had to lap up their food from bowls like dogs. If anyone was caught moving his lips in prayer, he was beaten: for the Reds thought the Trappists had learned to communicate with one another by lip reading. And all along the way the soldiers taunted them:

"You believe in God! If your God exists, why doesn't He help you? Why doesn't He get you out of here? You say that God made you! God can't make anything because He doesn't exist. If a man and woman are strong, they have children. If they are not strong, they don't have children, and God doesn't have anything to say about it. . . ."

The Red soldiers told them how Our Lady of Consolation had gone up in flames. They said, "Soon there will be no more Christian churches left in China."

When the monks did not believe that Yang Kia Ping had been burned, their captors took a party of them all the way back to see the ruins with their own eyes. It was all too true. Nothing was standing except a few blackened walls, stark and terrible in the wild valley. The Reds had set fire to the building the day the monks had left—and that very evening a rescue party of Nationalist troops had arrived. They were twelve hours too late.

On September 6, Father William, a seventy-year-old French priest, died on the road and was buried at Lai Hsun Hsien, in the mountains. In the next ten days two of his compatriots, Father Stephen and Father Alphonse, followed him. The latter was a former Jesuit missionary who had felt that deep, undefinable attraction that brings men from the active life into the cloister, and he had become a Cistercian at Consolation. An exemplary monk, he had suffered greatly in his last days, tortured by dysentery and kept in solitary confinement, where no one could give him any care.

The Trappists were not even allowed to dig deep graves for their dead, and wolves came during the night and dug up the bodies.

By the end of September the "trials" of the Trappists had

ceased to interest the population. The Reds, satisfied that they could now release some of them without "loss of face," summoned five of the brothers and told them they would be sent away, with freedom to make their way through the Nationalist lines if they wanted to run the risk of getting shot.

Before they left, the Trappists were told: "You are not so much to blame as the old fathers. They have deceived you. They have taught you to think incorrectly. And that is the whole trouble with you people: you do not think straight. But now, perhaps, you have learned some sense." But the Red leaders added: "Do not make the mistake of entering another monastery or seminary and don't get yourselves made into priests. We will soon have the whole of North China under our control, and if we catch you in another monastery, we won't be so gentle with you next time."

On October 4, seven more brothers were sent away with the same instructions. Seven brothers and young monks followed them on the 13th. The latter group was released at the edge of no man's land, between the two armies and in a coal field northwest of Peiping. As they approached the Nationalist lines, machine-gun bullets made the earth jump all about them, but they were untouched. A sentry brought them before his commanding officer, and they explained who they were. Soon they were put on a freight train headed for Peiping. They arrived in the city October 18, ragged and emaciated, and presented themselves at the college of the Marist Brothers.

After a time the various groups of Trappist refugees in Peiping gathered together and were given a small dairy farm in the suburbs. Here, they settled down in great poverty to live their communal life as well as they could. All of them were lay brothers or young monks not yet ordained priests. The Reds had kept all the surviving priests at Mu Chia Cheng. With them, were twenty-three other Cistercians. All were rated as "dangerous" prisoners and were frequently clubbed or flogged. Of the seven Europeans who had been in the community, three were dead, and two still remained behind. The latter were getting near the end when the young monks were released, and news of the death of one, Father Augustine, an aged Frenchman and the novice master of Yang Kia Ping, was reported soon after. The last European survivor was a Dutch Trappist from Koeningshoeven, Father Aelred Drost, who died in October 1947.

The position of the monks in Peiping was anything but secure, but they soon had the joy of welcoming Dom Paulinus Li, the Chinese prior of Our Lady of Liesse; he came from south China, where he had established a refuge for his monks in the province of Sze-Chuan. Plans were made to bring the survivors of Our Lady of Consolation to south China, where they would form a single community with the other refugees.

A month and a half later, the news of the martyrdom of Yang Kia Ping reached Europe and America. In the chapter rooms of all the monasteries of the Order, the names were read of those who were known to be dead. The first list had twelve names on it. It was soon followed by a second with four more.[4]

A circular letter from the abbot of Consolation, Dom Alexis Baillon, who was in France, gave the Cistercian Order a bare outline of the story that has been told here and added only a few words of comment, impressive in their Trappist economy:

[4] On the first list were three French priests, fathers Stephen, William, and Alphonse, and one Chinese priest, Father Emile. The rest were brothers, all Chinese: brothers Conrad, Mark, Bruno, Aloysius, Bartholomew, Clement, Jerome, and Philip. On the second list were Brothers Anthony, Malachy and Amedeus, all Chinese. In October Fathers Michael (the prior), Bonaventure, Odilo (Chinese) and Aelred died. On the twenty-eighth of January, 1948, five others were horribly murdered—their brains dashed out by stones. They were Fathers Seraphin and Chrysostom, Brothers Alexius, Roch and Eligius.

Between February and May of the same year the following died or were executed: Fathers Maurus, Simon and Theodore, Frater Hugh, Brothers Irenaeus and Martin (all Chinese). There remain six whose death notices have not yet reached us at the time of this writing. This material is mostly based on an article by Rev. C. McCarthy, S.J., which gave a full account of the events at Yang Kia Ping, as told to him by Frater M. Joachim, O.C.R., one of the monks who was released. We saw the article in manuscript.

We hardly dare to recommend the deceased to your prayers, for they seem to us to have died as martyrs. But we especially recommend the living that they may have the courage to suffer and that the good God may deliver them.

No one with an enlightened faith can doubt that the sufferings and sacrifices of the Chinese Cistercians have added to the great increment of merit that has accumulated in the Order in these last fifteen years of anguish and persecution and has contributed to the intense spiritual and material vitality that is filling the whole organism of the Order and the Church. The blood of martyrs is proving to be the seed of Cistercians.

Two Cistercian monasteries in Yugoslavia fell into the hands of the Communists when the armies of Marshall Tito took over the country. One of these was the great monastery of Mariastern and the other was Our Lady of Liberation. The Communists, of course, took over both monasteries. Full details of what happened to the monks have not yet reached us. It is known that many escaped to Germany and are in Cistercian monasteries there. Some were last heard of working in the secular priesthood in Yugoslavia and others are known to have been imprisoned in concentration camps.

The monastery of El Athroun was in the midst of the fighting in Palestine in 1948 and has been, for many months, in serious danger. Although theoretically "respected" by the combatants, it has suffered damage under fire, and at least one member of the community has been killed.

The new monastery in Utah sprang up and began its flourishing growth on the very day when the crucifixion of Yang Kia Ping got under way; in the very days of December when the news from China was being read to the monks in our American houses, we also heard of still another foundation in our own country.

The bright colors and the characteristic American light-heartedness that marked the arrival of four Trappists in New

Mexico present a strange but encouraging contrast to the grim scene that was then nearing its conclusion in North China.

Early in December, 1947, a big, dusty, Ford truck pulled into Santa Fe, New Mexico. It had Rhode Island license plates, and the four men in it—wearing plain suits or overalls—were looking for the archbishop. These men were Cistercians from Our Lady of the Valley in Rhode Island. They were thus the lineal descendants of Father Vincent de Paul Merle and his Nova Scotia foundation, and they were there to accomplish a work that probably added much joy to the happiness of that old veteran of La Val Sainte in heaven.

The Rhode Island monastery had made no little sensation in the Southwest by buying up a well-known dude ranch in the Pecos Valley, some twenty miles out of Santa Fe. These monks had come to prepare the way for a regular colony of Trappists. They knew nothing, yet, of what had been going on in China: but what they were about to do was a Providential commentary on those events. They were going to show anyone who might be interested the quiet and effective way Christian communism has of liquidating capitalist institutions and replacing them with something more healthy and fruitful in the moral order.

Seven thousand feet above the sea, on the banks of the Pecos River and at the foot of the Sangre de Cristo range, this isolated ranch was bounded on three sides by a government forest. A few miles beyond their gate the road came to a dead end at the government fish hatchery. And the Pecos River is considered to be the finest trout stream in the Southwest.

Among the cottonwood trees of the ranch were many cabins and tennis courts and riding stables. The ranch house itself contained a dining room that could accommodate three hundred guests. More than that, it sheltered several billiard tables and a great mahogany bar, well stocked with all those things that usually belong in a bar.

The stationery bore the legend, "Valley Ranch—The Finest Playground in America."

But Father Vincent de Paul's descendants had not come to New Mexico to play. They sold the cases of Scotch and rye and the boxes of cigars. They got rid of the billiard tables, the saddle horses, and all the other toys that the sportsmen had left. They dismantled the cabins and the big mahogany bar, and one of the monks, an architect, drew up the blueprints that would turn all that into a cloister and a chapel and a chapter room and a refectory and a library and dormitories.

The monks were bringing order to that peaceful valley. They were delivering it from the emptyhearted restlessness of people with more money in their pockets than happiness in their souls. The deep and intelligent silence of contemplatives would now swallow up the last echo of the banal conversations that had once been heard in those groves. The hammers of carpenters and the sound of peaceful work would make those trees forget the dull noise of secular amusement, and the adolescent racket of third-rate swing music would be lost in the mature measures of Gregorian chant.

The tide of that clean culture which had once touched the edge of these desert mountains, when Spanish Franciscans brought Christ to the Southwest, had turned again with a promise of monasticism and contemplative life: a life centered on God and immersed in His worship, a society of men capable of fulfilling the highest destiny for which men were created.

There are not a few people in our world and in our country who dare to find hope for the future in such signs as these. And the New Mexico foundation, dedicated to Our Lady of Guadalupe, is the most symbolic of them all. It would be too much to expect that a whole nation might follow in the direction Valley Ranch took when it allowed itself to be transformed from a dude ranch into a Trappist monastery. Nevertheless, the trend is there, and it is something that belongs to our age. Perhaps it may, in time, come to be one of the lesser characteristics of our age, its greatest paradox and its happiest surprise, the consolation in the depths of our tragedy.

But such things as these have been dearly paid for in blood

and lives. They are the fruit of martyrdoms. As such, they have only one destiny: to bear the same kind of witness to God that is borne by martyrs: to praise Him at no less cost than that of the wild, perfect, supreme love that transcends every other love, every other work, every other desire, to lose itself entirely from the eyes of men in that profound abyss which is known as adoration.

PART TWO

PART TWO

XII. CISTERCIAN LIFE IN THE TWELFTH CENTURY

To UNDERSTAND the Cistercian life, you need a general idea of the way a monastery is organized. Once you have that, the rest is easy. A twelfth-century monastery of the Cistercian Order plainly and effectively tells its own story, even if all its monks are gone and half the walls are in ruins. And you can almost grasp the purpose of the monastery when you see the site where it was built, even if there is practically nothing left of the ruins.

The tradition of the White Monks was to build in lonely, wooded valleys. There were several reasons for this. But it would be just as well to say at the outset that they did not seek out such places for the sake of the scenery. That was something the twelfth century would not altogether have understood, even though St. Bruno, the founder of the Carthusians, allowed the landscape of southern Italy a place in his contemplations.[1] And it is true that St. Bernard confessed he had learned all his wisdom from the "oaks and beeches of the forest" and invited the schoolmaster of York, Henry Murdach, to come to Clairvaux and "learn something from the woods that you will not find in books." [2] Nevertheless, the monks of

[1] Letter to Raoul de Verd, in Migne, *P. L.*, Vol. 152, col. 421b. He gives a beautiful description of the view from the hermitage in Calabria, where he died, and admits that he found it helpful to relax his mind by gazing at the pleasant countryside when his spiritual exercises became too much for him.

[2] *Quidquid in Scripturis valet, quidquid in eis spiritualiter sentit, maxime in silvis et in agris meditando et orando se confitetur accepisse; et in hoc nullos aliquando se magistros habuisse nisi quercos et fagos joco illo suo gratioso inter amicos dicere solet.* William of St. Thierry, *Vita Bernardi*, I, iv, 23. St. Bernard wrote to Henry Murdach: "*Aliquid*

the Middle Ages did not go into the wilds looking for the beauties of nature. Father Vacandard [3] tells us what we are to think of St. Bernard's supposed "love of nature." He shows us clearly enough that the founder of Clairvaux and of the Cistercian school of mysticism was far from being a twelfth-century Wordsworth. Rather, the solitude and peace of the forest gave his mind freedom to contemplate God in His revelation.

But there is one error far worse than this one. It is the mistaken idea that the Cistercian fathers liked to build in marshy and unhealthy places so that the monks would always be ill. This condition would enable them to do penance and would keep death, their last end, inescapably before them, and they would long for their deliverance with undimmed ardor. This theory has a frail foundation. It is based on a sentence attributed to St. Bernard in a letter of one of his contemporaries, his next successor but one in the abbatial chair of Clairvaux. The writer, Fastrad of Gaviamez, was giving a younger abbot a piece of his mind for leading a life that savored of relaxation. His language is dramatic and rhetorical, and the sentiments he attributes to St. Bernard seem to be rather heavily colored by his own penitential cast of mind. [4] A closer acquaintance

---

amplius invenies in silvis quam in libris. Ligna et lapides docebunt te quod a magistris audire non posses." Epistola 106, No. 2.

[3] *Vie de Saint Bernard* (Paris, 1895), p. 57.

[4] The words attributed by Fastrad to St. Bernard are: *Nec sufficit monacho infirmitatem allegare. Sancti enim Patres, majores nostri, valles humidas et declives monasteriis exstruendis indagabant, ut saepe infirmi monachi et mortem ante oculos habentes securi non viverent.* Among the letters of St. Bernard, *Epist.* 478, No. 4. From the same letter comes the famous quotation in which St. Bernard says that the monk would water every morsel of the bread he ate with his tears if he realized the obligations of his state. The tenor of the letter is given by Fastrad's etymological definition of a monk as one dedicated to solitude and sorrow: *Monachi etymon est solitudo et tristitia.* He chides his young abbot friend for eating "fresh-caught fish" under pretext of being ill, when one of their companions in the novitiate had refused to ask for an egg to relieve his hunger until he was actually at the point of death. Fastrad closes by warning his correspondent that "if your soul were in God's grace your body would not be so weak."

with the abbot of Clairvaux would show that although he may have said these words to Fastrad, they need to be balanced against the saint's serious and explicit teaching about discretion: *mater virtutum et consummatio perfectionis* ("the mother of virtues and the seal of perfection").[5]

Whatever the first Cistercians may have believed about penance—and their life was certainly most austere—they never favored a spirituality that sought perfection in suicide. On the contrary, St. Bernard was one of the most determined defenders of Christian sanity against the Manichaeism revived by the Albigenses, who condemned the body and all its works as essentially evil.

In any case, history records more than one occasion when St. Bernard ordered a monastery to move to a healthier site, after the original location proved harmful to the monks. One instance of this was at Belleperche, in marshy, low-lying country near Montauban, in southern France.[6]

The true reason the White Monks escaped to wild places and built their monasteries in mountains and forests was to get away from the world. And the reason they wanted to get away from the world was primarily to find not suffering for themselves but joy. They were looking for freedom: freedom from all the cares and burdens of worldly business and ambition. They desired this freedom not for its own sake but for the sake of union with God by contemplation.

[5] The real doctrine of St. Bernard is found in his sermons. This quotation comes from the third sermon on the Feast of the Circumcision, No. 11, in which he says that those who have reached the degree of the spiritual life in which penance is a pleasure to them, sometimes sin by excess and ruin their interior life by making themselves unfit to live as contemplatives: *Timendum est ne . . . corpus destruat per immoderatam exercitationem; ac deinde necesse habeat, non sine magno spiritualis exercitii detrimento, circa debilitati curam corporis occupari.* Cf. *In Cant.*, Serm. xlix, No. 5. However, see his remarks on false "discretion," which is only a disguise for the "wisdom of the flesh." *In Cant.*, Serm. xxx, Nos. 10-12.

[6] See Marcel Aubert, *l'Architecture Cistercienne en France* (Paris, 1946).

The Cistercian manifesto that was the *Exordium Parvum*—probably written by St. Stephen Harding himself—tells us this clearly several times. Pope Paschal II, issuing a bull in approval of the new foundation, commended them for throwing off the burden (*angustias*) of worldly life and of mitigated monasticism and ordered them officially to continue in the way they had chosen, "in order that being all the more free from the disturbances and pleasures of secular life you may the more eagerly strive to please God with all the powers of your mind and soul." *Ut quanto a saecularibus tumultibus et deliciis liberiores estis, tanto amplius placere Deo totis mentis et animae virtutibus anheletis.*[7]

The monks themselves made a point of appealing to St. Benedict's precept *a saeculi actibus se facere alienum* ("to become strangers to the business of the world") when they rejected the care and usufruct of parishes, manorial estates, tithes, and all the other intricacies of ecclesiastical feudalism.[8] And then, in order to give themselves to a simpler and more interior way of prayer,[9] they even rejected the excessive activity which the liturgical pomp of Cluny imposed upon the monks. The attitude of the founders of Cîteaux is summed up in one sentence by the author of the *Exordium*. He describes the satisfaction with which they arrived in the marshy woods that had been granted them by the Duke of Burgundy, and observed that the brush was too thick to encourage visitors. It was inhabited only by wild beasts, and the monks congratulated themselves on having found a place that was all the more perfect for their life because it was repugnant and inaccessible to seculars.[10]

Nevertheless, when the world tried to follow them, and the Duke of Burgundy signified his desire to come and visit the

[7] *Exordium Parvum*, xiv, Guignard, p. 70.

[8] *Ibid.*, xv, p. 71.

[9] *Ibid.*, xii, p. 68.

[10] *Tanto religioni . . . habiliorem, quanto saecularibus despicabiliorem et inaccessibilem. . . . Ibid.*, iii, p. 63.

monks in state, with his whole court, Stephen Harding risked the whole future of the monastery and the Order by inform- ing His Grace that he was not wanted unless he came alone, to pray.

It is understandable, then, that the founders of the Cistercian Order considered this matter so important that they wrote it into their original statutes [11] at the very beginning of the list. It is the first recorded item in the formal legislation of the General Chapters.

To pay for their solitude the White Monks were willing to accept the most unhealthy and uncomfortable situations. But that does not mean that they resigned themselves to pine away there and die. On the contrary, they took land that their con- temporaries were afraid even to approach and entirely trans- formed it by their labor from a wilderness into fertile farms. They drained valleys that were too moist, they irrigated land that was too dry. They cleared forests. They even performed almost unbelievable feats of engineering in order to get them- selves settled in difficult mountain passes. For example, the builders of Bonneval, in the rugged uplands of south central France,[12] built a terrace supported by gigantic blocks of granite in order to be able to place their monastery and its necessary gardens on the flank of a steep, wooded hill dominating a ravine.

When St. Bernard and his companions were sent out by St. Stephen Harding in the early summer of 1115 to make the third foundation from Cîteaux in three years, they crossed the plateau of Langres to the valley of the Aube and found a wooded vale which penetrated the hills to the depth of a

---

[11] The first collection of statutes, the *Instituta* of 1134, begins with these words: "*In civitatibus, castellis, villis, nulla nostra construenda sunt cenobia, sed in locis a conversatione hominum semotis.*" The same rule is found in the present *Constitutions* of the Cistercians of the Strict Observance.

[12] It is in the diocese of Rodez and the modern department of Aveyron. In modern times it has become a convent of Trappistines. See Mgr. Auvity, *L'Abbaye de Bonneval* (Rodez, 1947).

mile or so on the left bank of the river. The place had a bad reputation. It was supposed to be frequented by robbers. Perhaps that was only a legend. But in any case, Bernard was not moved to settle there by any such considerations as were attributed to him by Fastrad in the letter we have mentioned. It was watered by pleasant streams and sheltered from the world and from the weather. Closed off on three sides by hills, it opened south and eastward to catch all the sunlight of the day. Only late in the afternoon, when the sun began to sink behind the western slopes with their ancient oaks, did shadows steal across the simple little abbey built by the pioneers. Up to that moment it had been storing up light and heat all day.

True, not all of Bernard's daughter houses enjoyed the same advantages. When his cousin, Godfrey de la Roche, founded Fontenay, he had to drain the swampy valley and collect its waters into many ponds before building his charming abbey— which was, according to the meaning written into its name, to "swim upon fountains." [13] These valley monasteries developed within the Cistercian Order a beautiful spiritual symbolism by their names alone, eloquent and harmonious names full of poetry and simple mysticism, in which the image of "waters" and "fountains" and "springs" plays a very important part. It was before St. Theresa of Avila wrote her famous allegory of contemplative prayer and the various *aguas* by which the soul is irrigated. This concept is more than traditional: Christ Himself gave His Church that figure of grace and the interior life in His own preaching, as His Spirit had also revealed it before to the prophets. He spoke to the Samaritan woman of the "water that would become a fountain springing up [in the believing soul] to life everlasting" [14] and repeated the figure later, when preaching to the crowds at the feast of Tabernacles. His Evangelist explicitly tells us what He meant: "Now

[13] The beautiful fancy of monks of a later generation led to the inscribing of these words of Genesis over the entrance gate: *Spiritus Dei ferebatur super aquas* ("And the Spirit of God moved over the waters"). Gen. i:2.

[14] John iv:14.

this He said of the Spirit which they should receive, who believed in Him." [15]

Steeped in the language and imagery of Scripture, the Cistercians were acutely alive to the spiritual and poetic possibilities of their surroundings, which they condensed into names like Fountains, Clairvaux ("Clear Valley," or "Valley of Light"), Trois Fontaines ("Three Fountains"), Vauluisant ("Shining Valley"), Aiguebelle (*Aqua Bella*, "Beautiful Water"), Senanque (*Sana Aqua*, "Clean Water"), Clairmarais ("Clear Marsh"), Bonaigue (*Bona Aqua*, "Good Water"), Fontfroide ("Cold-Spring"), Mellifont ("Fount of Honey")— not to mention other such names as La Benisson Dieu ("God's Blessing"), La Grace Dieu ("God's Grace"), Beaulieu, Bonlieu, Bonport, Cherlieu, Rosières, Clairfontaine, and hundreds more, all of them ingenuous yet full of meaning, bearing witness to a deep spiritual ideal.

Surely, there is nothing in these names to indicate any deliberate intention of dying of malaria. . . .

When the monks had found their homes, they not only settled there, for better or for worse, but they sank their roots into the ground and fell in love with their woods. Indeed, this love of one's monastery and its surroundings is something integral to the Cistercian life. It forms the object of a special vow: stability. When the monks of Melleray inscribed over their door *In nidulo meo moriar* ("Let me die in my little nest"), they were expressing something that has been in the heart of every true Cistercian since St. Alberic, whom St. Stephen praised as being a "lover of the brethren and the monastery, the *place*," *amator fratrum et loci*.

It is difficult not to succumb, at least temporarily, to the charm of the typical Cistercian valley. Look at the poem Tintern inspired and what the eighteenth-century English water-colorists got out of Fountains and Bylands and Rievaulx and Jervaulx and Furness and the rest! Or look at Senanque, in the deep Provençal valley, near Petrarch's Vaucluse, where

[15] *Ibid.*, vii:39.

boxbushes and dwarf oak cling to the hillsides among the pale outcrops of rock burnt white and ocher by the gorgeous sun. You will find the same attraction about the monasteries in Kentucky, Utah, New Mexico.

It all adds up to one thing: peace, silence, solitude. The world and its noise are out of sight and far away. Forest and field, sun and wind and sky, earth and water, all speak the same silent language, reminding the monk that he is here to develop like the things that grow all around him: he is planted in the garden of the Lord, *plantatus in domo Domini,* and his existence has now one meaning only: to reach out for the light of truth and the waters of grace, to sink his roots into God and raise his branches into God's good air and breathe heaven and absorb its wonderful rays.

So, from the very outset, even the site of a Cistercian monastery is, or ought to be, a lesson in contemplation. And the monasteries built by the White Monks made it all more explicit.

At this point we are not so much concerned with the architectural beauty and austerity of the twelfth-century Cistercian abbey, except to say that it was not only in keeping with the natural surroundings but largely influenced by them. You cannot put a basilica on the scale of Cluny or Vezelay in a narrow valley or a mountain ravine. Nestling in a wooded hollow between hills, the Cistercian abbey was a structure in low elevation and had no stone tower. Towers were forbidden by the General Chapter in one of the few pieces of explicit legislation on architectural matters.[16]

The monastery conformed to a well-established type and was always a simple, four-sided group of buildings around a cloister garth, dominated by the monastic church with its low belfry generally perched on top of the transept crossing. There was usually a rose window in the façade of the church, another at the end of each transept, and a fourth at the end of the apse if, as was so often the case, it happened to be rectangular. But on the whole, one was struck by the lack of large windows in

[16] *Institutiones* 1240, d I, 2. (*Nomasticon,* p. 287.)

the rough stone walls of the exterior. All around the outside
of the buildings you met a sober, austere bareness, broken up
by small windows arching to rounded tops, as if questioning
the traveler with the simplicity of peasant children. The sun
poured down on the mellow brown tiles of the roofs. The
place was so quiet you wondered at first if it were inhabited,
until you heard the sound of hammering or sawing or some
other work.

Not till you got inside did you realize, suddenly, that the
whole monastery was lighted from within. That is to say, it
was centered upon a quiet pool of pure sunlight and warmth,
the cloister garth. All around this central court, invisible to
anyone outside, the wide bays and handsome open arches of
the cloister allowed the light to pour in upon the broad flagstones of the floor, where monks walked quietly in their hours
of meditation or sat in corners with vellum manuscripts of St.
Augustine or the Old Testament prophets.

For the rest of the buildings, light was no particular problem. In church the monks chanted the offices mostly from
memory, and in any case, the most important of the canonical
hours were sung in the middle of the night. Often the windows
did not open into the nave itself but into the side aisles. The
sanctuary, however, was lighted by a big, simple rose window
or by three or more small arched windows, through which
the morning light poured in upon the altar as the ministers
ascended for the conventual Mass. Since the church was always
orientated, the rays of the rising sun shone into the apse and
shot long spears of light at the monks gathered under the bare
stone arches to sing the hymn of Prime, *Jam lucis orto sidere*.
In most Cistercian churches all the side altars were so arranged
that the priest saying Mass faced the rising sun.

The chapter room opened into the cloister and had some
fair-sized windows of its own. The refectory was sufficiently
lighted by a few high windows. The only person who really
needed a good light in the refectory was the monk appointed
to read aloud to his brothers. He usually sat in a lectern built

into the wall and reached by a flight of steps let into the wall itself, and lighted by its own little window. Light was not important in the warming room. This was where the monks were allowed to gather around the only fire accessible to them in cold weather, although they could not stay there for any length of time or read books there. Still less were large windows needed in the dormitory; here, the high stone ceiling gave the monks a cool and pleasant gloom for the midday siesta so necessary in summer, when they had longer hours of work and less nighttime sleep.

Everything in the monastery was centered on the cloister and dominated by the church. It was in the church that the monks prayed, in the cloister that they lived. The cloister was, in a certain sense, the most important of all. It was the meeting place of all the different elements of the monk's life, the clearinghouse where he passed from material to spiritual things and settled down for the moments of transition between work and prayer, prayer and work.

He came in from the fields, took off his wooden *sabots*, and sat under the sunny arches to read and meditate while the tension induced by activity seeped out of his muscles and while his mind retired from exterior things into the peaceful realms of thought and prayer. Then, with this preparation, he passed into the dark church, and his mind and will sank below the level of thoughts and concepts and sought God in the deepest center of the monk's own being as the choir began to chant, with closed eyes, the solemn, eternal measures of the liturgy.

When the monk returned from the inscrutable abyss of a contemplation which he himself could scarcely fathom, he emerged once more to the cloister, to sit or walk silently under those sunny arches or in the open garth itself, while the fruit of his prayer expanded in him and worked through his whole being like oil in a woolen fabric, steeping everything with its richness and life.

Yet, we must not think of the cloister as something altogether esoteric, a place filled with the same kind of sacrosanct hush you expect in a museum. It was a place where men *lived*. And the monks were a family. The cloister was not exempt from the noises of a society that was at the same time monastic and rustic. The young monks might practice difficult passages of chant that they had not yet mastered by heart. Others might be engaged in their laundry (for each monk washed his own clothes) or in repairing their shoes. Others might take it into their heads to bring their blankets down from the dormitory and beat the dust out of them. So, although they did not speak, the monks had to know how to be contemplatives in a busy and not altogether noiseless milieu.

The monk's life was lived on three different levels. On each, there was the common element of constant prayer, constant union with God by the simple intention of love and faith that sought Him in all things: but apart from that, the three levels were characterized, respectively, by the predominance of *bodily* activity out at work; of *mental* activity in the readings and meditations of the cloister, and *spiritual* and *affective* activity in the church. If the monk happened, also, to have the grace of infused contemplation, he would be able at times to rise above all these levels and all these activities to a pure contact with God above all activity. But ordinarily speaking, even the contemplative monk lives and loves and therefore *acts* on these three levels.

Now, the cloister was the scene of the monk's most characteristically human mode of being. It was there that he met God and his brothers as a social and thinking and affective and perhaps affectionate creature: St. Ailred testified that the bond between brothers might be expected to be warmed by a glow of genuine and holy fondness. But in any case, all these elements made the cloister the place where the monk was most truly on his own level as a human being. That was why it was the solvent, the common denominator, of everything else in his monastic life.

The cloister was his base of operations. It was from the level appropriate to the cloister that he set out on his flights into the areas above and beyond his nature, in church and liturgy. It was also from there that he went forth to the realms in which he commanded natures lower than himself and, by the work of his hands, diverted the things of the woods and the fields to the material uses of his brethren.

So, the Cistercian monastery became the perfect picture of the soul of the contemplative. Perhaps it was because the Cistercians were such refined psychologists [17] that they could not help building themselves houses that reflected all the interests that most intimately concerned their own hearts. But the cloister, with its adjacent chapter room, symbolized the soul operating in its own human mode by a free play of the reasoning intellect and the affective will—making practical and speculative judgments and carrying them out in the light of reason and grace—always drawing strength and meriting fresh grace from the operation of the social and Christian virtues so necessary in the monastic community.

Firmly established in peace and harmony within himself, when all the powers of his soul are united by grace and virtue, the contemplative receives into his soul, into his intellect and will, the choice graces of God's light and love.

Under the impulsion of these forces within him, he can go out of his cloister into the exterior world and do his share of the world's activities, performing good works for Christ and the Church and enriching himself still more with the fruits of his activity.

But he does not stay active all day. Outside his cloister, he has no place to rest; he is only a wanderer, and soon he returns

---

[17] The Cistercians were fond of treatises *De Anima*, which were, at the same time, tracts in mystical theology, or the psychology of mysticism. It has been remarked that St. Bernard's *De Gratia et Libero Arbitrio* was in reality a *De Anima*, and it is certain that it lays the foundations for a psychology of contemplation. But all St. Bernard's works do that. This was one of his predominant interests.

to the peace of recollection, where he is again flooded by the light of God's grace.

This time, however, he is drawn further within and above himself. He passes from the cloister of his active faculties to the church—or innermost substance—of his soul—which the Cistercians called the *memoria*. By that word, they did not mean memory. It was the term they had inherited from St. Augustine to describe the very essence of the soul considered as the *actus primus* from which the faculties emanate and pass into action.

It is by the activity of our mind and will that we know and love: it is in the cloister that the monk finds his sunlight and companionship and books. But above activity, in the dark church of the *memoria* where there is no explicit thought, and where acts of the will are mute as in the depths of their ultimate causes, the soul meets God in the ineffable darkness of an immediate contact that transcends every activity, every intuition, every flame of virtue or love. Not that love and intellection have here ceased, but they have been drawn up to a level so transcendently simple that the soul acts without knowing that it acts, and loves and knows all at once in a movement so pure and so free of all expense of human energy that it seems not to be acting or knowing or loving at all.

It is in the inner sanctuary of the spirit that the monk achieves the supreme purpose of his whole life and really fulfils his vocation—by union with God in perfectly pure and disinterested love that seeks no reward, because God Himself is its reward; the soul now loves God with His own love of Himself.

But just as the monk could not enter his church except by passing through the cloister, so the ordinary preparation for perfect union with God was the exercise of his faculties in the knowledge and love of God and his brethren, in which are included all virtues. *Plenitudo legis est dilectio.*

The Cistercian fathers looked upon the monastery as a

school in which men acquired the supreme art that transcends all others, the art of love, *ars artium, ars amoris*.[18]

The cloister and chapter room, centers of the community life, as such, were also properly the school where charity was learned by humility, obedience, and brotherly love. Here, the monk was taught by other men, the abbot, the novice master, and the example of all his brethren. But nothing he could learn from them would be anything but a preparation for the real knowledge of God (Who is Himself substantial love) taught by experience in a union with Him consummated in the very substance of the soul by His own Holy Spirit.

Everything in the Cistercian life, every detail of the Rule of St. Benedict, was ordered and interpreted and understood in relation to that one end: perfect union with God.[19]

This explains the austerity which banished sculpture and painting and stained glass and mosaic from the Cistercian abbey: the monk must not only be stripped of all right to own rich and beautiful and precious things, but his mind and imagination must be delivered from all attachment to, and dependence upon, the means that led to God by a less direct road. Only the Crucifix remained for him to fix his eyes upon, if he could not close them and find God in the depths of his heart. All the rest was proscribed with a severity that nevertheless had its point. The General Chapter explained the reason for the ban on pictures and statues and stained glass in any part of the monastery by remarking that they often interfered with the profit of a good meditation: *Dum talibus intenditur utilitas bonae meditationis vel disciplina religiosae gravitatis saepe negligitur.*[20]

The White Monks were applying principles that have also

---

[18] William of St. Thierry, *De Natura et Dignitate Amoris*, I, i. On the cloister as school of charity, see also Gilson, *Mystical Theology of St. Bernard*, pp. 60 ff., 200.

[19] *Ausculta o fili precepta magistri . . . ut ad eum per obedientiae laborem redeas, a quo per inobedientiae desidiam recesseras. . . . Rule*, Prologue.

[20] *Statuta*, 1134, No. xx.

been made famous by St. John of the Cross. The Spanish Carmelite, like St. Bernard of Clairvaux, admitted the usefulness and even necessity of sensible means to awaken the spiritual life in beginners and even certain advanced souls, but he declared that, for those who wanted to progress in the ways of mystical prayer, the time would come when God would demand the sacrifice even of one's own interior fancies and images and concepts and memories:

> Since no created things can bear any proportion to the being of God . . . nothing that is imagined in their likeness can serve as a means of *proximate union with Him,* but quite the contrary. All these imaginings must be cast out from the soul, which must remain in darkness as far as this sense is concerned in order to attain to divine union.
>
> In order that one may attain supernatural transformation it is clear that he must be set in darkness and carried far away from all that is contained in his nature, which is sensual and rational . . . The soul must be like to a blind man leaning upon dark faith and taking it for a guide and leaning upon none of the things which he understands, experiences, feels and imagines. For all these are darkness and will cause him to stray; and faith is above all that he understands and experiences, feels and imagines.
>
> And thus a soul is greatly impeded from reaching this high estate of union with God when it clings to any understanding or feeling or imagination or appearance or will of its own.[21]

It was simply an extension of the monk's flight from the world. The need to build a monastery in physical solitude was supplemented by the much more fundamental need for interior solitude and exspoliation. Hence, too, the need for silence, for humility, for fasting, for subjection to superiors: all this was to help the monk to divest himself of every selfish desire, every shred of human attachment, because he knew that, once he was empty of self-love, he would be filled with the love of God.

[21] St. John of the Cross, *Ascent of Mount Carmel,* II, 12 and II, 3.

Thus every human affection in the saints must, in an ineffable way, melt away from itself and flow over entirely into the will of God. Otherwise how is God to be all in all if in man there remain something that is still man? [22]

We have been speaking of the cloister. Certainly it was a rugged life the monks led, under those stone arches open to all winds. That was their place of rest and reading and meditation in winter as well as in summer. True, it was the north side of the cloister, opening to the noonday sun, that was the usual place of reading. It was here that the books were kept in their *armarium*. It was also the most convenient place for prayer, for the church door was close at hand, and if one were moved to lay aside the book and enter into the silence of contemplative prayer, one could slip into the dark sanctuary—provided the book was left outside.

Remember, too, that the Cistercians had monasteries in Norway and Sweden and Denmark, not to mention the Highlands of Scotland, the Alps, the Carpathians, the Apennines. However, the usages explicitly allowed them to wear several robes and both their cowls in cold weather.[23]

They had longer labor and longer fasts than the Cistercians have today. The ordinary workday in Lent began with several consecutive hours of reading and study after Prime, but the community went out to work in the fields, still fasting, about half-past nine in the forenoon, and worked until the tenth hour, which came late in the afternoon, about four or half-past four. Only then did they return home and sing Vespers and

[22] *Sic omnem in sanctis humanam affectionem quodam ineffabili modo necesse est a semetipsa liquescere atque in Dei penitus transfundi voluntatem. Alioquin quomodo omnia in omnibus erit Deus si in homine de homine quidquam supererit?* St. Bernard, *De Diligendo Deo*, x, No. 28.

[23] *Monacho in hyeme tribus tunicis induto liceat scapulare superinduere non tamen sine duabus cucullis. Consuetudines*, lxxiv. Guignard, p. 176. The scapular was worn at work only in the twelfth century, and that is why it was permitted only with all these qualifications, as a last resort, when the monk had already exhausted the rest of his wardrobe trying to keep warm.

take their single meal of the day. By the time they rose from table in the refectory and made their way to church through the cloister, chanting the *Miserere*, the shadows of twilight were enveloping the gray walls and tile roof of their monastery, and the setting sun was withdrawing the little light that still touched the tops of the hills or the crowns of the budding trees. In a moment it would be time for Compline, and the community would retire to their straw mattresses. However, once they were there, they might perhaps get a longer sleep than the Trappist does today. It varied with the time of sunset, because they were in bed half an hour or so after the sun was down and rose at the eighth hour of the night. That granted them, in the wintertime, at least eight hours' sleep; but in summer, sunset was much later and "hours" were much shorter.[24]

We who live in an age that has developed so many accurate instruments for measuring out all man's activities into exact periods of time and calculating the precise money value of every piece of work done and measuring the calories we consume and the vitamins we need, would find it hard to live by the easy and natural approximations of the Middle Ages. In a Cistercian abbey of the twelfth century the absence of the clocks and machinery and instruments and devices to which we have become conditioned gave the life of the monks a completely different tempo from ours. Their days had their own vital rhythm, something quite different from our own days—even where a modern monastery strives to keep the same Rule as the one they lived by.

The ordered sequence of prayer and work and reading and eating and sleeping into which the monastic day is divided could not be made to depend on any instrument. It followed the sun, the moon, the stars. It was integrated not into some

[24] The monks reckoned time according to the Roman system. The day was divided into twelve equal "hours" from sunrise to sunset, and the night was also divided into twelve hours from sunset to sunrise. Hence, in winter the twelve hours of night were much longer, and in summer it was the other way round.

abstract and mathematical norm of time but into the earth's actual journey around the sun.

Therefore, the rhythm of the monk's existence was something free and natural and organic. It was attuned to the waxing and waning seasons. It followed the sun's course along the ecliptic. It knew the same free moods of expansion and contraction that made the sap swell in the trees or the leaves fall from their branches.

Monastic historians have not given an altogether satisfactory answer to the question of just how the monks managed to get up at the eighth hour of every night, when the eighth hour fell each night at a different time. Perhaps the bell ringer or the abbot had developed some sixth sense that told him when to crawl out of his blankets and wake the brethren. Perhaps the first cockcrow, which is supposed to come a little after midnight, gave the necessary alarm. But in any case, the Rule provided for the accident of a late rising: the cantor would shorten the night office by cutting some of the "lessons" (*lectiones*) read aloud at each nocturn. And the bell ringer would do a suitable penance.

The night hours from about two o'clock (according to our modern reckoning) until daybreak were devoted to liturgical prayer. The hymns of the office attuned the monk's spiritual consciousness to the darkness around him and to the peril it symbolized. The stone vaulting of the church was lost in shadows. Only one small light flickered before some altar or near the ambo, where the lectionary lay open. The monks themselves were scarcely visible in the gloom. Sometimes the abbot went around the choir with a lantern to make sure that no one had fallen asleep.

And in that darkness the full, slow measures of the psalmody rose and fell with even cadences, each verse broken at the mediant by the long, significant pause which was typical of the Cistercian office. Between every pair of psalms the spell woven by the monotonous cadences was broken and a voice intoned the antiphon. With a momentary dash of color and flame this brief cry of melody was taken up by all those hidden voices, only to sink again into the austere monotony of the next psalm.

On most days of the year the canonical office was followed by the singing of the office of the dead. The choir broke up toward the end of the tenth hour of night for a period of reading, only to return for another office, Lauds, in which a new note of hope anticipated the coming of their Christ, their rising sun.

Sunrise, of course, changed the whole temper of the office and of the monk's day.[25] Now the chanting of the canonical hours went more quickly. Only three psalms were appointed for each hour. The hymn *Jam lucis orto sidere* hailed the risen sun, and those who were praying the office, roused from deep meditation on eternal truths, looked outward to the fields and workshops and begged God to send grace for the day's work. And soon the monks were on their way to the woods and pastures.

In all seasons of the year one or another of the day hours would be chanted in the fields by all those who were not working within easy reach of the church. Usually it was the midday hour of Sext (about noon), but in times of special work, such as harvesting, vintage, sheepshearing, Tierce and None might also be sung in the fields.

The monks could tell by the sun when it was near the time for Sext. When the bell was heard ringing in the distant abbey church, the heads of the various work groups would give the signal, and their helpers would gather together and begin chanting, after the usual silent prayers, standing in two choirs among the wheat sheaves or in the rows of vines, with their grape baskets resting in the shadow of the leaves; or if working in the olive groves, they would pray beneath the silver

[25] The bell for Prime was rung at daybreak. *Apparente die pulsetur signum*, etc. *Consuetudines*, lxxiv. The Carthusians of La Grande Chartreuse knew the time for certain exercises by the way the sun struck the tops of the mountains in the various seasons of the year.

foliage, bowing in their gray robes, their hard, brown hands on their knees.

Those who were working within the enclosure, splitting wood or digging in the garden, pruning fruit trees or copying manuscripts, tanning hides or making cheese, would gather in choir. If they were caught in the fields at the hour of None, they had the chance to sing these words: "Because thou shalt eat the labors of thy hands, blessed art thou, and it shall be well with thee." [26]

Meanwhile, toward the middle of the morning work the cooks had presented themselves to the prior and received his permission to leave the fields or the orchards or wherever they were working and return to the monastery. There, they washed up and began to prepare dinner for the community, after having broken their own fast with a chunk of black bread and a cup of wine.

The monks came in a few hours later and sang another hour of the office. Then, if the dinner was not yet ready, they sat down to read in the cloister. They had to be prepared for any kind of emergency in this matter, because all the monks took turns at cooking, and one could generally tell when the community would have to wait half an hour overtime for their food, or when the soup would be burned.

Once they were in the refectory, things were not rigidly systematic. Although perfect silence had to be observed, no one was allowed to walk about the room eating, and there were a few little points of monastic etiquette to be observed. It was not unlikely that the cellarer might come and put some extra portion before you—a wedge of cheese or some eggs or fruit. You were certain to receive an extra portion if you had been bled by the surgeon or had some other weakness or ailment, or if a feast day.

In the summertime the monks rested in the dormitory for

---

[26] Ps. 127:2. *Labores manuum tuarum quia manducabis beatus es, et bene tibi erit.*

an hour, or an hour and a half, while the sun was at its height. They would keep their own rakes and pitchforks by their bedside, for in harvest time the monks did not hand in their tools after work. If the work was heavy or far afield, the monks might take their dinner in the country and sleep out their siesta under the trees at the edge of a wheat field or under the roof of one of their granges. Sometimes they even spent two or three days away from the monastery, staying at a grange. If there was a chance of returning home the same day, they might sing Vespers in the fields, although this was very unusual. If they were obliged to stay at a grange, they found simple but clean quarters—a dormitory, refectory, and chapel. If they were there over a Sunday or feast day, they spent the day in reading, meditation, and prayer, as they would have done in the cloister. The usages insisted on the usual strict silence at the grange and restricted the use of sign language. Also, the monks were not allowed to wander off into the woods by themselves.

In summer and winter the monks' day ended with the setting sun, and they went to bed a little after dark had fallen. However, before they retired, St. Benedict wanted all the various activities of the monastery to fold themselves back into a single unit. He wanted to gather his family together for the night. Perhaps it was again a spontaneous, unconscious reflection of the way the contemplative collects his faculties before entering into the darkness of his wordless prayer. But in any case, while the last rays of the sun still slanted down over the wooded hills and across the monastery, the monks and brothers gathered in the cloister, and one of their number read aloud to the whole family. This was called "collation," because St. Benedict had suggested that, among other works, Cassian's *Collationes* (*Conferences*) would be the most appropriate book for this time.[27]

----

[27] . . . *sedeant omnes in uno loco et legat unus collationes vel vitas Patrum*. . . . *Rule*, chap. 43.

As the light gradually waned, they listened to the last songs of the birds under the eaves and in the forest, punctuating the pauses in the reader's voice, while swallows flew about the garth and the belfry in the dusk. Finally, the abbot gave the signal to rise, and after a brief prayer they filed into the church, not to begin the office of Compline but only to conclude it: for that reading was a regular part of the office.[28]

The day finally ended with the murmur of corporate prayer pulsing through the shadows of the dark church, until the monks, blessed by their abbot in the shadows of the transept, ascended the steps that led directly from the church to the communal dormitory.

Nothing could be simpler than such a life. Yet it was never monotonous—any more than the seasons are monotonous, or the development of growing things. It was an austere life, without being rigid. There was enough sane latitude to keep formalism out of it, and it was so close to the earth and so bound up with nature that it had to be rich in spontaneity. It had to be genuine. And anyone who really gave himself to the Rule and to the prayer and labor and poverty and obedience it demanded, found himself deepened and broadened and matured more than he had ever dreamed possible. Without burdening himself with systems and rigid sets of pious practices, but simply by laboring and chanting the praises of God—and by reading the Scriptures and living in harmony with his brethren—and by taking the fasting and the heat and the cold and the poverty as they came from day to day—the monk grew and became strong in spirit and found his way, without realizing it, into the pure atmosphere of sanctity.

However, this could not be accomplished merely by the material and natural organization imposed upon the monks' life by the Rule. There was needed a special, formal element

[28] The short lesson from St. Peter in Compline in the Roman breviary is a vestige of this practice. The idea was to put some spiritual thoughts into the mind of the monk or priest after the business of the day, to prepare him for his night prayers.

of spirituality to draw all these material elements together and give them a higher life. And though the Cistercians would have been completely perplexed at the notion of inventing or devising a new system of spirituality or discovering a new way to God, they did, nevertheless, have a distinctive spirituality of their own. There was nothing in it of special method or new technique. It was simply St. Benedict and the Gospel over again: but in the Cistercian monasteries of the twelfth century, Benedictine simplicity was invested with a special vitality and purity and charm.

The result of this was that the Cistercians, without consciously intending anything of the sort, came upon a new and peculiarly delightful region of the spiritual life that was all their own. To attempt an explanation of how that came about would be the subject for a fascinating book all by itself. But it was the fruit of a Providential combination of natural and supernatural elements: the Gospel, the Rule of St. Benedict, the ferment of the twelfth-century renaissance, the woods of France and England and Belgium and Germany, the ardent and poetic souls of a Bernard of Clairvaux, an Ailred of Rievaulx, a William of St. Thierry, a Guerric, an Adam of Perseigne, an Isaac of Stella, a Baldwin of Ford. . . . But above all, the special grace of the Spirit of God was there, forming souls in these hidden monasteries to a life of charity and deep contemplation.

It was the Holy Ghost Who infused into these monks a special fire of inspiration which tempered with love the tremendous austerity of their reform. It was the Spirit of God, God's own love, that sweetened their sufferings with an indefinably powerful unction and raised them above the level of penitential drudgery and routine and formalism. And it was God's love that opened their eyes to new horizons in the interior life and replaced the gloom of the hardened ascetic with the serene, unbounded confidence of the mystic who dares to aspire to the possession of God and who, with impetu-

ous and unconquerable desires, cries out for the embrace of
His love and will not be denied.

It was the Holy Ghost Who taught these saints the one
magnificent truth that so many austere penitents had seemed
to forget: that if we love God, it is because God has first
loved us more, and that God has created us not so much to
fear Him and honor Him and worship Him, as to love Him,
since love is the perfection of all adoration and homage.
God would rather have us love Him than merely fear Him,
because fear keeps us far below Him, while love alone can
make us His equal. The Cistercians never grew tired of asserting it over and over again. Love makes man equal to God,
and God wants us to love Him in order that we may be equal
to Him and share His nature and all His infinite goodness and
joy. God wants us to love Him beyond measure, because then
He can give Himself to us beyond measure and our joy will
then know no measure, but will go on expanding inexhaustibly
forever as we lose ourselves more and more in the interminable
substance of Him Who is love. We are perfectly ourselves
only when we have lost ourselves in this pure love of God
for His own sake; and God calls us to Him in order to transform us into love. And when our whole life and being is nothing but a perfect act of love, we have become what God is,
and we share His ineffable joy—the joy of pouring ourselves
out and of giving ourselves without end. And the more we
give ourselves to Him, the more He gives Himself to us in
return. The exchange goes on forever, and the wonder of it
and the exultation increase without limit, for everything that
the soul has is given to God, and all that is God is given to the
soul: *quippe quibus omnia communia sunt, nil proprium, nil a
se divisum habentes.*[29] And so, God's love, flowing through the
soul, returns in the soul's love of God to its own principle, its
own fount, from which it never ceases to flow back into the
soul. *Magna res amor, si tamen ad suum recurrat principium,*

[29] St. Bernard, *In Cant.*, vii, No. 2.

si refusus suo fonti semper ex eo sumat unde jugiter fluat.[30]

God loves us that we may learn to love Him for love's sake, because He knows that pure love is the most perfect beatitude, and that is what He wants to share with us. *Nam cum amat Deus, non vult aliud quam amari: quippe non ad aliud amat nisi ut ametur, sciens ipso amore beatos qui se amaverint.*[31]

If contemplation and the pure love of God became the explicit end of the monastic life in the mind of St. Bernard and his school, the spirituality of the Cistercians was also characterized by certain particular means to this end. And this is the triumph for which St. Bernard is best known.

There were men of all kinds coming to Clairvaux and to the hundreds of monasteries of White Monks that sprang up all over Europe: men like the ones who alarmed William of St. Thierry by bringing the works of Abélard and William of Conches into the novitiate at Signy, and others like the unlettered knights who asked to be admitted to Clairvaux after an overnight visit. There were mature monks from Cluniac monasteries and young men, like Bernard's brother Nivard, who had little spiritual formation. There were intellectuals and soldiers, theologians and farmers, clerks and merchants and courtiers and serfs. But meditation and the ways of the interior life were laid open to them all by a method that transcended every method and obviated all difficulties and all intricacies from the very start.

There was nothing involved about it. You came to the monastery to learn, or rather to relearn, the love whose seeds were implanted in your very nature. And the best way to do this was to open the eyes of faith and gaze upon the perfect embodiment of God's love for men: Christ on the Cross.

Christ was the center of the Rule of St. Benedict. Christ had drawn St. Pachomius into the desert. Christ was with St. Anthony in the Thebaid.[32] The love of Christ is the center of

[30] *Ibid.*, lxxxiii, No. 4.   [31] *Ibid.*

[32] *Vita Pachomii*, v-vi, P. L. 73, 233. St. Athanasius, *Vita S. Antonii*, ix, P. L. 73, 132.

all Christian mysticism. Obviously it must be so, for that is
what the word Christian means. Nevertheless, it is true to say
that St. Bernard transformed and, in some sense, transfigured
Christian spirituality by filling it with that lyrical love of
Christ and His Virgin Mother which pervades the whole
Middle Ages. It is true that St. Bernard and his Cistercians
rediscovered that love of the Savior which had put such fire
into the Gospel of St. John and the Epistles of St. Paul. They
realized how close Christ is to us, not only as God but as Man,
and they were able to grasp the full meaning of the truth
that "no one comes to the Father but by Him." [33] They understood that God wanted to draw all men to Himself through
His Incarnate Word, through Jesus, the Son of Mary. *Nemo*
potest venire ad me nisi Pater qui misit me traxerit eum.[34] They
knew that all blessedness, eternal life, was to be found in the
knowledge of "the one true God and Jesus Christ Whom Thou
hast sent." [35] And they saw that in Christ alone was the gate to
all true spirituality, to all true mysticism. "Whosoever denieth
the Son, the same hath not the Father. He that confesseth the
Son hath the Father also." [36] *Qui videt me videt et Patrem.*[37]

That was why St. Bernard based all his teaching on that one
foundation, the love of Christ. He saw that Christ was the key
to everything that mattered in the universe: for all created
things, by their goodness and order and beauty, awake in our
hearts the love for the God Who made them and make us
obscurely desire the possession of Him. But that joy would
be forever impossible unless Christ were sent to take us back
to God and to teach us the way to love God by showing us
how God really loved us. Above all, it is only through the
merits of Christ's death on the Cross that we can obtain the
grace to rise above our own selfishness to the pure and selfless

[33] *Dixit eis Jesus: Ego sum via veritas et vita. Nemo venit ad Patrem*
nisi per me. John xiv:6.
[34] John vi:44.
[35] *Ibid.,* xvii:3.
[36] I John ii:22.
[37] John xiv:5.

love of God for His own sake, which is the very essence of mysticism for the Cistercians. And so, St. Bernard exclaims:

Great must be my love for Him through Whom I have existence, life and wisdom. If I am ungrateful to Him, then I am unworthy of Him. Worthy indeed of death is the man who will not live for Thee, Lord Jesus, and he is, in fact, already dead. And the man who has no sense of Who Thou art, is senseless. And the one who desires to live for anything else but Thee is living for nothing and is, himself, nothing. For after all, what is man, if he has no knowledge of Thee? [38]

St. Bernard was impatient of the dialectical wrangling that kept the great logicians and humanists of his day so busy with technicalities and abstractions that they forgot to live. The abbot of Clairvaux—who was himself one of the great intellectuals of the twelfth century—knew that the true perfection of the intellect did not lie there: these interminable analyses of the words and terms and the outer surface of revelation were only a blind alley; if the professors thought they could arrive at the full possession of truth by their debates, they ran the risk of getting nowhere.

God has not revealed Himself to us in Scripture and tradition in order that we may spend our lives haggling about the prepositions and conjunctions in the different manuscripts through which the deposit of faith came down to us. The Letter of Scripture must be studied and understood: but the content of revelation will not be exhausted when we have argued out all its terms and propositions to suit our own reason. To expect any such satisfaction would be hopeless from the start.

And so, St. Bernard taught his monks to read Scripture and the Fathers with an altogether different spirit. Searching the sacred text with the eyes of faith rather than with those of scholarship, they filled their minds and memories with the mysteries in the life of Jesus and with the prophecies and types

[38] *In Cant.*, xx, No. 1.

of Christ in the Old Testament. Then, in the silence of deep and humble meditation they sought to penetrate the surface and slake their thirst at the springs of living water which only God could lay open to them.

God, in His turn, seeing the soul's desire to know Him, and seeing its recognition of its helplessness to penetrate the mysteries which transcend its natural powers, rewards its love and faith by the gift of understanding. The light infused into the mind by the Holy Spirit, together with love that inflames the will, opens up deep and penetrating insights into the mysteries of God, until suddenly the soul becomes aware that God has made Himself present to the eyes of the mind in a manner that baffles all description and can only be understood by those who have tasted the experience.

St. Bernard tells us that this presence of God has nothing in it of an imaginary vision, nothing in it that appeals to sense or to mere emotion. *Vide tu ne quid nos in hac Verbi animaeque commixtione corporeum seu imaginatorium sentire existimes.* And he goes on to give a classical description of the way the Word is present to the soul in mystical experience:

Not in any figure, but infused into the soul: the Word is apprehended not under any outward appearance but by His effect. . . . He is a Word that does not sound in the ear but penetrates the mind; He does not speak, He acts; He does not make Himself heard in the senses but in the desires of the will. His face has not a visible form, but impresses a form upon the soul; it does not strike the eyes of the body but fills the heart with joy.[39]

The secret of Cistercian spirituality was simply to seek the perfect possession of God through the love of Christ: a love that expressed itself in the search to know Jesus in His mysteries and in all Scripture, and in the ardent desire to serve

[39] (*Verbum*) *non figuratum sed infusum; non apparentem sed afficientem; . . . Verbum nempe est non sonans sed penetrans; non loquax sed efficax; non obstrepens auribus sed affectibus blandiens. Facies est non formata sed formans; non perstringens oculos corporis, sed faciem cordis laetificans. In Cant., xxxi, No. 6.*

Him by the perfect observance of the Rule of St. Benedict. *Qui habet mandata mea et servat ea, ille est qui diligit me.*[40]

But it would be an error to think that, for St. Bernard, the whole contemplative life was summed up in the love of Christ *as Man*. This is only the beginning. It has a definite purpose: to prepare us for the infused and experimental knowledge of Christ in His Divinity as it has just been described. The importance of devotion to the Humanity of Jesus in Cistercian spirituality is that the White Monks considered it the simplest and most effective preparation for infused contemplation.

This is the point where a superficial study of the Cistercian spirit will generally go off the rails. As soon as we begin to talk about devotion to the Humanity of Jesus, we think of all the books of meditations and all the devotions and all the pious art that abound in our time, and we unconsciously assume that St. Bernard was thinking of all this when he urged his monks to cultivate an ardent love for Christ. Yet, we have already seen how rigorously all such means were banned from the Cistercian abbey church. The monks were not allowed to use books of devotion or even to meditate from books in church; they had no pictures to look at; they had their "devotions" but these were simple and unadorned, unlike those of our own day. There was not even a time prescribed for formal meditation. Yet, to tell the truth, there has never been such rich and vital and perfect interior life in Cistercian monasteries as there was in the twelfth century—the age of the great Cistercian saints and of the purest Cistercian mysticism. How did they manage to nourish their interior life under such conditions?

The answer is simple. The whole harmonious structure of regular observances, the monastic life we have been discussing, the simple round of prayer and labor and reading, the life of the cloistered cenobite, far from the activities of the world, close to nature and with God in solitude—all this was satu-

[40] He that hath My commandments and keepeth them, he it is that loveth Me. John xiv:21.

rated in Scripture and in the liturgy. In fact, the liturgy elevated and transformed every department of the monk's existence, penetrated to every recess of the monastery, and incorporated all the monk's activities into a vital and organic whole that was charged with spiritual significance. The monk lived by the sun and the moon and the seasons, granted: but all nature was elevated and made sacred by the liturgy, which gathered up all the monk's acts and all his experience, ordering and offering everything to God.

Perhaps, at first sight, that may look complicated: but it was really extraordinarily simple. The liturgy, far from complicating life with ritualistic functions, had been purified by the Cistercians and stripped down to its primitive essentials and was therefore doing the work it had done in the days when St. Benedict wrote his Rule. Nothing was plainer and at the same time richer than the liturgy of primitive Cîteaux, in which, stripped of all conflicting elements, the temporal cycle of the Church's year dominated all.

In other words, the Cistercian really worked his way through the liturgy of the fundamental seasons—Advent, Christmas, Septuagesima, Lent, Easter, and post-Pentecostal—in all their fulness. The mighty lessons taught by the Church in every Nocturn and every Mass had a chance to work themselves right into the blood and marrow of the monk's existence. In Advent he virtually lived and breathed Isaias. The words, which he knew by heart, sang themselves over and over in his mind and soaked themselves into the landscape of the season and its weather and its every aspect, so that when December came around, the very fields and bare woods began to sing the *Conditor alme siderum* and the great responsories of the night offices. In the snows of January, the triumphant antiphons of Christmas or the mysteriously beautiful responsories of the Epiphany followed the monk to the bare forest. Later, the office *Domine ne in ira* began to echo through his mind and prepare him for the austere and somber cycle of offices that would go from Septuagesima to Passion Sunday and Holy Week in an ever-increasing seriousness and dramatic power until the final anguished *katharsis* of Good Friday.

Then suddenly the dazzling joy of the Easter liturgy and its incomparable lightness and relief and triumph led the monk into spring, and the budding woods and the songs of the birds and the smell of flowers and the first green blades of the coming harvest filled the sunlight with silent *alleluias:* and on to another climax of confidence and vision and peace at the Ascension. Then Pentecost gave the whole interior life of the monk a new direction, and he entered the summer and the long series of Sundays that discussed, in poetry and music, every phase of Christ's public life and teachings, while in the night offices he chanted his way through the Books of Kings. In August he was in the Books of Wisdom; in September, Job and Tobias; in October, the Books of the Machabees, and in November, Ezechiel and Daniel.

The liturgical cycle took the monk through all Scripture, all the Old and New Testaments, with commentaries and explanations by the greatest of the Fathers, all of it chanted and prayed and absorbed and literally *lived*. The attitude of the Cistercians toward all this is doubly clear when we reflect that the books of the Bible sung in the church were also, at the same time, read in their entirety in the refectory during the same season.

In this way not only did the monk live in the midst of nature and the joys and beauties of the woods and mountains, but his whole life was steeped, besides, in perfect poetry and music, and his mind was filled with fascinating stories and images and symbols and pictures. He moved and breathed in the spiritual world of the prophets and patriarchs. He was familiar with Gedeon and Joshua and Moses and Aaron and Elias and Jeremias. He lamented with Job and he praised God with Daniel and he saw the heavens open in the wild, brilliant theophanies of Isaias and Ezechiel.

The Vulgate became so much a part of the monk's mind, that he could not help thinking in its language and seeing things in the light of its symbols and images, and gradually the whole universe became impregnated with the poetry and the meaning of Scripture. And this was all the more simple and easy because there was nothing else to get in the way. The monk had no other interests. All his other reading revolved around Scripture, because the monks read nothing that was not more or less a commentary on the Vulgate.

The influence of this kind of interior life is obvious the moment anyone reads a page of St. Bernard or St. Ailred. Bernard, especially, is a poet after the manner of Isaias (although his best poetry is all prose), for his language is full of the vegetal exuberance of the great prophet of the Incarnation. So fresh and rich and ingenuous and outspoken is the style of the abbot of Clairvaux that one wishes his sermons on the *Canticles* had been illustrated by Eric Gill.

Such is the atmosphere of all Cistercian spirituality: and it is incomparable.

The Cistercians transfigured the Old Testament with their one great obsession, the love of Christ. For it was precisely this that was their "method" of arriving at Christ and of keeping in touch with him. They did not have any systematic meditations on Christ—still less, scientific or psychological histories of Christ's life. But they developed the habit of seeing Christ in every page of the Bible, whether of the Old Testament or of the New. And carrying the substance of the Vulgate in their memories, they went about everywhere with an inexhaustible mine of material in which their faith found Christ under every symbol and every allegory and every image; all spoke to them of the union of the contemplative soul with the Word of God by pure love. What is more, the monks' simple faith and ardent desire often bore fruit in the one thing they longed for: the ineffable "touch" of the Divine Substance meeting the depth of their own being in the direct contact of mystical love, and filling their very substance with wisdom and with peace.

Infused contemplation was the end to which all this simple

and harmonious interplay of liturgy and prayer and reading and sacrifice and poverty and labor and common life was directed. Mystical prayer was the fullest expression of the Cistercian life: the end to which all were encouraged to aspire, although it was to be expected that not all, perhaps not even a majority, would reach it. If they did not taste the perfection of that experience on earth, that did not matter. What was important was to love God's will and live to do His will and contribute as best one could to His glory by the perfection of obedience and humility.

But the final result of this combination—a hundred or two hundred monks and brothers living out this existence in all its ramifications—was that for a few score of years and in a score of the most truly Cistercian of the Cistercian abbeys, the contemplative life was lived, and lived in community, with a simplicity and completeness and a perfection that had scarcely been known in the world since the days of the Apostles.

This still constitutes the peculiar function of the White Monks in the Church: to contemplate God as perfectly as it can be done by men living in common, to contemplate God day and night, winter and summer, all the year round, not merely as individuals in a community but precisely as a community.

And that is the Cistercian vocation.

XIII. THE CISTERCIAN
CHARACTER AND SANCTITY

THE Cistercian life of the twelfth century was a seamless garment, a perfect unity, whole and complete. It lacked nothing, and it was of a single piece. It was simple and it was total, and the whole integrated unit gave God the perfect praise He looks for from men living together on the face of His earth.

By the time the seventeenth century came around, that garment had been torn into many pieces in the decadence of the Order. And the pieces had been scattered. Father de Rancé managed to get most of the fragments together and connect them up more or less in the right relation to one another. The result was no longer the same seamless unit that it had been before. It was patchwork. But since it was a tour de force merely to get those pieces together again, it attracted much attention. The attention was directed, most of all, to the clever way all those segments had been joined and to the individual merits of each piece in relation to the others; as a consequence, men somehow lost sight of the wholeness and the simplicity which were the most characteristic qualities of the Cistercian life.

Ever since the seventeenth century, Trappists have tended to look at their life not as a single organic whole directed to the glory of God but rather as a complex assemblage of fragments, or "exercises," each one with some special purpose: one to obtain grace for the world, another to make the monk himself do penance, another to help him grow in this or that particular virtue, another to give edification to outsiders, and yet another to earn his daily bread.

But once the life was broken up into fragments, even the individual sections ceased to have quite the same meaning they ought to have if they were to be thoroughly integrated in an essential whole. Therefore, many Trappists were able to consider the offices in choir and, *a fortiori*, manual labor primarily as penances, and then to neglect the third essential element in the Cistercian life—reading—as something accidental and unimportant because it was restful rather than penitential.

That was why the periods devoted to *lectio divina* (spiritual reading) came to be spoken of as "intervals." It was as much as saying that these were moments grudgingly conceded to the body for rest, and that any excuse would serve for cutting them down or suppressing them altogether.

So, the old *Spiritual Directory* of the Trappists, written in the past century by a certain Father Benedict, who ended his days at Gethsemani in the time of Dom Benedict Berger, can sum up the life of a Cistercian monk in this strange sentence: "*All the exercises of the contemplative life combine to make ours an essentially penitential order.*" [1] Never was a cart put more squarely before the horse. Instead of penance serving as a means to contemplation, contemplation is offered to us as a means to penance.

In this sense, contemplation was something you measured by the clock. If you spent a certain number of hours in some formal kind of praying, you were a contemplative. And to judge by the words we have just quoted, the more your prayer exhausted you, the more truly could you be called a contemplative.

The Cistercian who carried this principle to its extreme was not the Abbé de Rancé but Dom Augustin de Lestrange. When he and his religious determined to sing the whole night office every day—a practice that had been abandoned for several centuries—it was not so much out of love for the liturgy —still less, of Gregorian chant—as out of a desire to spend

[1] *Directoire Spirituel, de l'Ordre des Trappistes*, p. 35.

more hours in a formal exercise of prayer which demanded
generosity and stamina and labor. In order to do this, they
got up earlier each night—rising before midnight on the big
feasts, for they still recited the little office. And then, to make
sure that they spent a certain fixed amount of time in choir,
the Val Sainte regulations stipulated that the night office must
never, under any circumstances, end before four o'clock. That
meant that it always lasted at least two and a half hours and
might last four, or four and a half. A similar ironclad injunction determined that the conventual Mass must end precisely
at eight-thirty (in the winter season). Among the many supplementary devotions introduced by Dom Augustin, we read
that the Litany of the Blessed Virgin was recited at eight-
forty-five on the mornings of Sundays and feast days and that
"this must always last about a quarter of an hour." [2] The beautiful *Salve Regina* was also subjected to this harsh treatment.
When sung properly, it takes about four minutes. The Trappists of La Val Sainte stipulated that it must be prolonged
for a quarter of an hour.

The timetable of the Val Sainte monks is one of the most
perplexing and complicated documents in monastic history,
and it is not made any clearer by some of the expressions they
used in measuring time. For instance, when they wanted to
say "seven and a half minutes to six," they were liable to put
it down as "three quarters and a half quarter after five" (*Cinq
heures trois quarts et demi quart*).

All these extras, of course, tended to whittle down the
monks' time for spiritual reading and private meditation. Where
St. Benedict and the *Consuetudines* of Cîteaux left the monks
one or two or even three hours at a stretch to meditate,
Dom Augustin and his followers seem to have exerted their
ingenuity in finding ways to break up every "interval" into
small segments of fifteen minutes or half an hour. The morning interval never seems to have been longer than an hour,

[2] *Règlements . . . de la Maison Dieu de la Val Sainte* (Fribourg,
1794), Vol. ii, p. 6.

and this period might be cut in half by a litany. This new system was designed expressly to prevent the monks from becoming too interested in their books or lapsing into a form of contemplation that was not in every way active and laborious. The afternoon interval was more or less suppressed by devoting the time to communal practice of Gregorian chant. Knowing the style of their books of chant, we can state with certitude that this, also, was more a penance than anything else. It was practically impossible to sing prayerfully from those chunky black notes, bunched into arbitrary spaces and having no notation of the neumes.

With the addition of various practices of their own choice, the monks of La Val Sainte succeeded, without realizing it, in making their day as overcrowded as the Cluniac schedule; this was one of the things that St. Robert and his companions had tried to escape when they left Molesme. By trying to be more Cistercian than Cîteaux, Dom Augustin had managed to devise a splendid method for defeating the true end of the Cistercian usages, which is contemplation.

This condition was intensified by one other notion that had the force of a *de fide* definition in the spirituality of De Rancé and Dom Augustin, namely, that the merit and value of the things a monk did were measured by the physical effort he had put into them. The monk was urged to drive himself through his heavy day and throw himself into every exercise "with all his might." As a corollary, if he noticed that he was actually *enjoying* what he did, he must do something to spoil his joy, and work up some degree of compunction. If anything was pleasant, there was probably something wrong with it. These Trappists could not be persuaded that merit and joy could go together. To be meritorious in the sight of God, your activities had to make you miserable. Said De Rancé to his monks:

I have often told you that monks should live in groanings; that they were obliged to weep not only for their own offenses but also for the iniquity of the world; that their whole life was nothing else but a state of dolor and compunction; but again I repeat that if monks only realized the extent of their obligation to lament, and if they thought about the account they will be called upon to render God in this matter, they would ask Him for compunction without ceasing and their greatest sorrow would be that they did not have enough of it to weep in torrents.[3]

And he added:

Bathe your faces constantly in the bitter waters of penance. Take no care for anything else but to shed tears and leave God to wipe them away. . . . Take heed to avoid everything that might dry up the fountain of your tears. Have no business or employment or occupation that might be capable of dissipating your sorrow and compunction: but rather make use of everything that can feed and strengthen them.[4]

The Abbé de Rancé's notions about sanctity and the monastic life can also be judged from the lives of the monks who died at La Trappe, in his time, with the reputation of saints. The series of their short biographies [5] fills several volumes, and most of the stories came from the pen of De Rancé himself.

It is a long time since these books, once so popular, have been read even by Trappists, and the reason is not far to seek, for they are extremely gloomy. These grim ascetics pass across the scene, one after the other, all looking alike, speaking alike, fasting alike, mourning alike, and dying alike. They are stiff, frozen-faced creatures, and if they have any expression, it is one of earnest and emaciated scrupulosity. They are obsessed by one idea: they have come to the monastery to die, and they must be about their business as quickly as possible. Therefore, they overwork and underfeed themselves, and their abbot permits them to do it; he feels that self-chosen austerities are

[3] *De la Sainteté et des Devoirs de la Vie Monastique* (Paris, 1847), p. 366.

[4] *Ibid.*, p. 374.

[5] *Relation de la Vie et de la Mort de Quelques Religieux de l'Abbaye de la Trappe.* 6 vols. (Paris, 1775).

the very essence of the monastic life and that, if they are inspired to ruin their health, they must be allowed to do so because it will make saints of them.

The reformer of La Trappe defended his views on this point quite explicitly. He asserted that, in his opinion, the monastic life by its very nature was supposed to be unhealthy, and that extraordinary penances were essential to the monk's vocation. These are his words:

This truth [that it is permitted to undertake austerities which attack the health and shorten life] can be remarked in all monastic observances since the holiest and most renowned of them contain in their institution . . . rigors and burdens and penitential practices so severe that it is scarcely possible to observe them for long with exactitude and conserve one's life and health.[6]

Even St. Benedict's famous discretion does not deter the abbot of La Trappe from trying to prove that the Rule of the patriarch of monks is also ordered to this same end: to sanctify monks by destroying their bodily life.

He cites as an "assured proof" of his contention such interior exercises as meditation on death and hell; the prohibition of jokes and of words that provoke laughter, and the preservation of silence, which he thought St. Benedict had prescribed as "perpetual." He sums up all these mortifications with the statement that a Benedictine monk's time "is so filled with regular occupations and exercises that he does not have a single moment for any recreation or relaxation of mind."

This way of life, he tells us, was destined to bring men to an early grave. This is his conclusion:

No one can fail to agree that a life so painful and laborious can hardly last long and that nature, crushed by this series of interior and exterior mortifications, must be constrained to succumb in a short time.[7]

---

[6] *Sainteté et Devoirs*, p. 699.
[7] *Ibid.*, p. 701.

St. Benedict realized he was writing a much easier rule than had been followed by the monks of Greece and Egypt. His constant concern was to temper all things so that the weak would not be discouraged and the strong would be stimulated to do more. Also, he made careful provision for the care of the sick and the aged and the little children. He would have been surprised at the Abbé de Rancé's interpretation of his aims.

Another aspect of De Rancé's emphasis on externals was the great importance he attached to mortifications that seem trivial, at least on paper. Not content with the traditional modesty of the eyes, he describes a trait in one of his monks for which he might well have coined the term "modesty of the feet":

He [Brother Dositheus Leroy] made use of his feet with the same restraint and the same reserve as his hands and his eyes; he went nowhere except precisely where he was supposed to go; his gait was neither too slow nor too fast; one could notice in it neither languor nor levity, in such wise that he gave evidence of a modesty that edified all.[8]

After the restoration of La Trappe by Dom Augustin, various picayune mortifications were detailed in the Postulants' guide. Among the terrific vigils and fasts of La Val Sainte we find this:

You will be very hot in summer without being allowed, at least in public, to wipe the sweat from your brow with a handkerchief; you will only be allowed to turn the drops aside with your finger to keep them from rolling into your eyes and impeding your vision. . . . You will never be allowed to lean against the wall when sitting down, no matter how tired you may be. . . .[9]

The story is told that Father Benedict, the author of the old *Spiritual Directory*, and a Trappist of the same stamp, had gone from France to England and was planning to settle down

[8] *Relations*, II, 309.
[9] Quoted in *La Bretagne Cistercienne, by Comte de Warren* (Saint Wandrille, 1946), p. 160.

at Mount St. Bernard. While he was standing in choir, he saw one of the monks raise his hand and chase a fly from the top of his shaven crown. Father Benedict realized at once that a monastery where men were so dissolute as to swat flies was no place for him. So he hastened to Gethsemani, then under the iron rule of Dom Benedict Berger and swarming with the most persistent flies in the world.

However, we must guard against taking the writings of De Rancé and the spirit of his generation too literally. The reformer of La Trappe was never the inhuman creature that his own rhetoric sometimes makes him seem. We must remember that tears and lamentations were already coming to be something of a literary fashion even in the *Grand Siècle,* and the *Relations* of La Trappe have a certain affinity with the graveyard literature that was to prepare the way for romanticism in England, Germany, and France. Yet the abbot of La Trappe was not really morose. On the contrary, the famous portrait of him by Hyacinthe Rigaud shows Armand de Rancé to have been a sprightly and vivacious little monk whose face could light up with an expression of happy candor. His monks all had a great affection for their father abbot, and the atmosphere of La Trappe, in spite of the lugubrious competitions in penance that occupied the minds of the religious, still had the warm congeniality of a very happy family. In fact, people who visited the place were often amazed by the cheerfulness of these penitents. It is even said [10] that De Rancé once officially urged his monks to be cheerful and to cultivate smiles. And although the Trappists of the seventeenth, eighteenth and nineteenth centuries did not have all the warmth of the devotion to Christ and His Virgin Mother that was so characteristic of the Golden Age, yet it was La Trappe that started the charming custom, which still prevails, allowing every monk and brother to add the name of Mary to the particular name he takes in religion.

[10] I have this on the authority of Dom Gabriel Sortais, who assures me that it is true, although he also admits that he has never been able to make anybody accept it without protest.

The Trappist is never merely "Father Moses" or "Brother Macarius," he is "Father Mary Moses," or "Brother Mary Macarius." It is a gesture of ingenuous homage to the Queen of Heaven. The Trappists have never omitted her Little Office, and say a special Mass in her honor every day of the year except Good Friday. The Rosary has become one of the unwritten essentials of Cistercian life.

It is characteristic of Cistercian monks in all times to be filled with a deep peace, on whose tide they are carried above suffering, even though sickness and trials may bear down tremendously upon their bodies and souls. They achieve a heroism which is not the indifference of a stoic or the insensibility of a yogi, but the fortitude born of supernatural love. It is something infused by the Spirit of God: it is beyond the reach of human nature alone. It brings with it a deep simplicity and humility.

In the last fifty years there have appeared many scattered biographies of Trappist monks and lay brothers who lived out their vocations with the enthusiastic generosity which makes men saints. In those pages—most of the books are little known and long since out of print—we can see the real effect of De Rancé's reform without having to make allowances for the exaggerated style of De Rancé's own writings. Looking at the Trappist life through other eyes than those of the reformer himself, we are able more clearly to discern the true Trappist character.

The Trappist tree is recognized by its good fruits: these are the monks and brothers who have come to the monastery because they love God and trust Him to lead them—through the Rule of St. Benedict and the guidance of other men—to Himself. They do not insist on any peculiar program of prayers or penances either for themselves or for others. They love the Rule, they accept its hardships, they fast and work and do what they are told, they pray, they read and meditate, according to the grace God gives them, and gradually, imperceptibly, the hidden power of God takes hold upon them.

Through the simplicity of the Rule, the harmony of the seasons, the liturgy, the action of the Sacraments, and the graces of prayer and sacrifice, they become true Cistercians. They do not, perhaps, realize it themselves: they have lost all but the last trace of self-consciousness. They do not regard themselves as great ascetics; they merely "keep the Rule." They have their work and their prayer and their books to keep their minds occupied; but in and through these things, in the garden and the barns, in the woods and the fields, they are united to God—just as much as they are in church or cloister. They do not lose His presence. It envelops them in a cloud of peace. That presence is the source of an immense and constant, though intangible, strength; it is the source of light, knowledge, understanding, and counsel when they need it most.

These Trappists are humble in the truest sense: they have forgotten themselves. The secret of their humility and peace is obedience. They have had the courage to give up their own wills and their own way of doing things, and they let the details of their lives be determined by their Rule and their superiors. In return, God has made them free. Their freedom consists not so much in liberty to choose between things as in a deliverance from the necessity of such choice. They are no longer concerned with the innumerable dilemmas of sense and appetite. They are free to taste joy and rest in God, Who is the source of all the good things that appeal to sense and appetite. Instead of dividing its energies among a million reflections of the goodness of God, the soul retains and intensifies all its vitality by concentrating itself in one act of love, which possesses all created goods in their source.

Yet, these Trappists are busy men. They have much to do. The holiest monks and brothers quite often are those who have the hardest and most responsible positions in the community. The reason is that these posts demand a more complete obedience to the first superior and exact a more uncompromising sacrifice of one's own will. Then, too, the difficult business of accommodating oneself to the needs of a family of a hundred or more brothers has its humiliations, and it demands more than ordinary patience and kindness and tact. No one can be a good cellarer or a good novice master or a good prior or a good infirmarian unless he really loves the men he has to look after.

There is, perhaps, no such thing as a typical Trappist, in reality. But it is easy enough to sketch two or three who have come close enough to an imaginary type. Some were more evidently "saints" (in a human sense, at least) than the others. Perhaps one or two were "characters" rather than saints. But all of them represent Trappist life as it is, or as it was in the last century. All of them bear witness to the deep vitality of De Rancé's reform.

Dom François d'Assise, one of the early abbots of Port du Salut,[11] is much more like a figure in the *Fioretti* than a character in De Rancé's *Relations*. Perhaps this abbot's patron saint had obtained for him a liberal endowment in the same spirit of simplicity and joy which was his own. At any rate, the semi-legendary stories that have come down to us about the abbot of Port du Salut have a distinctly Franciscan flavor about them. There even exists a long, mock-heroic poem from the hand of some Trappist or Trappistine [12] commemorating the day when Dom François commanded some swallows and was obeyed.

It seems that there were hundreds of swallows nesting under the eaves of the church and chapter room and all around the cloisters of Port du Salut. Besides the many other inconveniences they caused, the birds used to disturb the meditations of the monks and Dom François's own addresses to them in chapter, by their incessant twittering. One day the abbot was trying to give his daily explanation of the Rule and was not making much headway against the competition of the

[11] He died on June 19, 1854.

[12] Manuscript in the archives of the Trappistine convent, N. D. de l'Immaculée Conception (Laval, France).

swallows. Finally, he turned to the open window and raised his voice and exclaimed:

"Now listen to me, you swallows! Stop all that noise at once. Get away from here and don't come back. In future I forbid you to build any nests in this part of the monastery. Keep to the outhouses and barns."

It is asserted that, since that day, the swallows have been content to nest in the barns and outhouses of Port du Salut and never come near the cloister or the church. . . .

The story is not presented as an article of theological faith. It makes no difference whether you believe it or not. The thing that matters is that such a story exists—and is a definite contrast to anything found in De Rancé's *Relations*.

Another and even stranger tale is told of Dom François d'Assise. He is supposed to have carried on a long correspondence with a Protestant lady in America whom he converted to the Catholic faith. There is nothing so strange about that. What is peculiar is the way the letters are supposed to have been delivered. The postal service was too slow for the zeal of this fervent abbot. So, when his letters were written and sealed, he placed them inside the Tabernacle of the high altar in the abbey church. When he went back a few days later, he would find a reply from his penitent across the Atlantic. . . . Even the credulity of his most devoted clients seems to have hesitated at this tale, however. In the manuscript in which it is recorded we find a marginal note in a firm Trappistine hand: *Il faut passer toute cette histoire des lettres* ("Skip all this business about the letters").

Feeling that these words were left as a directive for readers in convent refectories, we have been bold enough to disobey them, and once again it is in order to draw attention to the fact that such a story could exist.

Dom François passed out of the world and went to his reward with all the humility and compunction of a true Trappist—but also not without a certain sardonic humor. He left detailed instructions as to what was to be done with him. He insisted on being buried in the habit of a lay brother, in the part of the cemetery allotted to the lay brothers, and not in the manner prescribed for priests. He asked that there be no mound on his grave: he wanted people to be able to walk over it without inconvenience. His epitaph was to be the sentence: *Domine miserere super peccatore qui pertransiit malefaciendo* ("Lord, have mercy on this sinner who went around doing evil"). He thanked all the monks and brothers for having put up with him for so long and assured them that they had thereby earned a huge reward for themselves in heaven.

In the middle of the last century there was a brother blacksmith at the abbey of Bricquebec in Normandy. He was called Brother Abel. A powerful, bearded man, he was one of the best blacksmiths in the district. But above all, he was a real Trappist. The novices who were sent to him to be trained at shoeing horses had to be content with absolute silence. Ordinarily, in a case like that, permission to talk was allowed, but Brother Abel believed in the rule of silence, and the novices had to do their best to pick up his system of signs.

He worked with a rosary in one hand and a hammer in the other. When the iron was in the fire, the beads would run through his blackened fingers as he prayed to the Mother of God.

He was a man of deep prayer, this blacksmith. Vocal prayer was only a stopgap. He was happiest when the bell for the end of work called him back from the smithy to the monastery. There, he would wash up and swing his brown cloak over his shoulders and go to kneel down in the quiet church. He would turn his swarthy, bearded face toward the tabernacle and sink into a deep absorption that held him there, motionless, during practically all of his free time. This muscular and practical man, skilled in his craft and one of the best workers in the monastery, had the gift of deep contemplation. His abbot knew it and appreciated it and even allowed him to take three quarters of an hour from his work each day and devote the time to prayer.

When Brother Abel grew old and fell sick and had to lay down his hammer, he was sent to the infirmary. He would get up about four o'clock each morning and pray by his bed before going to hear Mass in the infirmary chapel. One day, one of the brothers noticed that he did not come to the chapel, and he went to see what was wrong. Brother Abel was kneeling by his bed as usual. But he was dead. He had died in the middle of his prayer. It was November 13, 1879, the feast of all the saints of the Order.

About that time there were two old monks in the infirmary at Bricquebec whose devoted companionship was typical of Cistercian simplicity. One of them, Father Stephen Hurel, had gone stone blind from getting lime in his eyes while mixing fertilizer in the fields. He was completely helpless. He depended for practically everything upon Father Paul Enée, who was crippled and could get around only with the aid of a couple of walking sticks. The two monks spent their days together, taking care of each other in every way. They teamed up for all the usual spiritual exercises, and their spiritual reading was also a communal affair. Father Paul read aloud for both of them. During the War of 1870 they said many extra rosaries together for peace.

Occasionally they could be seen together in the monastery, coming slowly along the cloister on their way to the community chapter or to their father abbot's room. Father Paul would lead the way, shuffling along gravely with his two canes. His companion would be in tow, clinging to the ample sleeve of Father Paul's cowl.

For all De Rancé's truculent insistence that the Rule opened the way to an early death, one of the most familiar and characteristic Trappist "types" is that of the ancient priest or lay brother who has long since celebrated the jubilee of his entrance into the novitiate. He is far too weak to follow the community in its various functions, but he refuses to be confined entirely to the infirmary. With pathetic insistence, he pleads for permission to struggle down to choir and stand in his old stall, at least for the conventual Mass. Or if he can no longer make the bows and go down on his knees, and if it wears him out just to stand there trying to sing, he can at least sit in the choir of the infirm. Perhaps he is so far gone that he comes down in a wheel chair, and then only on the very great feasts. When the monks file out into the cloister behind the acolytes and the torchbearers and the deacon with the cross and the thurifer with his fuming censer, all singing the first responsory for a solemn procession, there will be the old father, hiding around a corner in his wheel chair, blinking at the young monks and realizing that there are faces among them which he has never before seen.

There is something deeply touching about an old monk's affection for every detail of the community life; perhaps the most affecting of all is the fact that his love for every precept of the Rule, every rubric of the liturgy, is the fresh, wide-eyed love that a child has for all the things that go on in his own household. To be in the infirmary, with a cell all to himself, with a softer bed, and with meat for dinner is no pleasure for a monk who has prayed and labored and meditated for fifty or sixty years with his brethren. His heart is down in the cloister and the choir and the monastic scriptorium. This is, indeed, one of the classic Cistercian types, and the literature of the Order in the twelfth and thirteenth centuries shows us plenty of such characters.

Perhaps one of the most indomitable of all diehard Trappists was the founder of Bricquebec Abbey, Dom Augustin Onfroy. Born in 1777, he had gone through the French Revolution as a militant, if not truculent, Catholic, was ordained priest and, after peace was restored, was given a country parish in Normandy. He had always dreamed of being a Trappist. But this was the period when the monks were struggling to get themselves re-established in France. Instead of merely entering one of the monasteries that Dom Augustin de Lestrange had reopened, Father Onfroy started a monastery of his own. He bought a mill at Bricquebec in 1824 and moved into it with a couple of disciples and began to live the Rule as best he knew how. Eventually they were received into the Order.

But the first days of that foundation were marked by the most phenomenal poverty. Thirteen Trappists had only twelve shirts among them. When they were short of vegetables, they would try to give substance to their soup by throwing some of the more edible forest leaves into the pot. They ate a great deal of "salad"—which means dandelion leaves—and when these ran short, they tried the shoots of young ferns. Their bread was so coarse that the abbot of La Trappe, after an official visitation of Bricquebec, took a loaf home to his own abbey and put it on display with the notice: "This is the kind of bread they have to eat at Bricquebec: so stop complaining about what you get here."

But above all, Dom Augustin was a tireless laborer. He not only led his monks out to work in the fields, he was often there before them. In the spring he would take one of the lay brothers with him and hitch up an ox team to a plough and start turning up the fresh, stony earth of their fields as the sun came up over the hills. Peasants in the district remembered seeing Dom Onfroy ploughing at four o'clock in the morning in 1848, when he was seventy-one years old. But he, like other diehards in the Order, gave trouble to his superiors when it came time for him to accept mitigations that doctors said he needed. When the Vicar General of the Trappists ordered him to follow his doctors and eat meat in his old age, he obeyed with such fuss and unwillingness that he could well be called *non parum obstinatus*. But that was the way he had been formed.

The Trappist of the nineteenth century was cut on the De Rancé pattern. Penitential practices, vocal prayers, and farm labor—or perhaps one of the monastic industries that began to flourish in that age—these were what filled his mind. These were his life. He was practical and intensely energetic. He was extremely austere and not a litle rigid. He was intolerant of less muscular conceptions of the monastic life than his own, and his ambition was to take heaven by storm, carry off the prize of a supernal crown by an onslaught of irresistible energy. Underneath all that, he was intensely simple, and in his soul burned the vigorous faith of a child. He was content with his life and his penances and his work. The deepest needs of his soul were satisfied by these things, and they did not usually present any particular problem to him: if he managed to survive the life long enough to make his vows, he turned out to be equipped to stand all that the Rule had to offer in the way of austerity. Those who could not do so had found it out long before and had quickly dropped out of the running. The Order—or rather its various congregations—did not number very many monasteries, and the selection of vocations seems to have more or less taken care of itself. If you could stand the life you became a monk, and if you could not you went somewhere else. Apart from that, the monasteries were poor, and the life of the monks was dominated by the labors necessary to keep body and soul together. So they did not leave us any special record of their spiritual problems.

However, the old *Spiritual Directory* survives as a witness to the solid and serious character of their austere spirit. The monk who wrote it had read deeply in St. Bernard, although he had used the saint chiefly as a quarry of suitable quotations in defense of penance and austerity—without arriving at any special appreciation of his doctrine on the contemplative life.

At the end of the nineteenth century, and especially after the reunion of the three congregations, the interior life of the Order entered upon a new stage of growth, and we soon observe its effects in the lives of the monks themselves. Among the young men who entered Cistercian monasteries about the time the spiritual tide was changing, we find certain difficulties and problems of adjustment. The new generation includes not a few souls who do not readily fit into the mold devised by the Abbé de Rancé, and their maturing is attended with much anguish. In many cases that anguish contributes to a deeper and purer spirituality, and this in turn leavens the whole Order and contributes to a new spirit, until finally the Cistercians become conscious of their new direction and begin to formulate new aims. The monks come to realize an essential lack in a life that claims to be contemplative yet makes its contemplation consist in a multitude of "devotions" and "practices" and, above all, "macerations." They seek a solution of the problem in the Cistercian writers of the twelfth century and gradually acquire some sense of the scope and depth and beauty, as well as the sane and healthy simplicity, of Cistercian mystical theology. A whole new doctrine of contemplation opens out before them, and the Cistercian vocation takes on an entirely different meaning. . . .

But even today this is a work that has barely been begun, although it has been maturing slowly for some fifty years. The movement has not yet reached maturity in all the monasteries. The full warmth of the new fire has not yet spread to the remotest parts of the Order, where the members of the body still are somewhat stiff and cold with the formalism of an earlier day. But there can hardly be a house of Cistercians that has not, to some extent, begun to exchange the new spirit of confident love of God for the old rigid concentration on one's own sins and on one's own penances to destroy sin.

If Father Joseph Cassant is ever canonized—and there is a possibility of it, since his process has been passed on to Rome by the archdiocese of Toulouse—it will be because of what he suffered in the beginnings of this new development. The soul of Father Joseph Cassant is given to us as a living psychological case history of the transition. Not that the transition was by any means fully worked out in his life. It was never to be so. He died too soon. Only the conflict was there, sketched out in its broad lines: and underneath the conflict a modern observer can easily work out the essentials of a Cistercian solution—so that Dom Etienne Chenevière, the present abbot of La Grande Trappe, has been able to write an illuminating study of Father Joseph specifically as a Cistercian.

L'Ame Cistercienne du Père Marie-Joseph Cassant [13] is more than the usual pious biography. It brings to life the soul of a young man who had very few natural gifts, yet was haunted by a deep, spiritual ideal. Instead of trying to dress up Father Joseph into something that he was not, Dom Etienne takes every opportunity to let him speak for himself in his own tortured and often ungrammatical language. Father Joseph left a couple of boxes of notes, most of which were quotations from the books he had read; but the pile also included spiritual observations and, especially, records of the desires and resolutions that took shape in his soul at various points in his religious life. These documents give us a fascinating insight into the heart of a monk of our own time in various stages of formation.

Father Joseph was the son of a southern French farmer. His character was strong and positive and practical: and he had his countrymen's love of clear-cut decisions. His whole life was a struggle of will to get things worked out and in their proper places, in spite of the slowness of his mind. He was meant to be a priest and a saint, and there seemed to be an infinite number of obstacles in his way. One of the greatest was the fact that it almost required a miracle for him to pass the necessary examinations. Then, too, his health was so poor there was a chance that he would not live long enough to realize at least the first half of his ideal.

His realistic and energetic character predisposed him to embrace Trappist asceticism. He had all the courage, but none of the strength, necessary for this. And his sense of the concrete made it a temptation to attach great importance to penances and labors which showed a tangible result—at least to the extent that they made you *feel* the price you were paying to carry them out. Father Joseph Cassant labored under such physical and spiritual handicaps that things which the

[13] Published by the abbey of Sainte-Marie du Désert (Bellegarde, Haute Garonne, 1938).

other monks took in their stride could be negotiated by him only with extreme effort and patience.

If he had fallen into the hands of the wrong kind of director, Father Cassant would have been six feet underground within a year. Fortunately, his novice master, who later became his spiritual director, belonged to the new generation of Cistercians. Dom André Malet (he was later abbot of Sainte-Marie du Désert) was a priest of benign and gentle and prudent character, wise with the wisdom of charity. Without diminishing anything of his penitent's ideals, he knew how to restrain and canalize his generous will and lead him on in the ways of a more fruitful sacrifice. Thanks to his guidance, Father Joseph did not exhaust himself beating the air but took up arms in an ascetic campaign against his real enemies. And it is a tribute both to the clear-sightedness of the director and to the docility of the penitent that Father Joseph was able to recognize the biggest obstacle to his sanctity in what we, today, would call an "inferiority complex." He was keenly sensitive of his lack of gifts; but the supernatural realism of his interior life made him able to see, when it was pointed out to him, that this was precisely the providential tool with which God intended him to forge his sanctity.

Instead of trying to beat his way through a stone wall in a vain effort to do the spectacular and heroic things that he read about in the lives of great ascetics, he would have to accept his handicaps, his weakness, his slow mind, and devote his life to the task that was to demand of him an obscure and laborious heroism: keeping the Rule of St. Benedict and living the ordinary, everyday life of a Cistercian with the most perfect dispositions God's grace could afford him.

His novitiate began with a dramatic scene characteristic of La Trappe. Amid all the tenseness and emotion with which a newcomer to the monastery tends to devour the spiritual food that is presented to him, Father Joseph was following the annual retreat of the community. During the retreat an old lay brother died in the infirmary. The stark austerity of the

Cistercian burial rites made a shattering impression on the young man, and his father master found him afterward in tears. Joseph threw himself with ardor into the monastic life, and his desires for perfection led him to try and overdo everything. As a result, he was in danger of straining and exhausting his mind or falling into scrupulosity. Without the guidance of a wise director, his vocation would soon have been lying around him in ruins. But we read in his notes: "Penance does not consist in fasting but in following the Rule exactly in order to please God. . . . It is an act of virtue to take necessary care of one's health with the intention of serving God better, but not to make oneself singular by useless care for the body. . . . Self-love has several skins. As soon as you peel off one of them the next one shows up. . . . If I can't find time for my studies or haven't got the brains, I will always do the will of Jesus without worrying about the future. . . . It doesn't do any good to conquer your body if you still feel anger in you."

True, in the early days he put down some of those wild statements that De Rancé's Trappists were so often encouraged to make about themselves: "I am the greatest sinner. Can't spend an hour without offending God." But soon his entire spirituality became absorbed in one thought: the confident love of Christ. His attention belonged rather to the Redeemer, in Whose presence he lived, than to his own failings and his struggles and his efforts to become a saint. After vain attempts to keep up a constant stream of vocal prayers while he was out at work in the fields, he realized that there was a much simpler way of praying and keeping united with God—by the intention with which he did all things: "If I can walk, I owe it to Jesus. If I am a man, if I breathe, etc., it's all a gift of Jesus. So it is my intention that all these things should be acts of love, of thanksgiving, repeated over and over."

His deeply practical and concrete outlook on life led him to adopt a form of active contemplation, a burning faith that finds Christ's love coming to us in all the events of our lives.

If anyone was good to him, it was because Jesus wanted it so. If he had to suffer anything, that suffering was something he needed. It came to him from Christ's love and was meant to do him good. By accepting it, he could prove his love for Jesus, he could show his gratitude. In everything, he looked beyond secondary causes to the First Cause, without Whom nothing else in the universe can stir. *Il n'arrive que la volonté de Jésus semper.*[14]

Finally, he reached the point where his whole spiritual life could be summed up in an obedience which allowed God to work on him and guide him through his superiors. No matter what they did—and sometimes their decisions were very painful—it was God that acted on him, through them. Even when it seemed impossible to believe such a thing, he believed it. And his trust saved him from taking all the false roads he might have taken; it brought him to the altar as a priest, allowed him the happiness of offering for a few months the Sacrifice of the Mass; then, with his interior life entirely simplified and disengaged from all the conflicts and useless efforts that had tended to divide and sap his spiritual energies in the first years, Father Joseph spent his last days not merely accepting with patience the most intense suffering but rising above it and dominating it, together with all the things of time, by a blind and pure faith, a simple and total love for Christ that kept him absorbed in a contemplation that was almost entirely in the will. There is almost no intellectuality in this simple, yet intensely practical soul, and the element of vision is almost lacking from his contemplation—which boils down, in the last analysis, to one thing: a simple, resolute, constant direction of the will, with all its energies, to God. And the God Whom that will seeks and finds is not even hidden in the cloud of a

[14] "Only the will of Jesus is what happens, all the time." Father Cassant liked the Latin word *semper*. It is scattered through all his writing. With the clangor the word acquired in the mouth of a southern Frenchman, it had a much more emphatic sound than the French *toujours* (always).

definite mystical experience: He is reached through the faith of Christ's little ones, on the most ordinary level of religious experience, by means that could almost be called banal. Father Joseph Cassant had always relied very much on books and holy pictures and all the sacramentals to aid him in his prayer: he did still, but it was now entirely simple, consisting in the renewal of a glance and the refreshing of a constant and powerful intention.

On the afternoon of June 17, 1903, the body of Father Joseph Cassant was lowered into its grave in the *préau* of Sainte-Marie du Désert. Someone had thrown into the grave a few bright handfuls of petals from the flowers that had been scattered before the Blessed Sacrament in the cloister procession that same day—for it was the octave of Corpus Christi. Otherwise, it was a very ordinary Trappist funeral. Yet, in 1935, the General Chapter of the Order unanimously voted the introduction of his cause.

Of all the Trappists who have lived and labored and suffered in monasteries since De Rancé reformed the Cistercian life in the seventeenth century, it was this humble little father, one of the most obscure and prosaic of them all, who first really attracted attention by his sanctity. Compared with the utterly fantastic adventures and labors of a Dom Augustin de Lestrange, a Dom Urban Guillet, a Father Vincent de Paul, a Dom Augustin Onfroy, a De Rancé, or all the ascetics shaped by the great reformer, the life of Father Cassant was apparently nothing at all. Dom Urban Guillet had accomplished more spectacular feats of daring self-sacrifice in a week than did Father Cassant in his whole life. The monks of La Val Sainte had lived for years under a regime that would have killed this poor little monk in a month. Dom Augustin de Lestrange had led his men from Switzerland to Austria to Poland to Russia and then to the West Indies and America and back to France again—and Father Cassant had only struggled breathless in the vineyards of Sainte-Marie du Désert, not even able to keep up with the rest of the community. He had to start home early so that he would get back to the monastery at the same time as the rest. And when there was danger that the Waldeck-Rousseau legislation against religious orders would mean the expulsion of the monks, the mere thought of having to cross the border to some house in Spain nearly overwhelmed him with despair.

Yet, it is Father Joseph Cassant who is talked of as a prospect for beatification rather than the Abbé de Rancé, or Dom Augustin de Lestrange, or Dom Urban Guillet. . . .

The problem that was barely sketched out in the life of Father Cassant was worked out more fully in one of his contemporaries, a Trappistine nun. Father Cassant's death and burial, which marked the solution of all his difficulties on earth, came at the precise moment when Mother Mary Berchmans Piguet was having the struggle of her life to keep her vocation together. This very gifted young nun had been sent from the convent of her profession, Our Lady of the Immaculate Conception, in Laval, France, to a new foundation in Japan. She had arrived at Hakodate in the winter of 1902 and was now living with a small pioneer community in a wooden frame building in the hills outside the city. Mother Berchmans's spiritual director at Laval had discovered in her the ardent soul of one who needed, above all things, to find God in a pure and entire love, the only thing that was capable of delivering her from attachment to objects that were less than He. Her director had sent her to Japan because he wanted her to be a "victim," a "martyr." He believed the sacrifices imposed on her by the struggles of a new foundation would be the quickest way of purifying and preparing her soul for the great things that were destined for her.

Mother Berchmans, whose interior life had been marked by nothing so much as her strong attraction to silence and prayer, now found herself deeply involved in all the activities and responsibilities and distracting cares of a new foundation. Under the strain of overwork her health began to collapse, and neither the climate of Japan nor anything else about the country appealed to her nature or agreed with her physical constitution. She had almost all the important jobs anyone can have in a Trappistine convent except that of prioress, and the last years of her life were taken up with the training of the first Japanese novices that came to Our Lady of the Angels— a task which demanded heroic sacrifice, as she was gradually dying of tuberculosis.

But the crux of Mother Berchmans's problem was not in having to exchange peaceful contemplation for activity and suffering and sickness. She wanted with her whole heart to accept the situation that was pointed out to her by God's will. But the real source of her suffering lay in the fact that the only *way* she knew of accepting it did not seem to be the right one. She argued that the only thing to do was to force herself to like the things she hated. That was what it meant to be a "victim soul" and a saint: you proved your love for God by pushing your way blindly and by main force through every repugnance. That was what was called generosity. And the more hatred and disgust you felt for your lot, the more enthusiastically you told yourself that you liked it. And if you were generous, then everything would soon come easily. If it did not become easy, but remained just as hard and re-pugnant as before, that was your fault: it was all due to your weakness, to your tepidity. If you could not get to like sacri-fice, it was because you were a coward. And if God did not give you grace to overcome your cowardice, it was because you were a sinner.

So, the thing to do was to kneel down, day after day, and try to pull yourself apart and discover what it was that made you sin; to accuse yourself and humiliate yourself and lower yourself below all creatures into the dust and acknowledge what a miserable sinner you were. Then, maybe you would not be such a coward, and everything would be easy, every-thing would be wonderful; you would be able to make all those sacrifices without turning a hair, and you would soon have real evidence that you were a saint. . . .

When Mother Berchmans had been in Japan a couple of years, she discovered that things did not work that way in the religious life.

It was a thing that hundreds of monks and nuns have discovered before her time and since. She had run up against that same blank wall where, too often, monastic fervor lies down in despair; where monks wake up and find that they are mediocrities and can see nothing else to do but stay that way—or else go crazy.

It was the same dead end toward which Joseph Cassant had headed with such zealous haste at the beginning of his novitiate, and from which he had been saved by a good director.

But Mother Berchmans had to face the problem more or less alone. Her new confessor was a hardheaded, matter-of-fact person with a series of cut-and-dried solutions for all problems, and he did not give her much sympathy, because he was a very busy man: he had several convents on his hands, and he was a trifle suspicious of nuns, anyway. They had too many imaginary woes. He told her to be more generous. If she would only say, "Thy will be done," and mean it, all her problems would be at an end.

It was not her confessor or her superior or her sisters in the convent that saved this nun from giving up the struggle in disgust—or else driving herself out of her head from strain. It was a book. It was the same book that accomplished the merciful office of rescuing so many religious of that same generation. It was *The Story of a Soul*, the autobiography of St. Thérèse of Lisieux, who was only just being discovered by the Church at large.

In her simplicity, this Carmelite contemplative had not been afraid to start a quiet but extremely effective spiritual revolution all by herself in her cloister. With the serene confidence of one guided by the Holy Ghost, and without bothering to consider how her message would be disseminated through the world, she had set down on paper certain ideas of the spiritual life that were in conscious opposition to the kind of stereotyped rigorism that had been the fashion for several centuries. She was struggling against that current that still flowed through the Church bearing the pollution of a thinly disguised Jansenism: a formalistic spirit that set up many barriers between God and the souls of Christians. She was in complete reaction against systems of spirituality that placed inordinate emphasis upon sin and made people fix their attention on themselves and their own miserable souls and their own penances, instead of teaching them to believe in God's love and trust His infinite mercy and allow themselves to be guided by His wise Providence.

This message came to Mother Berchmans, in her little convent in Japan, as a liberation. At once the young Trappistine realized the futility of concentrating her attention on her own limited efforts and feeble strivings and failures in the spiritual life. There is only one thing that matters in religion, and that is love: not our love for God but, above all, God's love for us. For if we try to give Him a love that has not first been given to us by Him, our love is nothing. Everything comes to us from Him and from His love.

The aim of the spiritual life should be, therefore, not to keep us far from God, trying to placate His anger by an Egyptian slavery of penances, but to bring us close to Him, purifying our hearts by a perfect love that casts out all fear and consumes all desire for anything but God alone and, therefore, at the same time fills us with confidence in Him. "And we have known and have believed the love which God hath for us. . . . Fear is not in charity: but perfect charity casteth out fear, because fear hath pain. And he that feareth is not perfected in charity. Let us therefore love God, for God hath first loved us." [15]

Without realizing it, Mother Berchmans, in putting into

[15] I John iv:16-19.

practice the doctrine she read in the autobiography of the new Carmelite saint, had come very close to a truth which is at the very center of Cistercian mysticism: that confidence born of divine love is the secret of sanctity, as it is also the secret of contemplation. In the words of Etienne Gilson, concerning the theology of St. Bernard:

This *fiducia* (confidence), offspring of charity, is an essential factor in St. Bernard's doctrine. Penetrated with charity we become even in this world, in virtue of the gift, what God is in virtue of His Nature; and how then should we fear His judgment? . . . Hence we see why St. Bernard's contemplation moves by way of consideration of the judgment, and how the precise point where the fear of Divine chastisement gives way to *fiducia* marks the entrance of the soul into ecstasy. We see also why, to put it more simply, the progress of love consists in the passage of a state in which a man is the slave to fear (*servus*) to another in which he purely and simply loves.[16]

With this discovery, Mother Berchmans found that all her spiritual faculties were set free from the withering restrictions of formalism and reliance upon external practices and labors and penances, and were able to concentrate on the *unum necessarium*, the one all-important duty of the contemplative —to love God in all things and make everything contribute to His glory. And although the "confidence" of St. Thérèse of Lisieux might not be quite the same as St. Bernard's *fiducia*, nevertheless the results in practice were very much alike. In reading the Little Flower, Mother Berchmans and her whole generation came much closer than they realized to St. Bernard and the first Cistercians.

[16] *The Mystical Theology of St. Bernard*, p. 24. However, we must be warned against attempting to draw a strict parallel here between Cistercian mysticism and the teaching of St. Thérèse of Lisieux. There is one fundamental difference: for St. Bernard, *fiducia* is intimately linked with mystical experience and is, in fact, only known by such an experience, while the confidence of St. Thérèse is a virtue and can constitute a habitual *state* in the soul, a habitual condition of peaceful abandonment. That is not what St. Bernard meant by *fiducia*. See Gilson, *ibid.*, p. 142 ff.

And so, love once again came to occupy the place of honor that belonged to it in the spirituality of Cîteaux.[17]

It was after she reached this solution that Mother Berchmans first came under the more or less direct guidance of a Cistercian abbot who was to exercise a most powerful influence in the spiritual development of the Order after the reunion. Dom Vital Lehodey, as superior of Bricquebec, was also father immediate of most of the houses in the Far East and was consequently responsible for their regular visitation.

Dom Lehodey, justly famous in the modern Church for two classical works—one on abandonment, *Le Saint Abandon*, and the other on mental prayer, *Les Voies de l'Oraison Mentale* [18]—was then at the height of his career. Perhaps no one in the Order was more keenly sensitive to the new development in spirituality, the ferment of new life that had begun to make itself so evident immediately after the reunion. Already profoundly versed in the secrets of contemplation and of contemplative souls, he learned from his contact with the many monks and nuns of the Order who acknowledged him as their spiritual father what the Holy Ghost was preparing for the Cistercian family. He was able at once to verify, in the soul of Mother Berchmans, the same movements, the same tendency toward a deeper and simpler and purer life of union with God that was beginning to burn high in so many other monasteries. He could detect the stirrings of infused contemplation—that vitally important element in the life of a contemplative order —which had been suffered to lie dormant or unrecognized at La Trappe. He was able, then, to give Mother Berchmans all

[17] Another important influence in the life of Mother Berchmans was the "Cistercian" mystic, St. Gertrude the Great, who has many affinities with St. Thérèse of Lisieux. She stands about midway between St. Bernard and the modern Carmelite, placing the same stress on trust in God.

[18] *Le Saint Abandon* (Paris: Lecoffre); English translation: *Holy Abandonment* (Dublin: Gill). *Les Voies d'Oraison;* English translation: *Ways of Mental Prayer* (Dublin: Gill).

the encouragement she needed to speed her along her course with serenity and courage and peace of heart.

Already, at Bricquebec, Dom Vital had discovered this deep contemplation flourishing almost unheeded in some of his monks and brothers. There was Brother Candide Villemer, for instance, nearing the end of his forty years as a Trappist. The old brother had been one of those typically saintly Trappists, serving the monastery year after year in quiet and patient labor. First, he had learned the blacksmith's trade from that champion of silence, Brother Abel, the one who worked with a hammer in one hand and a rosary in the other. Then he became the monastery miller for several years, and after that he passed on to the guest-house kitchen—a job that he had dreaded because he loved silence and seclusion and did not want to come in contact with outsiders, to whom he would be obliged to speak. He spent thirteen years in that employment. All through his religious life he had been remarkable only for his simplicity and quiet demeanor. He was one of those brothers who have absolutely nothing outwardly extraordinary about them—no special traits, no particular austerities, no remarkable devotions. He disappeared into the community. He achieved that perfect anonymity which belongs to the most unobtrusive member of a group of men. He spent much of his time in the church, motionless in prayer. Perhaps that was the only thing people wondered at: that perfect stillness, that deep, restful absorption. They did not realize that at those moments Brother Candide was in another world.

Dom Vital discovered that this brother had had to suffer an obscure and terrible interior agony at the beginning of his religious life. He had entered upon the ways of mystical prayer in his first days in the monastery. He was perfectly simple and docile and did not have any elaborate notions of what was going on in his soul. He never thought of himself as a mystic, and perhaps the term "infused contemplation" was unknown to him. All he knew was that the love of God worked and expanded within him and drew him down into the depths of a vivid and suave darkness that was full of rest and yet full of life: a deep cloud that enveloped his whole being and in whose center he came face to face somehow with God. It was not that he *saw* anything or *heard* anything, but his whole being was pervaded with the loving sense of God's presence. And God, with the power of that indefinable nearness, drew all his mind and will to Himself, so that words became useless and thoughts ceased to have meaning and memories became a nuisance and all the earth vanished into insignificance and only one thing mattered: the silence, the deep fruitful silence, of adoration and love with which his heart was full.

But that was in 1865. He was in a Trappist monastery in the full tradition of De Rancé. When his superiors and confessors discovered how Brother Candide was behaving at prayer, they did not give him their approval. They told him he should not be so idle. They told him he was wasting his time and laying himself open to the temptations of the devil, that he had better keep himself busy with pious thoughts and affections of the will. He should formulate acts of sorrow for sin and ask pardon of the God Whose justice was outraged by the crimes of the world. He should meditate upon the last things and the divine attributes and many other points that he would find in good spiritual books.

So Brother Candide, who was a simple and docile brother and perfectly obedient, did just what he was told.

And when love called him down again into the peace of that fruitful and silent darkness where he would be alone with his God, Brother Candide kept words in his mouth and sentences in his mind and forced his memory to keep turning over abstract truths about the Divinity or about the economy of salvation. And although he felt as if his soul were being torn to pieces by the teeth of a steel harrow, he kept on doing what his superiors had told him to do and he made acts and he said he was sorry for his sins. . . .

He suffered very much for years, fighting in anguish against

what his soul desired and his whole heart longed for, in order
not to displease God by disobeying his superiors; but finally
God brought the torture to an end, and Brother Candide
found understanding and peace and encouragement when he
went to receive spiritual direction from young Father Vital
Lehodey, one of the new priests in the monastery. Then his
heart expanded with joy, and he gave himself up without fear
to the love of God that so quietly, yet so urgently, demanded
to possess his whole being: and as he stood in choir, his heart
followed the chanting of the monks with an ardor that did not
speak and did not sing, because it was too deep for speech and
for song: it surged and swelled like the waves and the tides
of the sea.

XIV. *PARADISUS CLAUSTRALIS*

THE kings and the dictators and the mighty of the world accomplish their works with great noise, with speeches and drums and loud-speakers and brass and the thunder of bombers. But God works in silence.

Nations, dynasties leave their mark upon the world by tearing pieces out of the map, by killing men and sending them into exile or slavery. But while armies destroy with great terror and confusion, God builds life where they have sown death and brings sanctity out of the poisoned stream of their hatred.

The spirit of the world, which is selfishness and envy and conspiracy and lust and terror, makes men loud from the fear of their own hollowness. But the Spirit of God gives them peace, teaches them not to be afraid of silence but to find themselves in quiet. The spirit of the world, which is avarice and oppression, arms men against one another and divides them against themselves and against others: it splits the world into armed camps. But the Spirit of God draws men together and unites them in peacefulness and teaches them to work together and to carry one another's burdens and to honor one another, in spite of their faults and their weaknesses and their infirmities. It teaches them to be compassionate and to obey one another for the sake of God's love and His peace.

While the world is drunk with the great chalice of the Whore of Babylon, which is war, God brings His chosen ones, His elect, into hidden monasteries to refresh them with the peace that is born of the love of brothers living together in unity.

But the world envies them their peace. Such happiness is a reproach. It condemns the spirit by which the world lives. It accuses the rich men of their injustice and the Communists of their inhuman and complacent hatreds and the humanists of their insufficiency. It denies everything that the world stands for.

There are two ways in which the world gets its revenge. One is by open hatred, by direct attack. That is useless. It does no more harm to the monastic Order than the vintner does to his vine when he prunes it in the spring. In fact, it is God, in silence and wisdom, Who uses the Church's enemies to perfect His saints and purify His religion.

The other kind of revenge is more subtle, because it is not even conscious: it comes not from hatred that is aware of itself as hatred, but from a love that is misdirected and turns to hatred without realizing it. For that is the way the world loves: it destroys what it loves, because its love is selfish and can be satisfied only by devouring its object.

That is what happens when the men who live in monasteries pay more attention to the gifts of men than to the gifts of God; when they begin to depend on the example and the tactics of the world and to attach more importance to money and power and health and comfort and visible forms of heroism than to the means which God has given them. For the monk has only one thing, in the last analysis, that he can depend on: and that is not a thing, it is God.

That is the key to the Cistercian life, the secret of its austerity and its penances. The monk becomes poor and gives up the possession of all material things—houses, cars, books, clothes of his own, everything: he even renounces the possession of his own body and his own will. But the only reason why he makes himself poor and struggles to keep himself that way is in order to be immensely rich. For, when he owns nothing, God becomes his fortune, and he owns and enjoys all things in God, their Creator. When the monk ceases to rule and dominate his own life, for the sake of God, it is God Who assumes command of his life and his body and his soul: but to be commanded and ruled entirely by God is to be endowed with

His tremendous love, for, whatever God touches, He floods it with the riches of His infinite actuality.

Therefore, the worst misfortune that can befall the Cistercian monk is to acquire things, to regain that possession and control over his own person and his own being and his own faculties which he is supposed to have renounced and transferred into the complete power of God.

Now, for the Cistercians, poverty is a function of obedience and the common life. The temptation to gain possession of special objects in a monastery does not rise far beyond such things as books and fountain pens: but what is much more important is this interior, spiritual communism of the will. Exterior possessions are, after all, only a sign, an expression of interior ones: self-centeredness, selfish desires. A man cannot own other things unless he first owns himself with an unshakable attachment. And although it may be good to get rid of exterior things, it is useless to do that if you do not also mean to give up your own desires and become poor in spirit. For, if your will is attached to things, it is attached, and you are not free, whether or not you actually possess the things you desire.

Therefore, the world gains a much more subtle revenge on monks when it poisons them with its own spirit and teaches them to retain command of themselves instead of abandoning themselves to God.

Yet, because men are what they are, they always tend to go their own way and to live according to their own will, even when they think they are acting with the most disinterested purity. Even the holiest of things can become possessions when you love them for their own sake. Prayer can become a possession. So can penances. A monk may become just as attached to some little practice of devotion as a manufacturer is to his Packard: and with the same results. He will prefer the pleasure he derives from his private prayers to the good of his brothers and of the community, just as the rich man prefers his own cars and other luxuries to the welfare of the men he employs. A Trappist can be just as attached to some penance as a drunkard is to his bottle, and with the same sort of effect: for he may prefer his penance—which is the choice of his own sweet will—to some real duty, just as the drunkard would rather get drunk than go home and love his family.

And a contemplative can become attached to his contemplation. He may think that contemplation is the only thing in the world that matters. As long as he can be by himself and nurse that warm interior sweetness of rest in the center of himself—which may well be only an illusory shadow of true contemplation—the whole world can fall to pieces and the monastery with it, for all he cares. He will sacrifice everything else for that pleasure. Obedience will become a matter of no importance. Charity will seem absurd. And the love in his heart will dry up in the withering heat of his desire for his own complacent self-satisfaction. And he will be as trammeled as a millionaire.

There is only one reason for the monk's existence: not farming, not chanting the psalms, not building beautiful monasteries, not wearing a certain kind of costume, not fasting, not manual labor, not reading, not meditation, not vigils in the night, but only GOD.

And that means: love. For God is love. If we love Him we possess Him. Everything else about the monastic life is only a means to that end. When prayer and penance and all the rest cease to be means and become ends in themselves, the contemplative life stops dead and the monk begins to amble along the broad, dreary paths that are trodden by the multitudes of the world.

Therefore, there is a limit to the value of all the methods and means the monk uses to acquire the love of God. His external activities can be carried beyond what the economist would call a "point of diminishing returns." That holds for prayer as well as for penance, for fasting as well as for contemplation, for the liturgy as well as for manual labor: all these things are valuable only up to a certain point. Beyond that limit they do harm instead of good. What is the limit? St. Bernard long ago explained to monks that the exterior acts prescribed by monastic rules were valuable only to the extent that they favored the growth of interior charity.[1] It is no good to fast beyond the point where fasting and charity come in conflict, or to pray when it interferes with the love you owe to your brothers or to God.

But there is one thing in life that has no limit to its value, one virtue that can be practiced without any need for moderation. And that is *love:* the love of God and the love of other men in God and for His sake. *There is no point at which it becomes reasonable to abate your interior love for God or for other men, because that love is an end in itself: it is the thing for which we were created and the only reason why we exist.* Only the exterior acts which are means to this end have to be moderated, because otherwise they would not serve as means and would not bring us to the end. But when the end itself is reached, there is no limit, no need of saying, "It is enough." [2]

In fact, if you discover any kind of love that satiates you, it is not the end for which you were created. Any act that can cease to be a joy is not the end of your existence. If you grow tired of a love that you thought was the love of God, be persuaded that what you are tired of was never pure love, but either some act ordered to that love or else something without order altogether.

The one love that always grows weary of its object and is never satiated with anything and is always looking for something different and new is the love of ourselves. It is the source of all boredom and all restlessness and all unquiet and all misery and all unhappiness; ultimately, it is hell.[3]

[1] St. Bernard, *De Praecepto et Dispensatione*, chap. 1, No. 5.
[2] Cf. St. Thomas Aquinas, *In Epist. ad Romanos*, xii.
[3] *Cesset voluntas propria et infernus non erit.* St. Bernard, *Serm. iii in Temp. Resurrectionis*, No. 3.

There is one thing and one alone which the monk never wearies of seeking, and that is the one love of which he can never grow weary. But there will he find this love? The answer to that question is the very heart of Cistercian mysticism and the Cistercian vocation.

For the eternal, insatiable, unlimited, and unlimitable love for which the monk lives is to be found within the monastic community itself.

Indeed, that love is the very life of the monastery, as it is the life of the whole Church. It has brought the monks into this place before they were ever capable of realizing or understanding what it was that was drawing them here. *Congregavit nos in unum Christi amor.*[4] This love holds them together and is the one life principle which vitalizes and perfects them all in one. "And the glory which thou hast given me," said Jesus to His Father, "I have given them that they may be one as We also are one." [5] But most tremendous of all is the fact that this love, which is the life of all and the unity of all and the bond of their perfection, is God Himself. It is the Spirit of God, the Holy Ghost, *Vinculum perfectionis.* And by that Spirit of Love men are brought together to form a spiritual organism which is the Body of Christ. The monastery is that Body in miniature. "If we love one another God abideth in us and His charity is perfected in us. In this we know that we abide in Him and He in us because He hath given us of His Spirit." [6]

The only problem that remains is to distinguish this love from the false love which is selfishness and which can, nevertheless, disguise itself in so many apparently holy enthusiasms. It is a problem of that most important monastic virtue, discretion. But St. Bernard, trained in the wisdom of the great St. Benedict, gave his monks a concept that was the key to the whole problem.

[4] The love of Christ has brought us together.
[5] John xvii:22.
[6] I John iv:12-13.

If the false love which ruins our peace and destroys all unity among men is self-love or our own will, *voluntas propria*, it seems that the true love which gives peace and unites us all to one another and to God is its exact opposite. But the opposite to the private will of one is the common will of all—not the will of all men, but of God and of all men who agree with Him. For the will of God alone embraces the perfect good of all and can be said to be the true will of all things that are capable of love. It is what they would all want if they could see the true order of things.

The problems of the monastic life are all resolved in this concept. The one thing the monk needs to live for is that *common will*—the will which is not peculiar to him alone, which does not seek his own momentary benefit or convenience, but which seeks the good of all in the will of God.

What really matters in a monastery, then, is not prayer, not penance, not fasting, not vigils, still less the farm and the chickens and the tractors and the buildings, but the common will, *voluntas communis*. As soon as two or three Christian men are gathered together, there can be all the essentials of a monastery. The common life can begin. "Where two or three are gathered together in My Name, there am I in the midst of them." [7]

And that, incidentally, is one of the reasons why the least effective way to try and abolish Cistercian life is to put the monks into concentration camps, where are to be found precisely the conditions under which monasticism becomes heroic!

When one first becomes a Cistercian, one is kept occupied for several months with the business of getting used to the fasts and labors and the rest of the routine. Generally, the whole two years' novitiate is passed under special conditions—and with special graces—which tend to keep the novice something of a hothouse plant. Nevertheless, the big trial of the novitiate and the crucial test of a vocation is obedience: and

[7] Matt. xviii: 10.

in obeying the father master, the novice learns the first elementary steps in following the "common will" at the cost of his own. Generally, he does not quite see whither it is all leading; but at the same time he is eager to do what is expected of him, and the trials are too obviously trials to be very surprising.

It is after profession that the Cistercian really begins his training as a mature monk. He is simply thrown more or less on his own in the community; if it is a big community, he is like a fish in a deep, silent sea. He sees his abbot once a week or so, speaks to his confessor once or twice a week, and he might sometimes open his conscience to the father prior as well. But on the whole, he is left face to face with a huge, inscrutable, and perhaps terrifying force which surrounds him on all sides and which is the community, the common will.

This can develop into a terrifying trial to a young monk who does not realize what it is all about. To live in a house full of a hundred, or a hundred and fifty, completely silent men who are always together yet never speak to one another: to move about in this amorphous yet vital mass which stirs into action at the sound of bells rung at precise intervals of the day and applies itself with a mysterious energy to all its communal activities . . . if you do not acquire deep faith and supernatural common sense, a couple of years in a Trappist monastery will do strange things to you!

Men who have not been properly trained to the life in their novitiate—or have not been able to absorb the training given to the novices—either twist and warp under the pressure of what they cannot understand, and become eccentrics, cranks, seeking refuge in a skein of peculiarities. Or else they jump over the wall and run away.

A man who is more adaptable and who has something of a foundation of interior prayer may react against the community in a subtler way: but in the end it boils down to the same thing. He will argue: "I am a solitary, living in community. The community exists for one reason, to purify my heart by making me suffer and giving me opportunities for patience. All right. I will be patient. I will show them I can take it. But as for my interior life, that is my own. I am a solitary and I will live as one, inside myself, even though I have to exist in the midst of all these other people."

It is not exactly a sinful solution, but it is a very imperfect one. It is the same as saying that monks live together for two reasons: one is purely negative: they are to act as hair shirts on one another. The other is more positive: community life is safer. They huddle together, so to speak, for protection against the devil. There is safety in numbers.

But this is merely a caricature of the cenobitic life. If you live like that, the vital flow of charity, which is supposed to unite you to all the rest of the monks and all of them together to God, will be largely sterilized, and God's work will be left almost without fruit.

The trials that a young professed monk may have in his first years of life in community often reduce themselves to a refusal to give himself up entirely to the love of God as expressed in the *voluntas communis*. He may think it is sufficient to conform externally to the others without loving them and their life, in his heart, more than himself and his own life. He thinks he is being virtuous. He thinks he is trying to preserve "purity of heart" and "detachment" in order to love God better; actually, he is refusing the complete sacrifice of himself and his own will to God's will, which flows through the community and expresses itself in the demands made on the individual not only by the Rule but by *every smallest circumstance of the common life*.

This is the sort of thing that ought to be written all over Cistercian monasteries in letters of fire because, no matter how often it is preached to the monks, it can never be preached enough; it is never sufficiently understood and never thoroughly learned except by a minority.

But the ones who learn it and really put it into practice are saints.

Strangely enough, it is a Carthusian hermit who has written one of the deepest and most beautiful sentences ever printed about the Cistercian common life. Dom François de Sales Pollien,[8] writing at the time of the reunion of the Cistercian congregations, said these words:

In a [Trappist] monastery through which there circulate powerful currents of spiritual life, the soul of the monk, ever carried onward by the stream from which no instant, no occasion ever withdraws him, finds itself lifted up without realizing how, and transported into the regions of divine life with greater simplicity and less preoccupation with itself.

That is very true. The monasteries through which these streams of intense life flow are the ones in which the monks have renounced themselves most completely and have abandoned themselves with the most generous and unquestioning faith to the common will, or, if you prefer, to God's will expressed by the Rule and the desires of their superiors and the needs of their brethren.

In practice, this involves the deepest, most searching sacrifices. It is relatively easy to renounce a world whose pleasures are boring and whose ambitions are a waste of time and effort. It is not too hard to give up licit satisfactions when the sacrifice soon finds more than ample compensation in the delights of interior freedom and the taste of supernatural things. But when we have to renounce our plans and aspirations for the highest and most spiritual goods and devote ourselves, under obedience or out of charity, to some trivial and distracting series of far less perfect tasks, then the sacrifice can be supremely difficult. It is all the more so when it turns out that our spirit of faith, being far less pure than we imagined, is not strong enough to enable us to see God's will in duties that do not flatter our self-esteem.

For a cenobite, sanctity resolves itself into the practice of the most ruthless communism ever devised. A Cistercian monk

[8] *La Vie Contemplative, son Rôle Apostolique* (Montreuil, 1900), p. 93.

who lives his vocation to the limit retains absolutely nothing he can call his own, not even his judgment or will or the most intimate depths of his soul. He gives up things a Marxist has never even heard of, things which no amount of human violence or political strategy could ever take away.

As long as the monk retains private ownership of any corner of his own being, he is that far short of the freedom and purity of love found only in union with the common will. As long as there is any refuge where he can curl up by himself and hug some private good that nobody else is allowed to share, there remains in his heart a cranny in which the dirt of selfishness accumulates. Before he realizes it, he is blinded and stifled by the refuse his subconscious egotism collects. He can no longer see by the light of true faith or breathe the clean air of divine charity, wherein all spiritual health is found.

St. Bernard saw that the love of God could never tolerate these private crannies. Searching the depths of undeliberate attachment to spiritual consolations, the abbot of Clairvaux wanted to sweep out the last traces of proprietorship from the hearts of his monks and set them free by spiritual poverty, which possesses the kingdom of heaven.

Wherever there is proprietorship [he said], there is singularity. Where there is singularity there is a private corner, and in any such corner there is bound to be dirt and rust.[9]

A problem immediately arises. What about the interior solitude essential to contemplation? All tradition agrees that without at least interior solitude a man cannot reach deep interior union with God. But interior solitude seems to imply a complete interior withdrawal from the community. One lives in the monastery as if alone. Indeed, mystical writers advise the contemplative to live as if there were nobody in the universe but himself and God. Taken literally, such advice would turn monastic life into a hell on earth. Yet, correctly interpreted, it contains a truth on which contemplation depends. But would

[9] *De Diligendo Deo*, chap. xii, No. 34.

any such conception have been admitted by twelfth-century Cistercians? William of St. Thierry said the charity that was the soul of a monastic community simply excluded all solitude. Love did not permit a cenobite to be alone. *Nullum inter se patiuntur esse solitarium ne dicat ei Salomon, Vae soli!* [10]

What does this mean? Did the cenobites of the twelfth century frown and shake their heads whenever one of their number tried to go off and pray by himself? When some monk found a quiet place where he could meditate without being bothered by others, did the rest of the community come after him, wearing expressions of pain and concern, and explain to him, somewhat stiffly, that he was not showing the right spirit, that he ought to stay with the brethren, even though they were a distraction?

The doctrine of the common life taught by St. Bernard and his school did not aim merely at making the monks "good mixers." At Clairvaux the common life was viewed as a preparation for contemplative union with God. And the early Cistercians agreed with all contemplatives in admitting that contemplation was impossible without interior solitude. Consequently, there could not possibly have been any opposition, in their minds, between their notion of the *voluntas communis* and the interior solitude of the true contemplative.

St. Bernard, always ready to discourage monks who wanted to become hermits (he was one of the greatest champions of the cenobitic life), taught that solitude had an extremely important place even in the life of a contemplative cenobite. *Nil tibi et turbis*, he exclaims; *nihil cum multitudine caeterorum.* On the whole it is rather startling to find this theologian of the common will telling his contemplatives to have "nothing to do with the crowd, nothing to do with the common run of other men. *O sancta anima, sola esto!* "O holy soul, remain alone! Keep thyself for Him alone Whom alone thou hast chosen for thyself from among all others. Fly from

[10] *De Natura et Dignitate Amoris*, chap. ix, No. 25.

public view, fly even from thy own household, from thy inti-
mates and friends. . . ." He admits he wants this solitude to
be interior above all, but he does not deny that physical solitude is also desirable, even for a Cistercian, if the opportunity
should present itself, and especially when he wants to pray.
*Et corpore interdum non otiose te separas cum opportune
potes, praesertim in tempore orationis.*[11]

So, St. Bernard and William of St. Thierry, who certainly
agreed on the principles of mystical and ascetical theology,
seem to be contradicting themselves and each other when
they insist the cenobite can never be a solitary, yet must be
a solitary in order to arrive at the logical term of his vocation—
mystical union with God. The answer is that there are two
kinds of solitude, one which is not permitted and the other
which is not only permitted but absolutely necessary.

The first kind of solitude, the wrong kind, is a man's isolation from other men by selfishness and pride. William of St.
Thierry clarifies his own statement, *Nullum inter se patiuntur
esse solitarium,* by explaining what he means by a "solitary" in
this context. It is, he says, a monk who refuses to let anybody
else in on the movements of his interior life and who upsets
the community with eccentric devotional practices.[12] It is the
contemplative who imagines he is the only one in the monastery who knows anything about the spiritual life, believes
no one else is capable of directing him, and insists on directing
everybody else, beginning with the abbot. St. Bernard, in a
famous passage, describes the false solitaries with a text from
St. Jude: "These are they who segregate themselves, brute
beasts, not having the spirit of God."[13] He explains that these
"solitaries" are contentious, evil-tempered men who spend
their time raising Cain in the community, and he goes on to
show why "the Spirit of God is not in them":

[11] *In Cant.* Serm. 40, No. 4.
[12] *De Natura et Dignitate Amoris,* chap. ix, No. 24.
[13] Jude, i:19.

Consider the soul of a man, how it gives life to all the members of the body in their union with one another. But separate any one member from its union with the rest, and see how long it will continue to receive life from the soul! . . . But that is what happens to every man who is cut off from unity [i.e., love, the common will] with other men: there can be no doubt that the spirit of Life withdraws from such a one.[14]

The Holy Spirit, the living bond of charity which unites all the saints into one Mystical Body in Christ, does not enter into the soul of the monk who does not love God in his brothers. Consequently, that monk's soul is dead. To be separated from the living vine, from the source of life without which we can do nothing, is not a very desirable form of solitude.

The other kind of solitude, which the cenobite *must* desire, is the exact opposite. True interior solitude is simply the solitude of pure detachment—a solitude which empties our hearts and isolates us from the desires and ambitions and conflicts and troubles and lusts common to all the children of this world. And so, in urging his monks to leave the world and all it stands for, St. Bernard insisted they should concentrate on being unlike the common run of men and enter into the loneliness of the saint, whose heart, isolated above the level of the world, exists in a rarefied atmosphere where there is no desire but the desire of God alone.

However, the more a monk is able to isolate himself from the desires and agitation of the world, and the more he isolates himself in the will of God, the more he becomes one, by charity, with all the others who are united in the same love of God. So, the whole problem clears up like magic. The solitude which St. Bernard recommends, far from being opposed to the common will, *is*, after all, the common will seen from a different point of view.

Thus, in the "communism" of the Cistercian cenobite, even

[14] Serm. i, *in Festo S. Michaelis*, No. 5. Cf. *De Gradibus Humilitatis*, No. 7 and Serm. 46, *in Cant.*, No. 6.

solitude and silence and interior contemplation are viewed as functions of the common life. Each monk is taught, therefore, to treasure certain moments of deepest silence and recollection and even physical solitude, that he may enter into communion, in the depths of his own soul, with the spirit of God, Who is the common life of the monastic community and of the whole Church of God. His solitude, therefore, instead of separating him from his brothers, unites him more closely to them. The closer the contemplative is to God, the closer he is to other men. The more he loves God, the more he can love the men he lives with. He does not withdraw from them to shake them off, to get away from them, but, in the truest sense, to *find* them. *Omnes in Christo unum sumus.*

In its highest expression, the fraternal charity of the contemplative seeks a union with other men far beyond mere benevolence and mutual tolerance and good fellowship. It is a union in which all souls are fused into one—into the soul of the Mystical Christ, in Whom they all become one Person.

Now, the true end of the monastic vocation is the perfection of this Mystical Person, not only the perfection of individual sanctity. To view the monastic life merely as a school of individual perfection would be a serious diminution of the Cistercian ideal. The monastery does not exist just to form individual saints and contemplatives, but to form one Saint, one Contemplative, Who is the little Mystical Body of the monastery itself. Each monk contributes to the spiritual perfection of the whole by the purity of his contemplation and by the sanctity of his life: if God has made him a contemplative and a saint, it is, ultimately, that he might so contribute. Needless to say, the monastery is only a member in the great Mystical Body of the Church. Therefore, in the long run, the purity of heart produced in each monk by the monastic rule, by obedience, humility, labor, charity, solitude, recollection, and prayer, adds to the sanctity of the whole Church.

Nothing could more clearly demonstrate this thesis than the fact that individual prayer, in a Cistercian monastery, is always subordinated to the liturgical praise of God, "to which nothing is to be preferred." [15] In the *opus Dei* the voice of the monastic choir, uniting the voices of many monks, blends into the chant of the one Mystical Christ; and one of the chief reasons why a monk ought to purify his heart in private, solitary contemplation is that this public praise, which he is officially delegated to offer in the name of the Church, may be more pure and efficacious in obtaining grace for the world.

What a transformation is worked in a community of men by the marvelous power of charity and contemplation, by the power of that pure, disinterested love which is a created participation in the sublime life of God! It turns monasteries into Edens where men recover the lost innocence of their father Adam. It turns the cloister into a Paradise where the monks begin, even on earth, to imitate the contemplation and praise of the nine choirs of angels—and the angels, remember, are cenobites. One of the greatest joys of monastic life, as of heaven itself, is the consciousness that all this happy contemplation is *shared*. Even if the monk cannot talk or write, and so cannot communicate the joy of his own vision of God to his brethren and to the world, nevertheless the whole atmosphere of the cloister is charged with supernatural happiness and radiant with an indefinable sense of vision which belongs to all: because the whole community is one Contemplative, one Hermit, one Angel, one Seraph in the whole hierarchy of choirs that behold and laud their Creator with tremendous and eternal praises!

Here are the words in which William of St. Thierry describes a community of contemplative monks:

The harmony of their lives and of their virtues and of their holy desires seems to be based not on the rules of music but on those of love. And they offer up this harmony to God as a perfect sacrifice, perfect because it is His likeness. In the grace which shines through all their faces and bodily movements and even

[15] *Nihil operi Dei praeponatur. Rule,* chap. 43.

flows in the folds of their garments, they show forth the presence of love of God dwelling within them, and that presence inspires them all with delight. And in this manner they live together like the Seraphim, setting each other on fire with the love of God. And they strive to honor one another and to do good to one another with such ardor that no honor and no favor done to another is capable of satisfying the desires of him who wishes to honor and do good to his brother.[16]

In this atmosphere, far from being crushed in a mold that destroys individuality and stifles the gifts of nature and grace, men are, on the contrary, set free to grow and develop in the air and light of supernatural peace and fecundity. Only the monk who refuses to give himself without reserve to the "common will" becomes cramped and warped and turns into a caricature. It is only in a community where formalism has inhibited the true life of prayer that men are forced into a mold. False ideals of asceticism can disfigure the common will, the life of union with God in all its Benedictine simplicity. False and limited notions of spirituality can corrupt a monastic rule and turn the community into a monster which does not give life to individual monks but devours them. But where love governs the monastery, and union with God is the ideal of all who live there together, formalism is washed away by the healthy life stream of common charity. Individuals who correspond to the demands made upon them by such a community do not lose anything vital, but spiritually find themselves in God; they find all the rest of mankind there as well and learn to love everyone in Christ. Then they begin to prosper and grow to an unbelievable extent. And their eyes discover new horizons of joy that would be forever unattainable outside the claustral school of charity.

Nothing, then, could be more alien to the spirit of the cloister than regimentation. The Rule is not designed to blot out individual differences by superimposing a fixed pattern

16 *De Natura et Dignitate Amoris,* chap. ix, No. 25.

of piety. On the contrary, the purpose of Cistercian asceticism is to liberate each monk's true self and allow his personality to develop, supernaturally, in its deepest and most vital capacities. The reason for the strict obedience which is the foundation stone of Benedictine spirituality is not to kill anything good or vital in the person of the monk. Nothing of value is ever destroyed by the Rule when it is properly observed and applied. Monastic obedience and labor and fasting and penance and silence and all the rest are directed against the enemies of a man's true self, and their purpose is to clear away the obstacles that stand in the way of the healthy development of his personality.

After all, what *is* your personal identity? It is what you really are, your real self. None of us is what he thinks he is, or what other people think he is, still less what his passport says he is. Many of us think, no doubt, that we are what we would like to be. And it is fortunate for most of us that we are mistaken. We do not generally know what is good for us. That is because, in St. Bernard's language, our true personality has been concealed under the "disguise" of a false self, the *ego* whom we tend to worship in place of God. The monastic ascesis is entirely directed against this *ego*. To the worldling, who knows no other "self" than this shadow of himself, the Cistercian life will evidently spell the destruction of everything he is accustomed to think of as his real personality. But the monk who has given himself, without return, to God and to the formation prescribed by the Rule soon discovers that monastic obedience and penance are rapidly delivering him from the one force that has prevented him all his life from knowing his true self.

We are what we love. If we love God, in Whose image we were created, we discover ourselves in Him and we cannot help being happy: we have already achieved something of the fulness of being for which we were destined in our creation. If we love anything else but God, we contradict the image born in our very essence, and we cannot help being unhappy, because we are a living caricature of what we are meant to be.

Now, this liberation of true personalities is not the work of one monastic rule alone. All the religious rules are destined to fulfil the same function in different ways. They are all designed to perfect the sanctity of the Mystical Body by forming its members into saints.

The various orders use different means to arrive at the same ultimate end. Their success depends on their fidelity to the means variously assigned to them by God. What is good for a Jesuit will not necessarily be good for a Sister of the Good Shepherd, and what is perfect for a Lazarist may be imperfect for a Carmelite. A Carthusian cannot perfect his monastic personality by living the life of a Capuchin missionary, nor were the Camaldolese hermits founded to carry out the same work as the Christian Brothers.

So it is with the Cistercian. Insofar as he becomes involved in functions which have no place in his own Rule and tries to carry out labors not assigned to him by the Church, he tends, at least *per se*, to diminish the efficacy of his hidden apostolate of prayer and penance and to jeopardize his chances of interior liberation and divine union. The Cistercian cannot slake his thirst at anybody else's well: and the six centuries since the Order began to decline in the 1200's have proved that the proverb *Bibe aquam de cisterna tua* ("Drink the water of thy own well") can be applied to the White Monks as truly as to anybody else.

That is why the great Abbots General since the reunion have insisted on a return to the integrity of the Cistercian life in its letter and spirit. They have insisted at the same time on the austerity and contemplative warmth of the first Cîteaux. They have ceaselessly urged the Cistercians of our day to love the simplicity and balance and rugged energy of the life led by their founding fathers. They have never despised the great work of the Abbé de Rancé or neglected to pay their debt of gratitude for his work and that of Dom Augustin, without whom the Order would not exist today. But their gaze goes back through the centuries to the days of St. Bernard and the school of Clairvaux, when the name Cistercian was synonymous with the pure contemplative adoration of God—the adoration offered by the cenobite, whose contemplation was a kind of communism and whose chief function on earth was to unite with his brothers in the great work of liturgical praise, which was an imitation of heaven. As the late Abbot General, Dom Hermann-Joseph Smets, declared: "Our apostolate is marked out for us by our Fathers of Cîteaux: and I mean our Fathers of the *old* Cîteaux, of the golden age, and not those of the age that was gilded by the fascination for exterior works—those activities which have too often paved the way for our decadence. . . . It is the old spiritual wine made by our Fathers that we are called to drink, and no one, having drunk old wine, straightway hath a mind for new, for he saith: the old is better. *Nemo bibens vinum vetus statim vult novum; dicit enim, vetus melius est.*" [17]

Call it wine, if you like, or call it water. It comes to the same thing. For there is intoxication in the waters of contemplation, whose mystery fascinated and delighted the first Cistercians and whose image found its way into the names of so many of those valley monasteries that stood in forests, on the banks of clean streams, among rocks alive with springs.

These are the waters which the world does not know, because it prefers the water of bitterness and contradiction. These are the waters of peace, of which Christ said: *"He that shall drink of the water that I shall give him, shall not thirst for ever. But the water that I shall give him shall become in him a fountain of water, springing up into life everlasting."*

These are the Waters of Siloe, that flow in silence.

> FRATER M. LOUIS, O.C.R.
> *Feast of All the Saints of*
> *the Cistercian Order, 1948*

[17] Circular Letter, Sept. 8, 1929. The scripture text is from Luke, v:39.

BIBLIOGRAPHY

Acey, L'Abbaye de N. D. d'. Acey, 1946.

Acta Sanctorum Bollandiana.

Aelredi, S., *Opera*, in Migne, *Patrologia Latina*, Vol. 195.

Alani ab Insulis, *Opera*, in Migne, P. L., Vol. 210.

Amedei, B., *Homiliae in B. V. M.*, in Migne, P. L., Vol. 188.

Antoine, Vie du R.P.D., anon. Paris, 1840.

Association Bourguignonne de Sociétés Savantes, "Saint Bernard et son Temps," *Recueil de Mémoires et Communications*, 2 vols. Dijon, 1929.

Astorga, Ignacio, O.C.R., *De la Paz del Claustro al Martirio*. Cóbreces, 1948.

Aubert, Marcel, *L'Architecture Cistercienne en France*, 2 vols. Paris, 1946.

Auvity, Mgr. Fr., *L'Abbaye de N. D. de Bonneval*. Rodez, 1947.

Bazy, Annoncia, *Vie du Vénérable Jean de la Barrière*. Paris, 1885.

Bégule, Lucien, *L'Abbaye de Fontenay*. Lyon, 1912.

Bélorgey, Dom Godefroid, O.C.R., *La Pratique de l'Oraison Mentale*. Paris, 1945; Vol. II, 1946.

—— *L'Humilité Bénédictine*. Paris, 1947.

Berlière, Dom Ursmer, *L'Ascèse Bénédictine*. Maredsous, 1927.

Bernardi, S., *Opera Omnia*, in Migne, P. L., Vols. 182–185.

Besse, Dom, *Les Mystiques Bénédictins*. Maredsous, 1922.

Boylan, Eugene, O.C.R., *A Mystic Under Arms*. Cork, 1945.

Brémond, Henri, *L'Abbé Tempête, Armand de Rancé, Réformateur de la Trappe*. Paris, 1929.

Bricquebec, Petites Fleurs Cisterciennes de, anon. Cherbourg, 1909.

Brunonis, S., *Opera Omnia*, in Migne, P. L., Vols. 152, 153.

Caesarii Heisterbacensis, *Dialogus Miraculorum*, 2 vols. Coloniae, 1851.

Canivez, Jean-Marie, O.C.R., *Statuta Capituli Generalis Ord. Cisterciensis*, 8 vols. Louvain, 1933 ff.

Catholic Encyclopaedia, The, 15 vols. New York, 1907.

Chautard, Dom Jean Baptiste, O.C.R., *Les Cisterciens Trappistes.* Conférence de DRAC, 1931.

—— *The Soul of the Apostolate,* new translation. Gethsemani, 1946.

Chenevière, Dom Étienne, O.C.R., *L'Ame Cistercienne du P. Joseph Cassant.* Bellegarde, 1938.

Chronicon Villarensis Monasterii, in Martène, *Thesaurus Novus Anecdotorum,* Vol. iii.

Cistercian Contemplatives, Monks of the Strict Observance at Gethsemani, Ky., Our Lady of the Holy Ghost, Georgia, Our Lady of the Holy Trinity, Utah. Gethsemani, 1947.

Cistercienser Chronik (periodical). Bregenz, 1889 ff.

Collectanea Ordinis Cisterciensium Reformatorum (periodical). Westmalle, 1932 ff.

Courtray, D. A., *Histoire de la Val Sainte.* Fribourg, 1914.

Cram, Ralph Adams, *The Substance of Gothic.* Boston, 1925.

Dalgairns, J. B., Lives of St. Stephen Harding, St. Ailred, St. Robert of Newminster, St. Waltheof, in Newman's *Lives of the English Saints.* London, 1901.

D'Arbois de Jubainville, Henry, *Étude sur l'État Intérieur des Abbayes Cisterciennes . . . au xiie Siècle.* Paris, 1858.

Daumont, Octave, O.C.R., *Le P. Maxime Carlier, O.C.R.* Chimay, 1921.

Déchanet, Dom J.-M., O.S.B., *Guillaume de Saint Thierry, l'Homme et son Œuvre.* Bruges, 1942.

Delatte, Dom, O.S.B., *Commentary on the Rule of St. Benedict,* trans. by Dom Justin McCann, O.S.B. New York, 1921.

De Rancé, Armand, *Relations de la Vie et de la Mort de Quelques Religieux de la Trappe,* 6 vols. Paris, 1741.

—— *De la Sainteté et des Devoirs de la Vie Monastique.* Paris, 1846.

—— *La Règle de Saint Benoît Nouvellement Traduite et Expliquée,* 2 vols. Paris, 1703.

De Visch, Caroli, *Bibliotheca Scriptorum S. Ord. Cisterciensis.* Coloniae, 1656.

"Dialogus inter Cluniacensem Monachum et Cisterciensem," in Martène et Durand, *Thesaurus Novus Anecdotorum*, Vol. v. Col., 1571.

Dictionnaire de Spiritualité. Paris, 1932.

Dimier, Anselme, O.C.R., *Clarté, Paix et Joie, les Beaux Noms des Monastères Cisterciens*. Lyon, 1946.

—— *La Sombre Trappe*. Saint Wandrille, 1946.

—— *Saint Hugues de Bonnevaux*. Tamié, 1940.

—— *Saint Pierre de Tarentaise*. Tamié, 1935.

Directoire Spirituel des Cisterciens Réformés, Vulgairement dit Trappistes (the "old" *Directory*). Paris, 1869.

Directoire Spirituel des Cisterciens Réformés, revised. Bricquebec, 1910.

Estienne, Yvonne, *Les Trappistines*. Paris, 1937.

Exordium Magnum, in Migne, *P. L.*, Vol. 185.

Exordium Parvum, in *Nomasticon Cisterciense* (*q.v.*) and in Guignard (*q.v.*).

Farrow, John, *Damien the Leper*. New York, 1937.

Federal Works Agency (W.P.A. project), *Kentucky: A Guide to the Blue Grass State*, Harcourt, Brace, New York, 1939.

Fontaine, Georges, *Pontigny, Abbaye Cistercienne*. Paris, 1928.

Gaillardin, Casimir, *Histoire de la Trappe*, 2 vols. Paris, 1844.

Gallia Christiana in Provinciis Distributa, 16 vols. Parisiis, 1715–1865.

Garraghan, Gilbert J., S.J., "The Trappists of Monk's Mound." *Illinois Catholic Historical Review*, Vol. viii, no. 2 (Oct., 1925).

Garrigou-Lagrange, Reginald, O.P., *The Three Ages of the Interior Life*, 2 vols., St. Louis, 1948.

Gethsemani, a father of the Abbey of (M. Alberic), *Compendium of the History of the Cistercian Order*. Gethsemani, 1944.

—— a monk of (M. Amedeus, O.C.R.), *Dom Edmond Obrecht*. Gethsemani, 1937.

Gethsemani Magnificat, Trappist, Kentucky, 1949.

Ghellinck, J. de, S.J., *L'Essor de la Littérature Latine au Moyen Age*, 2 vols. Paris, 1939.

Gilleberti de Hoilandia, *Opera*, in Migne, *P. L.*, Vol. 184.

Gilson, Étienne, *The Mystical Theology of St. Bernard*. New York, 1940.

—— *The Spirit of Medieval Philosophy*. New York, 1936.

Grolleau, Ch., et Chastel, Guy, "L'Ordre de Cîteaux, La Trappe," in collection, *Les Grands Ordres Monastiques*. Paris, 1932.

Guerrici Abbatis, B., *Sermones*, in Migne, *P. L.*, Vol. 185.

Guignard, Philippe, *Les Monuments Primitifs de la Règle Cistercienne* . . . Dijon, 1878.

Guigonis i, Prioris Cartusiae Majoris, *Consuetudines*, in Migne, *P. L.*, Vol. 153.

Guillet, Vie du R.P.D., anon. La Chapelle-Montligeon, 1899.

Hélyot, H., *Histoire des Ordres Monastiques, Religieux* . . . Paris, 1847.

Holmes, Fred L., *The Voice of Trappist Silence*. New York, 1941.

Hubrecht, Alph. C.M., *Une Trappe en Chine*. Peiping, 1937.

Huvelin, Abbé, *Quelques Directeurs d'Ames au 17e Siècle*. Paris, 1917.

Janauschek, Leopold, *Origines Cistercienses*. Vindobonae, 1877.

John of the Cross, Saint, *Works*, trans. by E. A. Peers, 3 vols. London, 1933.

Knowles, Dom David, O.S.B., *The Monastic Order in England*. Cambridge, 1940.

Lac, Abbaye de Notre Dame du, anon. Montreal, 1906.

Le Bail, Dom Anselme, O.C.R., *Le Moine Soldat, Bulletin du Cistercien aux Armées*. 1914–1918.

—— "La Spiritualité Cistercienne." *Cahiers du Cercle Thomiste Féminin*, Paris (April, 1927).

—— *L'Ordre de Cîteaux, La Trappe*, in collection, *Les Ordres Religieux*. Paris, 1924.

—— "Saint Bernard," in *Dictionnaire de Spiritualité*.

Lehodey, Dom Vital, O.C.R., *Le Saint Abandon*. Paris, 1919.

—— *Les Voies d'Oraison Mentale*. Paris, 1908.

Lenssen, M. Seraphin, O.C.R., *Hagiologium Cisterciense*. Tilburg, 1948.

Luddy, M. Ailbe, O.C.R., *Life and Times of St. Bernard*. Dublin, 1927.

—— *The Order of Cîteaux*. Dublin, 1932.

Luddy, M. Ailbe, *The Real De Rancé*. Dublin, 1931.

—— *The Story of Mount Melleray*. Dublin, 1932.

Manrique, Angelus, *Annales Cistercienses*, 4 vols. Lugduni, 1642.

Martène, Dom, et Durand, Dom, *Voyage Littéraire de deux Bénédictins*, 2 vols. Paris, 1717.

—— *De Antiquis Monachorum Ritibus*, 2 vols. Lugduni, 1690.

—— *Thesaurus Novus Anecdotorum*, 4 vols. Paris, 1717.

Mattingly, Sr. Ramona, "The Catholic Church on the Kentucky Frontier." *Studies in American Church History*, Vol. xxv. Catholic University, Washington, D. C., 1936.

Merton, Thomas, *Exile Ends in Glory*. Milwaukee, 1948.

—— "Poetry and the Contemplative Life," in *Figures for an Apocalypse*. Norfolk, Conn., 1948.

Montalambert, Count, *The Monks of the West*, 2 vols. Boston, 1872.

Nogues, Dom Dominique, O.C.R., *Mariologie de S. Bernard*. Paris, 1935.

Nomasticon Cisterciense, Séjalon, ed. Solesmis, 1892.

Odyssée Monastique, Dom Augustin de Lestrange et les Trappistes pendant la Révolution. La Grande Trappe, 1898.

"Orval, La Resurrection d'." Edition de luxe de la revue *L'Art Belge*, Brussels (1943).

Perkins, William Rufus, *History of the Trappist Abbey of New Melleray*. Iowa City, 1892.

Pourrat, P., S.J., *La Spiritualité Chrétienne*, 4th ed., 4 vols. Paris, 1947.

Proust, Dom Eutropius, O.C.R., *Gethsemani Abbey, a Narrative of the Late Abbot Eutropius*, O.C.R. Gethsemani, 1899.

Raymond, M., O.C.R., *The Man Who Got Even with God*. Milwaukee, 1941.

—— *Burnt Out Incense*, New York, 1949.

Religieux Chartreux, un, (Dom François de Sales Pollien), *La Vie Contemplative, son Rôle Apostolique*. Montreuil, 1900.

Religieux Cistercien, un, *Dom Augustin Onfroy*. Cherbourg, 1902.

Rousseau, François, *Moines Bénédictins, Martyrs et Confesseurs de la Foi pendant la Révolution*. Maredsous, 1926.

Schneider, Fulgence, O.C.R., *L'Ancienne Messe Cistercienne*, Tilbourg, 1929.

Schrepfer, Luke, O.S.A., *Pioneer Monks in Nova Scotia.* Tracadie, 1947.

Spalding, Martin J., *Sketches of Catholicity in Kentucky.* Louisville, 1844.

Spirit of Simplicity, The: Report to the General Chapter of the Reformed Cistercians, new translation. Gethsemani, 1948.

Spiritual Directory for Religious, translation of the *Directoire Spirituel* (the "new" *Directory*) by a monk of New Melleray, reprint. Gethsemani, 1946.

Stapehill, a religious of, *La Trappe in England.* London, 1935.

Talbot, Hugh, O.C.R., *The Cistercian Abbeys of Scotland.*

Tamié, L'Abbaye de, anon. Tamié, 1943.

Thérèse of Lisieux, St., *The Story of a Soul.* New York, 1927.

Trappist Life at Our Lady of Gethsemani, anon. Gethsemani, 1946.

Us des Cisterciens de la Stricte Observance. Westmalle, 1926.

Vacandard, Abbé, *Vie de Saint Bernard,* 4th ed., 2 vols. Paris, 1910.

(Val Sainte), *Règlements de la Maison Dieu de N. D. de la Trappe mis en Nouvel Ordre et Augmentés des Usages Particuliers de la . . . Val Sainte.* Fribourg, 1794.

Visitation, a Sister of the, *Most Rev. Clement Smyth, Second Bishop of Dubuque.* New Melleray, 1937.

Walsh, E. H., *The Monk of Gethsemane Abbey.* Brooklyn, N. Y., 1893.

Webb, Hon. Ben J., *A Century of Catholicity in Kentucky.* Louisville, 1884.

Whalen, Rev. Charles W., *The Trappist Way.* New Melleray, 1945.

William of St. Thierry, *Opera,* in Migne, *P. L.,* Vols. 180 and 184.

—— *The Golden Epistle,* trans. by William Shewring. London, 1930.

—— *Méditations et Prières,* trans. by Dom J.-M. Déchanet, O.S.B., Brussels, 1945.

Williams, Watkin, *The Mysticism of St. Bernard of Clairvaux.* London, 1931.

GLOSSARY OF SOME
MONASTIC TERMS

ABBEY. A monastery canonically erected by the Holy See and the Major Superiors of the Order and enjoying a certain independence and autonomy, under the control of its own ABBOT. The Abbey is the most complete and self-sufficient social unit that exists in the structure of monastic life.

ABBOT. Regular first superior of an Abbey, in charge of the temporal and spiritual affairs of the whole community.

ABBOT GENERAL. Superior at the head of a monastic Order.

AMBO. A bookstand, usually in an elevated position, used in liturgical services. (Also called *"Jube"* in Cistercian monasteries.)

ANTIPHONER. A large liturgical book containing the text and musical notation for the ANTIPHONS, short melodic chants sung in between Psalms in the Choral Office. The Antiphoner also contains the text of RESPONSORIES, or longer chants, in which certain verses are repeated. These chants are interspersed between the readings of LESSONS from the Fathers or from Scripture. The Lessons (read from the *Ambo*) are contained in another volume called the LECTIONARY.

APOSTATE. A member of a religious Order who has left the Order without the proper dispensation, or a member of the Catholic Church who has left the Church, or a member of a religious Order who has left both his Order and the Church.

ASCETICISM. The doctrine and practice of self-discipline and control of all the natural faculties in order to arrive at moral, intellectual and spiritual perfection. In the highest sense, asceticism means the effort of man's soul, aided by God's grace, to deliver himself from every attachment and desire that falls short of God himself. Actually, in a contemplative Order, asceticism is the active practice of virtues, with the help of God's grace, preparing us for or accompanied by mystical contemplation, in which the chief work is performed passively in the soul by God Himself.

BENEFICE. A permanent sacred office, constituted by ecclesiastical authority, and giving right to a determined revenue connected by its nature with that office (see Code of Canon Law, C. 1409).

BREVIARY. A small liturgical book serving as a compendium of all that is contained in the larger liturgical books (v.g. the Antiphoner, Lectionary, Psalter, etc.) designed to help priests and monks to recite the Office conveniently when they are by themselves and not in choir.

CANONICAL HOURS. The different sections of the Divine Office, properly so called, as distinguished from the various "Little Offices." There are seven canonical hours: Matins with Lauds, Prime, Tierce, Sext, None, Vespers and Compline. The Canonical Office is the total of psalms, hymns, lessons, antiphons, responsories, etc., officially instituted by the Church and imposed as a matter of obligation, to be recited daily by all monks and other religious under solemn vows as well as by clerics in major orders (subdeacons and above).

CENOBITE. A monk who lives the "common life," that is, who lives in a community with other monks and shares with them all the daily exercises of prayer, labor, study, meals, and so on. In the strict sense, the cenobitic life is altogether common, and the monk has no private cell of his own.

CHAPTER (*Capitulum*). The monastic Chapter, strictly speaking, is the group of monks under solemn vows who have active voice in determining the affairs of the community. The Chapter Room is the place where they meet. In the broader sense, the "Chapter" is the daily meeting of the monastic community in the Chapter Room, after Prime, for the recitation of prayers and an exhortation by the Abbot or PRIOR.

CHAPTER OF FAULTS. A session in which the monks accuse themselves and one another of violations of the Rule, and receive suitable penances from the Superior.

CHARTERHOUSE (*Chartreuse*). A monastery of Carthusian hermits.

CLOISTER. A covered arcade, usually quadrangular and open to the weather. By extension, the term is applied to the whole monastery or convent.

COLLATION. Originally this was a short period of public reading, for which the monastic community gathered before Compline. Today the term is used to signify a light refreshment, taken in place of supper on fast days, consisting of some bread, a little fruit and a hot drink.

COMMENDAM. The practice of giving the revenues of an Abbey or Priory to an absentee who was an Abbot only in theory and who might, perhaps, never even see the monastery, let alone become a monk. The chief cause of this abuse was that many monasteries came into the power of secular princes who distributed their revenues to their court favorites, much as a modern political boss shares out "graft" with his underlings. Those who became abbots in this way were called COMMENDATORY ABBOTS and the monasteries were said to be held *In Commendam*. This abuse no longer exists.

COMMON OBSERVANCE. The distinction between Cistercians of the Strict and Common Observance grew up in the sixteenth and seventeenth centuries. The Common Observance was the mitigation of the Cistercian Usages permitted by several Popes, and it is followed by several Cistercian congregations today. The Cistercians of the Common Observance do not lead as strictly contemplative a life as the Reformed Cistercians. They engage to a great extent in parish work and education, and have excelled in historical scholarship in the past hundred years. This volume intends no criticism of the present-day Cistercians of the Common Observance, for they are to be considered as a thoroughly legitimate development of Cistercian life and have the full approval of the Holy See. There are two houses of the Cistercians of the Common Observance (otherwise called Sacred Order of Cistercians, S.O.C.) in the United States.

COMPLINE (*Completorium*). The last of the canonical hours chanted each day by the monks. It is the evening prayer of the monastic community, after which all retire to bed.

CONTEMPLATION. In the broadest sense it is a "simple intuition of the truth" (*simplex intuitus veritatis*) in which the mind is content to rest in a reflective gaze, without specific acts of reasoning, in the way an artist stands gazing at a picture. In the strict sense, contemplation is a simple intuition of God, analogous to the natural process described above, but produced immediately in the soul by God Himself and giving the soul a direct but obscure and mysterious experimental appreciation of God as He is in Himself.

CONTEMPLATIVE LIFE. A life in which everything is ordered to favor the development of contemplation in the strict sense, and therefore a life in which exterior activities are supposed to be kept at a minimum.

CONVENTUAL MASS. A Mass which is celebrated in the presence of the whole monastic community. It is generally a High Mass, chanted by the community assembled in choir. In the Cistercian Order there is one Conventual High Mass each day of the year. On Sundays and Feasts there are two Conventual Masses, one of which is a Low Mass.

CORPUS CHRISTI. Literally "the Body of Christ." A term for the Sacrament of the Holy Eucharist, in which Christ becomes substantially present under the accidents or species or outward appearances of the Host when the words of consecration are pronounced over them by the priest at Mass. The Feast of Corpus Christi occurs in May or June, and on these occasions the mystery of the Blessed Eucharist is fittingly celebrated with a special liturgical Office and Mass. In Catholic countries the Blessed Eucharist is carried in procession through towns and villages on this day and on the Octave Day of the feast (eight days later). In Cistercian monasteries this procession is held in the cloister in all countries.

CROZIER. A staff surmounted by a crook, symbol of the pastoral office of a bishop or abbot.

DETACHMENT. The habitual disposition of one who is not enslaved by the appetites and necessities of human nature. While remaining subject to the limitations and needs of a human body and soul, the man who is "detached" is not dominated by the desire of pleasure or the fear of pain; his will is able to function freely without being dominated by self-interest. The acquisition of detachment is the proximate end of all asceticism. Christian detachment is distinguished by its supernatural character. It is ordered not merely to the perfection of the individual but to the love and service of God and, ultimately, to union with God in contemplation.

DEVOTIONS. A term used loosely to cover all kinds of pious practices, especially prayers and meditations centered upon particular mysteries, saints or holy objects. Generally a "devotion" implies the use of set forms of non-liturgical prayer in the special cult of its object. In a broader sense, any habitual religious response to a special appeal exercised upon the soul by this or that saint or mystery is called a "devotion."

ENCLOSURE. The limit defining the separation between the monastery and the "world." It is usually a high wall or some such barrier, in which the doors are kept locked. In strictly enclosed communities, members of the opposite sex are forbidden to enter the enclosure under pain of excommunication.

EUCHARIST. See Corpus Christi.

EXCOMMUNICATION.. An ecclesiastical penalty by which one is deprived of the rights and privileges of a member of the Catholic Church. A monk may also be excommunicated from his monastic community without being expelled from the cloister.

FATHER IMMEDIATE. The Abbot of a monastery that has founded other monasteries is called the "Father Immediate" of those monasteries, and he exercises a certain supervision over them, visiting them each year to make sure that the Rule is being observed.

FRATER. Latin for "Brother." In some religious communities this title is given to the young monks who are not yet priests, or to the novices to distinguish them from the "Fathers" (priests) on one hand and the "Brothers" (lay-brethren) on the other. In the Cistercian Order, as well as some others, all the members, whether priests or not, use the title "Frater" (or simply "Brother") before their own names, even when called "Father" by others.

GARTH. An open courtyard or garden, surrounded by the cloister.

GENERAL CHAPTER. A legislative and judicial body made up of the Abbots and other titular superiors of the whole Order.

GRANGE. A group of farm buildings with a chapel and living quarters generally tenanted by lay-brothers working in outlying parts of the monastery farm. These "granges" were necessary in the Middle Ages when the monasteries owned much more land and when communications were difficult.

HEBDOMADARY. A monk deputed to a certain function for an entire week. St. Benedict speaks of the "Hebdomadary Cook," the "Hebdomadary Reader" (in the refectory), etc. Today the term is only applied to the priest who is appointed to sing the Conventual Mass for the week.

HERMIT. A person dedicated to a life of absolute solitude, for the sake of prayer, penance, recollection and closer union with God.

HOST. A small wafer of unleavened bread used in the Holy Sacrifice of the Mass.

INDULT. A decision of the Holy See granting certain rights,

privileges or exemptions to an individual or a community.

INFUSED PRAYER or CONTEMPLATION. The term infused, applied to prayer, contemplation, knowledge, love, etc., is generally synonymous with "mystical," and signifies an effect that is directly produced in the soul by God without active intervention on the part of the soul, which is moved passively to a knowledge or love of God completely transcending all the faculties of human nature. However, when speaking of "infused" virtues, whether moral or theological, Catholic writers use the term in a broader sense, to signify habits produced in the soul by God gratuitously, since they are supernatural, but in which the active cooperation of the soul plays an influential part.

LAVABO. A ceremony in the Mass, in which the priest washes his fingers reciting part of the 25th Psalm, beginning with the words *"Lavabo inter innocentes manus meas . . ."* It symbolizes the purification of body and soul with which he must approach the most sacred and essential part of the Mystery.

LAXIST. A moral theologian who excels in finding ways to evade moral obligations, and is so excessive in this respect that he cannot safely be followed by a Christian conscience.

LAY-BROTHER. A member of a religious Order who, though he makes simple or solemn vows, remains technically a layman in the sense that he is not destined to the clerical state, or Holy Orders, or at least to the public celebration of the Divine Office. Lay-brothers devote to labor the time that monks and clerics spend in prayer and study.

LITANY. A long prayer consisting of a series of invocations and responses. Traditionally, a Litany is supposed to be sung in a moment of special need.

LITURGY. The system of prayers and sacred texts and ceremonies established by the Church as the official vehicle of her public worship of God precisely as a group, or, better, as the mystical body of Christ. The Liturgy is essentially official, social and symbolic. It is also essentially concerned with the Mysteries of the Christian Cult, which are the chief and most immediate means by which both individuals and society are sanctified and brought into intimate participation in the life and contemplation of God. Quite distinct from the Liturgy are private and even public devotions which do not have this official and symbolic character and are not directly concerned with the Sacred Mysteries.

MASS. The central Mystery of the Christian Faith. It is the liturgical action in which the priest, as the representative of Christ, renews the offering to God of Christ's own Sacrifice of Himself on Calvary, Christ Himself being present on the altar, under the species of bread and wine, by virtue of the words of consecration.

MATINS. The canonical hour which is chanted soon after midnight. The longest of the hours.

MEDITATION. Mental Prayer. A process which aims to bring the soul to a closer union with God by means of thought, reflection and affective activity of the mind and will, cooperating with ordinary grace. Mental Prayer is prescribed, as a matter of duty, in the religious Orders and Congregations and in clerical life. It is essential to an integral Christian life and therefore should be practised by laymen also.

MISERERE. The fiftieth psalm. It begins with the words "*Miserere mei Deus . . .*" (Have mercy on me, O Lord!)

MISSAL. Book containing the prayers and readings prescribed in the celebration of Mass.

MITER. Ceremonial headdress of bishops and abbots. The average dictionary will endeavor to show you what a miter looks like.

MONASTIC ORDER. The term "Monastic Order" is used in two ways: first to signify the whole structure of monasticism, and second to signify a religious Order whose members are monks. Monasticism, the life of the monastic religious Orders, is distinguished from other forms of religious life by the relative stability and the patriarchal and agricultural character of the vocation. The Monastic vocation implies retirement from the world and from the active ministry (at least to a great extent), and permanent residence in a family of monks dwelling in the country, governed by a Superior elected for life, living by the labor of their hands, in poverty, with common ownership of all property, and having as their principal purpose the Liturgical praise and contemplation of God, not only for the sanctification of their own souls, but as representatives of the whole Church before the throne of God.

MONK. A religious dedicated to God by vow in the monastic life. Essentially the word monk implies the contemplative rather than the active life. The term monk is only correctly applied to the members of the monastic Orders, Benedictines, Carthusians, Cistercians, etc. Members of the Mendicant Orders, dedicated to the life of teaching and preaching, like the Dominicans, Franciscans and Carmelites, are properly called *Friars.* Other Orders, designed for the active life, and in which common exercises and the community life are considerably reduced (for instance the Jesuits) do not use the name "monk" or "friar" for their members. These are simply called "religious."

MORTIFICATION. The virtue by which we "mortify"—that is "put to death"—the rebellious desires and appetites of our soul in order to liberate our potentialities for good, that they may be elevated to high perfection by the action of God's efficacious grace.

MYSTICISM. A way of prayer, or of contemplation, or simply of living, in which the direct action and influence of God tend to dominate and absorb the activity of our natural faculties, raising them to a habitually supernatural level. The characteristic external mark of true Christian mysticism is not a succession of flamboyant experiences and phenomena, but a life of constant peace, recollection, absorption in God, charity, humility and, last but not least, balance and common sense, even in the midst of great trials, distracting duties, or heroic suffering.

NIGHT OFFICE. The psalms, hymns, lessons and other prayers chanted or recited by the monks during the hours between midnight and dawn. This usually includes the canonical hours of Matins and Lauds. Distinguished from the "Day Hours."

NONES (or *NONE*). The fourth of the "Day Hours," an office that should, properly speaking, be chanted in the early afternoon. It is the office of the "Ninth Hour" (2:30 or 3:00 P.M.).

NOVICE. An aspirant to vows in a religious Order who has been canonically admitted to the prescribed course of training in the novitiate.

NOVITIATE. The house or part of a house assigned to the novices as their place of residence and training.

NUN. Strictly speaking a "Nun" (*nonna*, Latin equivalent of the title "Mother") is a religious woman who has taken *solemn* vows in an Order. Religious women professed in Congregations, and having only simple vows, are more properly called "Sisters."

OBLATE. A lay-person who desires to share, to some extent, in the life of prayer and the spiritual benefits of a monastic Order. In the Cistercian Order, oblates live in the monastery and lead the life of the monks, with certain small modifications and without any vows or other formal religious obligations. Many Trappist monasteries receive young boys as oblates and give them their primary and secondary education, as a preparation for the religious life. This is not done in any of the monasteries of the United States.

OCTAVE. The prolongation of a liturgical feast over a period of eight days.

OFFICE. The sum of daily prayers, psalms, lessons, etc., to which the monk or cleric is bound as a duty (*officium*). The term may refer to the whole public prayer of the Church at large. It may refer to the special prayers assigned to a given day: "the Office of the day." It may refer to a particular canonical hour: "the Office of Prime." It may refer to those prayers which are a matter of immediate obligation to an individual: "I must go and say my Office."

ORDER. A religious society established under the authority of the Holy See, and in which the members are bound by solemn vows. This is the point which distinguishes an *Order* from a *Congregation.* In the latter the members only take simple vows. (Code of Canon Law, C. 488.) All Orders are approved directly by the Holy See. Congregations may have only diocesan approval.

PARISH. The fundamental territorial unit in the Catholic Church. It is a district, having its own Church and Pastor, who may be a secular priest or a member of a religious Order. A parish forms part of a diocese (Code of Canon Law, C. 216).

PENANCE. The virtue by which one endeavors to destroy the effects of sin or moral disorder by self-correction and amendment and reparation to God. In another sense, we speak of *a* penance, meaning a penalty imposed by a confessor or ecclesiastical superior in reparation for a fault. By virtue of the communion of all Christians with one another through sanctifying grace and incorporation in the Mystical Body of Christ, certain members of the Church who may, themselves, be without serious sin, can do penance for others, vicariously. This will not wipe out the sins in the souls of others, but it can congruously merit grace for them to make the necessary acts of repentance themselves. In any case it will serve as a reparation for their sins in the sight of God.

PONTIFICAL HIGH MASS. A High Mass celebrated with the pomp and rites reserved to a Pontiff (Bishop, Archbishop). Abbots of monastic Orders have the privilege of celebrating Mass Pontifically.

POSTULANT. One who has applied for admission to a religious Order. A postulant is usually received into the Guest-House and then into the community for an initial period of trial, before the novitiate begins.

PRÉAU. See Garth.

PRIME. The first of the "Day Hours," supposed to be chanted about dawn (the "first hour").

PRIOR. There are two kinds of Priors in the Cistercian Order: 1) Titular Priors, who are the highest superiors in independent Priories. 2) Cloistral Priors, who are second superiors, appointed by the Abbots in their own Abbeys.

QUIETISM. A heresy which distorted the Catholic teaching on contemplation by asserting that the way to sanctity was to abandon all interior and exterior activity whatever and remain completely inert, empty and passive without thinking or desiring anything, even eternal salvation.

REFECTORY. Place where members of a religious community gather for meals.

ROSARY. A method of prayer combining meditation with the recitation of the *Hail Mary* and *Our Father*, in honor of the chief events in the life of the Blessed Virgin Mary. In order that the counting of vocal prayers may not complicate the meditation of the mysteries, the one saying the rosary passes a string of beads through his fingers as he recites the vocal prayers, one bead for each prayer. Each meditation is accompanied by ten "Hail Marys" and it is easy to tell when to pass on from one subject to another by a glance at the beads.

SALVE REGINA. ("Hail, Holy Queen.") An antiphon in honor of the Blessed Virgin Mary. In the Cistercian Order it has been the custom since the thirteenth century to sing the *Salve Regina* after Compline, every evening, before the monks retire to the dormitory.

SECULAR. Anyone or anything not associated with the religious state. A secular priest is one who is not a member of a religious Order or Congregation, but is subject to a Bishop and works among Catholics in the world.

SEXT. The third of the "Day Hours," chanted about nine o'clock in the morning (the "third hour").

USAGES. A set of monastic customs, determining ceremonies and conduct in all the aspects of communal monastic life.

VESPERS. The most important of the "Day Hours." Vespers is chanted in the late afternoon.

VOCAL PRAYERS. Prayers in which words are actually spoken, or at least vocalised without sound.

VOWS. Promises made to God to perform a virtuous act or embrace a higher state of life. A dedication of one's self or one's actions to God. Solemn and perpetual religious vows are made publicly in the presence of representatives of the Church and impose a serious obligation upon the one who makes them. The obligation of Simple vows is less onerous, juridically speaking, than that of solemn vows. In either case, public vows involve a contract between the individual and the Church, with mutual obligations, and all vows, public or private, bind the individual to God by a special tie of religion. Vows may be dispensed by a competent authority. The more public and solemn they are, the more difficult it is to obtain a dispensation. Thus a private vow may ordinarily be dispensed by a confessor, but solemn religious vows can be dispensed only by the Holy See.

INDEX